MW01378367

Desire in Dante and the Middle Ages

LEGENDA

LEGENDA, founded in 1995 by the European Humanities Research Centre of the University of Oxford, is now a joint imprint of the Modern Humanities Research Association and Routledge. Titles range from medieval texts to contemporary cinema and form a widely comparative view of the modern humanities, including works on Arabic, Catalan, English, French, German, Greek, Italian, Portuguese, Russian, Spanish, and Yiddish literature. An Editorial Board of distinguished academic specialists works in collaboration with leading scholarly bodies such as the Society for French Studies and the British Comparative Literature Association.

MHRA

The Modern Humanities Research Association (MHRA) encourages and promotes advanced study and research in the field of the modern humanities, especially modern European languages and literature, including English, and also cinema. It also aims to break down the barriers between scholars working in different disciplines and to maintain the unity of humanistic scholarship in the face of increasing specialization. The Association fulfils this purpose primarily through the publication of journals, bibliographies, monographs and other aids to research.

Routledge
Taylor & Francis Group

LONDON AND NEW YORK

Routledge is a global publisher of academic books, journals and online resources in the humanities and social sciences. Founded in 1836, it has published many of the greatest thinkers and scholars of the last hundred years, including Adorno, Einstein, Russell, Popper, Wittgenstein, Jung, Bohm, Hayek, McLuhan, Marcuse and Sartre. Today Routledge is one of the world's leading academic publishers in the Humanities and Social Sciences. It publishes thousands of books and journals each year, serving scholars, instructors, and professional communities worldwide.

www.routledge.com

Desire in Dante and the Middle Ages

EDITED BY MANUELE GRAGNOLATI, TRISTAN KAY,
ELENA LOMBARDI AND FRANCESCA SOUTHERDEN

LEGENDA

Modern Humanities Research Association and Routledge
2012

First published 2012

Published by the
Modern Humanities Research Association and Routledge
2 Park Square, Milton Park, Abingdon, Oxon OX14 4RN
711 Third Avenue, New York, NY 10017, USA

LEGENDA is an imprint of the
Modern Humanities Research Association and Routledge

Routledge is an imprint of the Taylor & Francis Group, an informa business

© Modern Humanities Research Association and Taylor & Francis 2012

ISBN 9-781-907747-96-0 (hbk)

CONTENTS

ACKNOWLEDGEMENTS

The symposium and conference at which the papers contained in this volume were first presented took place in April and June 2010 at the University of Oxford. For funding both of these events, we would like to thank the Paget Toynbee Fund of the Department of Medieval and Modern Languages, Oxford, and the Oxford Society for the Study of Medieval Languages and Literature. We would like to thank Somerville College, Oxford, the Department of Italian Studies at Wellesley College, the Department of Italian Studies at Dartmouth College, and the Faculty of Arts at the University of Bristol for sponsoring the publication of this volume. We are also grateful to Martin McLaughlin and Graham Nelson for their advice in conceiving and preparing the manuscript. Finally, we wish to express our gratitude to everyone who, from many places and in different ways, took part in the Oxford symposium and conference and contributed to their success.

M.G., T.K., E.L., F.S., November 2011

NOTES ON THE CONTRIBUTORS

Daniela Boccassini is Professor of Italian and French at the University of British Columbia, Vancouver and Associate Head of the Department of French, Hispanic, and Italian Studies. Her research interests focus on the Medieval and Renaissance periods, and in particular on the exploration of the ways in which the act of writing preserves the memory of complex cultural processes, involving various disciplines, different cultural traditions, and multiple epistemological transitions. Among her most recent publications are *Il volo della mente. Falconeria e sofia nel mondo mediterraneo: Islam, Federico II, Dante* (Ravenna: Longo, 2003) and 'I sogni di Dante e l'ombra di Aristotele: Riflessioni sulla fenomenologia della visione nel *De ignorantia* di Petrarca', *Italica*, 84 (2007), 137–61.

Bill Burgwinkle is Reader in Medieval French and Occitan Literature at the University of Cambridge and Head of the French Department. His research thus far has focused on Medieval French and Occitan literature, gender and sexuality, and critical theory, and his new project is a collaborative AHRC-funded study on Medieval Francophone literary cultures outside of France. He is the author of *Sodomy, Masculinity and Law in Medieval Literature, 1050–1230* (Cambridge: Cambridge University Press, 2004), *Love for Sale: Materialist Readings of the Troubadour Razo Corpus* (New York: Garland, 1997), and *Razos and Troubadour Songs* (New York: Garland, 1990) and he has recently co-authored, with Cary Howie, *Sanctity and Pornography in Medieval Culture: On the Verge* (Manchester: Manchester University Press, 2010). He is also the co-editor of *Significant Others: Gender and Culture in Film and Literature, East and West* (Honolulu: Hawaii University Press, 1992) and *The Cambridge History of French Literature* (2011). He is a Fellow of King's College, Cambridge.

Fabio Camilletti is Assistant Professor in Italian at the University of Warwick. He specializes in nineteenth-century European literature and culture from a comparative perspective. His research interests include Dante, Leopardi, Aby Warburg, courtly/romantic love, literature and psychoanalysis. He has worked extensively on Dante Gabriel Rossetti and the Pre-Raphaelite metamorphoses of Dante, and in 2005 published the monograph *Beatrice nell'Inferno di Londra* (Trento: La Finestra). In 2010, he co-edited with Manuele Gragnolati and Fabian Lampart the volume *Metamorphosing Dante: Appropriations, Manipulations, and Rewritings in the Twentieth and Twenty-First Centuries* (Berlin and Vienna: Turia + Kant). He is currently finishing his second book, entitled *Dante's Book of Youth: The Vita Nova and the Nineteenth Century (1840–1907)* (forthcoming with IGRS Books), and working on a new monograph on *Classicism and Romanticism in Italian Literature: Leopardi's Discourse on Romantic Poetry* (forthcoming with Pickering & Chatto), conceived within the frame of a new research project on paradigms of historicity in Bourbon Restoration Italy, financed by the British Academy.

Peter Dent is a lecturer in the History of Art at the University of Bristol. He previously held a Henry Moore Foundation Postdoctoral Fellowship at the University of Warwick and a British Academy Postdoctoral Fellowship at the Courtauld Institute of Art in London, where he worked on a research project entitled 'Sculpture and the Senses in Late Medieval Italy'. His recent publications include: 'Chellini's Ears and the Diagnosis of Technique', in '"una insalata di più erbe": A Festschrift for Patricia Lee Rubin', ed. by S. Nethersole, P. Rumberg, and J. Harris (London: Courtauld Institute of Art, 2011); '"[P]er concorrenza d'una [...] da un Tedesco": Giovanni Pisano, Vasari and the Competitive Motive at Pistoia, *c.* 1301', *Zeitschrift für Kunstgeschichte*, 74.1 (2011); and (with Ettore Napione) 'Il Maestro di Santa Anastasia e la produzione di tabernacoli: due inediti', *Verona illustrata*, 23 (2010). He is editing a forthcoming collection on Sculpture and Touch and is a completing a monograph on Sculptural Encounters in Dante's World.

Manuele Gragnolati is Reader in Italian at the University of Oxford and Fellow of Somerville College. His research interests include the relationship between identity and corporeality in Dante and medieval eschatology, the intersections between language, desire, and subjectivity, and contemporary appropriations of Dante. He is the author of *Experiencing the Afterlife: Soul and Body in Dante and Medieval Culture* (Notre Dame, IN: Notre Dame University Press, 2005) and the editor of *The Power of Disturbance: Elsa Morante's 'Aracoeli'* (Oxford: Legenda, 2009; with Sara Fortuna); *Aspects of the Performative in Medieval Culture* (Berlin-New York: de Gruyter, 2010; with Almut Suerbaum), *Dante's Plurilingualism: Authority, Knowledge, Subjectivity* (Oxford: Legenda, 2010, with Sara Fortuna and Jürgen Trabant), and *Metamorphosing Dante: Appropriations, Manipulations, and Rewritings in the Twentieth and Twenty-First Centuries* (Berlin and Vienna: Turia + Kant, 2010; with Fabio Camilletti and Fabian Lampart). He has collaborated with Teodolinda Barolini on an edition of Dante's *Rime* (Milan: Rizzoli, 2009) and is currently editing the volume *Another Europe: Pier Paolo Pasolini's Euroeccentricity* (Berlin and Vienna: Turia + Kant, 2012; with Luca Di Blasi and Christoph Holzhey) and working on a book entitled *Identità dantesche: linguaggio, desiderio e corporeità in Dante, Pier Paolo Pasolini ed Elsa Morante*. He serves as Advisor to the Director at the ICI Berlin institute for Cultural Inquiry.

Tristan Kay completed his doctorate in Dante studies at the University of Oxford and is now Mellon Postdoctoral Fellow in the Department of Italian Studies at Dartmouth College. His publications include 'Dido, Aeneas, and the Evolution of Dante's Poetics', *Dante Studies*, 129 (2011); 'Dante's Ambivalence towards the Lustful', in *Dante and the Seven Deadly Sins*, ed. by John C. Barnes (Dublin: Four Courts Press, forthcoming); '"Una modesta Divina Commedia": Dante as Anti-model in Cesare Pavese's *La luna e i falò*', in *Metamorphosing Dante: Appropriations, Manipulations and Rewritings in the Twentieth and Twenty-First Centuries*, ed. by Manuele Gragnolati, Fabio Camilletti, and Fabian Lampart (Berlin and Vienna: Turia + Kant, 2011); and 'Redefining the "matera amorosa": Dante's *Vita nova* and Guittone's (anti-)courtly "canzoniere"', *The Italianist*, 29 (2009). He has co-edited the volume *Dante in Oxford: The Paget Toynbee Lectures* (Oxford: Legenda, 2011) and is currently revising his doctoral thesis for publication as a book entitled *Dante's Lyric Redemption*.

Giuseppe Ledda is *Ricercatore* of Italian Literature in the Faculty of Arts and Humanities at the University of Bologna. His main research field is Dante and medieval literature. His recent publications include *Dante* (Bologna: Il Mulino, 2008) and *La guerra della lingua: Ineffabilità, retorica e narrativa nella 'Commedia' di Dante* (Ravenna: Longo, 2002). He has also recently edited: *La poesia della natura nella 'Divina Commedia'* (Ravenna: Centro Dantesco dei Frati Minori Conventuali, 2009), and *La Bibbia di Dante: Esperienza mistica, profezia e teologia biblica in Dante* (Ravenna: Centro Dantesco dei Frati Minori Conventuali, 2011). He is a co-editor of the journal *L'Alighieri*.

Elena Lombardi is Senior Lecturer in the Department of Italian at the University of Bristol. Her main research interests are Dante and the medieval theory of language. In particular, she focuses on the intersection between theories of language and theories of desire in the Middle Ages. She has published essays on early Italian poetry (the Sicilian school and Guido Cavalcanti) and a book entitled *The Syntax of Desire: Language and Love in Augustine, the Modistae, Dante* (Toronto: University of Toronto Press, 2007). Her new book, *The Wings of the Doves: Love and Desire in Dante and Medieval Culture*, is forthcoming with McGill University Press in 2012.

Jonathan Morton is currently completing a D.Phil. in the Department of Medieval and Modern Languages at the University of Oxford, working on a thesis entitled *'Le Roman de la Rose': Poetry and Philosophy in Thirteenth-Century France*. His research focuses on Aristotelian ideas about nature and the natural, and how those questions are answered differently in philosophy and in literature in the context of the University of Paris in the thirteenth century, with a particular focus on Jean de Meun's continuation of the *Roman de la Rose*. Other research interests include medieval allegory, the medieval representation of animals, and the relationship between gender and academic discourse in the *Roman de la Rose* and elsewhere.

Monika Otter is Associate Professor of English and Comparative Literature at Dartmouth College. Her research focuses primarily on Latin, French, and English literature from England and Northern France in the eleventh to thirteenth centuries. She has worked on historiography, saints' lives, and romance, and the complicated interfaces between these genres; the development of 'fiction' as an idea and as a category of literature; women's literature and gender issues; and translation theory. Her publications include *The Book of Encouragement and Comfort: Goscelin's Letter to the Recluse Eva* (Cambridge: Boydell and Brewer, 2004); *Inventiones: Fiction and Referentiality in Twelfth-Century English Historical Writing* (Chapel Hill: North Carolina University Press, 1996); and 'Entrances and Exits: Performing the Psalms in Goscelin of St. Bertin's Liber Confortatorius', *Speculum*, 83.2 (April 2008), 283–302.

Francesca Southerden is Assistant Professor of Italian Studies at Wellesley College. She received a D.Phil. in Italian Literature from the University of Oxford, where she also held the post of Mary Ewart Postdoctoral Research Fellow at Somerville

College (2007–10). Her research interests include Dante, Petrarch, and their legacy in the twentieth century; modern Italian poetry; and literary and critical theory (especially psychoanalysis and the philosophy of language). She is the author of *Landscapes of Desire in the Poetry of Vittorio Sereni*, forthcoming with Oxford University Press, and has published several articles on the relationship between subjectivity, language, and desire in the poetry of Dante, Petrarch, and Sereni.

Robert Sturges holds a Ph.D. in Comparative Literature from Brown University (1979). He has taught at M.I.T., at Wesleyan University, and at the University of New Orleans, and is currently Professor and Associate Chair in the English department at Arizona State University, where he teaches medieval literature, critical theory, and gender and sexuality studies. His books include, as author, *Medieval Interpretation: Models of Reading in Literary Narrative, 1100–1500* (Carbondale: Southern Illinois University Press, 1990); *Chaucer's Pardoner and Gender Theory: Bodies of Discourse* (New York: St. Martin's Press, 2000); and *Dialogue and Deviance: Male–Male Desire in the Dialogue Genre (Plato to Aelred, Plato to Sade, Plato to the Postmodern)* (New York: Palgrave, 2005); and, as editor, *Law and Sovereignty in the Middle Ages and the Renaissance* (Turnhout: Brepols, 2011). He is completing an edition of *The Middle English Pseudo-Augustinian Soliloquies and its Anti-Lollard Commentary*.

Almut Suerbaum is Fellow in German at Somerville College, University of Oxford. She has worked on twelfth- and thirteenth-century narrative literature, medieval women's writing, and on the relationship between Latin and the vernacular language. Current projects include a collaborative study on fourteenth-century literature from the German South West, and the use of dialogue in medieval narrative texts. Her publications include *Innenräume in Der Literatur Des Deutschen Mittelalters: 19 Anglo-deutsches Colloquium*, ed. with Burkhard Hasebrink, Hans-Jochen Schiewer, and Annette Volfing (Tübingen: Max Niemeyer, 2008); 'Fabel', in *Kleine literarische Formen in Einzeldarstellungen* (Stuttgart: Reclam, 2002), 89–111; and 'Structures of Dialogue in Wolfram's "Willehalm"', in *Wolfram's 'Willehalm': Fifteen Essays*, ed. by Martin H. Jones and Timothy McFarland (Rochester, NY, and Woodbridge: Camden House, 2002), 231–47.

Paola Ureni is Assistant Professor at the CUNY College of Staten Island. She earned her Ph.D. in Italian Studies from New York University with a dissertation entitled *Memoria e pensiero: Cavalcanti e Dante, Tozzi e Gadda*. Her primary area of interest is medieval philosophy and poetry, but she also works on twentieth-century Italian literature. Her research focuses mainly on medieval and twentieth-century theories of memory as exemplified by literary works in relation to the philosophical debate of both periods. She has published several articles, mainly in the journal *Studi danteschi*, exploring the relationship between Dante's *Divine Comedy* and medieval medical science as well as theology. She has also published articles on the work of Italian writers of the twentieth century, such as Federigo Tozzi and Pier Vittorio Tondelli.

Annette Volfing is Professor of Medieval German literature at the University of Oxford and Tutorial Fellow in German at Oriel College, Oxford. She has a particular interest in later medieval religious, mystical, philosophical, or allegorical writing. Current research projects include Albrecht's 'Jüngerer Titurel' and the 'Tochter Syon' material. She has also written articles on the 'classic' narrative texts by Heinrich von Veldeke, Wolfram von Eschenbach, and Gottfried von Straßburg. She is the author of *Medieval Literacy and Textuality in Middle High German: Reading and Writing in Albrecht's 'Jüngerer Titurel'*, Studies in Arthurian and Courtly Culture (New York: Palgrave Macmillan, 2007); *John the Evangelist and Medieval German Writing: Imitating the Inimitable* (Oxford: Oxford University Press, 2001); and *Heinrich von Mügeln: 'Der meide kranz'. A Commentary* (Tübingen: Niemeyer, 1997). She has also edited, with Almut Suerbaum, *Amicitia: Friendship in Medieval Culture. Papers in Honour of Nigel F. Palmer*, Oxford German Studies, 36.2 (2007).

Marguerite Waller is Professor of Women's Studies and Comparative Literature at the University of California, Riverside. Her articles in the areas of feminist theory, contemporary women's activism, Italian and Central European cinema, new media, border art, feminist performance, Dante, Petrarch, and European Renaissance literature have been widely published, and she is the author of *Petrarch's Poetics and Literary History* (Amherst: University of Massachusetts Press, 1980). Her recent research focuses on transnational women's activism and filmmaking and on Dante's *Commedia*. With Jennifer Rycenga, she is the co-editor of *Frontline Feminisms: Women, War, and Resistance* (New York: Routledge, 2001), with Frank Burke of *Federico Fellini: Contemporary Perspectives* (Toronto: University of Toronto Press, 2002), with Sylvia Marcos of *Dialogue and Difference: Feminisms Challenge Globalization* (New York: Palgrave 2005), and with Amalia Cabezas and Ellen Reese, *The Wages of Empire: Neoliberal Policy, Repression, and Women's Poverty* (Boulder, CO: Paradigm Publishers 2007).

EDITIONS

Unless otherwise stated the following editions of Dante's works have been used:

Com.   *La Commedia secondo l'antica vulgata*, ed. by Giorgio Petrocchi, 2nd edn, 4 vols (Florence: Le Lettere, 1994)

Conv.   *Convivio*, ed. by Franca Brambilla Ageno (Florence: Le Lettere, 1995)

DVE   *De vulgari eloquentia*, ed. by Pier Vincenzo Mengaldo, in Dante Alighieri, *Opere minori*, 2 vols (Milan and Naples: Ricciardi, 1979–88), II, 1–237

Inf.   *Inferno*, in *Commedia*, ed. Petrocchi

Par.   *Paradiso*, in *Commedia*, ed. Petrocchi

Purg.   *Purgatorio*, in *Commedia*, ed. Petrocchi

Rime   *Rime*, ed. by Domenico De Robertis, 3 vols (Florence: Le Lettere, 2002)

VN   *Vita Nuova*, ed. by Domenico De Robertis, in *Opere minori*, I, i, 1–247

INTRODUCTION

Transforming Desire

Manuele Gragnolati, Tristan Kay,
Elena Lombardi and Francesca Southerden

Mapping Desire

Dante's *Commedia* has been appropriately termed 'the poem of desire',[1] not only because it features desire as the fundamental *trait d'union* between the self and God, but also because it covers the whole semantic area and the many implications of this vast and multifaceted concept. Although rooted in the pilgrim's sensual (if not erotic) love for a woman, it also encompasses the theme of the rational desire for knowledge, and combines the two in the spiritual drive towards the divine and the transcendental. Indeed, the importance and ubiquity of desire in Dante's universe can hardly be overstated, shaping as it does the gamut of experiences and encounters, both human and divine, up to and including the revelation of human origins in something universal and cosmic: 'l'amor che move 'l sole e l'altre stelle' [the Love that moves the sun and other stars] (*Par.* XXX, 145). Dante's masterpiece thus paradigmatically explores the multiple tensions — between lack and fulfilment, absence and presence, and earthly and divine love — through which the notion of desire has been articulated and discussed in diverse cultural fields since antiquity and which, as this volume attests, continue to reverberate in modern theories.

Dante's formulation of desire in the *Comedy* is the result of his long meditation on this concept in his other works (*Vita Nuova, Rime, Convivio, De vulgari eloquentia*), as well as his reception of many other discourses of desire in the Western Middle Ages. Indeed, from courtly literature to theology, from medicine to mysticism, from spirituality and devotional practices to political theory, the question of desire is central to medieval culture, matching — perhaps even surpassing — our contemporary fascination with it. While desire in each of these fields has a particular significance and its own terminology, it also goes beyond the borders of these single areas and is a truly inter-discursive feature of medieval culture.

The present volume takes Dante's multifaceted discourse of desire as a platform in investigating medieval concepts of desire in all their multiplicity, fragmentation, and interrelation. Originating from an international conference held at the University of Oxford in June 2010, it attempts to establish greater intellectual dialogue between Dante specialists and scholars working in other languages (German, French, Occitan, English, and Latin) and other disciplines, including art history, philosophy and critical theory. The result is an interdisciplinary collection that seeks to explore and contextualize notions of desire from the Middle Ages to the present through the study of complementary fields and discourses, encompassing language, sexuality, corporeality, subjectivity, perception, and knowledge. For all their diversity in terms of context and methodology, the volume's essays bring to light patterns, interconnections, and paradigms that are grouped into three sections — 'Transformations', 'Senses and Intellect', and 'Textuality and *Translatio*' — detailed below. Yet the essays also transcend these collocations in contributing to a common and multiple figuration of desire as a condition of endless movement and a protean agent of change. While the term 'desire' suggests a linear journey towards a given end-point or destination (where it might be fulfilled or at least appeased), it is often the journey itself — resisting linearity or closure, modifying its own trajectory — that emerges as a source of fascination for medieval thinkers. For it is the journey of desire that brings the subject into an active awareness of its own potential; a potential, that is, to reactivate desire in new and transformative ways. Thus, desire in this volume is conceived not simply as a discrete 'theme' in medieval studies, but as a fruitful means of going beyond conventional categories to reconfigure texts and open them up to innovative forms of critical interrogation.

Part 1: Transformations

Part 1 focuses on the role desire plays in a series of metamorphoses of language and, in particular, of selfhood. It shows how desire transforms to the degree that it collapses existing boundaries and goes beyond paradigms. A blueprint for this transformative capacity can be found in *Paradiso* XXX's image of the river of light which, as Dante-pilgrim drinks of it, transforms itself into a circle in an imperceptible but staggering reorientation, whereby what is taken within transforms everything within and without. Several essays in this section consequently establish paradigms which in the end are shown not to hold or which necessarily break down as the authors under discussion (from Dante to Hadewijch to 'Attār) probe the question of what happens after a close encounter with the divine and what it means to enter into a completely new state of mystical and sensual being or to 'live' in a new love of God beyond any previously known limit. Does this experience end in a radical dissolution (near cataclysm) of the subject after the Event or in its preservation in and through the event? Is it a losing of the self or, as Bill Burgwinkle argues, following Leo Bersani, a loss of the self that may yet entail its rediscovery elsewhere, as something new and different? Wherever the experience leads the individual, however, it emphatically does not cancel out the existence of desire itself, which is transformed by the paradisiacal experience but never absent, static, extinguished, or uniform. Indeed, the object of desire seems at times to be desire itself, the subject paradoxically fulfilled through deferral and unfulfilled in possession. Satiety in desire is consequently only one possible goal, which may be more or less present in the diverse texts explored. Transformation may occur as movement towards (peace) or beyond (lack), or it may be explosive and multidirectional as it seeks to encompass that which regenerates and reconstitutes it from within.

Bill Burgwinkle's 'Modern Lovers: Evanescence and the Act in Dante, Arnaut and Sordello' has a twofold focus in its exploration of Dante's notion of desire and subjectivity: first, it seeks to illustrate how this notion can be seen to foreshadow certain modern theories of desire and selfhood in a more profound sense than is typically suggested; and second, it identifies the roots of this proto-modern treatment of desire in the poetry of the troubadours. Burgwinkle first explores the Dantean resonance of Alain Badiou's notion of the Event, understood as a moment in life when subjectivity is overturned: 'a moment that leads to a loss of orientation and identification and institutes a new affiliation to the particular moment or event that provoked this momentous change.' For Dante, Burgwinkle shows, this event is surely love: the vital force in the development of the pilgrim's subjectivity and his evolving relationship to the Divine. Burgwinkle traces Dante's 'post-evental' fidelity to love back to his troubadour precursors, and especially to Arnaut Daniel and Sordello, both of whom appear as characters in the *Purgatorio*. Burgwinkle foregrounds in both poets a loyalty and surrender to the Event of love which anticipates and informs Dante's own. From the troubadours, Burgwinkle moves to another modern thinker, Leo Bersani, and to the applicability of his writings, especially as informed by queer theory, to the dissolution of stable categories and the temporary erasure of subjectivity which defines the pilgrim's experience of Paradise: the condition to which Dante's fidelity to love ultimately leads. Burgwinkle's essay paints the Dante of the *Paradiso* as a true radical, both 'modern lover' and queer theorist *avant la lettre*.

Daniela Boccassini's '"L'ora che volge il disio": Comparative Hermeneutics of Desire in Dante and 'Attār' also considers the transformative role of desire in collapsing the boundaries between self and Other. She begins from a Dantean syntagm, 'L'ora che volge il disio' (*Purg.* VIII, 1), in order to offer a comparative reading of the visualization of desire in Dante's *Commedia* and in the Islamic mystical narrative in verse, *Mantiq al-Tayr* [*The Conference of the Birds*] by Faridoddin 'Attār. The 'turning of desire upon itself' common to both texts, and to several other works in the Islamic tradition, Boccassini argues, is akin to an awakening in the desiring soul of a revealed knowledge of its own divine origin. The way to *trapassar dentro* [move into] the Divine truth, beyond the 'veil' of reality — if approached in the right manner — is also a mirror for perceiving the divine within the human: the 'visible face' of the Transcendent within the Immanent. The journey that appears to take the soul from within to without in a moment of ec-stasis is in fact an inner and circular transmutation that takes the subject beyond any linear conception of desire (as centred on a specific object) to a cosmic union with the divinity. Boccassini maps the implications of these two trajectories for understanding the nature of desire in Dante and 'Attār, and especially their culmination in a final 'meaning event' in which the 'ontologically unfathomable relation between the self and God' is testament to the miraculous turning of the will upon desire, and desire upon itself, as registered in the concluding tercet of Dante's *Paradiso* and in the last vision of 'Attār's poem. In Boccassini's final analysis, both texts are seen to climax in a moment of mystical union, one which coincides with the soul's reconciliation to itself through refinding, and merging with, the divine origin: a fluid state of pure motion and pure desire beyond any notion of subjectivity, yet not completely dissolving the experience of individuality.

The notion of desire as a movement that seeks to incorporate the divine within the human leads us to **Annette Volfing**'s essay, 'Ever-Growing Desire: Spiritual Pregnancy in Hadewijch and in Middle High German Mystics'. She discusses the motif of 'spiritual pregnancy' in the writings of Middle High German mystics, and in particular Hadewijch, in order to elucidate the complex interplay between gender, corporeality, and desire at the basis of their discourses, particularly where they describe the soul's desire to embrace a Marian role in relation to the Christ-child. She demonstrates how the Mariological aspirations of (especially, though not exclusively, female) mystics would often manifest themselves as the will to identify with Mary, to share in her desire to mother Christ and interact with him as Mary did (first carrying him within their heart/womb, then watching him grow up), a spiritual paradigm to rival that of bridal mysticism. Hadewijch's treatment of her own 'spiritual pregnancy', in which she puts greatest emphasis on the time of gestation and growth of the foetus within (the nine months used to structure her poem), is a significant case since she also fully develops the notion of the soul as womb, in allegorical terms, in describing the growth of love within the soul and the soul's own transformation through loving. Yet Volfing shows that by focusing on the process rather than the outcome of her spiritual pregnancy, the speaker of Hadewijch's poem (implicitly, though not solely, gendered female) relishes being in a permanent state of transition and growth and resists articulating (metaphors of) actual parturition, which is potentially seen as a splitting or separation of the self and the termination of a desire that actually thrives on a cycle of deferral and renewal.

In '"Quali colombe dal disio chiamate": A Bestiary of Desire in Dante's *Commedia*', **Giuseppe Ledda** explores various instances in the poem in which the medieval bestiary tradition can help shed light upon the full implications of Dante's use of animal images to reflect upon questions of desire. Drawing upon a wide range of medieval sources, from encyclopedias to theological texts, Ledda argues that Dante's animal similes cannot be understood simply from a 'realistic' or naturalistic perspective traditionally adopted by critics, but must instead be interpreted with close reference to medieval writings on animals and their perceived characteristics. In this vein, Ledda shows how Dante carefully exploits various animals' diverse connotations to convey the transition through the three realms of the *Commedia* and the different notion of desire we find in each of them, from loss via lack to satiety. While birds are used in Hell's circle of the lustful to convey a chaotic, disordered desire, and in Purgatory birds were found in flight towards a longed-for destination, the nightingale and eagle similes of the *Paradiso* are used precisely to articulate a desire that is no longer destructive or exclusively carnal, but redemptive and fulfilled. Images of animal life in the *Commedia* are thus — like the classical and romance literary traditions in which Dante roots his 'poema sacro' — renewed and redeemed from within, pointing to the transformation but also to the enduring centrality of desire witnessed in the pilgrim's journey through the three realms of the afterlife.

Fabio Camilletti's 'Dante Painting an Angel: Image-making, Double-oriented Sonnets and Dissemblance in *Vita Nuova* XXXIV' begins by examining nineteenth-century reinterpretations of the thirty-fourth chapter of Dante's *Vita Nuova* —

including Dante Gabriel Rossetti's painting, *The First Anniversary of the Death of Beatrice*, and Robert Browning's poem, *One Word More* — to argue that a dialogue between the *libello* and its post-Enlightenment re-appropriations unveils subterranean tensions within Dante's text itself. Camilletti's essay focuses on the episode in which Dante draws figures of angels on the first anniversary of Beatrice's death in order to examine a pivotal constellation in the text between death, desire, and memory, and the status of the simulacra as a means to compensate for an original loss. Reading the 'double-oriented' sonnet of the *Vita Nuova*, 'Era venuta', in light of Dante's concerns with image-making and the temporal doubleness of the *Vita Nuova* itself, here evident in the tension between time (death and loss of the beloved) and the eternal (immortalization of her), Camilletti discusses the possibility of interpreting the episode through the psychoanalytical category of sublimation and interrogates Dante's representation of Beatrice to show how it oscillates between abstraction and disembodiment, conveying a sense that the object of desire can never be successfully recuperated through the work of art, or at least not until the experience of the *Paradiso*. There, where all previous categories of representation collapse in the face of a new, incarnational poetics based on the immanence of the object of desire, the aporias of *Vita Nuova* XXXIV find their final resolution in light of a new understanding that goes beyond any notion of mimesis of either language or image.

Part II: Senses and Intellect

Part II, 'Senses and Intellect', investigates the ways in which these two dimensions of human experience ultimately work to articulate desire beyond dualism. Emphasized in this section is the mobility of desire as process, whether in the body or through the senses (vision, touch) or as transposed into the realm of knowledge or cognition. Yet desire is also manifest as transgression and non-containment, whether speaking of identity, sexuality, or the relationship to the Other/other. The gaze emerges as a particularly significant index of desire in that it enables a privileged understanding of the relationship between the (perceiving, but simultaneously perceived) subject and the object of desire. Desire and perception together reveal certain fundamental ideas about identity, foregrounding or prefiguring the increasingly inter-subjective experience of desire as it is mapped in Dante's *Purgatorio* and *Paradiso*, while exploring the implications of a body and mind made permeable by desire, as against those reified by more negative experiences of desire, including those trapped in phallocentrism or immobilized through passivity. Together, the essays in this section map what Marguerite Waller terms a matrix of subject positions, which shed light not only on issues of epistemology (knowledge and understanding) but also on questions of gender and selfhood. What emerges is a new understanding of the mechanisms that contribute to defining identity and the potential for desire to disrupt or even radically subvert the status quo.

Peter Dent's 'The Call of the Beautiful: Augustine and the Object of Desire in *Purgatorio* X' concentrates on the role played by the marble reliefs on the first terrace of Dante's Purgatory in stimulating and directing the pilgrim's desire, especially insofar as that desire is understood as spiritual motion, which, in Augustinian terms, can be directed rightly or wrongly in the soul's journey toward God. In analysing the relationship in *Purgatorio* x between subjectivity, optics, and spiritual ascent, Dent traces the evolution of a paradigm that has its roots in classical and medieval theory connecting beauty, voice and gaze, and is mediated through Book 10 of Augustine's *Confessions*. Reading *Purgatorio* x alongside Augustine's theory of desire, Dent shows how the 'call of the beautiful' — understood as that which binds creation to Creator, and the desiring subject to its object of attention — is central to an understanding of the pilgrim's encounter with God's art on the terrace of pride, especially as a 'visibile parlare' [visible speech]. In particular, Dent argues, Dante brings together the visual and the verbal in a special sign that is first perceived outwardly and then processed inwardly by the pilgrim, transforming the perceiving subject through a process involving attention, interpretation and the correct reading of God's visible (and invisible) signs. Desire, as it is elicited and elaborated through the 'call of the beautiful', demands at the same time an active response; the relationship between the subject and its object of desire is not fixed but evolving, as in the whole of Dante's second realm.

Questions of perception are also at the heart of **Robert Sturges**' essay 'Desire and Devotion, Vision and Touch in the *Vita Nuova*'. Sturges looks both forwards and backwards from Dante's treatment of vision and its relation to desire in his first major work, seeking to better contextualize its complex notion of visuality within the later Middle Ages and to draw attention to the ways in which this notion may be seen to anticipate modern psychoanalytical theories of the gaze, particularly those of Jacques Lacan and Laura Mulvey. Since antiquity, theories of vision have been divided into those of intromission, whereby light is emitted from the object and passes through the air to the observer's eye, and those of extramission, whereby the gaze is embodied in rays emitted by the eye that reach outwards and 'touch' the body of the object being viewed. Late-medieval thinkers, including the Dante of the *Convivio*, largely understood vision as intromissive, yet Sturges highlights the *Vita Nuova*'s occasional use of an extramissive model in describing its subject's visual experience of Beatrice. The somewhat surprising presence of extramission in the work is related by Sturges to fourteenth-century devotional literature, closely informed by Augustine's visual theory, which described spiritual vision in the 'tactile' terms typical of classical extramissive models. Moreover, it is seen to foreshadow the (phallic) male gaze as theorized in the work of Mulvey on scopophilia. Yet intromission also has an important role in the *libello*, with Dante describing on occasions how the subject is rendered abject and powerless by his vision of Beatrice, anticipating the radical openness to the other and the dissolution of the ego associated with Lacan's writings on the gaze. Sturges argues that the *Vita Nuova*'s handling of vision is above all reciprocal and inter-subjective, drawing upon models both intromissive and extramissive, scientific and devotional, and anticipating diverse and competing psychoanalytical models in its delineation of the complex desiring relationship between the gaze and the divine.

Identifying another dynamic nexus common to both medieval and modern thought, **Paola Ureni**'s 'Intellectual Memory and Desire in Augustine and Dante's

Paradiso' explores the connection between memory and desire in the last cantica, investigating how both sustain the pilgrim's journey to the vision of God. Although Dante seemingly derogates memory at the beginning of *Paradiso* (I, 5–9), separating it from intellect and desire (the two motors of the journey), Ureni argues that it is possible to trace the development of a form of intellectual memory that is at work throughout the canticle. Ureni's essay develops along two tracks: a philosophical reading based on the formulation of memory given by Augustine chiefly in the last books of the *De Trinitate*, and a rhetorical inquiry into the concept of *transsumptio*, an extended metaphor in which the theological and the poetic coincide in their attempts to represent the transcendent experience of the soul in its encounter with the divine. In her final textual example from *Paradiso* XXXIII, Ureni shows how the rhetorical and the philosophical converge in the transumptive language of Paradise, which becomes itself a medium between divine and human memories and desires.

Marguerite Waller's essay, 'Sexualities and Knowledges in *Purgatorio* XXVI and *Inferno* V' addresses the interdependence of sexual desire and epistemology in Dante's *Commedia*. Centring on the pilgrim's encounter with the poets of erotic love in *Purgatorio* XXVI, it concludes with a rereading of certain aspects of *Inferno* V. Drawing upon feminist and queer theory and recent philological and critical Dante scholarship, Waller argues that in *Purgatorio* XXVI, 'heterosexual' and 'homosexual' penitents alike are engaged in purging the phallic dimension of their eroticism. The elaborate and associatively rich figures used to characterize the love poets in *Purgatorio* XXVI (Caesar in triumph and Pasiphaë in her wooden cow) link this process of purgation to the issues of knowledge production, historiography, and political power so prominent throughout *Purgatorio*. The purging of the sin of both groups in *Purgatorio* XXVI, Waller suggests, includes revealing the performances and masquerades that constitute social identity as meaningful only within a matrix of subject positions and relationships that themselves need to be read as contingent and political. Phallic, patriarchal sexualities that are not read this way effectively deny sexual difference and the epistemological richness it enables. According to Waller, because Dante's Francesca never got to experience this difference, she never came to know her socially transgressive and potentially transformative sexual desire as salvific.

Part III: Textuality and *Translatio*

The productively transgressive potential of desire, and the possibilities it has for creating integrative models which do not, however, deny difference, are also at the heart of the final part of the volume, 'Textuality and *Translatio*'. The essays in this section all explore the dialogic relationship between desire and various aspects of textuality, including inter-textuality and *translatio*, understood in the broadest terms as the practice of the transfer of language(s), culture, and knowledge(s). Part III consequently focuses on the reinterpretation and recreation of paradigms of desire, whose elements are freely combined and reconfigured, and in which desire again emerges as movement and irresistible surplus (especially in linguistic terms, or those of translation, where something necessarily remains irreducible to language). Just as during the Middle Ages as a whole, translation describes the process whereby authors actively re-appropriate and rewrite, rather than passively or faithfully transmit material from their original sources, so desire in the texts discussed resists unproblematic transposition from one domain into the other, often foregrounding instead the slippage between them. In between the hope or possibility of arriving at a 'full' desire, or its fullest expression, and the uncovering of an unbridgeable gap (in language or desire), desire exists as an all-powerful mover nonetheless immoveable in its enduring presence at the heart of the (writing) subject and its identity, even when every other condition of existence has been fulfilled. Indeed, as the entire volume attests, textuality and desire are inseparable, especially where desire incorporates the desire *of* language.

Almut Suerbaum's paper, 'Between "Unio" and Alienation: Expressions of Desire in the Strophic Poems of Hadewijch', investigates Hadewijch's lyric poetry, composed around the middle of the thirteenth century and exceptional in exploring aspects of mystical union with the divine not just through the medium of visions and discursive tracts, but also in a lyric form. Hadewijch draws on literary contexts which are clearly inspired by Northern French courtly love songs, and directly or indirectly by Occitan lyric, a literary milieu with which the author, probably from Antwerp, may have been familiar thought her aristocratic family. The paper assesses how Hadewijch transforms motifs form the courtly love lyric — especially the relationship between the (male) lyric 'I' and the (female) beloved — within the theological framework of her songs, and articulates a central element of mystical theology by means of the secular discourse on love: the paradoxical relationship between desire for 'unio' as a movement transcending the gap between the created world and God, and an awareness that because of the fundamental difference between the human soul and the divine creator, such desire is inherently unrequitable. This transforms desire beyond a more linear and contingent interaction, centred on the 'I''s determination to move the desired object to fulfil its demands, to a dedicated cycle of renewal and self-renewal (mobilized through giving rather than receiving), in which only the suppression of the individual will (i.e. the relinquishing of demands upon the Other and the recognition and embracing of one's necessary helplessness) allows for the possibility of union with the beloved. Suerbaum thereby shows that, for Hadewijch, it is not the satiety produced by joy, but hunger and suffering that are the expression of perfect desire which is hence paradoxically closest to achieving the ultimate goal.

The intersection of secular and sacred discourses of love is also central to **Tristan Kay**'s essay, 'Desire, Subjectivity, and Lyric Poetry in Dante's *Convivio* and *Commedia*', which examines the radical synthesis of erotic and spiritual commitment that defines the poetics of Date's masterpiece. Proceeding from a reflection upon the Florentine's theory of vernacular language, Kay proceeds to reframe the tension between the *Commedia* and the unfinished *Convivio*, less in terms of their respective theological and philosophical foundations than in terms of the very different ways in which they handle desire and in particular its relationship to poetry in the mother tongue. The *Convivio*, a philosophical treatise in the vernacular nevertheless informed substantially by the modalities of Latin exegetical culture, is shown to define desire in a much more conservative and restrictive fashion than either the earlier *Vita Nuova* or the later *Commedia*, continually establishing an opposition between love and intellection that is deeply at odds with the integrative aspirations of the two other works. This notion of desire is very consciously reformulated in the *Commedia*, where the 'miraculous' Beatrice serves as an agent of synthesis in aligning Dante's corporeal and spiritual desires and redeeming his vernacular poetics, overcoming the limitations imposed by the obdurate mode of allegory employed in the earlier treatise. In tracing this poetic and ideological development, Kay draws attention to the author's careful negotiation and eventual transcendence of a courtly paradigm of desire and conversion, associated in a Dantean context with Guittone d'Arezzo and Folco of Marseille — poets whose pursuit of moral rectitude saw them sever themselves from a genealogy of romance lyric poets to which the Dante of the *Commedia*, in spite of his 'divine' subject matter, continues to declare his affiliation. It is ultimately in the redemption (and not the rejection) of desire for the *donna* that Dante is shown to situate his own uniqueness and pre-eminence as a vernacular poet.

In **Francesca Southerden**'s 'Desire as a Dead Letter: A Reading of Petrarch's *RVF* 125', desire emerges as an unmoveable and irreducible condition of lack, which cannot be fully translated into language or the logical experience of signification. Focusing on the nexus in Petrarch's poem between estrangement, loss of voice and the petrification of meaning, Southerden analyses 'Se 'l pensier che mi strugge' ['If the thought wasting me'] in light of a network of inter- and intra-textual references to desire, which extends from Augustine's *Confessions* and *The Trinity*, through Dante's *rime petrose* and *Commedia*, to Petrarch's own *RVF* 23. Whether recreating the linguistic and erotic fall embodied by the memory of Dante's *petrose* or evoking as his counter-model the miraculous scene of redemption of the subject and his language in the Earthly Paradise cantos of the *Purgatorio*, Petrarch repeatedly denies the possibility of reaching (self-)knowledge through poetry, or of being reconciled to himself or to God. The 'dead letter' of desire represents all those 'signs' in Petrarch's poem that fail to yield up any meaning beyond their own frozen status: receptacles for a melancholy desire fixated on an unattainable and unsymbolizable lost object which remains buried in a prehistoric dimension closed off to the subject. At the same time, Southerden shows how in their static, phantasmatic totality, those 'signs' — the grass and flowers fetishized as metonymic substitutions for the absent beloved — do allow for some ghostly reanimation or reimagination of what modern psychoanalytic discourse would call an 'original fantasy' (Laplanche and Pontalis), which re-enacts the play of loss and hallucinatory compensation corresponding to the advent of desire-in-language as a moment of unhealable fracture. From the resistance to speaking, through the resistance to moving, to the final stasis of the vision itself, Petrarch's poem works against the principles of articulated discourse, simultaneously redefining that teleology of desire and language that in Augustine's and Dante's conception would ultimately lead to the reconciliation of the (fallen) self to God and the rediscovery of its pristine unity. Desire for Petrarch is, by contrast, a counter-conversional impulse, one that gains in intensity to the degree that it resists transforming into something else.

Jonathan Morton's 'Queer Metaphors and Queerer Reproduction in Alain de Lille's *De planctu naturae* and Jean de Meun's *Roman de la rose*' is a comparative study of Alain de Lille's *De planctu* and Jean de Meun's continuation of the *Roman de la rose*, which can be considered a rhetorical and interpretative 'translation' of aspects of Alain's text in a new form. In particular, Morton examines both authors' use of 'queer' metaphors as part of each text's concern with representing (and in Alain's case, of extirpating) the unspeakable subject matter associated with the term 'sodomy'. Working from the concept of 'queer' as it relates to the demands and limitations of 'reproductive futurism' (Lee Edelman), which it uproots and transverses producing a troubling 'infinity' akin to the plural and unstable functioning of metaphor, Morton analyses the multiple presentations in each text of metaphors of writing and sex, both 'natural' and 'unnatural', straight(forward) and deviant. Focusing on the figure of Genius as it is portrayed in the *De planctu* and reinterpreted in Jean de Meun's *Roman de la rose*, alongside the figures of Orpheus and Pygmalion, Morton highlights the artistic potentialities of queer reproduction, considered an apt metaphor also for the practice of translation and other forms of poetic discourse that transcend the linearity of binary or syllogistic reasoning. Translation, in this analysis, emerges as unstable, open to what Morton terms 'sodomitical deviation', and subject to metaphorical and linguistic slippage. The proliferation of meanings that results from the undecidability of this process is at once a loss and a gain: the disturbing recognition of the impossibility of recovering a totality through 'perfect, lossless translation', and the pleasure of revelling in the profusion and plurality of an irreducible 'otherness' or 'beyondness'.

In 'Desiring Tales: Two Vernacular Poetics of Desire', **Monika Otter** also considers the productive slippage occurring in the interstices between words, or at the borders of complementary discourses or rival textualities, as opening a window onto desire. She considers the way in which Gottfried von Strassburg and the English poet Layamon — near-contemporaries (early thirteenth century), but almost certainly unaware of each other's work — formulate strikingly similar poetic projects in the prologues of their respective works, the *Tristan* and the *Brut*. Both authors describe their poetic enterprise in strongly affective terms; both link this description explicitly and directly to elements of the plot, creating complex and shifting homologies between the desires of author, reader, and characters. Both are, self-consciously and explicitly, translators so that the 'desire' is also that of the translator/redactor/active reader for the original text. Both go so far as to cast the ideal communion of author, reader and text in Eucharistic terms. But both depict this ideal as elusive, never quite to be attained: it is in this gap between full achievement and real text, that the desire of the text is kept alive and informs the entire poem. Otter demonstrates this through her study of the figure of Petitcreiu, in Gottfried: the little dog from fairyland whose consolatory magic fails, but necessarily so in order for his poem to continue, and in her analysis of the recurrent motif of an urgent, yearning search for the elusive Merlin in Layamon. In turn, the poetics of desire that emerges in these moments of the texts mirrors that of each author in the face of their quest for an original, French source they each claim to follow. Otter concludes that translation, in both modern and medieval understandings, plays with (or persists despite) unresolvable paradoxes of sameness and difference; the translation seeks to match its original, to the point of identity, while being perfectly conscious of the impossibility of that enterprise. It is consequently the perfect image of the asymptotic yearning for unicity and concord that is called 'desire'.

Note

1. The formulation is taken from the title of Franco Ferrucci's book, *Il poema del desiderio* (Milan: Leonardo, 1990). Other in-depth recent studies of desire in Dante's work include: Lino Pertile, *La punta del disio: Semantica del desiderio nella 'Commedia'* (Florence: Cadmo, 2005); Teodolinda Barolini, *Dante and the Origins of Literary Culture* (New York: Fordham University Press, 2007); Elena Lombardi, *The Syntax of Desire: Language and Love in Augustine, the Modistae, Dante* (Toronto: University of Toronto Press, 2007), and *The Wings of the Doves: Love and Desire in Dante and Medieval Culture* (Montreal: McGill University Press, 2012).

PART I

Transformations

CHAPTER 1

❖

Modern Lovers:
Evanescence and the Act
in Dante, Arnaut, and Sordello

Bill Burgwinkle

Dante is not a dualist.[1]

The question of Dante's notion of desire, at least as it pertains to his own case as a lover and author, can only really be approached at a bias: firstly, because he tells us so much and yet so little about his own erotic history; and secondly, because what he does tell us comes almost always filtered through the figure of Beatrice and his imaginary relations with her. Beatrice, the purported object of desire in life, becomes in Dante's retrospective and touched-up vision: an inspiration, a bait, a mask, a pair of spectacles, a view-scope, an illusion, a holograph, a film image, a mother, a child, a nurse, a visionary, a fortune teller, a knight, a protector, and possibly even a father.[2] How he moves from one of these fantasies — in which he is the active instigator and follower of his own desire, seeking her out for purposes of scopophilic gratification — to the other — in which he is the relative beneficiary of her superior wisdom, purity and privileged relation to the Divine — is, I suppose, the story of the interplay between the *Vita Nuova* and the *Commedia*, the two principal texts in which he sketches his views on desire and its importance to the development of subjectivity. Following Teodolinda Barolini's initiative,[3] then, my aim is to de-theologize this topic — not by denying that there is theology in the foreground *and* background of Dante's work, but by emphasizing just how frequently that theological base is equally at play in the secular critical theory that I will be addressing here: psychoanalysis, poetics, and some forms of queer theory.

To begin with a Lacanian point of view: Beatrice, the Ego Ideal if ever there was one, serves as a sort of guardian angel who watches over the pilgrim both in this life and in the after-world, a figure whose blessing and approval he yearns for *and* a stern mistress whose gaze will forever demand satisfaction.[4] On a slightly more simplistic level, Dante's narrative of self-destitution and subsequent reconstruction in the *Commedia* works as a clever retelling of the mirror stage. The pilgrim begins the journey as less than whole, then reconstructs the self through mimetic bonding with a series of interlocutors who also serve as ego ideals, figures whom he either admires and seeks to please, or who admonish him, straighten him out, deliver him from danger. But in the reshaping of psychoanalysis that is characteristic of Leo

Bersani's thought, the version that most interests me here, this early psychic setting (or re-setting) of the dials would amount to the construction of a template for paranoid suspicion rather than a therapeutic 'cure'. As Bersani sees it, the key idea that sets in early and shapes consciousness for a lifetime is that someone, somewhere, has deliberately withheld the truth of the subject's being and will refuse forever to reveal it. The anticipation of psychological mastery that accompanies maturation thus begins with a drama of loss or theft that will invariably lead to resentment.[5] Bersani owes this notion of paranoid subject formation to Jean Laplanche, who emphasized an 'enigmatic signifier' in the process of subject formation: an allusion planted in the child by the unknowing parent to the 'unconscious and sexual significations' of the adult world. Laplanche claims that the child will thereafter imagine that these secrets are crucial to his or her own task of mastery and self-protection.[6] They will forevermore colour his or her placement in the world with a 'degree of nostalgia for the narcissism they have presumably given up';[7] and it is this nostalgia for narcissism that Bersani claims Freud saw at the root of the interest that men — heterosexual men — show in women:

> Because what the man must appropriate as his is the woman's exclusion of him, he can narcissistically suppress her only by an intense, mimetic attention to her self-absorption, her utterly private pleasure in her own image.[8]

As inadequate as this embryonic explanation of what Beatrice really means to the pilgrim and to Dante the poet might be, it offers an interesting pathway into examining Dante's attitudes toward desire. Given the breadth and complexity of that topic, however, I am going to divide the rest of this paper into three sections. In the first I will be looking at the notion of the event, as theorized by Alain Badiou, in order to evaluate the importance of the subject's fidelity to that event and its potential application to the pilgrim's mid-stream change of life. In the second, I will be looking briefly at two of Dante's troubadour models: Arnaut Daniel and Sordello, both of whose songs might be read as examples of 'evental' thinking and its relation to the scatological, the corporeal and the pornographic; and finally, in the third section, I will return to that idea of the event, having passed it through a troubadour sieve, to relink with Bersani's reformulation of desire as inevitably tinged by paranoia. The fundamental notion that emerges from the *Commedia* is that love and desire alone can offer a solution to the subjective destitution that we might today call a life crisis or a depression or a loss of faith by spinning that loss of self in a positive sense, as a necessary wearing-away of the controlling ego, a productive and mystical merging within a larger collective that Dante calls the divine. With that, let us begin with Badiou.

Badiou

Reading Dante through Alain Badiou is not nearly as reductive and inappropriate as it may first sound. Badiou, like so many French philosophers/theorists is, after all, the product of a religious background and he has spent his life working in a country steeped in religious thinking, no matter how much it might protest otherwise. Though Badiou is best known for his Maoist political leanings in the 1970s and his contentious yet close affiliation with Louis Althusser and Jacques Lacan, he has shown particular interest in his writings since the mid-1980s in moments of transcendence, sometimes political but more often experienced through an encounter with art. His latest book is entitled *Éloge de l'amour*, which is, after all, a title that would suggest some affinity with Dante's project.[9]

What most interests Badiou are those moments in life when subjectivity is overturned: moments that lead to a loss of orientation and identification and institute a new affiliation to the particular moment or event that provoked this momentous change. This moment or event becomes known thereafter, retroactively, as Truth and those who adhere to that truth become known as believers. Such moments frequently display a strong link with what Lacan and Slavoj Žižek have at different times in their writings referred to as an *Act*. An Act, in this sense, is something unforeseen and unpremeditated, an impulsive turn towards doing something that everyone who loves you would probably counsel against. Jumping into a burning building to save a baby, diving into a freezing body of water to retrieve a would-be suicide, undergoing torture rather than renounce one's beliefs, carrying explosives onto an airplane in order to incinerate it and oneself: all of these are, at least potentially, Acts that puzzle and fascinate a larger public, and with good reason. They are impulses probably not even fully understood by their perpetrators; or that, at least, is what they tell us when asked after the fact to explain why they did what they did, how they summoned the courage or strength of character or single-mindedness required for such a deed. Acts such as these challenge the very notion of a contained and containable subject, one who is responsible for his/her actions. How, after all, can one take responsibility for an action when one barely knows that one performed it? How can one accept adulation for courage, knowing that no foresight went into the fatal decision to dive into the figurative flames? When we map this notion of the Lacanian Act, this moment of subjective destitution *par excellence* onto the Badiouan 'event', I believe that we are approaching the state of mind of the *Commedia*'s pilgrim in the opening cantos of the *Inferno*. Having wandered off the straight path and into the darkest woods, the pilgrim is presented as having done so not so much by plan but as if he had somehow been directed by another source. He cannot explain how he got where he is; he was simply 'sleepy', 'straying', turned away by beasts that blocked his path, until he meets Virgil and follows closely on his heels for the next sixty-one cantos.[10]

This following of Virgil could be seen as the first manifestation of what Badiou would call *fidelity to the event*, a fidelity that leads us through the three canticles and on to the sanctification and salvation of the pilgrim himself. This act of turning away from everything he had once known and been and this resolution to turn himself around in accordance with this new Truth or Event, comprised by the encounter with Virgil and through him Beatrice, provides an illustration of what Badiou means when he says that his philosophy is 'built on the simple and powerful idea that any existence can one day be transfigured by what happens to it, and can commit itself from then on to what holds for all.'[11] In this case, the pilgrim's fidelity to the event, figured by his fixation on Beatrice as the sign of his past and his future, is portrayed as a properly religious event, one that will determine the rest of his life through its instantiation of what then becomes, retrospectively, an encounter with Truth. This affiliation to the truth, no matter how it is generated and regardless of its localization, transforms completely what Badiou calls the 'situation of being' in which the subject previously found himself. Thinking that he has recognized the importance of the profound experience he has gone through, the subject is called upon to make an evental declaration ('I am a believer') that will henceforth make of him a figure of fidelity and it is within that new identity or place marker that he will construct a new subjectivity ('I am who I am because I am now a believer in the Event that I have experienced').[12] Peter Hallward rightly calls Badiou:

> [...] the untimely descendant of a long line of interventionist thinkers whose central insight is that access to truth can be achieved only by going against the grain of the world and against the currents of history — a group of thinkers that includes Saint Paul, Pascal, Claudel...[13]

And Dante, of course. The 'break' with life as lived before the event — with family, habit, history, even identity itself — is at the very root of the *Commedia* and is conceptualized in the gradual disintegration of identity categories in the closing cantos of *Paradiso* to match those in the opening cantos of the *Inferno*.

Love is by definition one of the privileged areas of Badiou's investigation because it is almost always commensurate with an event. As Badiou admits:

> Love does not exist naturally; it can only exist by change. [...] The sexual belongs to the order of being, of nature; and love belongs to the order of the event. [...] Love is always excessive; and it is the event that constructs for a situation of being the truth of that situation of being. [...] love is the truth of sex and not, as in the case of the pessimistic French moralists, sex is the truth of love. [*sic*][14]

I presume that he means that love is the truth that follows the event, the event being an always 'accidental' encounter that comes ex-nihilo. Love is thus the pretext for an Act having taken place. It is, in fact, an after-effect of experience that can never be verified quantitatively. Badiou, as opposed to most twentieth-century continental philosophers, believes in Truth but only as a subjective experience that attains its truth-value posthumously. Love, the after-effect of chance, according to Badiou, is reconstructed as the central event around which the subjective landscape and contours of identity are reorganized. It thus becomes a supplement for the lack of the sexual relation itself: not a fusing of identities, or a two-in-one subject, but a way of compensating for the fact that such a fusion will never actually take place.

In his book on Saint Paul, Badiou echoes some of this evental thinking in a more consciously religious mode. Though an atheist himself, he considers Paul's conversion to be *the* archetypal event, a moment in which the subject is born through a refusal of law, an act of rebellion against the automatism of cultural norms and unconscious drives that keep us in a state of desire, a state which is in his terms equivalent to the state of death:

> The gist of it is that when the subject as thought accepts the grace of the event — this is the moment of subjectivation (faith, conviction) — he who was once dead returns to the place of life. He takes up once again the attributes of power that had been ceded to the law and which were understood subjectively as sin.

> He recovers the living unity of thought and action. This act of taking back makes of life itself a universal law. Law returns as a figure of life for all, the way of faith, law beyond law. This is what Paul calls love.[15]

Badiou furthermore claims that the event that transpires and that rocks our world is very often an *artistic* event involving music, dance, poetry or, importantly, science. Art, science, politics and love are, in fact, the four categories that he singles out as singularly able to shake our foundations and catapult us into a new truth event. Love might be the most unexpected of the four, given that it gets little notice in much contemporary philosophy and is often lumped with inessential 'humanist' concerns, but this is where Dante comes in as an essential contributor to this discussion: Dante, like Badiou, sees love as deadly important. In his fictional universe, love is not only the God himself whose recognition the pilgrim seeks, but it is the problem and the solution to the situations he encounters, the key to understanding not only human but divine truth as well. Fundamental to the notion of being oneself, even to an understanding of vices and virtues, love is, if anything, over-indulged in the *Commedia*. Yet Dante never really addresses the physical and sexual side of love at all. Instead, love is seen as a delicate psychological and theological state to be treated with the utmost care. In my next section, I will argue that while Dante inherited this predilection for endless discourse on love and its perils from his immediate predecessors in Florentine and Sicilian poetry, it was from his Occitan models, those alter-egos, counter-egos, and ideal-egos whom we meet in the *Purgatorio*, that he learned to mix the grace with the grime.

The Occitan Models

It is striking that in the *De vulgari eloquentia* Dante chooses Arnaut Daniel as his model of the love poet who writes in the illustrious style. Arnaut, whom many still consider a less than logical choice, is the poet not only of exuberance in style but in subject matter as well. Though Dante acknowledges Arnaut as his model for writing continuous rhyme and innovations in poetic language, he does not quite admit that there are many *other* qualities that he enjoys about Arnaut's poetry and much more that he learned from him as well. He cites Arnaut only four times in the *De vulgari* (though that is more than any other poet apart from himself), and he refers to only four of his eighteen known songs, but I suspect that he knew more than these four songs and two of them, in particular, are worthy of a closer look. Arnaut could in many ways be seen as the poet of the Event, both by virtue of his extravagant post-evental poetics and his sometimes strange and incomprehensible subject matter. The first of these tendencies is fairly well known as it encompasses the very traits that most romantic critics particularly disliked about Arnaut; and that poets, rather than critics, generally tend to admire. Listen for a moment to the sonic explosions that Arnaut conjures up in this song, referred to simply as 'Sols sui...' as well as the imagery of these first four stanzas:

Sols sui qui sai lo sobrafan que.m sortz
al cor d'amor sofren per sobramar
que mos volers es tant ferms et entiers
c'anc non s'esduis de celliei ni s'estors
cui encubic al prim vezer s'e puois:
c'ades ses lieis dic a lieis cochos motz;
puois quand la vei non sai, tant l'ai, que dire.

I alone know the overwhelming pain that overtakes
my loving heart, suffering from over-loving,
for my will is so firm and whole
that it has never parted or grown distant from her
whom I craved at first sight, and ever since:
still now without her nearby, I recite to her my
                        burning words;
then, when I see her, I don't know what to say,
there is just so much to be said.

D'autras vezer sui secs e d'auzir sortz
q'en sola lieis vei e aug e esgar,
e jes d'aisso no.ill sui fals plazentiers
que mais la vol non ditz la boca.l cors;
qu'eu no vau tant chams, vauz ni plans ni puois
qu'en un sol cors trob aissi bos aips totz,
qu'en lieis los volc Dieus triar e assire.

I am blind to other women and deaf as well
since only through her do I see, and hear and heed,
and in saying this, I am surely not just falsely praising,
for my heart desires her more than my mouth can say;
Nowhere, wherever I might roam — through fields
and valleys, plains and mountains —
shall I find in a single body all of those qualities
that God chose to set aside and place in her.

Ben ai estat a maintas bonas cortz,
mas sai ab lieis trob pro mais que lauzar:
mesura e sen e autres bos mestiers,
beutat, joven, bos faitz e bels demors.
Gen l'enseignet Cortesia la duois
tant a de si totz faitz desplazens rotz
de lieis non cre res de ben si adire.

I have been in many a good court,
but here by her I find much more to praise:
measure and wisdom and other good talents,
beauty and youth, worthy deeds and charm;
so well did kindness teach and instruct her
that it has rooted out from her every ill manner:
I don't think she lacks anything at all that is
                        worthwhile.

Nuills jauzimen no.m fora breus ni cortz
de lieis cui prec q'o vuoilla devinar,
o ja per mi non o sabra estiers
si.l cors ses dirs no.s presenta de fors,
que jes Rozers, per aiga qe l'engrois,
non a tal briu c'al cor plus larga dotz
no.m fassa estanc d'amor, quand la remire.

No joy would seem brief or short to me
if it came from her; I beg her to guess what I want;
for from me she will never hear it
unless my heart can reveal itself without words;
even the Rhone, when swelled with water,
cannot produce a roar like I feel in my heart
when weary with love, I hold her in my gaze.

(Song 15, p. 64, ll. 1–28)[16]

In this song we see not only the stylistic verve and audacity that Dante so admired but also something deeper — thematic concerns that emerge from the language itself. This love poet does not work in the pastoral mode; nor does his interest lie in simple imagery and hackneyed praise. The overwhelming sensation of 'Sols sui' is of destabilization, an overcoming of reason. Throughout Arnaut's poetry the battle between reason and subjective destitution rages and in this song he is barely holding his own. The opening stanza imitates the attacks on his sensibility, his silencing before the buzzing in his ears, the reduction of his speech to rote recitation, the denial that acts of communication are actually capable of transmitting meaning. Yet he remains firm and committed to his cause, unshakeable in his determination that 'she', the Lady, represents the only possible conduit *to his own senses*. It is through *her* that he feels, sees, thinks and perceives; and through her that he recognizes goodness, grace and well-being. His obsession with her has led to disability: to wandering, stuttering, mute wonder, and a total loss of sociability. Overcome by a flood of sensation — note the metaphor of the irrepressible and roaring Rhone when fed by mountain streams — he is quite simply at the *mercy* of nature, standing still while the world cascades around him, unable to move or speak, either to approach the lady or denounce her. Jacques Lacan characterizes Arnaut as the troubadour who 'push[es] desire to the extreme point of offering himself in a sacrifice that involves his own annihilation.'[17] I believe it is *this* side of Arnaut that caught Dante's attention and we catch echoes of that infatuation in the praise of Beatrice that we find throughout his *oeuvre*. The devastating effects of the Event of love have laid him open to assault by the world around him and it is his fidelity to that event, even unto his own undoing, that marks him as a believer.

The second song that I want to evoke, and admittedly with less grounding, is the scandalous *sirventes*, 'Puois en Raimons e.n Truc Malecs'. Dante does not mention this song in the *De vulgari eloquentia* but it is on the one hand an excellent example of the 'continuous ode' form that he professed to admire in Arnaut, in which one single rhyme sound works for an entire stanza, and on the other a song whose vocabulary reeks of the shaggy/hairy and combed combination that Dante claims pleased him so much in Arnaut's works ('For in fact it is the mingling of harsh and gentle rhymes that give tragedy its splendour').[18] It is also found in mss ADHIK, all of them Italian manuscripts from the late thirteenth century, the very same manuscripts in which 'Sols sui' is found; and in four of the five manuscripts, the song is explicitly attributed to Arnaut Daniel.[19] It is this other side to Arnaut that deserves an airing here because it seems clear that Dante took inspiration from its topic and form just as much as he did from Arnaut's exalted and sacrificial love poetry and that he likely conflated what he learned with his own poetics:[20]

Puois en Raimons e.n Truc Malecs	Though Raimon and Truc Malec
chapten na Ena e sos decs,	Are defending Lady Ena and her rights,
enans serai vieills e canecs	I'll be old and decrepit
ans que m'acort en aitals precs	before I'd ever agree with requests such as these,
don puosca venir tan grans pecs;	the source of such great wrongdoing:
c'al cornar l'agra mestier becs	for you would need a beak to blow on that horn,
ab que.il traisses del corn los grecs;	one that could excavate from the horn its bits;
e pois pogra ben issir secs	and meanwhile he could go blind just doing so,
que.l fums es fortz qu'ieis dinz dels plecs.	so potent are the fumes that emerge from within those folds.
Ben l'agra ops que fos becutz	He would certainly need to be beaked
E.l becs fos loncs e agutz,	and the beak would have to be long and sharp,
que.l corns es fers, laitz e pelutz	for the horn is wild, ugly and hairy
e nul jorn no estai essutz	and it is never dry
et es prions; dinz ha palutz,	and it is deep; it is like a marsh
per que rellent'en sus lo glutz	and things ferment in that muck;
c'ades per si cor ne redutz:	and all day long things flow there and harden:
e non vuoill que mais sia drutz	and I never want to hear it said that a man
cel que sa boch'al corn condutz.	who put his mouth to that horn could ever be a lover.

(Song 1, p. 2, ll. 1–18)

The bodily, in all its excess, 'the Thing' as Lacan called it, is here put boldly on display with a relish that still surprises readers who pretend that the body was banished from courtly lyric or that if it does appear, it is only as an anomaly. Not the case here, as we see, with Arnaut jumping head first into the *tenso* between En Raimons and Truc Malecs to defend the right of the lover, Bernaut, to abstain from genital/oral contact, despite the request of his lady. Obstinately ambiguous, the song has attracted commentary over the years from critics anxious either to exculpate Arnaut or establish just what the parameters of this 'sexual' act might be — analingus, cunnilingus, fellatio, rimming, or just diarrhoea or menstrual flow? And once Arnaut gets his mouth around that horn or gets his 'beak' into that tunnel, we cease even to consider what *pleasure* might be had from the operation and instead relish the poet's delight in wiping our faces in the abject. The lessons Dante learned from Arnaut might then be dual: just as the hairy and the combed, the rough and the refined, became his model for language use in poetry, following Arnaut; so did muck and the abject quality of the body begin to matter just as much as the sublime: best demonstrated, I suppose, in the Malebolge cantos of the *Inferno*.[21]

The second poet I want to look at, also very briefly, is Sordello, best known since the writing of the *Commedia* as the Mantuan poet who embraces Virgil and leads the pilgrims up the mountain toward the gate of Purgatory in cantos VI–VIII of the *Purgatorio*. Dante mentions him as well in the *De vulgari* and between these two appearances, he emerges in Dante's eyes as a figure of nobility of spirit, refined linguistic tastes and fidelity to the values of the past. If one had not read Dante, however, Sordello would probably still be known, as he was in his time, as a poet on the make, always in the right place at the right time and quick to follow opportunity when it knocked. The Occitan *vidas* found in mss AIK introduce him as a talented young nobleman in need who used and cheated on ladies and patrons in his climb to the top. He is supposed to have fallen in love with Cunizza (again best known through her appearance in *Paradiso* IX), the sister of the tyrant Ezzelino da Romano and his brother, Alberico, though she was already married to the Count of San Bonifacio. On the brothers' urging, already unhappy with their in-laws, Sordello is said to have kidnapped Cunizza from her husband and to have settled with her and her brothers back in Verona for a short time before eloping with the sister of other friends of his, the brothers Strasso, and settling in Treviso. When his life was subsequently threatened by the husband and brothers of his two paramours, he put up a good show of nonchalance but was eventually forced to leave the country and settle in Provence. This love story, infamous at the time of Dante, even to the point that Dante felt able to include mention of Cunizza amongst the formerly lustful in the Heaven of Venus in *Paradiso* IX, was probably as important in Dante's selection of Sordello as a featured character as the upstanding verse of the Mantuan poet. Once again, it seems that Dante is particularly taken by the extreme nature of the love affair: the kidnapping, elopement, threat of murder, exiled wandering, and the severe blow to the reputations of the lovers. Absolute fidelity to the event of love, blended with the commitment to truth and acceptance of its consequences, would seem to have saved both Sordello and Cunizza, at least in Dante's eyes. Let us look briefly at some of the more gnarly imagery used by Sordello in his famous *Planh*, imagery that might, once again, have so impressed the young Dante that he returned to it in his own poetry:[22]

> Planher vuelh en Blacatz en aquest leugier
> Ab cor trist e marrit, et ai en be razo,
> Qu'en luy ai mescabat senhor et amic bo,
> E quar tug l'ayp valent en sa mort perdut so;
> Tant es mortals lo dans qu'ieu non ai sospeisso
> Que ja mais si revenha, s'en aital guiza no;
> Qu'om li traga lo cor e que.n manjo.l baro
> Que vivon descorat, pueys auran de cor pro.
> Premiers manje del cor, per so que grans ops l'es
> L'emperaire de Roma, s'elh vol los Milanes
> Per forsa conquistar, quar luy tenon conques
> E viu deseretatz, malgrat de sos Ties;
> E deseguentre lui manje.n lo reys frances:
> Pueys cobrara Castella que pert per nescies!;
> Mas, si pez'a sa maire, elh no.n manjara ges,
> Quar ben par, a son pretz, qu'elh non fai ren que.l pes.
> Del rei engles me platz, quar es pauc coratjos,
> Que manje pro del cor; pueys er valens e bos,
> E cobrara la terra, per que viu de pretz blos,
> Que.l tol lo reys de Fransa, quar lo sap nualhos;
> E lo reys castelas tanh qu'en manje per dos,
> Quar dos regismes ten, e per l'un non es pros!
> Mas, s'elh en vol manjar, tanh qu'en manj'a rescos,
> Que, si.l mair'o sabia, batria.l ab bastos!

> [so, I want to mourn for Lord Blacatz in this pleasant tune
> Though I do so with a sad and heavy heart; and right I am
> For in him I lost a good friend and lord;
> And all the treasured traits of virtue have died with him.
> So mortal is this loss that I suspect
> That they are now gone forever, unless my plan is accepted:
> That we cut out the heart of the man and let the barons eat of it
> Those men who live in dishonour; that way they might
> imbibe some of his worth.
> First let's have the Emperor of Rome eat of the heart:
> That would be essential if he is were ever to conquer the Milanesi
> By force; for they think of him as already conquered:
> A man with no inheritance, despite his German friends.
> Then let's have the King of France take a bite:
> He might then be able to take back Castille, that he lost through ineptitude
> But if his mother doesn't approve, he won't go near it
> For it appears that, to his credit, he never goes against his mamma.
> The English King I like because he is short on heart/courage
> Let him get a good bite of that heart; then he will be good and valiant
> And he will get back his land — he now lives in disrespect —
> The land that the King of France took, useless as he is;
> And the King of Castille had better eat two whole ones
> Since he now has two kingdoms and he doesn't deserve even one!
> But, if he wants to eat one, he had better do it in secret
> For if his mother knew about it she would take a stick to him!]

> (Song 26, p. 108, ll. 1–24)[23]

There is good reason to believe that Dante might also have seen something of himself in the figure of Sordello. In exile for almost forty years in the Savoie and Provence, then visitor at the aristocratic courts of Spain, the Aquitaine, and finally an illustrious stay of twenty-five years at the itinerant court of Charles d'Anjou, brother of Louis IX, in his courtly centres in Provence, Sicily and Naples before his death in 1270, Sordello never really settled. By the time that Dante composed the *Commedia*, he had almost too much in common with the Mantuan poet/scholar/ diplomat, and very likely recognized himself in his fate. Speaking *ex cathedra*, casting judgement upon his contemporaries, especially his political contemporaries, Dante could easily have emulated Sordello's knack for directing invective against his enemies and all those guilty of degrading the courtly values upon which civic virtue depended. Most appealingly of all, both Arnaut and Sordello contain their wider interests within the framework of love, that capacious mistress within whose realm all else is contained and to whom they remain faithful, faithful enough to cast umbrage upon all those who fail to make the grade.

In the last section of this paper, I am going to take a closer look at this author figure who speaks from within the realm of love — or in Dante's terms, Paradise. If God's creation is a set, to return to some of Badiou's mathematical obsessions, what can lie outside of that set and still maintain intelligibility? How can an author speak from within that set while physically absent from the afterlife? And what is the status of the post-paradisiacal pilgrim, returned to earth and chastened by his experience in the heavens?

Bersani

> Psychoanalysis has conceptualized desire as the mistaken reaction to a loss; it has been unable to think desire as the confirmation of a community of being.[24]

> [...] sexual desire initiates, indeed can be recognized by, an agitated fantasmatic activity in which original (but from the start, unlocatable) objects of desire get lost in the images they generate. Desire, by its very nature, turns us away from its objects.[25]

It is the phrases of 'community of being' and 'turning away' that capture my attention in these two citations by Leo Bersani, particularly in how they relate to the *Commedia*. If sexual desire conjures up fantasies in which objects of desire get lost in the images that they generate; and if the consequence of that desire is that the objects that we think we desire get left by the wayside, then this might be seen as an apposite comment on Dante's wayward conclusion to the *Paradiso*. Many critics have tried to read Dante through psychoanalysis, though never with very convincing results, and I will probably be relegated to that heap myself, but I do want to distinguish myself from some of the more reductive accounts of Dante's Oedipal struggles by turning instead to Leo Bersani's philosophical, rather than clinical, reading of subjectivity. After a lifetime of writing on psychoanalysis and aesthetics, it is only in his latest collection, titled after one of his most celebrated essays, *Is the Rectum a Grave? and other essays*, that Bersani's thinking can be read as independent of standard psychoanalysis, both in his emphasis on the aesthetic as an alternative mode of being and in his incorporation of what, for lack of a better term, we could call queer theory. Dissolution of the subject, the aggression invoked by difference (especially sexual difference), and the folly of grasping at notions of stability and possession are among the touchstones of this later work and they bring us back to the central topic of subjective destitution with which I began. In the essay 'Sociality and Sexuality', for example, he says:

> In other words, I have been proposing that we think of the sexual — more specifically, of *jouissance* in sexuality — as a defeat of power, a giving up, on the part of an otherwise hyperbolically self-affirming and phallocentrically constituted ego, of its projects of mastery.[26]

While it might be hard to claim that Dante the poet ever completely gives up the quest for mastery, or for ego enforcement for that matter, I would contend that it is quite a different case when it comes to his pilgrim and it is to that topic that I now turn. We, or I at least, know nothing about Dante's sexuality or about his love interests or his family or even his sexual identifications; but he offers us a rather candid account of such things as they relate to his fictional pilgrim. That pilgrim, in his travels through the cantos and the worlds they represent, does, in fact, forsake mastery, a mastery that he seems to have lost even before undertaking the voyage. Instead of roaming the world, searching for the self in the other, as we might expect from a psychoanalytically informed reading, by the text's end he seems almost happy to endure the loss of phallic identity. He settles into an almost complete reliance on male mentors while retaining the parental guidance of the stern and virginal Beatrice and his almost obsessive reverence of love itself. This 'stripping of the body of its imposed and unnecessary sexual identity', what Bersani refers to as a process of 'corporeal clearance', does not in any way correspond to a desexualization of the *Paradiso*, as some might argue, or a necessary spiritualization or allegorization of what has been, throughout the voyage, an undeniably sensual and bodily experience.[27] Sexuality has instead become something that one submits to, something overwhelming and instigated from without, a cleansing whose aim seems to be the defeat, as Bersani would have it, of the subjective as such. The new type of sexual interaction one encounters in the *Paradiso* involves not only the temporary erasure of subjectivity, already familiar from the Lacanian notion of *jouissance*, but a more permanent and more traumatic entry into a state of mystical and sensual being, a state that entails not only the merger of the soul with another soul of superior worth but a merging within a collective of souls of light that implies a loss of interest in subjective control *tout court*.[28] One could read this experience as a theological allegory, of course, especially along the lines of Badiou's description of eventual truth-procedures, but it can also be read as an allegory of a new form of sexuality: one that retreats from the aggressive tension of Girardean mimetic triangles and Freudian Oedipal struggles to move into what Bersani calls a 'non-suicidal dissolution of the subject'.[29]

Rejecting psychoanalysis's dead-ended insistence on structural and irresolvable 'loss' and 'lack', Bersani turns instead to what he calls 'productive masochism': 'not [...] pleasure in pain so much as the pleasure of at once losing the self and discovering it elsewhere, inaccurately replicated.'[30] The boundaries and borders that tie up the ego, that hold together identity are violated not only as a masochistic phenomenon, but also as an effect of reaching towards one's own 'form' elsewhere. This self-dissolution is also self-accretion; it is self-incremental. And so, thanks to the non-psychoanalytic notion of the correspondence of forms, psychoanalysis is conceptually enriched by the category of a masochism identical to narcissism.[31]

In *Paradiso*, of course, this masochism translates into a form of body that is transported effortlessly by other bodies, a body that loses its sight and its orientation and is frequently overwhelmed by the razzmatazz of music and dance. The pilgrim becomes a passive voyager whose very success can be measured by the loss of his hold on sensual containment. And as his bodily senses are overwhelmed, his mental sensations are magnified. Desire for lost objects is replaced by fulfilment within a new community of being that makes those objects insignificant, one in which individual souls are encountered as almost identical puzzle pieces in a cosmic design of enforced contiguity and sociability. In this sense, we could claim Dante as a queer theorist *avant la lettre*, a designer of new models of social and sexual communities in which individual subjects, while they certainly exist, are less important than the communities from within which they operate and in which sex is essentially communal, ubiquitous, and non-volitional.

The communities of Dante's paradise are odd formulations principally because they no longer rely on social relations at all, but are permeated with what Lino Pertile calls 'daringly erotic terms'.[32] Everyone has his place in these communities but discourse seems to have been left behind. All conscious attention (if either of those words has any meaning in the context of the *Paradiso*) is focused on the centre alone, the source of love. The pilgrim, until the moment when he was finally able to surpass the subjective and the proprietary, had been just another quester, seeking the answer to the eternal mystery, the enigmatic signifier: What do you know that I don't? What do you have in mind for me that you have been hiding all these years? In rejecting those questions in the final cantos of the *Paradiso*, in suggesting that there will finally be a moment in which they no longer matter, Dante has taken a step toward a human, utopian, and mystical collective and away from what we might think of as more overtly psychoanalytical, religious, earthly explanations. Instead of roaming the world in search of the lost object of desire; instead of fantasizing that someone else holds the key to his inner sanctum, the pilgrim is simply inserted into a complex design and essentially disappears into the greater glory of the collective. So what is the lesson about desire that he can bring back to the mortals below? How can he live again according to our less evolved ethics? What, in essence, comes after the event?

The first part of any answer to these questions would be that choice as we know it would have little role to play. The post-eventual subject becomes a slave to the event, after all, not a free man exposed to the illusions of freedom. The pilgrim would almost certainly need to be an ascetic, or an artist, or both: someone clinging to the lessons that he had learned, seared by what he had seen. The things that had once motivated him would matter little by then — except perhaps for ambition, which might be thrown off in the highest heaven but can never completely be occluded when operating within the imperfect and incomprehensible realm below. Desire, however, would surely cease to operate according to the fundamental fantasies of imagined wholeness and mastery; yet love would retain its status as the one event to which he owed fidelity. And what form would that love take, given that it would have to extend to all of God's creation rather than being unidirectional? It would likely be a rather passive affair or at least an operation that aimed at self-erasure in some sense, a way of losing sight of the self — what Bersani called '*jouissance* as a mode of ascesis' or what Virginia Burrus calls 'an active passivity, a wilfully embraced humiliation'.[33] Marriage never seemed particularly high on Dante's list at any rate, and physical passion, especially sexual passion, is almost absent from most of his work.[34] Communal pedagogy, friendship, and exposure to mind-blowing art would instead seem the most propitious way to propagate sanctity, anything that guaranteed a winnowing away of the ego as well as desire in the banal, psychoanalytical sense. There would no longer be any need to find oneself in the beloved; no reason really to distinguish at all between individuals except by virtue of their adherence to the divine plan. Sex, in other words, is more or less defunct, at least as we know it, with no further use for the death drive and no need for imagined oneness once one had seen the real thing. Language would no longer be alienating, at least in so far as you would now have access to a non-linguistic form of communication that supplements its own lacunae. Finally, as I alluded to earlier, the newly born pilgrim would by necessity become an aesthetic subject, someone whose attentiveness to the ways in which God delivers his product is a constant source of wonder.[35] It is precisely in this sense that Dante can be read as a queer and modern author: non-dualistic in Barolini's sense, post-traumatic, challenging social and religious convention, communitarian rather than coupled, sensuously open to the world and freed from the reins of possession.[36] The fantasy that structures the *Commedia* is the fantasy of the post-eventual convert whose body, now imbued with the divine, leads him to vacate the interior space of consciousness to become instead a body of pure surface, a receptor of the waves of love that emanate from the material of creation.

Notes to Chapter 1

1. Teodolinda Barolini, 'Beyond (Courtly) Dualism: Thinking about Gender in Dante's Lyrics', in *Dante for the New Millennium*, ed. by Teodolinda Barolini and H. Wayne Storey (New York: Fordham University Press, 2003), pp. 65–89 (p. 67).

2. See Regina Psaki's excellent 'Love for Beatrice: Transcending Contradiction in the *Paradiso*', in Barolini and Storey, eds, *Dante for the New Millennium*, pp. 115–30.

3. See Teodolinda Barolini, *The Undivine 'Comedy': Detheologizing Dante* (Princeton, NJ: Princeton University Press, 1992).

4. See Dylan Evans's entry in *An Introductory Dictionary of Lacanian Psychoanalysis* (London and New York: Routledge, 1996), p. 52, and Leo Bersani's definition: 'at once loved as a source of narcissistic satisfaction (it possesses "the perversions which we have striven to reach for our own ego") and feared as a source of rageful moral (frequently moralistic) demands made upon the ego', in 'Sociability and Cruising', in *Is the Rectum a Grave? and Other Essays* (Chicago, IL, and London: University of Chicago Press, 2010), pp. 45–62 (p. 52).

5. Bersani, 'Sociality and Sexuality', in *Is the Rectum a Grave?*, pp. 102–19 (pp. 106–07).

6. Jean Laplanche, *Seduction, Translation, Drives*, ed. by John Fletcher and Martin Stanton, trans. by Martin Stanton (London: Institute of Contemporary Arts, 1992).

7. Bersani, 'Sociality and Sexuality', p. 106.

8. ibid., p. 106.

9. Alain Badiou and Nicolas Truong, *Éloge de l'amour* (Paris: Flammarion, 2009).

10. 'Io non so ben ridir com'i' v'intrai | Tant'era pien di sonno a quel punto | che la verace via abbandonai' [How I came there I cannot really tell, | I was so full of sleep | when I forsook the one true way] (*Inf.* I, 10–12). Translations of the *Commedia* are from: Dante Alighieri, *Comedy*, trans. by Robert Hollander and Jean Hollander, 3 vols (New York: Doubleday, 2000–07).

11. Alain Badiou, *Saint Paul et la fondation de l'universalisme* (Paris: Presses Universitaires de France, 1997), p. 70; translated by Ray Brassier as *Saint Paul: The Foundation of Universalism* (Minneapolis: University of Minnesota Press, 2000).

12. Peter Hallward, *Badiou: A Subject to Truth* (Minneapolis and London: University of Minnesota Press, 2003), p. 148.

13. Hallward, p. xxiv.

14. Alain Badiou, 'What is love? Sexuality and desire. 2008. 2/12' at: <http://www.youtube.com/watch?v=iPZeXfJQbQw> [accessed on 26 March 2010].

15. Badiou, *Saint Paul*, p. 92 (my translation).

16. Cited from Arnaut Daniel, *Sirventese e canzoni*, ed. by Giosuè Lachin (Turin: Einaudi, 2000), pp. 64–67 (all citations from Arnaut's poetry are taken from this edition and all translations are my own).

17. Jacques Lacan, 'Supplementary Note: A Curious Case of Sublimation', in *The Seminar of Jacques Lacan, Book 7: The Ethics of Psychoanalysis 1959–1960*, ed. by Jacques-Alain Miller and trans. by Dennis Porter (New York and London: Norton, 1992), p. 163.

18. 'Nam lenium asperorumque rithimorum mixtura ipsa tragedia nitescit' (*DVE* II, XIII, 12). Translation taken from Dante, *De vulgari Eloquentia*. ed. and trans. by Steven Botterill (Cambridge: Cambridge University Press, 1996). As for the hairy and combed distinction, Dante refers to these as 'yrsuta' and 'pexa' in *DVE* II, vii, 2.

19. In ms A, however, the song is attributed to Giraut de Borneilh and in CR it is attributed to Arnaut de Mareuil. See James J. Wilhelm, *The Poetry of Arnaut Daniel* (London and New York: Garland, 1983), p. 115.

20. Barolini refers to Dante's taste for 'degradation of the courtly world through juxtapositions that carry shock value', in 'Beyond (Courtly) Dualism', p. 78.

21. See Zygmunt G. Barański, 'Scatology and Obscenity in Dante', in Barolini and Storey, eds, *Dante for the New Millennium*, pp. 259–73.

22. Teodolinda Barolini, *Dante's Poets: Textuality and Truth in the 'Comedy'* (Princeton, NJ: Princeton University Press, 1984).

23. Wilhelm, *The Poetry of Sordello* (London and New York: Garland, 1987), p. 108.

24. Bersani, 'Sociality and Sexuality', p. 105.

25. Bersani, 'Is the Rectum a Grave', in *Is the Rectum a Grave?*, pp. 3–30 (p. 28).

26. Bersani, 'Sociality and Sexuality', p. 109.

27. '[...] we may feel justified in arguing that Freud initiated Foucault's major enterprise of what might be called corporeal clearance — that is, stripping the body of its imposed and unnecessary sexual identity and presenting it as a marvellously variegated surface of flesh available to as yet unarticulated pleasures suppressed and crippled by the at once authorized and prohibited excitement of something called sex': Bersani, 'Fr-oucault and the End of Sex', in *Is the Rectum a Grave?*, pp. 133–39 (pp. 136–37).

28. In a similar vein, Bersani refers to 'fucking as "a defeat of the subjective as such"', in 'Sociality and Sexuality', p. 109.

29. 'A conversation with Leo Bersani', in Bersani, *Is the Rectum a Grave?*, pp. 171–86 (p. 174).

30. ibid., p. 174.

31. ibid., pp. 184–85.

32. Lino Pertile, 'Does the *Stilnovo* Go to Heaven?', in Barolini and Storey, eds, *Dante for the New Millennium*, pp. 104–14 (p. 104).

33. Bersani, 'Is the Rectum a Grave?', p. 30, and Virginia Burrus, 'A Saint of One's Own: Emmanuel Levinas, Eliezer ben Hyrcanus, and Eulalia of Mérida', *L'Esprit Créateur (Sanctity)*, 50.1 (Spring 2010), 6–18.

34. Pertile, '*Stilnovo*', p. 106.
35. 'Art can in effect position us as aesthetic rather than psychoanalytically defined subjects within the world': Bersani, 'Psychoanalysis and the Aesthetic Subject', in *Is the Rectum a Grave?*, pp. 139–53 (p. 142).
36. Or, as Regina Psaki puts it: 'The created universe is simultaneously geocentric and theocentric (*Par.* 28). Heaven is both desire and satiation' (p. 124).

CHAPTER 2

'L'ora che volge il disio': Comparative Hermeneutics of Desire in Dante and 'Aṭṭār

Daniela Boccassini

'L'ora che volge il disio'

In the opening line of *Purgatorio* VIII Dante makes reference to that particular time of day when the soul experiences an inner stirring unlikely to happen during either daytime, when the rational mind is in control, or nighttime, when consciousness ultimately surrenders to higher powers. What happens at dusk, in that brief span of time which is no longer day nor yet night, and hence partakes of both, is a 'turning about' of desire: 'Era già l'ora che volge il disio'.[1]

I need to emphasize that Dante here is not evoking a turning of the mind towards one's emotional, semi-conscious attachment to an external object of grasping. Contrary to what is too often repeated by commentators, and even more disquietingly claimed by translators, in these celebrated lines Dante is not focusing on the seamen's supposed yearning for the sweet friends they left behind, nor on the pilgrim's alleged nostalgia. What Dante conjures up for us here is an inner event of a completely different nature: it is a turning of desire onto itself unconditionally. The individuals most prone to this experience of an awakening of desire to itself, Dante further declares, are those seafarers and pilgrims who have left their homes in earnest, but have not yet entered the deep waters of their journey proper.[2] In the twilight of the waning day they still see what they have left behind, with all the melancholy that this condition involves, but cannot yet make out where they are heading, with all the anxiety that this predicament entails.

Even more importantly, this uncanny turning of desire onto itself, within a consciousness that is hovering between the not yet and the no longer, is what causes the heart to become tender (''ntenerisce il core'), is what allows the soul to be pierced by love ('d'amore | punge'). It is, in other words, what lets one's field of consciousness become entirely open, what makes the mind grow purely reflexive, what allows one's life journey to become true onto itself.

The effects of this radical 'volgere' of desire are mirrored in the narrative scene that follows these lines: rather than contemplate the sunset and mourn 'il giorno che si more' [the dying of the day], one of the souls among the negligent princes turns her[3] longing eyes towards the East,[4] and focusing single-pointedly on the dark horizon whence the sun will rise again, invokes divine defence against the dangers that besiege human consciousness, notably at night.[5] The soul does so by intoning the canonical hymn of Compline, thus inviting the other souls to join in the singing. Such are the sweetness and devotion of the chant that Dante experiences ecstasy — literally, the removal of his self from his own mind (ἐκ-στασις; 13–15). This exit of oneself from one's mind is precisely what the turning about of desire elicits: a removal to elsewhere than one's individual consciousness (the shore), a sailing towards the vastness which is Truth itself (the deep waters), that is to say Ultimate Reality experienced directly for what it is: unmediated, unsayable Awareness.

At this precise moment Dante interrupts the narrative and summons the reader to 'aguzzar la vista', so as to *recognize* the veil, become able to 'trapassar dentro', and reach onto Truth itself (19–21).[6] As we all know, in the Western world the topos of the veil connotes the figurative interpretation of a text, whereby the reader is urged to extract inner, 'true' meaning from an outer, possibly 'false', certainly ephemeral, form. However, in the Indo-Mediterranean world at large this same image is universally understood as the veil of cosmic illusion, as 'what the Hindus call *Maya*, and the Sufis *hijāb*'.[7] In this larger perspective, which includes our narrower understanding as well, the veil stands for manifest existence, Reality itself, which simultaneously conceals Truth to those minds that get caught into what shimmers on the surface, and discloses Truth to those minds that recognize, in and through those same luminous shadows, the Divine Mind at play. Hence, '*Maya* is the supreme veil and also the supreme theophany which at once veils and reveals.'[8] In the words of Muhyiddin Ibn 'Arabī, the great thirteenth-century Sufi master: 'The universe is neither pure being nor pure nothingness. It is entirely magic: it makes you believe that it is god/God, and it is not god/God; it makes you believe it is creation and it is not creation, for it is neither this nor that in all respects.'[9]

When we as humans come to realize that it is precisely the uniqueness of our human nature which allows us to partake simultaneously of both dimensions of Reality, of Immanence *and* of Transcendence, then we also come to see ourselves as poised at the isthmus between these two inseparable, complementary perspectives. That, Dante suggests, is what we come to see in the now polished mirror of cosmic reality at dusk ('l'ora che volge il disio'), when our consciousness is still, and yet no longer caught in the gleams of the veil of cosmic illusion.[10]

On the Nature of Desire

If we were to ask *what* allows or prevents the advent of this miraculous 'trapassar dentro', which mirrors and complements the ἐκ-στασις, the exiting of the mind from its existential limits, the answer Dante provides should now be obvious: desire itself, in its different modes of manifestation. Desire illusorily conceived in a linear manner — that is to say in the form of a subject grasping at an object vainly perceived as ontologically existent — traps the mind into the desiring process itself, and causes consciousness to abide in ignorance: *avidya*, lack of understanding. But once desire turns onto itself and engages in a circular, self-reflexive motion, then consciousness exits from its illusory self-awareness, lifts the veil, and merges with the space of pure Self-Awareness: *vidya*, ultimate wisdom, where the two dimensions of Immanence and Transcendence become simultaneously manifest. That is where human desire comes to realize that its only yearning is to become one with divine desire, and yet also paradoxically understands that the only way to achieve that single-pointed aspiration is by abiding in the experience of human desire itself. A human desire which, however, is eventually to be experienced in its 'alchemically transmuted' form. This transmutative turning about of desire, this act of salvific self/Self-mirroring is what allows the soul to 'trapassar dentro' Maya's veil, what sets human consciousness on the journey towards the beyond of the worldly, contingent self. In this 'inside-ful' dimension, Immanence, far from being erased or negated, reveals itself as the visible face of Transcendence — that is to say the only face of Ultimate Reality we, as humans, can experience.

What I am saying here is that for Dante the path to salvation does not imply, could not possibly imply a *renunciation* of desire — desire being the stuff of life itself, and therefore ultimately un-renounceable. Rather, Dante insists on the necessity to subject human desire to a process of conversion (a radical 'turning about' of consciousness) whereby desire ignorant of itself transmutes into 'sanctified' desire, desire made whole/holy, hence fully cognizant of its fundamental nature as pure Self. In this way earthly desire becomes the means in and through which c/ Consciousness realizes the workings of cosmic desire. This transmutative process does not affect Reality as such, but rather human nature, in the form of an inner journey of return to the source — the inevitability, and universality, of which Dante himself had already stated in the fourth book of the *Convivio*,[11] before restating it endlessly in the unfolding of the *Commedia*.

What this journey of return implies is what lies at the core of any and all esoteric paths to the divine — should we wish to label them mystical, Gnostic, Neoplatonic, Avicennian, Sufi, Tantric and more: in all such instances the 'nuovo e mai non fatto cammino di questa vita' [new and never traveled road of this life] (*Conv.* IV, xii, 15) is what leads to enlightenment, to what Schuon calls 'metaphysical realization, by which man becomes conscious of that which has never really ceased to be, namely, his essential identity with the Divine Principle that alone is real.'[12]

It is in this universalizing perspective — a perspective that we can call esoteric insofar as it always privileges the inner aspect of reality over and through the outer, exoteric one[13] — that a comparative reading of Dante's *Commedia* becomes, to my mind, truly revealing. And especially so if we accept to read Dante's poetic journey against the backdrop of similar poetic narratives written within the context of the religious tradition towards which Dante always manifested a quite open animosity, namely Islam. But precisely because that animosity originated in what Dante perceived as a historical severing of the universal bond that ties all men to 'The One outside of whom there is no god' [*La ilaha illa 'llah*],[14] it is enthralling to see how convergent Dante's universalistic views are with those expressed by some of the most accomplished visionary poets of Islam, such as 'Aṭṭār, Ibn 'Arabī, Sanā'ī,

Rumī. Perhaps not surprisingly, all of these poets were either Dante's elders, or his contemporaries.[15]

But before I come to the Islamic medieval narrative that most emphatically addresses the issue of desire in relation to the dynamics of the journey of inner transmutation, I wish to quote a passage from a doctrinal treatise by a Sufi master of the early twelfth century, where the workings of 'great desire' through the dynamics of earthly desire are described in terms Dante would have unconditionally approved of:

> Desire is the quality of longing and affliction in the heart, which is activated by the representation of the beauty of its goal. This creates an inner movement and an emotion in the heart inviting it to go on until the goal will be attained. The wish for the beloved sets the heart into motion and makes it desirous. That desire attracting the heart carries on the body and helps the seeker to set out on his way till he sees that there is a better stage than the one he aspires to. Then he will see how he should move to reach that higher stage and orbit.[16]

As we can see, desire as longing is the primary, unchangeable constituent of life, springing from the heart: a space which, like a cup, yearns to be filled once it comes to the realization of its inherent emptiness. This is the 'gift of longing' that all human beings share, making every individual potentially fit for the journey. For that to happen, though, there needs to arise an inner representation of 'the beauty of the goal', an inner stirring which 'intenerisce il core', makes the heart open, receptive. This is what allows the soul to switch from an initial 'wish for the beloved' to the subsequent realization of a 'better stage than the one he aspires to', which in turn creates the conditions for the soul to engage on the path of inner transmutation and thus reach not the object — there is no more object here — but rather a 'higher stage and orbit'. The spiraling movement of desire turning onto itself unconditionally, and hence 'perfecting' itself, is clearly visible in this passage.[17]

Desire and/as the Journey

Let us now turn to Fariddoddin 'Attār's *Mantiq al-Tayr*, traditionally translated as *The Conference of the Birds*.[18] This is a late twelfth-century Persian mystic poem (*mathnawī*) that narrates how the souls-birds initially compelled to fly to their own beautiful object of desire — whatever that may be — end up soaring to a much higher, all-encompassing desire which takes them onto a quest for Ultimate Truth. The poem ends with an attempt to convey symbolically the ineffable realization that crowns the souls-birds' life-long journey to the abode of their longed-for sovereign.[19]

At the beginning of the *mathnawī*, then, we see countless birds gather around the Cosmic Tree and the Water of Life that springs from its roots. In this holy space the birds express their yearning for an absolute Principle that might confer meaning to their lives.[20] At this initial stage, the birds are helpless: neither do they know how to achieve their goal, nor can they fathom what their search will entail. Only the hoopoe, whose lifelong service as Solomon's messenger has opened her heart to a deeper understanding of the Real, sees through their predicament. She knows that their sovereign, the mythical bird Simorgh, does exist, but she also knows that finding him is a disproportionate task: 'The Simorgh lives, the sovereign whom you seek [...] His creatures strive to find a path to Him, | Deluded by each new, deceitful whim, | But fancy cannot work as she would wish. | [...] The journey asks of you a lion's heart' (*The Conference of the Birds*, pp. 33–34).

While the hoopoe's inspiring first speech arouses the birds' collective enthusiasm, a closer look at what lies ahead makes them recoil into their small, yet safe, familiar identity. Every bird declares his inability to embark on the journey by adducing a seemingly valid reason, pertaining to the fulfillment of his unique kind of earthly desire. The hoopoe skillfully values these contingencies in their noble potential, but dismisses them in their miserly outcome. Repeatedly, she urges the birds not to give up their desire — which makes them inherently 'worthy of the Simorgh's throne' — but rather to redirect it by opening their heart to a larger understanding of it. Only in this way will they embark fearlessly on the voyage to the unknown, following an untraced path: 'In drops you lose yourselves, yet you must dive | Through untold fathoms and remain alive. | This is no journey for the indolent — Our quest is Truth itself, not just its scent!' (p. 51).[21]

And yet, the birds will not embark on their journey until the hoopoe reveals to them 'what relationship obtains | Between [the Simorgh's] might and ours' (p. 52), so as to allow them to reach a direct understanding of that logically unfathomable relationship: the Simorgh is the sunlight, she declares, and they are his countless shadows — just like the Cosmos in its entirety is.[22] This revelation is embodied by the hoopoe in the worldly narrative of a sovereign, his subjects and the mediating power of mirrors, a narrative meant to help the birds move from an outer to an inner understanding of their own, outer and inner, finite and infinite, identity. The whole *mathnawī* is in turn mirrored in this dynamic. On the one hand, the metanarrative tells the story of how the birds do succeed in leaving behind their worldly lives while searching for their sovereign Simorgh and how that quest ultimately divests them of their former self.[23] On the other hand, the actual body of the poem is made up of a multitude of stories which, like infinite mirrors, illustrate how the workings of desire (including the reader's desire to read on) trigger a process of inner transmutation which cannot unfold except in and through the body: the universal body of manifest creation, the physical body of the seeker, the body of the poem itself.

As for Dante, he repeatedly declares that his journey through the beyond was an embodied one, whereby he eventually found himself to be same and yet other — other and yet the same — at the end as he was at the outset. Moreover, we see that the wayfarer's journey unfolds by way of innumerable encounters with souls who become manifest through an otherworldly 'shadow-body', thus allowing Dante and his readers to 'lift the veil' and peek into the nature of the relationship between time and eternity. By getting to see with Dante, in the mirror of his poem, that dimension of reality which neither he nor the souls could access while on earth, we are offered a chance to achieve an insight into the ultimate nature of Reality in a way fit for human understanding, that is to say simultaneously embodied and disembodying.

We are reaching here what lies at the core of Dante's quest, and, as we shall presently see, of 'Aṭṭār's souls-birds' quest as well: namely, that something which allows and sustains the unfolding of 'gran disio' through the earthly into the heavenly, as Dante himself declares when he realizes he has unknowingly entered with his body the first of the heavenly bodies, the Moon:

> Per entro sé l'etterna margarita
> ne ricevette, com'acqua recepe
> raggio di luce permanendo unita.
> S'io era corpo, e qui non si concepe
> com'una dimensione altra patio,
> ch'esser convien se corpo in corpo repe,
> accender ne dovria più il disio
> di veder quella essenza in che si vede
> come nostra natura e Dio s'unio. (*Par.* II, 34–42)

> [Into itself the eternal margarite | took us as water will receive a ray | of light, remaining, even so, all one. | If I was there in body (we can't grasp | how one dimension takes another in, | as — body snaked in body — needs must be) | that should ignite in us still more desire | to see that being where, as can be seen, | our human nature is at one with God.]

The 'being' Dante alludes to is of course Christ, and the mystery he grapples with is that of the Incarnation, central to the Christian faith. However, Dante is also saying something else here, something of the utmost importance but also rather suspect, within the official parameters of Christianity: namely, that man's desire to contemplate the supreme mystery of the Incarnation can be fully aroused only by a direct experience of what the Islamic world calls *tajallī*, that is to say Theophany, or Divine Apparition — *tajallī* being something *other* than, and yet akin to, Christ's Incarnation proper.[24]

Tajallī means that the Divine becomes visible to man by shining, as in a mirror, within the human form, or, for that matter, throughout the entire universe. Thus, the mystery of theophany is both revealed and concealed in ordinary, yet unfathomable contingencies such as a ray of light partaking of water, which allows us to realize how, conversely, water partakes of light. In other words, the Transcendent continually manifests itself, and therefore can be apprehended on earth, through and within its conjunction with the immanent — an untenable proposition in a fully orthodox Christological perspective, and yet one that informs the poetic expression of all *Fedeli d'Amore*, regardless of their religious affiliation. As we know, Dante had an enduring experience of *tajallī* in his youthful encounter with Beatrice, 'la gloriosa donna de la mia mente' [the glorious lady of my mind], which the *Vita Nuova* accounts for in terms that more often than not appear alarmingly coterminous with those used in Christianity to refer to the Son of God. In 'Aṭṭār's poem, the hoopoe *is* a *tajallī* for the birds that receive her teachings: they would have never found the Way without her.

However, such manifestation of the Infinite within and through the finite ceases to appear blasphemous, once man realizes (in the double meaning of the word) the relationship that 'in Reality' obtains between visible and invisible, between Immanence and Transcendence: in that non-dual mirror we come to see how we as humans are God's shadow and more generally, how the whole universe is but the manifestation of God's desire to be known through his unending theophany.[25] As the hoopoe reveals to the birds, still uncertain of their relationship to the Simorgh:

> Thus we were born; the birds of every land
> Are still his shadows — think, and understand.
> If you had known this secret you would see
> The link between yourselves and Majesty.
> Do not reveal this truth, and God forfend
> That you mistake for God himself God's friend.
> If you become that substance I propound,
> You are not God, though in God you are drowned;
> Those lost in Him are not the Deity —
> This problem can be argued endlessly.
> You are his shadow [...]
> Your heart is not a mirror bright and clear
> If there the Simorgh's form does not appear;
> No one can bear His beauty face to face,
> And for this reason, of His perfect grace,
> He makes a mirror in our hearts — look there
> To see Him, search your hearts with anxious care.
> (*The Conference of the Birds*, pp. 52–53)

God, then, becomes visible in the mirror of human speculation, and the supreme form of speculation (mirroring, reflection) man could hope for was, across the Mediterranean, the beatific vision of God's face, the realization of mystical union in the polished mirror of the heart.[26] Let us see, then, where the journey of 'Attār's souls-birds leads them: as we can by now surmise, to a realization of Transcendence as/in/through Immanence not all that different from Dante's.

The Voyage around the Unmovable Mover

'A world of birds set out — sings 'Attār — and there remained | But thirty when the promised goal was gained, | Thirty exhausted, wretched, broken things, | With hopeless hearts and tattered, trailing wings' (*The Conference of the Birds*, p. 214). However extraordinary the feat of having reached the Simorgh's abode may be, the birds' journey is far from over. Just as Dante has to confront a lifetime of short-comings before he can mirror himself into Beatrice's eyes,[27] and eventually reach onto God's face, the thirty birds now have to contend with a merciless guard who plans to send them back, and then, even more painfully, they must behold the unbearably true likeness of their own lives, as it shows on a page of divine script. The consuming power of shame eventually allows them to give up their will entirely. By 'rising free' of their past actions, they become ready to approach 'the eternal moment in which — in Meister Eckhart's terms — the divine is giving birth to itself in the soul.'[28]

Here is, in 'Attār's words, the birds' final vision. The thirty birds have now merged into one entity: gone is the hoopoe, and gone are her followers. The birds silently speak in one voice, yet maintain the use of the plural to express their multiple, yet unified, identity/-ies:

> There in the Simorgh's radiant face they saw
> Themselves, the Simorgh of the world — with awe
> They gazed, and dared at last to comprehend
> They were the Simorgh and the journey's end.
> They see the Simorgh — at themselves they stare,
> And see a second Simorgh standing there;
> They look at both and see the two are one,
> That this is *that*, *that* this, the goal is won.
> They ask (but inwardly; they make no sound)
> The meaning of these mysteries that confound
> Their puzzled ignorance — how is it true
> That 'we' is not distinguished here from 'you'?
> (*The Conference of the Birds*, p. 219)

The birds' final vision of the Simorgh thus coincides with the supreme revelation of the meaning of their journey, couched in the form of an anticlimactic wordplay, which I now must explain. In 'Attār's *mathnawī* the word Simorgh refers to the ancient, mythical bird who is 'the visible manifestation of the Divine'.[29] However, in Farsi the word *si* means 'thirty' and the word *morgh* means 'bird'. That is to say: although the word Simorgh as referring to the Lord of the birds probably derives from the Avestic *Saena Meregha* through middle Persian *Sēnmurgh*, 'Attār deliberately plays on the homophony between 'Simorgh' and 'si-morgh', so as to achieve a baffling final identity between the sovereign and his subjects.

But this is far from being the end of the matter. Rather, 'Attār masterfully turns a banal pun onto itself and generates a *shat'h* — that is to say a spiritual paradox aimed at awakening the mind of the seeker to a higher level of awareness. The homophony Simorgh/si-morgh is precisely what allows 'Attār to 'trapassar dentro' the shimmering surface of wordplay and approach the inner, esoteric dimension of the very notion of identity. Beyond the exoteric appearance, which may mislead one into believing that 'there is no Simorgh other than the thirty birds', lies an altogether different understanding of the issue: whose 'identity' is concealed and revealed to whom within the very notion of 'identity' between the two Simorgh/si-morgh?

What we are facing here is what Michael Sells calls a 'meaning event',[30] that is to say the poetic performance of that act of supreme mirroring which is the realization of mystical union, whereby being and existence, subject and object collapse into each other — as do human desire and cosmic desire at this final stage of the inner journey. In this verbal reflection of the mystical realization saying becomes unsaying, language manifests as apophasis:

> And silently their shining Lord replies:
> 'I am a mirror set before your eyes,
> And all who come before my splendor see
> Themselves, their own unique reality;
> You came as thirty birds and therefore saw
> These selfsame thirty birds, no less nor more;
> If you had come as forty, fifty — here
> An answering forty, fifty, would appear;
> Though you have struggled, wandered, traveled far,

> It is yourselves you see and what you are.
> (*The Conference of the Birds*, p. 219)

What the birds are *is and is not* what the Simorgh is, and what the Simorgh is *is and is not* what the birds are. As a further proof of such inexpressible reflexivity, the Simorgh reveals to the birds that their journey never happened elsewhere than in the all-encompassing expanse of his universal mind, the very centre of his transcendent being:

> Though you traversed the Valleys' depths and fought
> With all the dangers that the journey brought,
> The journey was in Me, the deeds were Mine —
> You slept secure in Being's inmost shrine.
> (*The Conference of the Birds*, p. 219–20)

In other words: not only do the thirty birds who have attained their lord's abode 'discover' themselves as greater than themselves in the mirror of the Simorgh, but they are also called upon to realize that their journey to the Simorgh through the Seven Valleys never took place in the way they thought it did, namely as a linear displacement of their earthly selves towards the otherness of the cosmic self. By being told that they slept secure in the Simorgh's heart all along, the birds are urged to see how their path, far from being linear, was in fact circular.[31] What they accomplished through their journey was nothing but a circumambulation of the centre, a 'uni-versalizing' of themselves by means of a revolution around a single point of attraction, which now reveals itself as the centre of the uni-verse: the unmovable mover of everything that turns around that centre with ardent desire, so as to finally recognize itself in it, as if in a mirror. Desire, then, is the force which unites the centre to the circumference and the circumference to the centre — a uni-versalizing force of reciprocal attraction.

In the Simorgh the birds eventually die, and in the Simorgh they eventually find eternal life, thus regaining 'the selves [they] were before'. 'Attār does not dwell on this final development, as no human language could possibly approach it.[32] And yet we sense that meaning here hinges on the very notion of 'before': to which unsayable selfhood does this final notion of return allude for the reader? In all likelihood, to that ineffable identity achieved through a further annihilation (*fanā*)/rebirth (*baqā*), which led Scot Eriugena (810–77) to state, paradoxically, on the authority of St Dionysus the Areopagite, 'that God himself is both maker of all and is made of all' and add to this statement the following comment: 'this was unknown and unheard of — by me, by many, by nearly all. For if this is so, who will not immediately burst out, exclaiming in this voice: "God is all things and all things God?" It will be considered monstrous even by those considered learned.'[33] And indeed it was. About half a century later, on the other side of the Mediterranean, the sufi mystic Mansur al-Hallaj (858–922) proclaimed 'Anā l-Haqq' ('I am the Truth'), and was crucified for having dared to utter such a blasphemy.

As for Dante, we now need to turn our attention to the final station of his journey, which begins after Saint Bernard ends his prayer to the Virgin, and the Virgin turns her gaze onto the eternal light, inviting her protégé to do likewise.[34] Here Dante the poet interrupts the narrative and declares:

E io ch'al fine di tutt'i disii
appropinquava, sì com'io dovea,
l'ardor del desiderio in me finii. (*Par.* XXXIII, 46–48)

[And drawing nearer, as I had to now, | the end of all desires, in my own self |
I ended all the ardour of desire]

This is a paradoxical utterance, packed with three ambiguous phrases: 'fine', 'sì com'io dovea' and 'in me', are all polysemous terms, leading in turn to two quite different readings of the sentence (and hence of the rest of the canto as a whole), as the diverging translations of this passage abundantly demonstrate.[35] The two diverging readings are complementary, of course, but somehow our human mind struggles to behold them simultaneously, were it not for Dante's subtle poetic wording, where they are allowed to silently face each other. In so doing they invite the reader to 'trapassar dentro' and reach further into the complexities of meaning and its time-bound unfolding. Here they are: 1) From the exoteric/narrative point of view, Dante the wayfarer is now approaching God, here called the end of all desires: consequently, he feels that the blazing of desire is coming to its end in him, as it should. However, we could also understand differently, and more esoterically: 2) now that he is approaching the goal of all desires, as he was meant to from the very beginning, Dante ends (or brings to its highest intensity) his ardent desire not onto God, as one would expect, but onto himself. How can this be? Let us read further. The spiritual realization that follows, the 'pathos' of the beatific vision, is compared to 'nothing but' a dream; a vision, that is to say, whose reality can only manifest itself in a dimension other than the wakeful one experienced by the interaction of the rational mind and the senses.[36]

We should be wary of dreams and visions, both in general and especially in Dante's case. Exactly like 'Attār's thirty birds in the presence of the Simorgh, Dante has entered the dark space wherein the transcendent light originates, he has been admitted into the secret of divine presence. Forgetting his own will, he now comes to the realization that he has been turned and tossed all along by Divine motion: his own ardent desire and the desire of the godhead of all desires have never been other than one and the same desire. But now, why does this imply a return to his own self, 'in me finii'? What kind of self-mirroring is this, if not the realization of mystical union? Is not this what Dante states again — and again paradoxically — further into the canto, when he declares: 'E' mi ricorda ch'io fui più ardito | per questo a sostener, tanto ch'i' giunsi | l'aspetto mio col valore infinito' [And therefore (I remember this) I grew | the braver as I bore that light, and joined | the look I had to that unending light] (*Par.* XXXIII, 79–81)? A bold leap if there ever was one, met with boundless acceptance: the ineffable merging of desire into Desire, of self into Self.[37]

Eventually, as we know, it is the impossible understanding of, and ultimate abiding into, the 'imago al cerchio' [the image to the circle], the surfacing of 'nostra effigie' [our human form] within the triple circulation of divine light, but still 'dentro da sé, del suo colore stesso' [deep in itself, of its own colour], that leads Dante's mind to reach onto the heart of his own desire, forcing his 'alta fantasia' [all powers of high imaging] to settle into silence (*Par.* XXX, 127).

But the canto is not over yet. Three more lines stand in and of themselves as the poem's completion. They represent the very *telos* of the *Commedia*, they are its own *tajallī*. These three final lines are the supreme poetic expression of the mystical realization recorded in the unfolding of a hundred cantos:

> Ma già volgea il mio disio e 'l velle
> sì come rota ch'igualmente è mossa,
> l'amor che move il sole e l'altre stelle. (*Par* XXXIII, 143–45)

> [By then my desire and will already spun | like a wheel being moved uniformly | the love that moves the sun and the other stars.] (My translation)[38]

Compared to our starting point — 'Era già l'ora che volge il disio' of *Purgatorio* VIII — the indicator of time here no longer occupies the position of grammatical subject in the sentence. Rather, through the sudden bursting out of the adverbial adversative 'ma già' we find ourselves plunged at the heart of a 'volgere' [turn about, spin, rotate, swirl, gyrate] whose inherent timelessness abruptly reaches self-awareness. We have entered the 'eternal now', a new perspective from which we see the rest of the verse float in a completely open syntactical space. The verb 'volgea' and the nominal group that follows it ('il mio disio e 'l velle') stand one after the other in a 'rotated/rotating' relationship. If we are, temporarily, at a loss for a syntactical connection, our discursive mind will by default attempt to read 'il mio disio e 'l velle' as the subject(s) of the verb 'volgea', thus leaving the verb in need of an object which the sentence, in its unfolding, simply fails to produce. In its pivoting and gyrating onto itself, the very last terzina of the *Commedia* enacts the 'meaning event' which mirrors Dante's innermost realization: the transmutation of will into desire, the turning of desire onto itself, and its final merger with cosmic Desire.[39]

At the beginning of canto I of the *Commedia* 'il mio disio e 'l velle' were the wholly human agencies which had vainly turned the wayfarer away from the 'selva oscura' [dark wood] towards the unattainable 'dilettoso monte' [lovely hill] (*Inf.* 1, 2 and 77) guarded by the three wild beasts. Virgil, as an emissary of divine love, had then appeared, so as to turn Dante's steps onto a different path. At the end of the hundredth Dante comes to realize how his own desire and will could never have been the sole agents of his release from earthly *avidya*. By renouncing the notion of subjectivity and accepting to see both will and desire as open to an altogether different expanse of existence, Dante merges with the only truly universal dimension of Being, that of the 'rota ch'igualmente è mossa' (*Par.* XXXIII, 145) — a perpetual circumambulation of all that simultaneously proceeds from and returns to the unknowable, unreachable centre. Here Dante lifts the veil of cosmic illusion, reaches the beyond out of which the labyrinth of phenomenal otherness originates, and sees himself into the mirror of cosmic reality, where no difference can any longer be discerned between desire and will, heart and mind, God, the sun and the other stars.

There is one last word we need to address, and that is 'il mio'. Up to the very end, Dante seems intent on making reference to his own, individual self. If we look at this wording — 'il mio disio e 'l velle' — from the outer side of Maya's veil, we are likely to misconstrue what could appear to be Dante's obsession with his own ego. But if we pass beyond that veil, then we get to see something altogether different.

How can the movement of conversion summoned by the verb 'volgea' occur other than through a direct, embodied experience — an experience that each of us can only call 'mine' and yet recognize as universally human precisely because of its inalienable individuality? This is the mystery that lies at the core of all mystical realizations; in Kerenyi's words, it is 'my ineffable mystery that I have in common with all men.'[40] Even more paradoxically, it is precisely that universal 'me' and 'mine' that the 'I' finally needs to surrender, if it truly wants to find its S/self.

The concluding paradox, then, lies in the non-dual relationship between subject and object that Dante finds in the act of S/self-mirroring which the verb 'volgea' makes possible in the first place. Once our individual desire and will have become one — once they have become each other's mirror — then the *difference* between my no-longer composite being, the cosmic being, and the love that moves the whole universe evenly, 'sì come rota ch'igualmente è mossa', ceases to carry the meaning we expected it would, and reveals something else. At the end of the journey, when human desire manifests itself as *nothing but* cosmic yearning, the veil becomes a mirror, in which we simultaneously see our self and our true, unsayable Self — that is to say, the subject/object of the ardent desire which sparked the quest in the first place. Should we wish to see Dante's final verse mirrored into Ibn 'Arabī's words, that same insight into the ultimate nature of Reality reads like this: 'The movement that is the coming into existence of the universe is the movement of love [...] Thus Being is perfect, the whole movement of the Cosmos being the movement of love for perfection.'[41]

Notes to Chapter 2

1. *Purg.* VIII, 1–6: 'Era già l'ora che volge il disio | ai navicanti e 'ntenerisce il core | lo dì c'han detto ai dolci amici addio; | e che lo novo peregrin d'amore | punge, se ode squilla di lontano | che paia il giorno pianger che si more' [It was, by now, the hour that turns desire around | to the seafarers and makes their hearts grow tender | the day they bid sweet friends farewell; | the hour that pierces the new pilgrim | with love if he hears, far off, the bell | that seems to mourn the dying of the day]. Translations of the *Commedia* are based on *The Divine Comedy*, trans. by Robin Kirkpatrick, 3 vols (London: Penguin Books, 2006–07), but with some occasional modifications.
2. From a mystical perspective, that journey proper would be the 'journey of no return', which takes place after death.
3. Although we do not know whether it is a male or female soul that sings the hymn, I follow Dante's use of the feminine gender, in conformity with the Italian language, for the word 'anima'.
4. On the symbolism of the spiritual East [*ishraq*] as opposed to the worldly West, see Henry Corbin, *Histoire de la philosophie islamique*, 2nd edn (Paris: Gallimard, 1986), pp. 290–94.
5. *Purg.* VIII, 10–15: 'Ella giunse e levò ambo le palme | ficcando li occhi verso l'orïente | come dicesse a Dio: "D'altro non calme." | "*Te lucis ante*" sì devotamente | le uscìo di bocca e con sì dolci note | che fece me a me uscir di mente' [She joined her palms and lifted them | fixing her eyes towards the orient | as if to say to God: 'For nothing else I care.' | '*Te lucis ante*' so devoutly | issued from her lips, and with notes so sweet, | that I was moved to move beyond my mind].
6. *Purg.* VIII, 19–21: 'Aguzza qui, lettor, ben li occhi al vero, | ché 'l velo è ora ben tanto sottile, | certo che 'l trapassar dentro è leggero.' [Here, reader, let your eyes look sharp at truth, | for now the veil has grown so very thin — | it is not difficult to pass within].
7. See Seyyed Hossein Nasr, *Knowledge and the Sacred* (Albany, NY: SUNY Press, 1989), p. 141.

8. Nasr, *Knowledge and the Sacred*, p. 141; see also pp. 189–214. Ibn 'Arabī, *Futuhat IV*, 151, as quoted by Patrick Laude, 'Creation, Originality and Innovation in Sufi Poetry', *The Eye of the Heart*, 2 (2008), 112–30 (p. 124). For further probing into the subject see Michael Barry, *Figurative Art in Medieval Islam and the Riddle of Bihzād of Herāt* (Paris: Flammarion, 2004), p. 246; Patrick Laude, *Divine Play, Sacred Laughter, and Spiritual Understanding* (New York: Palgrave Macmillan, 2005), pp. 9–16, and Charles Upton, 'Homer, Poet of *Maya*', *The Eye of the Heart*, 4 (2009), 87–96, for an arresting perspective on how this same view might well be at the (forgotten) core of ancient Greek, and hence Western, culture.

9. *Futuhat IV*, 151 (ed. Cairo 1329h.), as quoted by Laude, 'Creation, Originality and Innovation in Sufi Poetry', p. 124. In introducing the distinction god/God (a concept Laude clarifies in his discussion of this passage without highlighting it visually), I am following Michael Sells's graphic practice. Sells in turn does not discuss Maya as such, but dwells precisely on that which is at the root of the issue of Reality as cosmic illusion: 'the *aporia* — the unresolvable dilemma — of transcendence'. Michael Sells, *Mystical Languages of Unsaying* (Chicago, IL: University of Chicago Press, 1994), p. 2.

10. Therefore, the possibility of 'trapassar dentro' the veil of cosmic illusion occurs when the mirror of the heart is polished. On this last image and its foundational importance for Ibn 'Arabī see Sells, *Mystical Languages of Unsaying*, pp. 63–89. For an overview of the image and its spread through the Islamic world see Barry, *Figurative Art in Medieval Islam*, pp. 190–250; see also Henry Corbin, *En Islam Iranien, aspects spirituels et philosophiques. Tome III. Les Fidèles d'amour. Shîisme et soufisme* (Paris: Gallimard, 1972), p. 16: 'On sort victorieux de l'"épreuve du voile", lorsque le voile devient "miroir théophanique".'

11. See for example IV, xii, 14: 'lo sommo desiderio di ciascuna cosa, e prima da la natura dato, è lo ritornare a lo suo principio. E però che Dio è principio de le nostre anime e fattore di quelle simili a sé [...], essa anima massimamente desidera di tornare a quello' [The supreme desire of each thing, and the one that is first given to it by nature, is to return to its first cause. Now since God is the cause of our souls and has created them like himself [...] the soul desires above all else to return to him]. Quotations from *Convivio* are taken from Dante Alighieri, *Convivio*, ed. by Cesare Vasoli and Domenico De Robertis (Milan and Naples: Ricciardi, 1988). Translations are from Dante Alighieri, *Il Convivio/The Banquet*, trans. by Richard Lansing (New York: Garland, 1990), with slight changes when necessary.

12. Frithjof Schuon, *The Transcendent Unity of Religions*, rev. edn with an intro. by Huston Smith (Wheaton, IL: Quest Books, 1997), p. 39.

13. A perspective for which Michael Sells prefers the word mystical as relating to mystery: 'Mystery is a referential openness onto the depths of a particular tradition [its esoteric aspect], and into conversation with other traditions': *Mystical Languages of Unsaying*, p. 8.

14. This is a well-known Islamic expression, part of the Muslim proclamation of faith. For an easily accessible reading of its meaning in a Sufi perspective see <http://www.surrenderworks.com/ library/esoterics/kalimah.html> [accessed 8 July 2011].

15. Possibly the most well-known expression of these universalizing views, grounded in the all-pervasive power of desire, are these celebrated verses by Ibn 'Arabī: 'My creed is love; | wherever its caravan *turns* along the way, | that is my belief, | my faith' (my emphasis). For a full contextual reading of this passage see Sells, *Mystical Languages of Unsaying*, pp. 90–115.

16. Ibn Abbādī (1097–1152), *at-Tasfiya*, 140, which I quote from T. P. De Bruijn, *Persian Sufi Poetry: An Introduction to the Mystical Use of Classical Poems*. (Richmond: Curzon Press, 1997), p. 52. It should be noted that the rationale for this approach is in and of itself of an esoteric nature, standing at odds with the more exoteric (and 'orthodox') way of renouncing the world, hence desire altogether. In Ibn Abbādī's words again: 'If he went on foot, the seeker would soon be exhausted and lose the force to proceed. Therefore he needs a swift horse [i.e., desire] in order to persevere until he reaches his goal' (ibid.). See also Corbin, *En Islam Iranien*, tome III, pp. vi and 136–37, where a similar passage by Rūzbehān Baqlī Shīrāzī (1128–1209) is quoted. The Tantric path is grounded in the same principles.

17. Something similar can be seen at work in the *Convivio*, where Dante distinguishes between the desire for worldly goods ('desiderio de la ricchezza' [desire for riches] IV, xiii, 2), which remains compulsive and grows quantitatively over itself like a tumour ('e in questo errore

cade l'avaro maladetto, e non s'accorge che desidera sé sempre desiderare, andando dietro al numero impossibile a giungere' [and it is into this error that the accursed miser falls, by failing to perceive that he desires to continue desiring by seeking to realize an infinite gain] III, xv, 9, 'sì che nulla successione quivi si vede, e per nullo termine e per nulla perfezione' [so that no progression of goals reached or perfection attained is found here] IV, xiii, 2), and the desire for understanding ('desiderio de la scienza' [desire for knowledge] IV, xiii, 1) which is inborn in man ('tutti gli uomini *naturalmente* desiderano di sapere' [all men naturally desire to know] I, i, 1), and grows qualitatively as it advances, perfecting itself while expanding, 'avvegna che pochi per male camminare compiano la giornata' [even though few, because of many straying from the right path, complete the journey] (IV, xiii, 7). See also *Par.* IV, 124–35 on the dynamics of human desire to know and the attainability of that desire, 'se non, ciascun disio sarebbe *frustra*' [were that not so, then all desire would *fail*] (p. 129).

18. *Mantiq* means 'logic'. See commentaries on 'Attār's use of this word by Lucian Stone, in 'Blessed Perplexity: The Topos of *Hayrat* in 'Attār's *Mantiq al-Tayr*', in *'Attār and the Persian Sufi Tradition: The Art of Spiritual Flight*, ed. by L. Lewisohn and C. Shackle (London and New York: Institute of Ismaili Studies, 2006), pp. 95–111 (p. 107, n. 3). Patrick Laude highlights the implications of *mantiq* as poetry: 'poetry as *mantiq* or logic points to a human presence that is as if delegated by the divine Absent. Poetic logic is like a gift, or a legacy from God to man, so that man may recover something of the Divine Presence in the Divine Absence. This is, as it were, the human side of the poetic equation, the human reflection of the Divine Intellect' ('Creation, Originality and Innovation', p. 120). This is quite plainly what Dante himself sees as the essence of H/his poetry: see *Par.* I, 19 ff.

19. Quotations from *The Conference of the Birds* are taken from Dick Davis's classic verse translation (Harmondsworth and New York: Penguin Books, 1984).

20. For an enlightening reading of the most highly realized among the visualizations of 'Attār's gathering of birds, a late sixteenth-century miniature by Master Habīballāh of Mashhad, in itself a 'supreme expression of medieval Persianate pictorial art', see Michael Barry, 'Illustrating 'Attār: A Pictorial Meditation by Master Habīballāh of Mashhad in the Tradition of Master Bihzād of Herāt', in *'Attār and the Persian Sufi Tradition*, pp. 135–64.

21. Compare Dante's analogous, well-known address to his readers: *Par.* II, 1–15.

22. The notion of shadow is equally foundational in Ibn 'Arabī's thought: 'Know that what is "other than the Reality", which is called the Cosmos, is, in relation to the Reality, as a shadow is to that which casts the shadow, for it is the shadow of God, this being the same as the relation between Being and the Cosmos, since the shadow is, without doubt, something sensible': *The Bezels of Wisdom*, trans. by R. W. J. Austin and with a preface by Titus Burkhardt (Mahwah, NJ: Paulist Press, 1980), p. 123. Clearly, the shadow is yet another 'imaginal' variation on the theme of the veil of cosmic illusion: see Henry Corbin, *L'Imagination créatrice dans le soufisme d'Ibn 'Arabi* (Paris: Entrelacs, 2006), pp. 205–06.

23. In a similar manner, the souls of Purgatory are urged to rush to 'spogliarvi lo scoglio | ch'esser non lascia a voi Dio manifesto' [shed that skin | which won't let God be manifest to you] (*Purg.* II, 122–23).

24. Scot Eriugena, in the *Periphyseon*, places Theophany at the centre of his view of the 'nothingness of God': '[...] so long as [divine *bonitas*] is understood to be incomprehensible by reason of its transcendence it is not unreasonably called "nothing", but when it begins to appear in its theophanies, it is said to proceed, as it were, out of nothing into something, [...] and therefore every visible and invisible creature can be called a theophany, that is, a divine apparition' (I am quoting from Sells, *Mystical Languages of Unsaying*, p. 58). See also Corbin, *En Islam iranien*, vol. III, p. vi: 'La manifestation théophanique n'est point une incarnation divine; la perception théophanique est une perception de l'amphibolie (*iltibās*), du double sens de tout être manifesté, qui simultanément voile et révèle l'invisible. Privé de la conscience qui gouverne cette vision, on reste dans le monde de la dualité, des oppositions; le pieux croyant aussi bien que le théologien dogmatique sont alors, au fond, des polythéistes qui s'ignorent' (and also ibid., pp. 15–19).

25. The cornerstone of this view is to be found in the *hadīth qudsī*: 'I was a Hidden Treasure and I lovingly yearned to be known, and I created creation in order thereby to be known', especially important in Sufi spirituality (I quote from Barry, *Figurative Art in Medieval Islam*, p. 18).

26. See Bernard McGinn, 'Love, Knowledge and *Unio mystica* in the Western Christian Tradition', in *Mystical Union in Judaism, Christianity and Islam: An Ecumenical Dialogue*, ed. by Moshe Idel and Bernard McGinn (New York: Continuum, 1999), pp. 59–86.

27. I do not have space here to discuss the encounter of Dante and Beatrice in the Garden of Eden, but I must point out that Beatrice wants Dante to see how after her death he reverted to an acquisitive form of earthly desire, rather than remain steadfast to the expansive sapiential desire she had sparked in him.

28. 'For that birth to occur, the soul must be completely empty. But to be completely empty, the soul must be free of everything, including its desire and expectation of the birth. To give up such desire is to risk nothingness' (Sells, *Mystical Languages of Unsaying*, p. 211). This is the final result of a radical understanding of repentance, as Dante himself suggests by referring to a double washing in the waters of both Lethe and Eunoe.

29. Barry, 'Illustrating 'Attār', pp. 140 and 128; Hanns-Peter Schmidt, 'Simorgh', in *Encyclopedia Iranica* (Cosa Mesa: Mazda Publications, 2003), ad vocem.

30. Sells, *Mystical Languages of Unsaying*, p. 9.

31. Thus it could be said that what they accomplished were in fact seven circumambulations of the centre as the ritual way to identify both the centre and the circle around it. On the importance of the ritual as *the* means to attain higher realization see Fritz Meier, 'The Mystery of the Ka'ba: Symbol and Reality in Islamic Mysticism', in *The Mysteries: Papers from the Eranos Yearbooks*, ed. by Joseph Campbell (Princeton, NJ: Princeton University Press, 1955), pp. 149–68.

32. 'Those who can speak still wander far away | From that dark truth they struggle to convey | And by analogies they try to show | The forms men's partial knowledge cannot know' (*The Conference of the Birds*, p. 221).

33. Sells, *Mystical Languages of Unsaying*, p. 53.

34. On Saint Bernard as *the* authority on *unio mystica* and the twelfth-century heated debate over the issue itself see McGinn 'Love, Knowledge and *Unio mystica* in the Western Christian Tradition'.

35. Compared to Kirkpatrick's literal translation, Mandelbaum's rendition takes the evasive path towards orthodoxy: 'And I, who now was nearing Him who is | the end of all desires, as I ought, | lifted my longing to its ardent limit'. What happened here to Dante's problematic 'in me'? It has been conveniently expunged altogether. As for 'finii', although in Charles Singleton's wording (1975) 'the meaning of the verb in this verse is much debated' (an issue already raised by Scartazzini and Vandelli in 1929), by the time Singleton was writing his commentary there was, and still is today, near unanimous consensus among commentators in understanding 'finii' as meaning: 'I brought the ardor of my desire to its highest intensity' (see Hollander's translation and commentary, 2007; all references to commentaries are from <http://dante.dartmouth.edu>). Rather, what calls for commentary here are Singleton's disparaging remarks on mysticism's alleged 'passivity': '[T]he poet's conception of the final act is not that of the mystic passive surrender, or the ideal of nirvana. Grace from above descends to help the struggling soul, but it is a soul that itself *struggles* toward the final attainment. Some commentators (with a certain measure of justness) have viewed this final act of the poem as epic in its nature.' This (mis)reading, which typically inhabits the mind of *homo modernus*, (mis)understands mysticism (passive, effeminate, bad) as the antithesis to the epic ideal (active, manly, good). Hopefully, my juxtaposing of Dante's *Commedia* and 'Attār's *Conference of the Birds* has helped understand how epics and mysticism are in fact inseparable in the pristine spiritual landscape which *homo modernus* has systematically endeavoured to devastate through his conceited, blind speculations. As for the co-presence of the two apparently opposite, epic and/or mystical, meanings in 'finii', Sri Aurobindo's statements with regard to the highest levels of spiritual development may prove more enlightening than Singleton's: 'Life has to change into a thing vast and calm and intense and powerful that can no longer recognize its old blind eager narrow self or petty impulse and desire. Even the body has to submit to a mutation and be no longer the clamorous animal or the impending clod it is now, but become instead a conscious servant and radiant instrument and living form of the spirit': *The Synthesis of Yoga* (Pondicherry: Centenary Library, 1955), p. 10. This salvific relationship of body and mind — Lama Anagarika Govinda comments, wholly à propos here — is 'very much in contrast with the generally accepted idea of a body-reviling, ascetically

intellectual Buddhism, which has crept into the historical and philosophical representations of the Buddha-Dharma' (*Foundations of Tibetan Mysticism* (York Beach, ME: Samuel Weiser, 1991), p. 70) as well as, I, shall add, more in general into the (mis)reading of all literary teachings of inner transmutation, of which Dante's *Comedy* and 'Aṭṭār's *Conference of the Birds* remain to this day paramount examples.

36. 'Qual è colui che sognando vede, | che dopo 'l sogno la passione impressa | rimane, e l'altro a la mente non riede, | cotal son io' [Like those who see so clearly while they dream | that marks of feeling, when their dreaming ends, | remain, though nothing more returns to mind, | so am I now] (*Par.* XXXIII, 58–61). I cannot expand here on the issue of dreams vs. 'reality' in Dante and beyond, as I have done in 'Sogno e visione: mistero, "mania", magia, realtà', in *Sogni e visioni nel mondo indo-mediterraneo*, ed. by Daniela Boccassini, *Quaderni di Studi Indo-Mediterranei*, 2 (2009), 1–20.

37. On the issue of the 'complex semantics' of the word 'aspetto' here and elsewhere in the *Comedy*, and on the 'sphere of semantic undecidability' which Dante cultivates to emphasize what is currently called, after Wittgenstein, the 'aspectuality' of poetic language, see Sara Fortuna and Manuele Gragnolati, 'Dante After Wittgenstein: "Aspetto", Language and Subjectivity from *Convivio* to *Paradiso*', in *Dante's Plurilingualism: Authority, Knowledge, Subjectivity*, ed. by Sara Fortuna, Manuele Gragnolati and Jürgen Trabant (Oxford: Legenda, 2010), pp. 223–47 (esp. pp. 230–31). All of these issues are in fact contained in the notion of the veil of Maya, which I am evoking here as 'door' to the 'aspectuality' of desire itself; 'aspectuality', in other words, is the paradoxical core of meaning which beckons mystics and esotericists of all ages and traditions.

38. This is my own, literal translation of the *Comedia*'s last terzina; contrary to what all translators do, I have not altered the bewildering syntax of the original. The English version should leave the reader with the same sense of uncertainty as to the syntactical order of the syntagms that the original so powerfully triggers. All translators strive instead for a syntactically ordered sentence [but my | desire and will were moved already — like | a wheel revolving uniformly — by | the Love that moves the sun and the other stars] thus depriving the reader of Dante's final, powerful poetic displacement.

39. I therefore fully concur with Bruno Nardi's understanding of 'disio' as 'amor naturale' and 'velle' as 'amor d'animo': see *Nel mondo di Dante* (Rome: Edizioni di Storia e Letteratura, 1944), pp. 143–45. For a list of all commentators accepting this more esoteric reading of 'disio' see Chiavacci Leonardi's 1997 commentary. As the final paragraph of this paper argues, Nardi's view needs to be taken a step further in the direction of absolute non-duality.

40. Carl Kerenyi, 'The Mysteries of the Kabeiroi', in *The Mysteries: Papers from the Eranos Yearbooks*, 32–63 (p. 37).

41. *The Bezels of Wisdom*, pp. 257–58. This is Ibn Arabi's 'circumambulation' of the *hadīth qudzī* (a saying of Allah as revealed to his Prophet Muhammad): 'I was a hidden treasure, therefore I longed to be known,' quoted above in n. 25, which lies at the core of the Sufi path of love.

CHAPTER 3

Ever-Growing Desire:
Spiritual Pregnancy in Hadewijch
and in Middle High German Mystics

Annette Volfing

In *Die Erlösung* [*The Redemption*], a Middle High German account of salvation history, the Annunciation is immediately preceded by a scene in which Mary meditates on the promised birth of the Saviour and wonders which woman will be so fortunate as to be chosen as his mother.[1] Although well aware that she might be considered somewhat presumptuous, Mary prays that she might be the one selected:

> Rex, adonay dominus,
> herre, kuneclîcher got,
> werde dîn wille und dîn gebot,
> sint dû wilt hernider kumen,
> alse ich zû rehte hân vernumen,
> daz mir die gnâde wêr bedaget,
> daz dû mich vil arme maget
> zû mûder, herre, wildest haben,
> sô hette ich gnâden vil entsaben. (2654–62)

> [Rex, adonai dominus, lord, royal God, given that you wish to come down here, as I have rightly understood, let it be your will and your command that I should be granted the favour that you would have me, most humble maiden, as mother. Then I would have received great mercy.][2]

Mechthild von Magdeburg's *Das fliessende Licht der Gottheit* [*The Flowing Light of Divinity*] similarly suggests that Mary, rather than being taken aback by Gabriel's message, had already been imagining her possible future destiny as the mother of God.[3] The idea that even Mary had once yearned to 'become Mary' (in the sense of taking on a particular maternal role) legitimizes Mariological aspirations in others and presents a powerful illustration of how they might stake a claim to this same role: whilst medieval mystics could obviously not substitute for Mary in any historical sense, there was nothing to stop them seeking to appropriate the bundle of experiences associated with the three stages of carrying, bearing and raising the Christ child.[4] This appropriation could be enacted on a variety of levels, ranging from that of imaginative identification with Mary and visionary interaction with the

Christ child, to more cerebral deployment of pregnancy-metaphors or -allegories.[5] In all cases, the subtext of maternal yearnings combined with personal ambition provides a potent alternative to bridal mysticism as a paradigm for spiritual desire.

In the narrow sense, the term 'spiritual pregnancy' relates only to the first of the three stages just mentioned (i.e. to carrying, rather than to bearing or raising the Christ child). As a hagiographical motif, it tends to be associated with reports of literal physiological change — as when Ida of Louvain and Lukardis of Oberweimar reportedly swell up after focusing for a prolonged period on the idea of the infant Jesus,[6] or when Dorothea von Montau experiences distension of the womb and pains analogous to those of a woman in labour.[7] In earlier mystical allegory, by contrast, the motif of spiritual pregnancy features as an extension of the theological commonplace of the birth of Christ in each individual soul.[8] So, for example, the second sermon on the Annunciation by Guerric d'Igny extrapolates from the literal to allegorical conception, warning all pregnant souls to be careful to prevent moral damage or injury to the foetus inside them.[9] However, it would be misleading to distinguish too sharply between hagiography on the one hand, and allegory on the other; or indeed to separate the pregnancy stage absolutely from those of bearing and raising the child.[10] All of these are predicated on the fundamental desire somehow to contain or possess Christ, if not within the female body, then at least within the context of a mother–child relationship.

The urge for maternal ownership inevitably complicates the relationship with Mary, who is seen as a figure to be loved, admired, imitated — and then ultimately supplanted. The same Ida of Louvain who swelled up with longing was subsequently allowed to hold the Christ child as a special favour from the Virgin. When the time came to hand the child back, Ida refused and an unseemly scuffle ensued, until Mary succeeded in snatching her son back to heaven.[11] In general, stories in which individuals rejoice at managing to borrow the child should be also be understood as implicitly acknowledging this religious subject's desire to 'become' the mother. This applies equally to mystagogical texts which encourage their readers to engage imaginatively with this maternal role, as when the narrator of *Der saelden hort* [*The Treasure of Salvation*] urges his audience to travel spiritually to Bethlehem in order to kiss the child, cuddle it, and sing it lullabies.[12] This imaginative stance parallels the widespread devotion to actual Jesus dolls, of which the life-sized doll belonging to Margaretha Ebner is a particularly well-known example.[13]

Excitement about the child also leads to numerous texts and artefacts adopting an invasive approach to Mary's body during pregnancy. Gertrude of Helfta describes a vision in which Mary's womb appears transparent and crystalline, offering full visual access to all the inner organs and to the child itself.[14] As Jeffrey Hamburger has noted, this vision may be based on familiarity with statues, such as the Visitation Group from St Katharinenthal, in which the womb is represented by a crystal.[15] Similarly, in paintings of the Visitation, the impression that the onlooker enjoys x-ray vision may equally be achieved by the representation of the two foetuses on the surface of the clothes worn by Mary and Elizabeth.[16] Finally, some plastic representations of the pregnant Madonna (*Maria gravida*) have doors allowing the little figure inside to be seen, or even removed and handled. This blurs the distinction between foetus and infant, making both equally appropriable to outsiders.[17] Of course, to the extent that a religious subject fully engages with the Mariological role, it could be argued that this apparently prurient investigation of another person's womb actually constitutes a form of spiritual introspection, with the onlooker monitoring his or her own spiritual development.[18]

Furthermore, spiritual pregnancy may also have an invasive impact upon the religious subject. A very literal example is provided by the case of the Italian nun, Chiara of Montefalco, who was embalmed by evisceration after her death: once her heart was removed and investigated, it was found to contain a foetus-like figure on a crucifix.[19] Sometimes it is even Mary who is responsible for the invasion: in the *Offenbarungen* [*Revelations*] of Adelheid Langmann, a nun at Engelthal, the Virgin is said to have approached a group of three nuns, opened their hearts, and placed a Christ Child inside each one. The hearts were then closed.[20] The fact that Mary later refers to her own historical pregnancy in terms of her having carried Christ under her heart makes it clear that we are dealing with a form of spiritual pregnancy here.[21] However, the text also makes it clear that, just as with Chiara de Montefalco, these are birth-less pregnancies: the Christ Children remain permanently incubated in the hearts of the three nuns.[22]

This kind of permanent pregnancy is implicitly deemed better than actual parturition because the mother never has to be parted from her offspring. Whilst there is a certain logic to this (in the sense that it must be a good thing never to be parted from Christ), the notion of a birth-less pregnancy is also somewhat uncomfortable. Here, it is worth briefly considering the way in which this notion is also deployed in the epithalamium to Queen Edith in the late eleventh-century *Vita Ædwardi Regis*.[23] Although, or even because, Edith has no children of her own, the anonymous poet presents her religious foundation at Wilton as a form of ongoing pregnancy. Monika Otter comments on this awkward rhetorical strategy, which, rather than deflecting attention from the problem of the Queen's literal infertility, actually highlights it:

> The Virgin Mary echoes also help explain in part what must surely be the most striking, and perhaps the most off-putting, idea in the Wilton epithalamium: that of the non-birth of the 'children'. It refers, of course, to the church, or even the dormitory of the convent, which, unlike a real, human mother, can shelter its babies in a womb-like enclosure even after 'birth'. [. . .] Wilton/ Edith does not give birth, and there is something oddly frustrated, retentive, even physically uncomfortable, about that twist to the image. Not having to let go, or, from the children's perspective, never having to leave the womb, may be comforting, but in a slightly monstrous way, one that, far from Mary's miraculous fecundity, seems very barren indeed.[24]

Although spiritual pregnancy in the Christological sense is generally to be distinguished from other metaphors or allegories structured around the notion of spiritual offspring (e.g. in monastic or pastoral contexts or in the context of religious foundations), Otter's observations may also be applied to the cases of Chiara and of Adelheid and her fellow nuns.

Whilst pregnancy and maternity are quintessentially female experiences, the topos of spiritual pregnancy is not restricted to religious women. Goscelin's

Liber confortatorius, for example, describes how, for a certain monk, identification with Mary permeated his liturgical routine so entirely that he was left regularly imagining his own impregnation through the Angel Gabriel.[25] The *Gnadenleben des Friedrich Sunder* [*Blessed Life of Friedrich Sunder*] features an even more complex relationship between Mary and the male religious subject:

> Er ha͡t die gewonhait, wenn er vnsers herren lichnam wolt enpfähen jn der meß, daz er denn vil oft bat vnser frowen, daz sie ir liebes kint ba͡t, daz er wolt von siner sel gaistlichen geborn werden, als och oft geschach.[26]

> [He had the habit, when he wanted to receive the body of the lord in the mass, that he would then very often ask our lady to ask her dear child to be born spiritually from his soul. This did indeed happen frequently.]

In the following chapter, Mary then assists at the nuptial union of this infant and the soul of Friedrich Sunder.[27] Whilst the soul is gendered female when functioning as the mother or bride of the infant, the infant also addresses Sunder as his brother.[28] There are also cases of what one might call gender-free deployments of the pregnancy topos. For example, when the refrain to a song by Heinrich von Loufenberg addresses the Christ child as being present both in 'dinem kripselin' (4,6 [your little crib], i.e. the historical one in the stable) and in 'mim kripselin' (9,6 [my little crib], i.e. the spiritual crib in the soul of the speaker), this construction of the soul as an ungendered container for the baby is not fundamentally different from the notion of the soul as a womb.[29] Spiritual pregnancy should therefore not be seen as an isolated motif within medieval religious writing, but as part of a wider engagement with the problem of how the finite might contain the infinite.[30]

The notion of the soul as a womb is deployed with a striking mixture of abstraction and literal-mindedness in one of the 'Mengeldichte' (poems in rhymed couplets) by the Dutch Beguine sister, Hadewijch.[31] 'Mengeldicht' 14, which will be the main focus of this paper, takes an allegorical approach to the motif of spiritual pregnancy, using it as a framework for describing the growth of love within the soul. Unusually, this text is particularly interested in the temporal aspects of pregnancy, with the sequence of nine months providing the key structural paradigm. As a result, this poem clearly differs from the hagiographical texts mentioned above, in which the swelling up of the saint is reported in rather cursory terms, or in which the spiritual birth of Christ is something to be fitted in regularly before Mass. It also differs from secular allegories of love which often gloss over the transition from conception to birth.[32]

This detailed attention to the passage of time in 'Mengeldicht' 14 allows for the possibility of presenting pregnancy as a gradual process of change for the human subject. Although on one level this interest in personal transformation provides a link to the Eckhartian concept of 'Gottesgeburt', whereby the human subject effectively becomes deified through participation in the ongoing progression of the Word from the Father,[33] it should be stressed that Hadewijch differs from Eckhart precisely in the focus on time. Whilst the 'Gottesgeburt' represents an instantaneous connection with eternity, Hadewijch's gestation period is based on the principle of gradual, progressive psychological change.

The connection between spiritual *connubium* and spiritual pregnancy is complex.

Occasionally, as in the case of Dorothea von Montau, spiritual pregnancy may be associated with an intensively eroticized relationship between the religious subject and the heavenly bridegroom.[34] In most cases, however, spiritual pregnancy tends not to be sexualized or associated with erotic desire. This is possibly due to a reluctance to sexualize the role-model, Mary, specifically at the point of the Annunciation: Mary's role as bride of Christ tends to be dissociated temporally from the Incarnation, so as to be enacted either from eternity (i.e. outside normal time), or in heaven after her assumption.[35] This means that, despite the analogy with the natural world on which these motifs are predicated, it is not the case that *connubium* should be understood as the 'cause' of spiritual pregnancy or as an experience which must be precede it temporally. Indeed, in the Friedrich Sunder example quoted above, the order is reversed (birth first, then *connubium*), although the regularity with which Sunder gives birth means that one should not read too much into the sequence.

Ultimately this leads on to the question of how rigidly one separates the infant from the adult Christ. Sometimes, as in the cases of Chiara of Montefalco's crucified foetus, the two images or stages are simply fused. In many cases, however, there is a tendency to present veneration of the infant as primarily relevant for younger or more immature mystics. In *Das Fließende Licht der Gottheit*, for example, the Mechthild's persona presents bridal mysticism as a superior, or at least as a more 'adult', alternative to spirituality couched in maternal terms. Above all, the maternal stance is seen as de-sexualized or even as an antidote to erotic desire. In a key scene, the senses personified encourage the persona to control her desires precisely by associating herself with the figure of the lactating Mary:

> Vro^{v}we, went ihr úch minnekliche ku^{e}len, so neigent úch in der jungfro^{v}wen schos zu^o dem kleinen kint und sehent und smekent, wie der engel fro^{e}de von der ewigen maget die unnatúrlichen milch so^{v}g. (I. 44, p. 30)

> [Lady, it you wish to cool down in love, you should bend down to the small child in the lap of the virgin and see and taste how it, the joy of the angels, sucks supernatural milk from the eternal maiden.]

When the issue of desire is thus made pivotal to the choice between infant and bridegroom, the persona opts firmly for the latter:

> Das ist ein kintlich liebi, das man kint so^{e}ge und wiege. Ich bin ein vollewahsen brut, ich wil gan nach minem trut. (I. 44, p. 30)

> [That is a childish form of love, to suckle and rock a baby. I am a fully-grown bride; I want to go to my beloved.]

Hadewijch also tends to view devotion to the infant Jesus as a subordinate or immature form of spirituality. Her seventh vision discusses three stages of contact with Christ: initially he comes to her persona as a toddler, then he appears as an adult bridegroom, and finally she is transformed as he dissolves entirely in inner union with her.[36] Even 'Mengeldicht' 14, notwithstanding its extended allegory of pregnancy, makes it clear that Hadewijch is uninterested in the minutiae of child-rearing. Not only is there little anticipatory desire for a baby, but the text repeatedly stresses how the allegorical child is born 'volwassen' (102, 163, 165) and 'rike' [powerful] (102) at the end of the nine months. Even if *volwassen* means 'fully formed' (i.e. 'ready to be born') rather than 'fully grown' or 'adult', this emphasis on the completeness of the child eliminates any sense of its dependency on the parent. Accordingly, the soul that has just given birth does not have any particular nurturing duties and is free to concentrate introspectively on its own, newly divinized state (149). For a text structured around the notion of pregnancy, 'Mengeldicht' 14 thus exhibits a surprisingly ambivalent or even dismissive attitude towards children and maternity — an attitude which arguably also extends to issues of gender, corporeality, and desire itself. These aspects will now be considered in turn.

The poem consists of three parts. The second and longest of these (47–162) is structured around an allegorical interpretation of each of the nine months of pregnancy, along the lines of 'Getrouwe vrese es direst maent' [Faithful fear is the first month] (47), or 'Die seuende maent es gherechticheit' [The seventh month is justice] (107). The months thus function much like the rungs or steps familiar from other mystagogical allegories, and the more corporeal aspects of pregnancy are largely played down. It should also be stressed that the tone is not experiential: the speaker is not sharing personal history, but is describing how things would be for anybody. Indeed, the gender of the speaker is unclear from the text itself, although one tends to construe it as female by analogy with the sex of the author. The third part (163–86) consists of a short and (at first sight) somewhat anti-climactic allegorization of the four weeks of a month, and the seven days of a week. The first part (1–46) is the most complex, both regarding the self-stylization of the speaker and the justification of pregnancy motif. The poem opens with an epistolary introduction, in which the persona sends greetings to the addressees from, or concerning, Love personified (*minne*). However, as she is also sending a request to Love herself, she defines herself as a two-way mediator:

> Jn den hoghen name der minnen
> Die v hare wesen moet doen kinnen
> Sendic v hare hertelike groete,
> Ende bidde hare datse v al moete
> Hare wesen tonen toten gronde,
> Datmen nie ghegronden en conde. (1–6)

> [In the high name of Love,
> Who must make her being known to you,
> I send you her kindest greeting
> And beg her that she may show you all
> Her being to its depths,
> Which we could never fathom.]

The identity of the addressees is not made clear, nor is the relationship of the speaker to them. To some extent, she makes common cause with them, using the first person plural to describe how they all fail to meet the exacting standards of Love:

> Dat wij so slappelijc vorwert tiden,
> Ende met armen troeste leuen,
> Ende so luttel in storme van minnen gheuen. (12–14)

> [Because we stride forward so slowly,
> And live with feeble hope,
> And give so little in the storm of love.]

At the same time, the speaker distances herself from the addressees by claiming the authority to teach them about the workings of Love. As the speaker works through a series of spatial metaphors, the addressees are to some extent given conflicting instructions. On the one hand, we are encouraged to travel 'ter hogher minne grade' [upward to sublime love] (17), but are hampered by a lack of real fervour and by reluctance to accept pain. On the other hand, the speaker prioritizes travel in the downward direction, into humility and into the abyss. Unlike the ascent, which involves effort and energy on the part of the travellers themselves, the descent is understood in terms of free-fall and abandonment of effort and control. It is this spiritual stance which links the addressees to the figure of Mary and which introduces the motif of pregnancy — cf. the English idiom 'falling pregnant':

> Wildi dus vallen ende in allen nighen,
> So suldi volmaecte minne ghecrighen.
> Want dat haelde gode neder in marien,
> Ende mettien seluen soude hi noch lien,
> Die hem so neder in minne const hebben:
> Hine mocht hem sine hoecheit niet ontsegghen,
> Hi soudenne ontfaen ende draghen tghetal
> Also een kint in zijnre moeder volwassen sal. (39–46)

> [If you were willing to fall thus and to bow in all things,
> You would obtain perfect Love.
> For that brought God down into Mary,
> And he would yet acknowledge the same in one
> Who could hold himself so humble in love:
> He could not refuse his sublimity to him,
> But such a one would receive him and carry him for as long
> As a child grows within its mother.]

The account of Month One features further Mariological references:

> Dus ontfeetmen alse Maria ontfinc,
> Ende in allen so diepe oetmoedicheit daer bi:
> Dats "ecce ancilla domini". (60–62)

> [Thus the soul receives as Mary received,
> And in all this obedient service still deeper humility:
> That is, *Ecce ancilla domini.*]

Despite the association with Mary, this hypothetically humble religious subject is presented as male, at least grammatically.[37] Given that the human soul is normally gendered female in relation to Christ, Hadewijch's repeated use of male pronouns is surprising, especially given the overall context of spiritual pregnancy. This reluctance to feminize the religious subject may represent an attempt to distinguish this intellectually demanding allegory from more physiologically oriented or sentimental forms of *imitatio Mariae*.

Nonetheless, 'Mengeldicht' 14 does provide occasional formulations drawing the reader's attention back to the female body. For example, in Month Two, it allegorizes the way in which the body starts to expand:

> Want si [verduldicheit] doet meest wassen ende op gaen
> Dat vat daer minne in es ontfaen. (75–76)

> [For patience, more than anything else, causes to grow and dilate
> That vessel in which Love in received.]

Month Five contains a reference to 'Die suete dracht' [the sweet burden] (94). Finally, Month Nine mentions the birth of the child:

> Dat in die grote stat heuet gheleghen:
> Jnt diepste van oetmoede, int hoechste der minnen,
> Daer men met allen in allen sinnen
> Gode dus leeft met alre macht,
> Jn nuwe minne, dach ende nacht. (144–48)

> [Which has lain in that great place:
> In the depths of lowliness, in the heights of love,
> Where with all, in every way,
> The soul lives for God with all power,
> In new love, day and night.]

This passage initially evokes the uterus very specifically ('die grote stat' [that great place] in which the child has been carried), but the subsequent line immediately dissolves this image by introducing the image of the depths of lowliness and the heights of love; the containment of the child within a well-defined inner space is replaced by an evocation of an abstract and infinitely open expanse which encompasses the parent as well as the child. At the point of birth, the female body, which was treated with some suspicion throughout the text, looses even its allegorical relevance.

This raises the question of what the birth of child actually means in allegorical terms. Month six contains a rare reference to the subject's longing for the birth of the child:

> Die seste maent es toeuerlaet
> Daer men alle rijchiet af ontfaet
> Ende troest dat dat kint metter vrocht sal comen
> Volwassen, rike ende gheuen alle vromen;
> Dus te verlatene op minnen sach
> Ende te hakenne na den hoghen dach
> Dat gheboren werde dit edele kint
> Ende te vollen in vollen van vollen ghemint. (99–106)

> [The sixth month is confidence,
> From which the soul receives all wealth
> And consolation that that Child, with fruit, shall come
> Full-grown and powerful, and shall give all benefits;
> Thus to trust in Love with full reliance
> And to long for the high day
> When this noble Child will be born
> And to the full, in full, fully loved.]

However, the text tells us very little about what happens when the child has actually arrived. There is some suggestion that this introduces a new age in which, as we have already seen:

> Daer men met allen in allen sinnen
> Gode dus leeft met alre macht,
> Jn nuwe minne, dach ende nacht. (146–48)

> [Where with all, in every way,
> The soul lives for God with all power,
> In new love, day and night.]

One might expect the third, concluding part of the poem to expand somewhat on this new mode of existence. However, whilst this part apparently opens with a celebration of the birth, the child is very quickly side-lined:

> Nu es dit kint volwassen gheboren
> Dat bi oetmoedicheit was vercoren,
> Ende es volwassen in hogher minnen
> Ende IX maende voldraghen binnen.
> Ende elke maent heuet weken viere...
> Elc weke es van vij daghen ... (163–67; 175)

> [Now is born full-grown the Child
> Who was chosen by humility,
> And is full-grown in sublime Love,
> And carried to term nine months.
> And each month has four weeks...
> Each week is of seven days...]

Instead, we are left with an allegorization of the lunar month, as the speaker explains that there are four weeks in a month (signifying power, knowledge, wisdom, and affection respectively) and seven days in a week (signifying the seven gifts of the Holy Spirit). The speaker again reverts to the collective second person plural as she expounds on the practical application of these qualities (e.g. 'Met rade versteetmen der minnen ghenoech | Met crachte werctmen hare ghevoech' [With counsel we understand how to content Love | With fortitude we carry out her wish] (181–82).

This moralizing close to the poem might be read as a neat solution to the perennial literary problem of 'what happens next' after a close encounter with the divine. Just as in nuptial texts, the pleasures of *unio* do not continue indefinitely, so the allegorization of the month arguably constitutes a sober glossing of what it means to be deified or to live 'in new love' for God, at least in this life. In other words, the benefit of the birth would be that the soul is now better able to access the qualities signified by the weeks and the days.

This reading is, however, undermined by ambivalence in Part Three as to whether the birth is in the past or in the future. The deixis of line 163 ('Nu es dit kint volwassen gheboren' [Now is born full-grown the Child]) suggests that the perspective is post-*partum*, yet lines 167–70 imply that the soul still needs to prepare itself for the birth:

> Ende elke maent heuet weken viere
> Ende elke seghet ghereide ende chiere
> Jeghen den groten hoghen dach
> Dat minne volboren werden mach. (167–70)

> [And each month has four weeks,
> And each calls for preparation and adornment
> Before the great high day,
> So that Love can be born perfect.]

Furthermore, the very focus on the lunar month may in itself be taken as an indirect reference to the cycles of the female body and to the physiology of birth. In other words, even when one is living out the gifts of the Holy Spirit, this is part of the preparation for, and countdown towards, the birth.

This ambivalence about past and future means that the focus of the poem is placed firmly on process rather than on outcome. On this account, the motivation for the use of the pregnancy motif is not to harness conventional maternal desires to a spiritual agenda, but rather to highlight a process of deepening introspection and change. The subject, as presented by Hadewijch, relishes being in a permanent state of transition or growth. Although Hadewijch sidesteps the awkward issue of having the foetus permanently stuck inside the womb, her subject has little genuine interest in actual parturition (with its associations of splitting and separation). So, although the birth is said to take place, the subject somehow also carries on being pregnant (i.e. growing and expectant). To the extent that the process is fuelled by desire, it is therefore not the conventional one for a separate, or at least separable, object. Instead, as Hadewijch's interest is primarily in the spiritual alertness and responsiveness of the religious subject, one might perhaps speak of secondary-level 'desire for desire' — the key issue being that the religious subject should aim always to be in the state of provisional longing associated with pregnancy, but with fulfilment indefinitely deferred.

Notes to Chapter 3

1. *Die Erlösung: Eine geistliche Dichtung des 14. Jahrhunderts*, ed. by Friedrich Maurer, Deutsche Literatur. Sammlung literarischer Kunst- und Kunstdenkmäler in Entwicklungsreihen. Reihe: Geistliche Dichtung des Mittelalters, 6 (Leipzig: Reclam, 1934).
2. Translations are my own, except for translations from Hadewijch. These translations are taken (with occasional modification), from *Hadewijch: The Complete Works*, trans. by Mother Columba Hart (London: SPCK, 1981).
3. Mechthild von Magdeburg, *Das fließende Licht der Gottheit*, ed. by Hans Neumann with Gisela Vollmann-Profe, Münchener Texte und Untersuchungen, 100 (Munich: Artemis, 1990), v. 23, pp. 174–75: 'Mere disú juncfro^{v}we zoh únsern herren har nider mit einer su^{e}ssen stimme ir sele, und si sprach in irme gebete, do si was alleine, alsus: "Herre got, ich vro^{e}we mich des, das du komen wilt in also edeler wise, das ein magt din mu^{o}ter wesen sol. Herre, da wil ich zu^o dienen mit miner kúscheit und mit allem dem, das ich von dir habe." Do trat der engel Gabriel har nider in einem himelschen liehte' [Furthermore, this virgin drew our lord down here with a sweet voice of her soul and she spoke in her prayer, when she was alone, as follows: 'Lord God, I rejoice on account of the fact that you will come in such a noble manner that a virgin is to be your mother. Lord, in this respect I am willing to serve with my chastity and with everything which I have received from you.' Then the angel Gabriel stepped down here in a heavenly light.]

4. For the distinction between the historical and the mystical births of Christ, see for example Gertrude von Helfta (*Le Héraut*, in *Œuvres spirituelles*, ed. and trans. into French by Pierre Doyere and others, Sources chrétiennes: Série des textes monastiques d'Occident, 19, 25, 27, 48, 5 vols (Paris: Editions du Cerf, 1967–86), II–V (IV, 4.3.8, p. 56)) who distinguishes between those nuns who focus on a vision of the historical Jesus born in Bethlehem (*Dominum tempore suo in Bethleem natum*) and those who worship the Jesus born within their own hearts (*Domino in intimis suis, quasi spiritualiter nato*). Similarly, in *Das Gnaden-Leben des Friedrich Sunder, Klosterkaplan zu Engelthal* (in Siegfried Ringler, *Viten- und Offenbarungsliteratur in Frauenklöstern des Mittelalters: Quellen und Studien*, Münchener Texte und Untersuchungen, 72 (Zurich and Munich: Artemis, 1980), pp. 391–444), the infant Jesus describes Mary as 'min lipliche mu°tter' [my bodily mother] and Friedrich Sunder's soul as 'min gaistliche mu°tter' [my spiritual mother] (p. 415).

5. For useful surveys of birth- and pregnancy-related motifs, see Bardo Weiß, *Ekstase und Liebe: Die unio mystica bei den deutschen Mystikerinnen des 12. und 13. Jahrhunderts* (Paderborn: Schöningh, 2000), pp. 571–96; and Miri Rubin, *Mother of God: A History of the Virgin Mary* (London: Allen Lane/Penguin, 2009), pp. 262–66.

6. *Vita vera Idae Lovaniensis O.S.C.*, in *Acta Sanctorum*, ed. by Jean Bolland and Gottfried Henschen, rev. by Jean Carnandet and others, 60 vols (Paris: Victor Palmé 1863–1983), APRILIS II, pp. 156–89 (1,5,31, p. 166 and 3,1,10, p. 184); *Vita venerabilis Lukardis Monialis O.S.C. in Superiore Wimaria*, *Analecta Bollandia* 18 (1899), 305–67 (cap. xliii, p. 334). See Weiß, *Ekstase*, pp. 593–95.

7. For the different approaches to spiritual pregnancy in the Latin and German *vitae* of Dorothea von Montau, see Almut Suerbaum, '"O wie gar wundirbar ist dis wibes sterke": Discourses of Sex, Gender and Desire in Johannes Marienwerder's Life of Dorothea von Montau', in *Dorothea von Montau and Johannes Marienwerder: Constructions of Sanctity*, ed. by Almut Suerbaum and Annette Volfing, *Oxford German Studies*, 39.2 (2010), 181–97.

8. See Hugo Rahner, 'Die Gottesgeburt: Die Lehre der Kirchenväter von der Geburt Christi im Herzen der Gläubigen', *Zeitschrift für Katholische Theologie*, 59 (1935), 333–418. For metaphors and allegories of spiritual childbearing in the ancient world, see Verna E. F. Harrison, 'The Allegorization of Gender: Plato and Philo on Spiritual Childbearing', in *Asceticism*, ed. by Vincent L. Wimbush and Richard Valantasis (Oxford: Oxford University Press, 1998), pp. 520–34.

9. *Guerric d'Igny. Sermons*, ed. by John Morson and Hilary Costello, trans. into French by Placide Deseille, 2 vols (Paris: Les Éditions du Cerf, 1970), II, 126–45 (pp. 140–42, lines 193–97): 'Vos quoque, o matres beatae tam gloriosae prolis, attendite vobis ipsis donec formetur Christus in vobis; attendite ne qua foris offensa gravior foetum tenerum laedat, ne quid ingeratis ventri, id est menti, quod spiritum quem concepistis extinguat' [You too, o happy mothers of such a glorious child, take care until Christ has been formed within you lest any external blow strikes the delicate foetus too hard, and lest you ingest anything into your stomach, that, is, into your mind, which may extinguish the spirit which you have conceived.]. See also Kurt Ruh, *Geschichte der abendländischen Mystik*, 4 vols (Munich: C. H. Beck, 1990–99), I, 321–29. Whilst this sermon considers the problem of negligent harm to the foetus, an anonymous Middle High German sermon (Franz Pfeiffer, 'Drei Predigten aus dem XIII. Jahrhundert', *Germania*, 7 (1862), 330–50 (p. 345)) warns against the Herodian sin of intentional infanticide: 'Wan wizzent, daz hiute ein bôsheit ist Herôdis und ouch ist ez ein bôsheit von Babilôn, daz ein mensche wil erleschen die geistlîchen geburt in der sêle...' [For you should know that there exist today one of the sins of Herod — which is also a sin of Babylon — namely that a person wants to stifle the spiritual birth in the soul...]. Although the association with Herod implies that the 'baby' has already been born, it would also be possible to construe this sentence as being about spiritual abortion (i.e. intentional destruction of the foetus).

10. *Das St. Trudperter Hohelied: Eine Lehre der liebenden Gotteserkenntnis*, ed. and trans. into German by Friedrich Ohly, Bibliothek des Mittelalters, 2 (Frankfurt am Main: Deutscher Klassiker Verlag, 1998), 15, 1–3, pp. 48–50, moves seamlessly from the tasks of bearing the child to nurturing it: 'dar umbe gibet uns got | Christen zu geberne geistlîche unde ziehen in unde | vuoren in mit den heiligen tugenden' [Therefore God lets us bear Christ spiritually and raise him and nourish him with the holy virtues]. Note also the difficulty of distinguishing between infant and foetus in the Middle High German example quoted in n. 9 above.

11. *Vita Idae*, 1, 5, 23, p. 177. See Weiß, *Ekstase*, p. 587.

12. *Der saelden hort: Alemannisches Gedicht vom Leben Jesu, Johannes des Täufers und der Magdalena*, ed. by H. Adrian, Deutsche Texte des Mittelalters, 26 (Berlin: Weidmannsche Buchhandlung, 1927), lines 1601–05.

13. *Offenbarungen der Margaretha Ebner*, in *Margaretha Ebner und Heinrich von Nördlingen: Ein Beitrag zur Geschichte der deutschen Mystik*, ed. by Philipp Strauch (Freiburg im Breisgau and Tübingen: J. C. B. Mohr, 1882; repr. Amsterdam: Schippers, 1966), pp. 1–166 (p. 87)). See Ulinka Rublack, 'Female Spirituality and the Infant Jesus in Late Medieval Dominican Convents', *Gender and History*, 6 (1994), 37–57 (pp. 37–39); Rosemary Drage Hale, 'Rocking the Cradle: Margaretha Ebner (Be)Holds the Divine', in *Performance and Transformation: New Approaches to Late Medieval Spirituality*, ed. by Mary A. Suydam and Joanna E. Ziegler (Basingstoke: Macmillan, 1999), pp. 211–39.

14. Gertrude of Helfta, *Le Héraut* 4. 3. 4, pp. 50–52. See also Alexandra Barratt, 'Context: Some Reflections on Wombs and Tombs and Inclusive Language', in *Anchorites, Wombs and Tombs: Intersections of Gender and Enclosure in the Middle Ages*, ed. by Liz Herbert McAvoy and Mari Hughes-Edwards (Cardiff: University of Wales Press, 2005), pp. 27–38 (p. 31); Rubin, *History*, p. 262.

15. Jeffrey Hamburger, 'The Visual and the Visionary: The Image in Late Medieval Devotions', *Viator*, 20 (1989), 161–82 (p. 168 and Fig. 3); Caroline Walker Bynum, 'The Female Body and Religious Practice in the Later Middle Ages', in *Fragmentation and Redemption: Essays on Gender and the Human Body in Medieval Religion* (New York: Zone Books, 1992), pp. 181–238 (pp. 198–201); Jacqueline E. Jung, 'Crystalline Wombs and Pregnant Hearts: The Exuberant Bodies of the Katharinenthal Visitation Group', in *History in the Comic Mode: Medieval Communities and the Matter of Person*, ed. by Rachel Fulton and Bruce W. Holsinger (New York: Columbia University Press, 2007), pp. 223–37.

16. See Hildegard Urner-Astholz, 'Die beiden ungeborenen Kinder auf Darstellungen der Visitatio', *Zeitschrift für schweizerische Archäologie und Kunstgeschichte*, 38 (1981), 29–58; Rubin, *History*, Fig. 22, showing the altarpiece from Csegöld in Hungary.

17. For an overview of the iconographic type, see Gregor Martin Lechner, *Maria Gravida: Zum Schwangerschaftsmotiv in der bildenden Kunst* (Munich: Schnell und Steiner, 1981). For examples of removable Christ-figures, see also the catalogue *Frauen, Kloster, Kunst: Neue Forschungen zur Kulturgeschichte des Mittelalters: Beiträge zum internationalen Kolloquium vom 13. bis 16. Mai 2005 anlässlich der Ausstellung 'Krone und Schleier'*, ed. by Jeffrey F. Hamburger and others in association with the Ruhrlandmuseum Essen (Turnhout: Brepols, 2007), pp. 453–54 (Fig. 379). These are grouped with other objects related to the motherhood of Mary: for the iconography of Mary in confinement ('Maria im Wochenbett'), see pp. 454–55 (Fig. 380); for examples of Jesus dolls kept in nuns' cells, see pp. 457–59 (Figs 384–88). Note also the iconography of the *vierge ouvrante* (or *virgen abridera*): a statue of Mary that could be opened to reveal quite a different image on the inside (e.g. of the Trinity). See also Bynum, 'The Female Body', p. 217, Fig. 6.11; Rubin, *History*, p. 345 and Fig. 20.

18. Heinrich Seuse provides an example of a religious subject being granted a view of his own inner organs (when the persona is able to look into his own heart, as though through crystal, and sees Divine Wisdom seated next to his own soul). Heinrich Seuse, *Seuses Leben*, in *Heinrich Seuse: Deutsche Schriften*, ed. by Karl Bihlmeyer (Stuttgart: Kohlhammer, 1907; repr. Frankfurt: Minerva, 1961), pp. 7–195 (Ch. 5, p. 20). See Arnold Angenendt, '"Der Leib ist klar, klar wie Kristall"', in *Frömmigkeit im Mittelalter: Politisch-soziale Kontexte, visuelle Praxis, körperliche Ausdrucksformen*, ed. by Klaus Schreiner with Marc Müntz (Munich: Fink, 2002), pp. 387–98 (pp. 395–96).

19. For further discussion, see Katharine Park, *Secrets of Women: Gender, Generation and the Origins of Human Dissection* (New York: Zone Books, 2006), pp. 39–76.

20. *Die Offenbarungen der Adelheid Langmann, Klosterfrau zu Engelthal*, ed. by Philipp Strauch, Quellen und Forschungen zur Sprach- und Culturgeschichte der germanischen Völker, 26 (Strassburg and London: Trübner, 1878), p. 33.

21. *Offenbarungen der Adelheid Langmann*, p. 36.

22. *Offenbarungen der Adelheid Langmann*, p. 33.

23. *The Life of King Edward Who Rests at Westminster*, ed. and trans. by Frank Barrow, 2nd edn (Oxford: Oxford University Press, 1992).

24. Monika Otter, 'Closed Doors: An Epithalamium for Queen Edith, Widow and Virgin', in *Widows and Virgins in the Middle Ages*, ed. by Angela Jane Weisl and Cindy Carlson (New York: St. Martin's Press, 1999), pp. 63–92 (pp. 78–79).

25. Monika Otter, 'Entrances and Exits: Performing the Psalms in Goscelin's *Liber confortatorius*', *Speculum*, 83 (2008), 283–302 (pp. 284–86).

26. 'Gnaden-Leben', p. 414.

27. 'Gnaden-Leben', pp. 415–16.

28. 'Gnaden-Leben', p. 414: 'Ich bin nit din kind: ich bin din bru^ederlin' [I am not your child, I am your little brother].

29. Heinrich von Loufenberg, 'Jesus in dem kripselin', in *Das deutsche Kirchenlied von der ältesten Zeit bis zu Anfang des XVII. Jahrhunderts*, ed. by Philipp Wackernagel, 5 vols (Leipzig: Teubner, 1864–77), II, no. 777, pp. 599–600.

30. There are numerous examples of religious subjects rendered physically uncomfortable by the pressure of the spirit of God inside them, even when there is no suggestion of spiritual pregnancy. See Nigel F. Palmer, 'Herzeliebe, weltlich und geistlich: Zur Metaphorik vom "Einwohnen im Herzen" bei Wolfram von Eschenbach, Juliana von Cornillon, Hugo von Langenstein und Gertrud von Helfta', in *Innenräume in der Literatur des deutschen Mittelalters. XIX: Anglo-German Colloquium Oxford 2005*, ed. by Burkhard Hasebrink and others (Tübingen: Niemeyer, 2008), pp. 197–224 (pp. 204–08).

31. Hadewijch, *Mengeldichten*, ed. by Jozef van Mierlo (Antwerpen: N. V. Standaard Boekhandel, 1952). For an introduction to the works of Hadewijch, see Ruh, *Geschichte*, II, 158–232; Joris Reynaert, 'Hadewijch: Mystic Poetry and Courtly Love', in *Medieval Dutch Literature in its European Context*, ed. by Erik Kooper (Cambridge: Cambridge University Press, 1991), pp. 208–25.

32. For example, in *Die Minneburg*, ed. Hans Werner Pyritz, Deutsche Texte des Mittlelaters, 43 (Berlin: Akademie-Verlag, 1950), lines 301–02, this is covered in a single couplet, when a female statue is said to have gazed on a male statue with such desire 'daz sie zu hant wart swanger gar | und auch ein cluges kint gebar' [that she immediately became pregnant and also bore a beautiful child].

33. See Weiß, *Ekstase*, p. 595: 'Bei der geistlichen Schwangerschaft ist an eine leibhafte Vergegenwärtigung der geschichtlichn Empfängnis Jesu gedacht. In der Gottesgeburt dagegen geht der Mensch nicht mit dem Sohn Gottes schwanger oder gebiert ihn, sondern Christus wird in seinem Herzen geboren oder der Mensch wird in die ewige Geburt des Sohnes Gottes hineingenommen.' For a summary of the Eckhartian concept of 'Gottesgeburt', see Bernard McGinn, *The Presence of God: A History of Western Christian Mysticism*, 4 vols (New York: Herder & Herder, 2005), IV, 118–24 and 164–81.

34. See Suerbaum, 'O wie gar wundirbar', pp. 196–97.

35. For Philip of Harvengt's potentially problematic presentation of Mary's womb as a marriage-chamber in which her own marriage to Christ is enacted, see Rachel Fulton, *From Judgment to Passion: Devotion to Christ and the Virgin Mary, 800–1200* (New York: Columbia University Press, 2002), pp. 353–63.

36. Seventh vision, in *De Visionen van Hadewijch*, ed. by Jozef van Mierlo (Löwen: De Vlaamsche Boekenhalle, 1924–25), pp. 71–79 (pp. 77–79). See Weiß, *Ekstase*, p. 590.

37. 'Hi' [he] (27, 47); 'hem' [him] (43).

CHAPTER 4

'Quali colombe dal disio chiamate': A Bestiary of Desire in Dante's *Commedia*

Giuseppe Ledda

Recent years have seen the publication of numerous studies concerning the animal symbolism of the *Comedy*. In light of these, Dante's animal similes can no longer be studied simply from the 'realistic' perspective that was previously adopted by critics, but instead within the complex framework of animal symbolism in medieval culture.[1] The topic of desire is an especially rich one with regard to the use of animal imagery, represented as it is not only through the pervasive metaphor of wings,[2] which evokes the flight of a bird, but also through a number of other images of birds and animals. The aim of this paper is to provide an analysis of a selection of these images, both in relation to medieval animal symbolism and to the dynamics of desire in Dante's poem.

I shall begin with the simile to which I refer in the title of my paper, 'quali colombe dal disio chiamate' [As doves called by desire] (*Inf.* v, 82).[3] Dante offers this image as he gives us his first great meditation on love, erotic desire, and lust. In describing 'the carnal sinners, who subject reason to desire', Dante in fact offers a sequence of three ornithological similes,[4] as the lustful are compared to starlings ('stornei'), then to cranes ('gru'), and finally to doves ('colombe'):

> E come li stornei ne portan l'ali
> nel freddo tempo, a schiera larga e piena,
> così quel fiato li spiriti mali
>   di qua, di là, di giù di sù li mena;
> nulla speranza li conforta mai,
> non che di posa, ma di minor pena.
>   E come i gru van cantando loro lai,
> faccendo in aere di sé lunga riga,
> così vid' io venir, traendo guai,
>   ombre portate da la detta briga. (*Inf.* v, 40–49)

[And as their wings bear the starlings along in the cold season, in wide, dense flocks, so does that blast the sinful spirits; hither, thither, downward, upward, it drives them. No hope of less pain, not to say of rest, ever comforts them. And as the cranes go chanting their lays, making a long line of themselves in the air, so I saw shades come, uttering wails, borne by that strife.]

The first description of the souls carried by 'the hellish hurricane' is provided by the simile of the starlings, birds which had a negative connotation in medieval naturalistic literature: they fly in crowded and chaotic flocks and are considered dirty and noisy, especially during the sexual act.[5] But there is also a second group of damned souls, namely those who died violently because of their love, who are compared to cranes flying in an ordered line. In medieval bestiaries these large birds are always interpreted in a positive way. Their flocks were seen to form letters of the alphabet in the sky.[6] Moreover, as noted by Brunetto Latini, they display a perfect social organization: when they are flying, 'the first one leads, guides and instructs with its voice, and all the others follow it and obey the instructions. When the chieftain has grown hoarse and its voice is somewhat weak', it is replaced by another.[7] This is an image of political or spiritual leadership, taken on in a spirit of service and responsibility towards the community.[8] However this positive symbol is somehow overturned by the line of the lustful in Dante's hell. While they used to be great queens and kings, they did not act as models of good behaviour. On the contrary, in being controlled by lust, they acted against moral values and human laws.

In the long line of the 'shades whom love had parted from our life' (ll. 68–69) Dante notices two souls who, unlike the others, are flying in pair. Aroused by curiosity he calls them, and they come towards him:

> Quali colombe dal disio chiamate
> con l'ali alzate e ferme al dolce nido
> vegnon per l'aere, dal voler portate;
>   cotali uscir de la schiera ov'è Dido,
> a noi venendo per l'aere maligno,
> sì forte fu l'affettüoso grido. (*Inf.* v, 82–87)

[As doves called by desire, with wings raised and steady, come through the air, borne by their will to their sweet nest, so did these issue from the troop where Dido is, coming to us through the malignant air, such force had my compassionate cry.]

At first the image of the doves seems sweet and tender, but actually, like the entire representation of Paolo and Francesca, it is ambiguous and ambivalent and finally reveals a negative meaning. In classical and medieval culture the dove of course has several positive meanings, but also a significant negative significance, for doves were associated with Venus, the goddess of love, and often mentioned as an example of lust. As Isidore notes, doves 'stay often in the nest, and incite love by kissing'. The nest is mentioned several times as the place where the doves copulate and their kisses are seen as preliminary to the sexual act.[9] It is also frequently said that their name, *columba*, comes from the phrase *colens lumbos* [exercising the loins].[10] Finally instead of singing, they were believed to weep or utter a sigh.[11] The doves of Dante's simile are driven by desire and 'borne by their will to their sweet nest'. Thus we can see that the medieval bestiary tradition offers an important cultural background that should be taken into account when interpreting several elements present in the passage: lust and lechery, desire, the 'sweet nest', the kiss, and the intermingling of weeping and speech.

Cranes and doves are two of the few animals mentioned more than once in the *Comedy*. In the *Purgatorio* cranes once again refer to the lustful. In canto XXVI, the condition of the souls is described, like that of the lustful in hell, through a sequence of three animal similes: ants, cranes, and fish. The crane simile is immediately preceded by one referring to the ants:

> Lì veggio d'ogne parte farsi presta
> ciascun' ombra e basciarsi una con una
> sanza restar, contente a brieve festa;
>   così per entro loro schiera bruna
> s'ammusa l'una con l'altra formica,
> forse a spïar lor via e lor fortuna.
> [...]
>   Poi, come grue ch'a le montagne Rife
> volasser parte, e parte inver' l'arene,
> queste del gel, quelle del sole schife,
>   l'una gente sen va, l'altra sen vene;
> e tornan, lagrimando, a' primi canti
> e al gridar che più lor si convene. (*Purg.* XXVI, 31–48)

[There on every side I see all the shades making haste and kissing one another, without stopping, content with brief greeting: thus within their dark band one ant touches muzzle with another, perhaps to spy out their way and their fortune. [...] Then, like cranes that should fly, some to the Riphaean mountains, and others toward the sands, these shy of the frost, those of the sun, the one people passes on, the other comes away, and they return weeping to their former chants and to the cry that most befits them.]

It seems evident that with their 'basciarsi una con una' these penitent lustful souls correct in fraternal kisses the luxurious kisses described in *Inferno* v.[12] When referring to the ant simile commentators and scholars usually quote a passage from Book IV of Virgil's *Aeneid*:[13]

> Migrantis cernas totaque ex urbe ruentis,
> ac veluti ingentem formicae farris acervum
> cum populant, hiemis memores, tectoque reponunt:
> it nigrum campis agmen praedamque per herbas
> convectant calle angusto, pars grandia trudunt
> obnixae frumenta umeris, pars agmina cogunt
> castigantque moras, opere omnis semita fervet. (*Aen.* IV, 401–07)

[One could see them moving away and streaming forth from all the city. Even as when ants, mindful of winter, plunder a huge heap of corn and store it in their home; over the plain moves a black column, and through the grass they carry the spoil on a narrow track; some strain with their shoulders and heave on the huge grains, some close up the ranks and rebuke the delay; all the path is aglow with work.][14]

Critics usually note that from a formal point of view there is a strong relationship between Dante's simile of ants and Virgil's.[15] However it has not been noted that the importance of this Virgilian simile relies upon the context in which it appears, for in Book IV of the *Aeneid* it is used in order to represent the Trojans who are preparing to leave Carthage. After yielding to Dido's love, Aeneas obeys the gods and decides to leave the queen and to set off with his men: they run away from lust in order to accomplish their mission. Similarly the lustful in Purgatory run away from the vice of lust (a vice encapsulated by Dido) and start again their penitential journey through the fire in order to attain salvation. It is important to remember that Dido is always mentioned by Dante in the cantos devoted to love and lust: *Inf.* v, *Purg.* XXX, *Par.* VIII and IX.[16] I would argue that the ants simile also constitutes an additional reference to Dido and the penitents' flight from the sin she represents.

It is well known that in Dante's *Purgatorio* the idea of a penitential pilgrimage from captivity to freedom, from vice to salvation, is of the greatest importance.[17] Similarly, with regard to the animal similes used to describe the souls, we should observe that the bestiary of Dante's *Purgatorio* is a penitential bestiary, using animals that in medieval culture are linked to penitential symbolism: the swallow and the eagle in canto IX, the yoked oxen in canto X, the hawks with their eyes sewn up in canto XIII and the mole in canto XVII.[18] The ant and crane similes of canto XXVI form part of this trend.

Dante's animal symbolism also relates closely to the theme of pilgrimage. For example, avian migration is evoked in the second simile of *Inferno* v, in which the cranes are carried by the wind but lack a destination. By contrast, the purgatorial cranes hasten to their migration. The two groups of penitents go in opposite directions because they yielded to different types of lust during their lives. In the same way the examples of lust they shout are also different, though they commonly emphasize the bestiality of this sin.[19] Dante scholars usually read the three animal similes of *Purgatorio* XXVI in terms of this animalistic desire.[20] However, I believe that this degraded bestiality of desire is restricted to the *exempla* of lust, and that the animal images in these similes have a different function,[21] concerned less with the vice of lust the souls yielded to in the past than with the penitential situation in which they now find themselves, as they fly away from vice onwards towards penitence and salvation.[22] The flight away from vice, as it is specified by the simile of the cranes, has to be performed in opposite directions, but not because of different goals. The two groups of penitent souls/migrating cranes in fact share the same aim: to reach peace and heaven, where finally their longing will be satisfied.[23] So, when cranes are evoked again in *Paradiso*, they appear to have attained the goal of their migrating journey: they are happily fed and take flight in order to form the letters that compose a sentence from the Bible:

> E come augelli surti di rivera,
> quasi congratulando a lor pasture,
> fanno di sé or tonda or altra schiera,
>   sì dentro ai lumi sante creature
> volitando cantavano, e faciensi
> or *D*, or *I*, or *L* in sue figure. (*Par.* XVIII, 73–78)[24]

[And as birds, risen from the shore, as if rejoicing together at their pasture, make of themselves now a round flock, now some other shape, so within the lights holy creatures were singing as they flew, and in their figures made of themselves now *D*, now *I*, now *L*.]

The cranes, forced into an aimless flight by the hellish storm, and then migrating in a penitential pilgrimage in Purgatory, have finally reached their goal and no longer need to wander.[25] This moment is seen as so significant that Dante chooses to follow it with only the second invocation of the *cantica*.[26] As scholars have observed, the other passages alluding to cranes also refer to problems of poetics.[27] The invocation of *Paradiso* XVIII suggests then that in this passage the image of the cranes and the episode it introduces have a special metapoetic importance: the poet seeks now the help of the divinity in order to write a new kind of poetry, beyond the poetics of courtly love and stilnovism. Dante-*poeta* asks the Muse to help him to become a faithful scribe of divine dictation like the cranes who form sacred words in the sky.

Cranes are not the only animals that appear more than once in the poem: doves constitute another relevant example of animals that can be found in different cantos. They are mentioned in canto II of *Purgatorio*, where Dante, Virgil and the souls are seduced by Casella's singing of 'Amor che ne la mente mi ragiona', a *canzone* in which Dante spoke allegorically about his love for philosophy (*Conv.* III). They are all now harshly reproached by Cato and forced to fly away, just like scared doves which are compelled to interrupt their meal:

> Come quando, cogliendo biado o loglio,
> li colombi adunati a la pastura,
> queti, sanza mostrar l'usato orgoglio,
>   se cosa appare ond'elli abbian paura,
> subitamente lasciano star l'esca,
> perch'assaliti son da maggior cura;
>   così vid'io quella masnada fresca
> lasciar lo canto, e fuggir ver' la costa,
> com'om che va, né sa dove rïesca;
>   né la nostra partita fu men tosta. (*Purg.* II, 124–33)

[As doves, when gathering wheat or tares, assembled all at their repast and quiet, without their usual show of pride, if something appears that frightens them, suddenly leave their food because they are assailed by a greater care; so I saw that new troop leave the song and hasten toward the hillside, like one who goes, but knows not where he may come forth; nor was our departure less quick.]

In this way the poetic phase constituted by the doctrinal lyrics devoted to Dante's love for philosophy is now considered only partially effective and has to be replaced by a superior aim.[28] Finally, in the heaven of the fixed stars, Saint Peter and Saint James greet each other with affection like doves:

> Sì come quando il colombo si pone
> presso al compagno, l'uno a l'altro pande,
> girando e mormorando, l'affezione;
>   così vid' ïo l'un da l'altro grande
> principe glorïoso essere accolto,
> laudando il cibo che là sù li prande. (*Par.* XXV, 19–24)

[As when the dove alights beside its mate, and the one lavishes its affection on the other, circling it and cooing, so did I see the one great and glorious prince received by the other, praising the food which feeds them thereabove.]

These heavenly doves definitively correct the lustful love of the doves in *Inf.* v: their love is now brotherly and charitable. Moreover the ambiguous philosophical and earthly food in *Purg.* II, 'biado o loglio' [wheat or tares], is replaced by the true and pure heavenly nourishment.

There are other interesting aspects that emerge when examining the dove simile of *Inferno* v, with the allusion to the nest particularly significant since the nest is very often mentioned in medieval bestiaries as the place of doves' lust.[29]

As is well known, the correction of the lustful love between Paolo and Francesca is fully accomplished in the poem through the representation of the love between Dante and Beatrice. And it is in the first canto of the *Paradiso* that this rectifying process begins.[30] Here Beatrice looks at the sun and Dante tries to do so as well, but soon he is forced to desist. And yet he can look into Beatrice's eyes, which are still staring at the sun. Therefore the divine light which transforms Dante and raises him to heaven comes towards him in an indirect and mediated way, reflected in Beatrice's eyes. This moment is extremely meaningful both in terms of correction of the negative model of lustful and tragic love and in terms of the construction of a new model of virtuous and salvific love. It is in this context that we find the first animal simile used to describe Beatrice (there is in fact only one more animal simile referring to Beatrice in the entire poem). Fixing her eyes on the midday sun, Beatrice is compared to an eagle, a bird that according to medieval scientific tradition was able to gaze directly at the sun:[31]

> quando Beatrice in sul sinistro fianco
> vidi rivolta e riguardar nel sole:
> aguglia sì non li s'affisse unquanco.
> E sì come secondo raggio suole
> uscir del primo e risalire in suso,
> pur come pelegrin che tornar vuole,
> così de l'atto suo, per li occhi infuso
> ne l'imagine mia, il mio si fece,
> e fissi li occhi al sole oltre nostr'uso.
> Molto è licito là, che qui non lece
> a le nostre virtù, mercé del loco
> fatto per proprio de l'umana spece. (*Par.* I, 46–57)

[when I saw Beatrice turned to her left side and looking at the sun: never did eagle so fix his gaze thereon. And even as a second ray is wont to issue from the first, and mount upwards again, like a pilgrim who would return home: thus of her action, infused through the eyes into my imagination, mine was made, and I fixed my eyes on the sun beyond our wont. Much is granted to our faculties there that is not granted here, by virtue of the place made for humankind as its proper abode.]

The bestiary tradition attaches great importance to the eagle and considers its visual excellence as its main and most peculiar quality. For this reason the eagle was often interpreted as a symbol of the contemplation of divine truth. In this context it is worth noticing that there is another simile, in a passage that follows the one quoted above, which links Dante to the eagle. As a prompt reply to Beatrice's action, Dante fixes his own eyes upon the sun. Thus, Dante too is somehow becoming an eagle.

But this is only the first step of his transformation: he can gaze at the sun only for a few moments, because he cannot endure its overwhelming brightness and has to be satisfied with its indirect vision. Nonetheless, it is thanks to this reflected light that Dante's heavenly ascent can begin:

> Io nol soffersi molto, né sì poco,
> ch'io nol vedessi sfavillar dintorno,
> com' ferro che bogliente esce del foco;
>   e di sùbito parve giorno a giorno
> essere aggiunto, come quei che puote
> avesse il ciel d'un altro sole addorno.
>   Beatrice tutta ne l'etterne rote
> fissa con li occhi stava; e io in lei
> le luci fissi, di là sù rimote.
>   Nel suo aspetto tal dentro mi fei,
> qual si fé Glauco nel gustar de l'erba
> che 'l fé consorto in mar de li altri dèi.
>   Trasumanar significar *per verba*
> non si poria; però l'essemplo basti
> a cui esperïenza grazia serba. (*Par.* I, 58–72)

[I did not endure it long, nor so little that I did not see it sparkle round about, like iron that comes molten from the fire. And suddenly day seemed added to day, as if He who has the power had adorned heaven with another sun. Beatrice was standing with her eyes all fixed upon the eternal wheels, and I fixed mine on her, withdrawn from there above. Gazing upon her I became within me such as Glaucus became on tasting of the grass that made him sea-fellow of the other gods. The passing beyond humanity may not be set forth in words: therefore let the example suffice any for whom grace reserves that experience.]

An additional trait of the eagle often mentioned in the medieval bestiary tradition is its behaviour towards its offspring. This concerns one of the elements of the dove simile in *Inferno* V: the nest. According to medieval tradition, the eagle, in order to test the worthiness of its eaglets, 'forces its unfledged young to look at the rays of the sun' (as Pliny writes). And, as Isidore notes, 'Any that maintain their gaze without moving it keeps, but the others it rejects as degenerate', and they are cast out of the nest.[32] Dante, however, forced to withdraw his gaze from the sun, is not rejected by the 'eagle' Beatrice, who allows him to look at it in an indirect way. Beatrice represents here the human beauty in which divine beauty is reflected; Dante through his love for her terrestrial beauty can reach its divine source. This kind of love does not involve an idolatrous desire for the creature but corrects and redirects the desire towards the divine.

The second and final animal simile referring to Beatrice is found at the beginning of *Paradiso* XXIII. These animal similes concerning Beatrice thus appear in extremely pronounced positions: the eagle simile was situated at the beginning of the heavenly ascent, while this second simile opens the second part of Dante's heavenly experience, for it is in the heaven of the fixed stars that Christ descends from the Empyrean with his glorious body in order to make himself visible to Dante. Beatrice is here compared to a mother-bird perched on a branch, staring at the point where the sunrise is expected and anxiously awaiting the dawn in order to nourish her nestlings:

> Come l'augello, intra l'amate fronde,
> posato al nido de' suoi dolci nati
> la notte che le cose ci nasconde,
> che, per veder li aspetti disïati
> e per trovar lo cibo onde li pasca,
> in che gravi labor li sono aggrati,
> previene il tempo in su aperta frasca,
> e con ardente affetto il sole aspetta,
> fiso guardando pur che l'alba nasca;
> così la donna mïa stava eretta
> e attenta, rivolta inver' la plaga
> sotto la quale il sol mostra men fretta:
> sì che, veggendola io sospesa e vaga,
> fecimi qual è quei che disïando
> altro vorria, e sperando s'appaga. (*Par.* XXIII, 1–15)

[As the bird, among the beloved leaves, having sat on the nest of her sweet brood through the night which hides things from us, who, in order to look upon their longed-for aspect and to find the food wherewith to feed them, wherein her heavy toils are pleasing to her, foreruns the time, upon the open bough, and with glowing love awaits the sun, fixedly gazing for the dawn to break; so was my lady standing, erect and eager, turned toward the region beneath which the sun show less haste. I, therefore, seeing her in suspense and longing, became as he who in desire would fain have something else, and in hope is satisfied.]

In this context commentators usually quote a passage from the *De ave Phoenice* by Lactantius.[33] This seems fitting because the phoenix has a strong resurrectional and Christological resonance. I would argue, however, that the allusion is here to another bird: the nightingale, or *luscinia*, which is considered a solar bird in the bestiary tradition.[34] According to Isidore this bird 'gets its name because its song signals the end of the night and the rising of the sun', 'quasi lucinia' [as if bringing light].[35] Another important aspect of the medieval tradition concerning the nightingale is its maternal love. It is frequently noted that this bird sings during the night while watching its eggs and keeping them warm with the heat of its body. This praiseworthy behaviour is imitated by the poor and virtuous mother who works hard at the loom during the night so that her children will not lack bread.[36]

Dante adds to Lactantius's phoenix, as well as to the nightingale of the bestiaries, the lexicon of love and desire, which is sweet and maternal but also ardent and inflamed. In this passage we can find a definitive correction of some of the main features linked to the dove simile in *Inferno* V: among them the topic of desire and that of the nest as a place of love. The bestiary of Beatrice is closed by this maternal and solar image of the bird awaiting the rising of the sun (Christ) in order to nourish her beloved son, thus recalling the image of the eagle fixing its eyes in the midday sun. In this case Dante replies with the same gesture: that is, redoubling Beatrice's desire (13–15). At stake is no longer the painful anxiety of passional love, but a desire already satisfied in hope.

Notes to Chapter 4

1. No comprehensive book-length study of the animals in Dante's *Comedy* has yet been carried out. There are, however, many essays devoted to single animal images. These include: John Freccero, 'Casella's Song (*Purg.* II, 112)', *Dante Studies*, 91 (1973), 73–80; R. A. Shoaf, 'Dante's "colombi" and the Figuralism of Hope in the *Divine Comedy*', *Dante Studies*, 93 (1975), 27–59; Lawrence V. Ryan, ' "Stornei", "Gru", "Colombe": The Bird Images in *Inferno* v', *Dante Studies*, 94 (1976), 25–45; K. J. Knoespel, 'When the Sky Was Paper: Dante's Cranes and Reading as Migration', in *Lectura Dantis Newberryana*, ed. by Paolo Cherchi and A. C. Mastrobuono, 2 (1990), pp. 121–46; Giovanna Neri, 'Il bestiario contemplativo di Dante', *Intersezioni*, 10 (1990), 15–33; Guglielmo Gorni, ' "Gru" di Dante: Lettura di *Purgatorio* XXVI', *Rassegna europea di letteratura italiana*, 2 (1994), 11–34; Lino Pertile 'Il nodo di Bonagiunta, le penne di Dante e il Dolce Stil Novo', *Lettere Italiane*, 46 (1994), 44–75 (repr. in Lino Pertile, *La punta del disio: Semantica del desiderio nella 'Commedia'* (Florence: Cadmo, 2005), pp. 85–113); Paolo Valesio, '*Inferno* v: The Fierce Dove', *Lectura Dantis*, 14/15 (1994), 3–25; Teresa Gualtieri, 'Dante's Crane and the Pilgrimage of Poetic Inspiration', *Rivista di Studi Italiani*, 13 (1995), 1–13; Lucia Lazzerini, 'Bonagiunta, il nodo e la vista recuperata', in *Operosa parva per Gianni Antonini*, ed. by Domenico De Robertis and Franco Gavazzeni (Verona: Valdonega, 1996), pp. 47–54; Sonia M. Barillari, 'L'animalità come segno del demoniaco nell'*Inferno* dantesco', *Giornale Storico della Letteratura Italiana*, 111 (1997), 98–119; Annamaria Carrega, 'Immagini intessute di scrittura: Aquile dantesche', *L'immagine riflessa*, 7 (1998), 285–301; Lucia Lazzerini, 'L'"allodetta" e il suo archetipo: La rielaborazione di temi mistici nella lirica trobadorica e nello stil novo', in *Sotto il segno di Dante: Scritti in onore di Francesco Mazzoni*, ed. by Leonella Coglievina and Domenico De Robertis (Florence: Le Lettere, 1998), pp. 165–88; Umberto Di Raimo, 'Domande sul simbolismo delle gru nella *Divina Commedia*', in *Mappe della letteratura europea e mediterranea: I. Dalle origini al 'Don Chisciotte'*, ed. by Gian Mario Anselmi (Milan: Bruno Mondadori, 2000), pp. 135–54; Claudia Sebastiana Nobili, 'Dante e il repertorio narrativo medievale', in *'Per correr miglior acque...': Bilanci e prospettive degli studi danteschi alle soglie del nuovo millennio*, 2 vols (Rome: Salerno, 2001), II, 993–1006; Elisa Curti, 'Un esempio di bestiario dantesco: La cicogna o dell'amor materno', *Studi Danteschi*, 67 (2002), 129–60; Antonio Rossini, 'Rane e formiche nella *Commedia*: la leggenda di due antichi popoli fra tradizione ovidiana, mediazione patristica ed intertestualità dantesca', *Rivista di Cultura Classica e Medioevale*, 54 (2002), 81–88; Daniela Boccassini, *Il volo della mente: Falconeria e Sofia nel mondo mediterraneo: Islam, Federico II, Dante* (Ravenna: Longo, 2003); Claudia Carmina, ' "Ecco la fiera con la coda aguzza": La bestialità nel canto XVII dell'*Inferno*', *Dante*, 2 (2005), 99–111; Carlos López Cortezo, 'Metapoetica della lussuria: Le gru di *Purgatorio* XXVI', *Tenzone*, 6 (2005), 121–41; Nicolò Maldina, 'Api e vespe nella *Commedia*: Osservazioni sul bestiario dantesco', *L'Alighieri*, 29 (2007), 121–42; Francesca Baraldi, 'Il simbolismo dell'aquila nella *Commedia* dantesca', *I castelli di Yale: Quaderni di filosofia*, 9 (2007/08), 85–101; Mariangela Semola, 'Dante e l'"exemplum" animale: Il caso dell'aquila', *L'Alighieri*, 31 (2008), 149–59. See also Giuseppe Ledda, 'Per un bestiario dantesco della cecità e della visione: Vedere "non altrimenti che per pelle talpe" (*Purg.* XVII 1–3)', in *Da Dante a Montale: Studi di filologia e critica letteraria in onore di Emilio Pasquini*, ed. by Gian Mario Anselmi and others (Bologna: Gedit, 2005), pp. 77–97; Ledda, 'La *Commedia* e il bestiario dell'aldilà: Osservazioni sugli animali nel *Purgatorio*', in *La fabbrica della 'Commedia': Atti del Convegno Internazionale di Studi (Ravenna, 14–16 settembre 2006)*, ed. by Alfredo Cottignoli, Donatino Domini, and Giorgio Gruppioni (Ravenna: Longo, 2008), pp. 139–59; and Ledda, 'Animali nel *Paradiso*', in *La poesia della natura nella 'Divina Commedia': Atti del Convegno Internazionale di Studi (Ravenna, 10 novembre 2007)*, ed. by Giuseppe Ledda (Ravenna: Centro Dantesco dei Frati Minori Conventuali, 2009), pp. 93–135.

2. See Pertile, *La punta del disio*, pp. 115–35.

3. Translations from the *Commedia* are taken from Dante Alighieri, *The Divine Comedy*, trans. and with a commentary by Charles S. Singleton (Princeton, NJ: Princeton University Press, 1970–75).

4. See Ryan, ' "Stornei", "Gru", "Colombe": The Bird Images in *Inferno* v'; Valesio, '*Inferno* v: The Fierce Dove'; and Gualtieri, 'Dante's Crane and the Pilgrimage of Poetic Inspiration'.

5. Pliny, *Naturalis historia*, X, xxxv, 73: 'Sturnorum generi proprium catervatim volare et quodam pilae orbe circumagi omnibus in medium agmen tendentibus' (cited from Gaio Plinio Secondo, *Storia naturale*, ed. by Alessandro Barchiesi and others (Turin: Einaudi, 1983–88)); Albert the Great, *De animalibus*, XXIII, xxiv, 104: 'Sturnus avis [...] Gregatim volat et compresse qualibet ad aciei centrum propter timorem accipitris contendente: accipitrem enim superius vel a latere accendentem alis eventant et subtus volantem stercoribus opprimunt. In harenis et paludibus sedent et cum armentis vaccarum assidue sunt propter pascua quae de stercoribus colligunt' (and IV, ii: 'Garritus autem earum maxime est tempore coitus'). Cited from Albertus Magnus, *De animalibus*, ed. by Hermann Stadler (Münster: Aschendorffsche Verlagsbuchhandlung, 1916). See also Ryan, ' "Stornei", "Gru", "Colombe": The Bird Images in *Inferno* v', pp. 28–29.

6. See Ernst Robert Curtius, *Letteratura europea e Medio Evo latino* (Florence: La Nuova Italia, 1992), p. 381; Gorni, ' "Gru" di Dante: Lettura di *Purgatorio* XXVI', pp. 28–30; and Gualtieri, 'Dante's Crane and the Pilgrimage of Poetic Inspiration', pp. 96–97.

7. See Brunetto Latini, *Tresor*, I, 163: 'et tozjors vet une devant les autres ausi come confenoniers et guie des autres, et les moine et conduist et chastie de sa voiz, et trestoz les autres ensivent cele et obeissent a sa loi. Et quant le cheveteine est enroés et sa voiz est auques deffaillie, ele n'a pas honte que une autre soit misse en son leu, et ele vet par derriere avec les autres.' Cited from Brunetto Latini, *Tresor*, ed. by Pietro G. Beltrami and others (Turin: Einaudi, 2007).

8. See also, e.g., Bartholomaeus Anglicus, *De proprietatibus rerum*, XII, 15: 'Grus de propria voce nomen accepit, tali enim vocem sonat ut dicit Isidorus. Est autem avis alarum magnarum et fortis volatu, aeris alta petens ut videat, quas velit pergere regiones, ut dicitur in Hexaemeron. Est enim avis diligens suam speciem, et in societate vivens, habens regem et ordine literato volans, ut dicit Ambrosius. Ductor autem agminis quasi instigando et arguendo voce ad rectos volatus cogit agmen, et si forte raucescat, succedit alia grus quae supplet idem officium. Grues autem voce praeconia terram petunt, ut quiescant et cum sederint ad custodiam sui vigilias ordinant, ut aliae securius conquiescant. Vigiles autem super unum crus stant directe, et lapillum tenent in pede altero, a terra suspenso vel elevato, ut si casu aliquo dormierint, per casum lapillis excitentur' (cited from Bartholomaei Anglici, *De genuinis rerum coelestium, terrestrium et inferarum rerum Proprietatibus Libri XVIII* (Frankfurt: apud Wolfangum Richterum, 1601; repr. Frankfurt a.M.: Minerva, 1964)); Hugh of Fouilloy, *De avibus* (= Hugh of St. Victor, *De bestiis*) I, 39: 'Grues dum pergunt, unam sequuntur ordine litterato [...]. Illos autem significant, qui ad hoc student, ut ordinate vivant. Grues enim ordine litterato volantes designant ordinate viventes. Cum autem ordinate volando procedunt, ex se litteras in volatu fingunt. Illos autem designant, qui in se praecepta Scripturae bene vivendo formant. Una earum reliquas antecedit, quae clamare non desinit, quia praelatus, qui primum locum regiminis obtinet, suos sequaces moribus et vita praeire debet, ita tamen ut semper clamet, et viam bonae operationis sequacibus suis praedicando demonstret. Quae autem alias antecedit, si rauca facta fuerit, tunc alia succedit, quia praelatus si verbum Dei subjectis non praedicet, vel praedicare nesciat, cum raucus fuit, necesse est ut alius succedat' (PL 177, 40–41).

9. See Isidore of Seville, *Etymologiae*, XII, 7, 61: 'Aves mansuetae, et in hominum multitudine conversantes, ac sine felle; quas antiqui Venerias nuncupabant, eo quod nidos frequentent, et osculo amorem concipiant'. Cited from Isidoro di Siviglia, *Etimologie, o Origini*, ed. by Angelo Valastro Canale (Turin: UTET, 2004). The text is also found in the *Physiologus Latinus* (*versio BIs*), XXXII: 'Aves mansuete et hominum mansiones conversantes, ac sine felle, quas antiqui Venerias nuncupabant, eo quod nidos frequentent, et osculo amorem concitant' (*Bestiari medievali*, ed. by Luigina Morini (Turin: Einaudi, 1996), p. 76). See also Alexander Neckam, *De laudibus divinae sapientiae*, dist. II, 733–34: 'Lumborum cultum praecedunt oscula multa, | Hunc cultum causam nomini esse puntant'. Cited from *Alexandri Neckam De naturis rerum libri duo: With the Poem of the Same Author, De Laudibus Divinae Sapientiae*, ed. by Thomas Wright (London, 1863; repr. Nendeln/ Liechtenstein: Kraus, 1967); Bartholomaeus Anglicus, *De proprietatibus rerum*, XII, 6: 'Sunt autem columbae aves mansuetae [...], quas antiqui venereas nuncupabant, eo quod frequentent nidos et osculo amorem concipiant et Veneri multum vacant. Et ideo columba dicitur quasi colens lumbos [...] Columba avis est voluptuosa'; and in the marginal glosses: 'Nota contra luxuriam': see Baudouin Van den Abeele, 'Simbolismo sui margini: Le moralizzazioni del *De proprietatibus rerum*', in *Simbolismo animale e letteratura*, ed. by Dora Faraci (Rome: Vecchiarelli, 2003), pp. 159–83 (p. 175); Brunetto Latini, *Li Livres dou Tresor*, I, 156: 'Et esmuevent luxure par

baisier, et plorent en leu de chant, et font lor niz en pertuis entre pierres ou aucun flum soit voisins'.

10. In addition to the passages cited in the previous note, see Bernardus Silvestris, *Commentum Super Sex Libros Eneidos Virgilii*: 'dicuntur aves Veneris quia sunt luxuriose: unde dicuntur columbe quasi colentes lumbos', ed. by Bruno Basile (Roma: Carocci, 2008), p. 156; Albert the Great, *De animalibus*, XXIII, 32: 'Columba sic dicitur quia lumbos colit'.

11. See Brunetto Latini, *Li Livres dou Tresor*, I, 156: 'et plorent en leu de chant'.

12. The lexicon of the kiss is extremely rare in the poem; it appears only here (l. 32), in *Inf.* V (twice, ll. 134 and 136; in this context the importance of kisses in the representation of doves in medieval culture should be stressed), and in two other passages: *Inf.* VIII, 44 and *Purg.* XXXII, 153.

13. For some formal similarities see also: Ovid, *Met.* VII, 624–26: 'Hic nos frugilegas adspeximus agmine longo | grande onus exguo formicas ore gerentes | rugosoque suum servantes cortice callem'. Cited from Ovidio, *Le metamorfosi*, ed. by Guido Paduano and others (Turin: Einaudi, 2000). This Ovidian passage does not seem intertextually present in *Purg.* XXVI; however, it is strongly alluded to in *Inf.* XXIX, 58–66. See Rossini, 'Rane e formiche nella *Commedia*', pp. 81–83.

14. Text and translation are taken from Virgil, *Eclogues, Georgics, Aeneid 1–6*, trans. by H. R. Fairclough (Cambridge, MA: Harvard University Press, 1960).

15. Similarities between the Virgilian phrase 'nigrum agmen' and Dante's 'schiera bruna' are generally underlined. However it is worth noticing that another parallel can be found in the hurry of the greetings: compare the Dantean phrases 'sanza restar', 'contente a brieve festa', with the frenetic activity of the Virgilian ants who 'castigant moras' (l. 407).

16. See *Inf.* V, 61–62 and 85; *Par.* VIII, 11–12 and IX, 97–99. On the archetypical presence of Dido in *Inferno* V, see Claudia Villa, 'Tra affetto e pietà (per *Inferno* V)', *Lettere Italiane*, 51 (1999), 513–41. Of special interest is the allusion to the Virgilian line 'adgnosco veteris vestigia flammae' (*Aen.* IV, 23) in the very moment in which Beatrice appears to Dante in Eden (*Purg.* XXX, 48: 'conosco i segni de l'antica fiamma'): see Peter S. Hawkins, 'Dido, Beatrice, and the Signs of Ancient Love', in *The Poetry of Allusion: Virgil and Ovid in Dante's 'Commedia'*, ed. by Rachel Jacoff and Jeffrey T. Schnapp (Stanford, CA: Stanford University Press, 1991), pp. 113–30 and pp. 274–76.

17. See e.g. Charles S. Singleton, '"In exitu Israel de Aegypto"', in *Dante: A Collection of Critical Essays*, ed. by John Freccero (Englewood, NJ: Prentice-Hall, 1965), pp. 102–21; Peter S. Hawkins, *Dante's Testaments: Essays in Scriptural Imagination* (Stanford, CA: Stanford University Press, 1999), pp. 247–64 and pp. 333–36; Carlo Delcorno, '"Ma noi siam peregrin come voi siete": Aspetti penitenziali del *Purgatorio*', in *Da Dante a Montale: Studi di filologia e critica letteraria in onore di Emilio Pasquini*, pp. 11–30.

18. See Ledda, 'Dante e il bestiario dell'aldilà'.

19. This is particularly strong in the example of Pasiphaë: 'Ne la vacca entra Pasife, | perché 'l torello a sua lussuria corra' [Pasiphaë enters into the cow, that the bull may hasten to her lust] (*Purg.* XXVI, 41–42); 'Nostro peccato fu ermafrodito; | ma perché non servammo umana legge, | seguendo come bestie l'appetito, || in obbrobrio di noi per noi si legge, | quando partinci, il nome di colei | che s'imbestiò ne le 'mbestiate schegge' [our sin was hermaphrodite: but because we observed not human law, following appetite like beasts, when we part from them, the name of her who bestialized herself in the beast-shaped planks is uttered by us, in opprobrium of ourselves] (82–87).

20. See for example Michelangelo Picone, 'Canto XXVI', in *Lectura Dantis Turicensis: 'Purgatorio'*, ed. by Georges Güntert, and Michelangelo Picone (Florence: Cesati, 2001), pp. 407–22 (pp. 418–19); Gorni, '"Gru" di Dante', pp. 13–14.

21. As noted above the cranes were connected with the invention of the letters of the alphabet, so they have a strong link with writing. Dante's allusions to them are always in contexts in which the focus of the discourse is literature. See *Purgatorio* XXIV, 64–69, immediately after the definition of the 'dolce stil novo' in the dialogue between Dante and Bonagiunta Orbicciani, and canto XXVI, in which Dante meets the poets Guido Guinizzelli and Arnaut Daniel, with whom he speaks about literary topics. On the relevance of the image of the cranes in this canto in connection with poetry see Gorni, '"Gru" di Dante'; Gualtieri, 'Dante's Crane and the Pilgrimage of Poetic Inspiration'; and López Cortezo, 'Metapoetica della lussuria: Le gru di *Purgatorio* XXVI'.

22. On the cranes in the naturalistic and encyclopedic medieval literature, see Baudouin Van den Abeele, 'Migrations médiévales de la grue', *Micrologus*, 8 (2000), 65–78, who pays special attention to the symbolic meaning of their migratory habits. Some classical texts concerning the migration of the cranes probably present in the Dantean memory are: Statius, *Tebais*, V, 11–16 and XII, 514–18; Lucan, *Bellum civile*, V, 711–16.

23. For different interpretations of this passage, which give emphasis to the unnatural, aberrant and 'scandalous' direction of one of the two groups of cranes, see Gorni, '"Gru" di Dante', pp. 23–27; López Cortezo, 'Metapoetica della lussuria: Le gru di *Purgatorio* XXVI'.

24. See also *Par.* XVIII, 88–93: 'Mostrarsi dunque in cinque volte sette | vocali e consonanti; e io notai | le parti sì, come mi parver dette. || "*DILIGITE IUSTITIAM*", primai | fur verbo e nome di tutto 'l dipinto; | '*QUI IUDICATIS TERRAM*', fur sezzai' [They displayed themselves then, in five times seven vowels and consonants; and I took note of their parts as they appeared in utterance to me. *DILIGITE IUSTITIAM* were first verb and substantive of all the design; *QUI IUDICATIS TERRAM* were the last] (and see Sap 1, 1, for the biblical quotation). See also Lino Pertile, '*Paradiso* XVIII tra autobiografia e scrittura sacra', *Dante Studies*, 109 (1991), 25–49.

25. In addition to Gorni, '"Gru" di Dante', pp. 28–30 and Gualtieri, 'Dante's Crane and the Pilgrimage of Poetic Inspiration', pp. 96–97; see also Michelangelo Picone, 'Canto XVIII', in *Lectura Dantis Turicensis: 'Paradiso'*, ed. by Georges Güntert and Michelangelo Picone (Florence: Cesati, 2002), pp. 265–79 (pp. 273–74).

26. 'O diva Pegasëa che li 'ngegni | fai glorïosi e rendili longevi, | ed essi teco le cittadi e ' regni, || illustrami di te, sì ch'io rilevi | le lor figure com' io l'ho concette: | paia tua possa in questi versi brevi!' [O divine Pegasea, who give glory unto men of genius and render them long-lived, as they, through you, the cities and the kingdoms, illumine me with yourself that I may set forth their shapes, as I have them in conception; let your power appear in these brief lines.] (*Par.* XVIII, 82–87). On the invocations in the *Commedia* see Robert Hollander, 'The Invocations of the *Commedia*', in his *Studies in Dante* (Ravenna: Longo, 1980), pp. 31–38; Giuseppe Ledda, *La guerra della lingua: Ineffabilità, retorica e narrativa nella 'Commedia' di Dante* (Ravenna: Longo, 2002), pp. 30–55. The nine invocations are: *Inf.* II, 7–9; XXXII, 10–12; *Purg.* I, 7–12; XXIX, 37–42; *Par.* I, 13–36; XVIII, 82–87; XXII, 112–23; XXX, 97–99; XXXIII, 67–75. On this one in *Par.* XVIII see Pertile, '*Paradiso* XVIII tra autobiografia e scrittura sacra', pp. 35–37.

27. See e.g. Michelangelo Picone, 'Canto XXVI'; Gorni, '"Gru" di Dante'; Gualtieri, 'Dante's Crane and the Pilgrimage of Poetic Inspiration'.

28. See Freccero, 'Casella's Song'.

29. See the texts by Isidore, Bartholomaeus Anglicus and Brunetto Latini quoted above.

30. For a significant prefiguration of this moment, see also the characterization of Beatrice's eyes as 'smeraldi' [emeralds] in *Purg.* XXXI, 116: the emerald is well known in the tradition of the medieval lapidaries for its reflecting capacity. This context is very similar to that of *Par.* I: in Eden, Beatrice fixes her gaze on the gryphon; her eyes reflect the gryphon; Dante sees the true natures of the gryphon reflected in Beatrice's eyes. In addition, her eyes are explicitly compared to a mirror (*Purg.* XXXI, 121–23: 'Come in lo specchio il sol, non altrimenti | la doppia fiera dentro vi raggiava, | or con altri, or con altri reggimenti' [As the sun in a mirror, so was the twofold animal gleaming therewithin, now with the one, now with the other bearing]); and finally she is called 'isplendor di viva luce etterna' [splendor of living light eternal] (*Purg.* XXXI, 139), where 'isplendor' means technically 'reflected light' (see *Conv.* III, xiv, 5, and, for Dante's use of technical terminology and optical concepts, Simon A. Gilson, *Medieval Optics and Theories of Light in the Works of Dante* (Lewiston, NY, Queenston, and Lampeter: Edwin Mellen Press, 2000)). In the *Convivio* Dante recognized as well a similar capacity to reflect the divine to the donna-Sapienza to whom the canzone *Amor che ne la mente mi ragiona* is devoted (see *Conv.* III, xv, 1–5, with the quotation of Sap 7, 26).

31. See Aristotle, *Historia animalium*, IX, 34, 620a1; Plinius, *Naturalis historia*, X, 3, 10; Elianus, *De natura animalium*, II, 26; Jerome, *Comm. in Is.* XII, 40, CChL 73A, 467; Gregory the Great, *Moralia in Iob*, IX, 32, 48, CChL 143, 489; XXXI, 47, 94, CChL 143B, 1614–16; Isidore of Seville, *Etymologiae*, XII, 7, 11–12; *Phyisiologus Latinus, Versio BIs*, VIII; Rabanus Maurus, *De universo*, VIII, 6 (PL 111, 243); Hugh of Fouilloy, *De avibus* (= Hugh of St. Victor, *De bestiis*, I, 56, PL 177, 53–55); Hildegard of Bingen, *Physica*, VI, 8 (PL 197, 1202); Bartholomaeus Anglicus, *De*

proprietatibus rerum, XII, I; Thomas of Cantimpré, *Liber de natura rerum*, V, 2; Albert the Great, *De animalibus*, XIII, I (ed. by Stadler, p. 1433); Brunetto Latini, *Tresor*, I, 145, 2; Philippe de Thaün, *Bestiaire*, 2013–2142; Gervaise, *Bestiare*, 829–62; *Bestiario toscano*, XXXV; *Bestiario moralizzato* (*Libro della natura degli animali*), XXXIV. On the eagle in the tradition of the Christian bestiary see Maria Pia Ciccarese, *Animali simbolici: Alle origini del bestiario cristiano. I. (agnello-gufo)* (Bologna: EDB, 2002), pp. 109–35.

32. Isidore of Seville, *Etymologiae*, XII, 7, 10–11 ('Aquila ab acumine oculorum vocata. [...] Nam et contra radium solis fertur obtutum non flectere, unde et pullos suos ungue suspensos radiis solis obicit, et quos viderit inmobilem tenere aciem, ut dignos genere conservat; si quos vero inflectere obtutum, quasi degenere abicit'). See also Ciccarese, *Animali simbolici: Alle origini del bestiario cristiano. I. (agnello-gufo)*, pp. 111–12, pp. 114–16, pp. 130–31, who quotes many passages from ancient and patristic authors, among them: Aristotle, *Hist. an.* IX, 619b; Pliny, *Nat. hist.* X, 10; Lucan, *Phars.* IX, 902–06; Elianus, *De nat. an.* II, 26 and IX, 3; Ambrose, *Exaëmeron*, V, 18 (PL 14, 232); Gregore of Elvira, *De Salomone*, 5–6 (CChL 69, 254–55). For other references and discussions see Maria Pia Ciccarese, 'Il simbolismo dell'aquila', *Civiltà classica e cristiana*, 13 (1992), 295–333. For the presence in medieval authors see *Physiologus Latinus, Versio BIs* (VIII, in *Bestiari medievali*, p. 24); Rabanus Maurus, *De universo*, VIII, 6 (PL 111, 243); Hugh of Fouilloy, *De avibus* (= Hugh of St. Victor, *De bestiis*, I, 56, PL 177, 53); Philippe de Thaün, *Bestiaire*, 2027–42; 2093–2112 (in *Bestiari medievali*, p. 218; p. 220); Alexander Neckam, *De natura rerum*, XXIII; Bartholomaeus Anglicus, *De proprietatibus rerum*, XII, 1; Thomas of Cantimpré, *Liber de natura rerum*, V, 2; Brunetto Latini, *Tresor*, I, 145; Albert the Great, *De animalibus*, XIII, 1; *Libro della natura degli animali* (*Bestiario toscano*), XXXV (in *Bestiari medievali*, pp. 458–59); *Bestiario moralizzato*, XXXIV (in *Bestiari medievali*, p. 510); Cecco d'Ascoli, *L'Acerba*, III, 3.

33. See Lactantius, *De ave Phoenice*, 39–42: 'Tollitur ac summo considit in arboris altae | vertice, quae totum despicit una nemus, | et conversa novos Phoebi nascentis ad ortus | expectat radios et iubar exoriens'. Cited from *La fenice: Da Claudiano a Tasso*, ed. by Bruno Basile (Rome: Carocci, 2004). Other classical passages frequently quoted by the commentators are: Verg., *Georg.* I, 413–14; II, 523; *Aen.* VI, 272; XII, 474–75; Statius, *Achill.* I, 215–16.

34. See also Maurizio Perugi, 'Canto XXIII', in *Lectura Dantis Turicensis: 'Paradiso'*, pp. 363–71. On the nightingale in medieval literature see Wendy Pfeffer, *The Change of Philomel: The Nightingale in Medieval Literature* (New York and Frankfurt am Main: Peter Lang, 1985).

35. See Isidore of Seville, *Etymologiae*, XII, 7, 37: 'Luscinia avis inde nomen sumpsit, quia cantu suo significare solet diei surgentis exortum, quasi lucinia'; Rabanus Maurus, *De universo*, VIII, 6 (PL 111, 247): 'Lucinia avis inde nomen sumpsit, quia cantu suo significare solet diei surgentis exortum, quasi lucinia. [...] Haec forsan sanctos praedicatores typice significare potest, qui futurae lucis exortum pronuntiant et ad ejus adventum animo vigilanti intendere fideles quosque exhortantur'. See Pfeffer, *The Change of Philomel*, pp. 20–23; Jean-Marie Fritz, *Paysages sonores du Moyen Âge: Le Versant épistémologique* (Paris: Champion, 2000), pp. 421–23.

36. See Ambrose, *Exaëmeron*, V, 24, 85 (PL 14, 239): 'Quid autem de luscinia dicam, quae pervigil custos cum ova quodam sinu corporis et gremio fovet, insomnem longae noctis laborem cantilenae suavitate solatur; ut mihi videatur haec summa eius esse intentio, quo possit non minus dulcibus modulis, quam fotu corporis animare ova quae foveat. Hanc imitata tenuis illa mulier, sed pudica, in usum molae lapidem brachio trahens, ut possit alimentum panis suis parvulis non deesse, nocturno cantu moestum pauperpatis mulcet affectum. Et quamvis suavitatem lusciniae non possit imitari, imitatur tamen eam sedulitate pietatis'. See also Wernerius, *Deflorationes SS: Patrum*, II (PL 157, 1149–50); and Pseudo-Hugh of St. Victor, *De bestiis*, III, 33 (PL 177, 96): 'Luscinia nomen est avis inde sumptum, quia cantu suo significare solet surgentis exortum diei, quasi lucinia, est enim pervigil custos. Cum ova quodam sinu corporis et gremio fovet, insomnem longae noctis laborem cantilenae suavitate remittit. Et, ut mihi videtur, haec summa est eius intentio, ut possit, non minus dulcioribus modulis quam fomento corporis, fetum animare atque fovere. Hanc vitam videtur ducere mulier viduata, sed pauper et pudica, quae colum digitis trahens ut parvulis suis victum acquirat, nocturno cantu moestitiam paupertatis demulcet, et quamvis suavitatem lusciniae imitari non possit, imitatur tamen eam sedulo maternae pietatis officio'. See also Thomas of Cantimpré, *De natura rerum*, V, 76; Albert the Great, *De animalibus*, XXIII, 68 (ed. by Stadler, p. 1501).

CHAPTER 5

Dante Painting an Angel: Image-making, Double-oriented Sonnets and Dissemblance in *Vita Nuova* XXXIV

Fabio Camilletti

In Dante Gabriel Rossetti's watercolour *The First Anniversary of the Death of Beatrice* (1853),[1] modelled on the thirty-fourth paragraph of the *Vita Nuova*, Dante is portrayed suddenly lifting his head, surprised by the presence of other people in his room. Among them, beholding him pitifully, is a young woman — plausibly the 'donna gentile' who will dominate the following paragraphs of the 'little book', or even Gemma Donati, to whom Dante became engaged, according to Boccaccio's biography, precisely due to the intermediation of his friends, who were worried by his persistent mourning for Beatrice.[2] In his hand, Dante holds the figure of an angel that he has been drawing: a *figura* of Beatrice, sketched in a moment of mournful imagination as a tangible sign of her presence-in-absence.[3]

The watercolour resumed the subject of the first of Rossetti's artworks inspired by Dante, a drawing with the same title completed in 1849.[4] In this work, Dante is caught in the very same moment, but no woman is present. The drawing is detailed, sketched in pen and ink, and shading is minimal. The style follows an early Pre-Raphaelite *ligne claire*, inspired by Flaxman's illustrations of the *Comedy* and by Carlo Lasinio's reproductions of the *Camposanto* frescoes in Pisa, thereby aiming to convey a peculiar earliness in fashion. The room's furnishing replicates the description of an imaginary thirteenth-century Italian painter's studio that Rossetti had outlined in the first version of the short story *Hand and Soul*, written in the very same year, 1849:

> Beside the matters of his art and a very few books, almost the only object to be noticed in Chiaro's room was a small consecrated image of St. Mary Virgin wrought out of silver, before which stood always, in summer-time, a glass containing a lily and a rose.[5]

In Rossetti's fictionalized construction of the Italian Middle Ages as the space of an early purity that modernity has lost, the imaginary painter and the real poet shed reciprocal light upon one another, in drawing both inspiration from a sort of mystical meditation, favoured by the separate space of the room. In *Hand and Soul*, Dantean themes are freely re-elaborated, outlining an artistic mysticism that unavoidably reverberates back to Dante's *oeuvre*, helping us to understand the major features of its Pre-Raphaelite reception:

> in the ecstasy of prayer, it had even seemed to [Chiaro] to behold that day when his mistress — his mystical lady (now hardly in her ninth year, but whose solemn smile at meeting had already lighted on his soul like the dove of Trinity) — even she, his own gracious and holy Italian Art — with her virginal bosom, and her unfathomable eyes, and the thread of sunlight round her brows — should pass, through the sun that never sets, into the circle of the shadow of the tree of life, and be seen of God, and found good: and then it had seemed to him that he, with many who, since his coming, had joined the band of whom he was one (for, in his dream, the body he had worn on earth had been dead an hundred years), were permitted to gather round the blessed maiden, and to worship with her through all ages and ages of ages saying, Holy, holy, holy. This thing he had seen with the eyes of the spirit.[6]

These 'eyes of the spirit', through which the poet-painter beholds 'his mystical lady', clarify the way Dante's passage is read in 1849. The date is not accidental. A year before, in 1848, the paranormal phenomena produced by the Fox sisters in the United States had given birth to the movement later known as Spiritualism, which can be seen as a nineteenth-century and positivistic aftermath of those experiences that pre-Enlightenment ages interpreted as belonging to the domain of religious supernatural. The act of self-gathering exits from the domain of religious introspection and spiritual exercise to enter that of an uncanny trance, or even possession. Not by chance, while translating the *Vita Nuova* in the 1840s, Rossetti suppresses a short passage from *VN* XXXIV, 2: 'Quando li vidi,' Dante had written, 'mi levai, e salutando loro dissi: Altri era testè meco, perciò pensava' [When I saw them, I stood up and greeting them said: 'Someone was with me just now; that is why I was so deep in thought'].[7] In his translation, Rossetti elides the second part of Dante's answer, so that what remains is only a puzzling 'Another was with me',[8] which ambiguously suggests an unseen and uncanny presence of the departed lady. In editing this translation in 1861, within his anthology of *The Early Italian Poets*, Rossetti will add in a footnote: 'The majority [...] add the words "And therefore I was in thought:" but the shorter speech is perhaps the more forcible and pathetic'.[9]

In the nineteenth century, the main value to be preserved in the text is therefore its 'forcible and pathetic' component, through which the angel painted by Dante (of which no original is preserved, and no evidence can be found outside Dante's text) is constructed as a paragon for interrogating the challenges of post-Enlightenment subjectivity. In the meantime, *VN* XXXIV is used as a paradigmatic text for questioning the relationship between literature and the visual arts, and for enhancing a new model of the artist characterized by a double vocation (*Doppelbegabung*)[10] as a painter-poet who creates 'double works of art'.[11] On the one hand, the nineteenth-century understanding of *VN* XXXIV — which is not only Rossetti's — betrays the need for a 'visualization of Beatrice':[12] the naïveté of the Italian scholar Melchior Missirini, who proposed to individuate in Dante's angel the hidden model of female beauty in medieval Italian art,[13] shares the same longing for a displaying of the *gentilissima* as Rossetti's representations of Beatrice, aiming to fill the absence of any description in the *Vita Nuova* (where, as Gorni highlights,

Dante even eliminates the traditional topos of the Lady's beauty).[14] On the other hand, Dante's painted angel of *VN* xxxiv is used in order to question the limits of representability, and the possibility of depicting intellectual beauty. Through the genre of 'literary portraits', of which *Hand and Soul* can be seen as the first example in the English-speaking world (and of which *VN* xxxiv is constructed as an illustrious precursor),[15] literature aims at facing the challenges of nineteenth-century art in relation to mimesis and adherence to the real, and eventually the risk of solipsism in the process of artistic introspection, as evident in Balzac's short story *Le Chef d'œuvre inconnu* [The Unknown Masterpiece] in which Beatrice is precisely mentioned as a model of intellectual beauty (1831). In Robert Browning's poem *One Word More*, of 1855,[16] Dante's lost angel is constructed as a counterpart to the inexistent sonnets composed by Raphael, and both are precisely 'unknown masterpieces' that are endlessly more charming than the painter's Madonnas or than the poet's *Comedy*: 'You and I would rather read that volume, [...] | Lean and list the bosom-beats of Rafael, | Would we not? than wonder at Madonnas' (lines 18 and 20–21); 'You and I would rather see that angel, | Painted by the tenderness of Dante, | Would we not? — than read a fresh Inferno' (lines 50–52).

Most of all, the angel of *VN* xxxiv seems to probe the questions faced by the nineteenth century in its post-Enlightenment reconfiguration of the problems of desire, death and loss. By conceptualizing the figure of the angel as a crystallization of the departed lady produced by 'the tenderness of Dante', the process of image-making is seen as a compensatory act of the irrevocable loss of the object of desire. Dante's angel is therefore interpreted as a simulacrum in which the dead lady is sublimated. Surely, as Alison Milbank highlights, Victorian writers (but the consideration can be widened to the whole nineteenth century) use the *Vita Nuova* to embody their own relationship with the loss of their objects of love, as Rossetti's own experience epitomizes vividly.[17] Dante's angel would therefore be used as an anachronistic device for reconfiguring the ambiguities of desire in the pre-Freudian decades: once sublimated into the image of an angel 'that impure contact cannot touch' (Lacan),[18] the Lady is at the same time portrayed and elided, vanishing in the very moment of its representation,[19] in the century in which 'the fading metaphor' of the muse, '[which] used to put real alterity under erasure, [...] is revitalised by turning to real death'.[20]

We can however ask ourselves how much these rhapsodic vicissitudes of *VN* xxxiv may tell us about Dante's text, and to what extent it is legitimate to speak of 'death', 'loss', or 'sublimation' for a text such as the *Vita Nuova*. If Dante's first book is employed in the nineteenth century in order to frame the most crucial issues of post-Enlightenment subjectivity,[21] it is possible to ask ourselves how much the *Vita Nuova* allows us to do so, and whether it is acceptable to retrospectively project post-Enlightenment categories onto Dante's text.

In *VN* xxxiv, Dante is sitting alone, 'in parte', namely outside those spaces — streets, churches, private houses — in which the public dimension of the *Vita Nuova* is set. Physical isolation corresponds to a state of mental detachment: the private space — 'una mia camera' [a room of mine] (*VN* iii, 2), 'la mia camera' [my room] (xii, 2), 'la camera de le lagrime' [the room of tears] (xiv, 9) — is the venue of self-inquiry and meditation,[22] as well as the setting of vision and poetic writing in which the poet's relationship with the phantasms of his desire is made possible.[23] Dante is drawing ('disegnava'; *VN* xxxiv, 1): the imperfect tense underlines the undetermined continuity of the operation, in which Dante is so absorbed that he does not perceive the presence of several people, 'uomini alli quali si convenia di fare onore' [some men to whom all consideration was due] (*VN* xxxiv, 1), who 'riguardavano quello che io facea' [were looking at what I was doing] (*VN* xxxiv, 2), and 'erano già stati alquanto anzi che io me ne accorgesse' [had already been there some time before I became aware of it]. As Gorni highlights,[24] the gesture recalls Jesus's in the eighth chapter of St John's Gospel: while the Scribes and the Pharisees are interrogating him about the possibility of executing the adulterous woman by stoning, Jesus, with an apparently indifferent behaviour, 'inclinans se deorsum digito scribebat in terra' [bent down and began to write on the ground with his finger] (John 8. 6),[25] and then, abruptly, stands up ('erexit se'; 8. 7), pronouncing the famous, final words: 'qui sine peccato est vestrum primus in illam lapidem mittat' [Let the one among you who is without sin be the first to throw a stone at her] (8. 7). Similarly, Dante stands up abruptly (*VN* xxxiv, 1): the sudden turning to the past tense ('volsi gli occhi' [I turned my head']; 'mi levai' [I stood up]) highlights the quickness of his gesture. Dante justifies his behaviour with his enigmatic sentence before returning to his previous operation, again echoing John: 'ritornaimi alla mia opera' [I returned to my work] (*VN* xxxiv, 3); 'et iterum se inclinans scribebat in terra' [Again he bent down and wrote on the ground] (John 8. 8).

In suddenly intruding, the external world of the men who are unable to understand the true nature of Dante's meditation, therefore interrupts Dante's introspection. In parallel, it makes Dante's operation turn from the self-referential and fully absorbing act of drawing to the public dimension of poetic speech: 'faccendo ciò, mi venne uno pensero di dire parole, quasi per annovale, e scrivere a costoro li quali erano venuti a me' [while I was doing this a thought came to me to write some poetry in the form of an anniversary poem, and to address it to those men who had come to me] (*VN* xxxiv, 3). The episode is thus connected to the genesis of the sonnet 'Era venuta', which is therefore meant as an act of apology and as a more detailed clarification of Dante's answer. The prose frame of the *Vita Nuova* constructs a detailed and composite narration for justifying a text that, in its original shape, was merely a poem that, as Barolini points out, was essentially Cavalcantian in inspiration with some stilnovistic and theological touches.[26] In inscribing the poem within the new context of the book, Dante invests it with strongly evangelical implications, connecting it at the same time with the practice of image-making. Moreover, Dante, raising crucial issues about this particular locus of the text, enacts a completely new and never-attempted operation, by adding to the already circulated text a new initial *quartina* ('cominciamento'), and by incorporating both within the book ('questo sonetto, [...] à due cominciamenti' [this sonnet has two beginnings] (*VN* xxxiv, 3). On the one hand, as Barolini notes, we witness here a foundational example of authorial philology, through which Dante productively plays with the dialectic relationship between previous poems and new frame on which the *Vita Nuova* is articulated, thus staging in an evident way the remotest archaeology of his own writing.[27] On the other hand, the new beginning — explicitly oriented, as it has been highlighted, according to the programmatic textual strategies of the prose — [28] is placed as the first one, thus singularly inverting the chronological order of the composition. The two beginnings create two orientations toward the sonnet, and therefore two possible ways of reading the text.

The already published version focuses on the mourning for the departed Lady. We have absolutely no clue for identifying this 'donna gentil' [gracious lady], whose death Love laments, with Beatrice; she has come to Dante's mind ('mente'; line 1) in the very moment in which Love's power ('valore'; line 3) brought the unnamed addressees of the sonnet to 'riguardar quel ch'eo facia' [to see what I was doing] (line 4). We are still in a pre-Vitanovian perspective, in which the 'valore' still belongs to Love; the expression 'riguardar quel ch'eo facia', in being almost literally recuperated in the prose ('riguardavano quello che io facea' [looking at what I was doing]), shows however how this stanza provides a first hint for the construction of the prose episode. The new one concentrates instead on the Lady's celestial glory. The Lady is now, and for good, Beatrice: the 'valore' now belongs to her ('per suo valore | fu posta da l'altissimo signore' [because of her great worth was placed by his most lofty Majesty] [lines 3–4]),[29] and she has been placed 'nel ciel de l'umiltate, ov'è Maria' [in the heaven of humility where Mary is] (line 4), thus echoing the periphrasis employed by Dante for alluding to Beatrice's death in *VN* XXVIII, 1: 'lo segnore della giustizia chiamoe questa gentilissima a gloriare sotto la insegna di quella regina benedetta virgo Maria' [the Lord of Justice called this most gracious one to glory under the banner of the Blessed Virgin Mary].

This periphrasis is just one of the many through which Dante pursues one of the most remarkable operations of the *Vita Nuova*, namely the elision of Beatrice's death in favour of an insistence on a continuity between earthly life and celestial hereafter: 'la sua partita da noi' [her departure from us] (XXVIII, 2), 'l'anima sua nobilissima si partio' [her most worthy soul departed] (XXIX, 1), 'fue partita da questo secolo' [she departed from this world] (XXX, 1); 'questa donna era fatta de li cittadini di vita eterna' [this lady had become a citizen of the eternal life] (XXXIV, 1). The substantive 'morte' [death] and the adjective 'morta' [dead] themselves are excluded by the prose frame (namely, by Dante's perspective *a posteriori*) in relation to Beatrice, and are present only when they are not connected to her, or when mediated by another point of view than that of the prose, as that of Dante's lack of awareness before the final revelation of *VN* XLII: the death of Beatrice's friend in *VN* VIII and IX ('villana Morte' [villainous death] (VIII, 5); 'la morta ymagine avenente' [the dead, fair image] (VIII, 6); 'Morte villana, di Pietà nemica' [Brute death, the enemy of tenderness] (VIII, 8); 'la morte di questa donna' [the death of this lady] (IX, 1)); the mournful but fallacious dream of *VN* XXIII and the *canzone* 'Donna pietosa' (XXIII, 17–28); the poem 'Gli occhi dolenti' (XXXI, 8–17): 'chiamo Beatrice e dico: "Or se' tu morta?"' [I call to Beatrice, 'Are you dead?'] (line 55); the request of Beatrice's brother for an elegy of the departed one, in which the definition of Beatrice as 'una donna che s'era morta' [a lady who was dead] (XXXII, 2) has to be connected to Dante's use of indirect speech, and must therefore be attributed to the speaker's perspective.

The two beginnings of 'Era venuta' therefore embody one of the strongest tensions on which the *Vita Nuova* is articulated, that between the topos of the Lady's death, on which the first 'cominciamento' was focused, and the 'glorious' perspective of the prose frame, whose laconism elides every mention of Beatrice's corpse or of her sepulchre,[30] in accordance with Dante's authoritative reassessment of courtly themes. From the beginning, *VN* xxxiv depicts a scene of remembrance in which image-making and poetic composition are used in order to celebrate the anniversary of the Lady's death. The prose inscribes the act of thinking within the frame of mnemotechnical practice: as Dante systematically does in the *Vita Nuova*,[31] the poem's 'mente' [mind] is translated into the prose's 'memoria' [memory]: 'Era venuta nella mente mia' [came into my mind]; 'questa donna era già nella mia memoria' [this lady was already in my memory] (*VN* xxxiv, 7), thus constructing the act of thinking as a melancholic speculation around an *imago* situated within memory. In openly portraying his own behaviour in reference to the culture of melancholy, Dante displays an oscillation between private and public spaces, as well as between inner speculation and public speech: the episode stages an undulating movement, from interiority to exteriority, from visual culture to poetic speech, from abstraction to concretization and vice-versa. The desiring memory of the departed Lady is first channelled into an abstracted angel-like figure, thus turning the topos of the 'donna angelicata', from the mere reactivation of a rhetorical simile, into actual identification. After having been systematically intellectualized and subtracted from the domains of concreteness and visuality throughout the book, Beatrice is not portrayed in accordance with a mimetic paradigm, but rather as she is now, from the perspective of the eternal, in the same way as the book had taken as its intention not to transcribe all and actual events, but only their actual and true meaning ('la loro sentenzia'; *VN* I, I). If the Lady had already been disembodied within the poem into 'nobile intellecto' [noble intellect] (*VN* xxxiv, 11), the mention of 'figure d'angeli' announces a significant twist, sublimating the Lady into the most noble form of intellect. Second, memory is externalized as a concrete simulacrum that stands as an emblem of the object's absence: the abstraction from the memory of the Lady to 'intellectual image' is re-externalized into a new *figura*, as a product of men, in which memory is condensed. The nature of this *figura* is however peculiarly undetermined: Dante speaks first of one angel ('disegnava uno angelo'), and later of several angels ('disegnare figure d'angeli' [drawing figures of angels] (*VN* xxxiv, 3)), while the verb 'disegnare' and the mention of 'certe tavolette' [some panels] (*VN* xxxiv, 3) as a support seem to imply a preliminary nature to the operation, a first sketching for a further and never achieved work of art.[32] In parallel, as Gorni remarked, the double-oriented sonnet itself seems to allude to the unrepresented angel: the two beginnings and the body of the poem would compose the stylized figure of a winged creature.[33]

These underlying tensions that pervade the text — the angel and the angels, the drawing and the sonnet, the two beginnings, as well as the concurrent processes of abstraction and concretization, of inner speculation and of material externalization — can be read as the visible embodiments of a shifting and ambiguous position of the subject in relation to the absence of the object of desire, and could even legitimate, as has been cautiously done, the evocation of the Freudian notion of 'repression'.[34] In being grounded in an oscillation between mourning and celebration of the Lady's glory, the double-oriented sonnet could be seen as a bipolar and multistable textual object, as a compromise formation resulting from the two contradictory and irreconcilable instances of loss and faith in an afterlife survival. When analysing the Freudian notion of sublimation in his seventh seminar on *The Ethics of Psychoanalysis*, Jacques Lacan precisely connected it to that of courtly love, arguing that both are grounded in a tension between abstraction and concretization. On the one hand, we see a spatial displacement of the Lady according to the paradigms of ascension and abstraction. Courtly love creates what Lacan calls an 'inhuman partner'[35] — *sacer*, disembodied, divine — of which the angel can be seen as one of the most evident manifestations. The abstraction of the Lady into the angel-like 'nobile intellecto', is precisely this emptying of the object of love, its defeminization, its metamorphosis into the asexualised image of the angel 'that no impure contact could touch': in being a speechless and desireless creature,[36] the image of the angel elides the Lady's actual femininity, establishing in its place the emptiness that, as Žižek glosses, 'functions as a kind of "black hole" around which the subject's desire is structured'.[37] On the other hand, we perceive the embodiment of the Lady in a series of signifiers — the painted tablets, the poem, the image conjured by memory — that become simulacra of her presence-absence. Through the isolation of the subject from the external world, the material *figuræ* (the image in the heart, the painted image, the sonnet) become embodiments of the disembodied, 'object[s] [...] find[ing] [them]sel[ves] at the place of the impossible Thing' (Žižek).[38] 'The Object', Žižek adds, 'is attainable only by way of an incessant postponement',[39] through the artistic creation of fetishized anamorphic objects that obliquely allude to the original loss.

Still, it seems that there is something, in *VN* xxxiv, that exceeds and escapes these readings. In his 1990 book on Fra Angelico, Georges Didi-Huberman shows how the puzzling nature of the Florentine painter's religious works, although created in the fullest Quattrocento, can only be interpreted with reference to the tradition of medieval theology, and therefore dismantles the historicist illusion of a *Zeitgeist*, through which contemporary cultural experiences can be used in order to explain artistic phenomena and vice-versa. Cristoforo Landino, who writes about thirty years after Fra Angelico's death — and who could therefore be claimed as an authority for understanding the categories within which his artwork was conceptualized 'at the time' — shows instead an essential misunderstanding of the out-of-time nature of Fra Angelico's art, allegedly belonging to the culture of the Renaissance but actually imbued with the medieval theology that post-Vasarian art-history has omitted from its teleological perspective.[40] The same happens, I think, with the episode of *VN* xxxiv. First, as Giorgio Agamben pointed out, Dante is still situated in an anterior position with respect to the turning point epitomized by Petrarch, in which the

> essential textual tension of Romance poetry [...] displace[s] its center from desire to mourning: Eros [...] yield[s] to Thanatos its impossible love object so as to recover it, through a subtle and funereal strategy, as lost object, and the poem [...] become[s] the site of an absence.[41]

The categories of 'loss' and 'absence', reverberating from the tradition of Romance poetry even into psychoanalytical reflection, are therefore inadequate for describing an intellectual experience that, according to Agamben, should not be even categorized as 'poetry': reading Dante through Boccaccio and Petrarch would be the same as interpreting Fra Angelico through Landino, who moves from a completely different paradigmatic frame of mind. The same applies to the culture of memory and its artistic implications: Petrarch's inscription within the culture of memory,[42] and his connection with the world of visual arts (epitomized by *Rvf* LXXVII and LXXVIII), shows a profound departure from Dante's operation as described in *VN* XXXIV. The portrait of Laura painted by Simone Martini belongs to a radically mutated paradigmatic frame compared with Dante's painted angel: the connection between the two, leading to the parallel Petrarch–Martini and Dante–Giotto, is a fully nineteenth-century construction, grounded in a nineteenth-century fascination with symmetries.[43] Second, Dante is situated beyond the tradition of courtly love to which Lacanian psychoanalysis refers: the act itself of concretizing a courtly metaphor, that of the image in the heart, as depicted in *VN* XXXIV, announces a departure from that tradition and a radical newness in approach. Finally, the adequacy itself of the psychoanalytical discourse in relation to courtly love should be re-thought and reassessed, and precisely in relation to the very nineteenth-century culture that witnesses both the construction of courtly love as a literary category found in the medieval corpus[44] and the birth of modern dynamic psychology to which the origins of psychoanalysis can be retraced. In other words, analysing courtly love from a psychoanalytical perspective risks engendering a tautology, by which a nineteenth-century construction like the myth of medieval Provence and its 'revolution in love' is interpreted through a nineteenth-century discourse such as the psychoanalytical one. The notion itself of the 'inhuman' partner proposed by Lacan for the courtly Lady presupposes a specific conceptualization of humanity grounded in sexuality, and may recall what Francesco De Sanctis wrote apropos of Beatrice in 1869:

> Beatrice is [...] more than a woman, she is 'angeletta bella e nova' [maiden beautiful and rare]; she is the divine not yet humanized, the ideal not yet realized, the face or aspect of all that is beautiful, good, and true [...]. But that is precisely why Beatrice is less than a woman, why she is pure femininity, the genus or type and not the individual. That is why you may contemplate, worship, understand, explain her, but you cannot love her, you cannot possess her in pure aesthetic delight, but rather you stand aloof from her. This explains why Beatrice has never achieved popularity, but has remained an inexhaustible source of dissertations and pretentious nonsense. Francesca, on the other hand, acquired immense popularity even in the least cultured countries [...]. Francesca is a woman and nothing but a woman [...] in her case these traits are not mere epithets, but the true qualities of a real person, qualities that are operative and therefore alive.[45]

Thinking of Dante's angel as a mere emblem of a loss risks therefore reading Dante through Rossetti, and interpreting the ambiguities of *VN* XXXIV through the lenses of a poetic tradition that actually constructed Dante as a precursor, but to which he is in fact extraneous. As Federica Pich correctly acknowledges, the tension staged in *VN* xxxiv is the one between time and the eternal:[46] an experiment, that of the *Vita Nuova*, which was doomed to remain unfollowed, and ultimately deactivated through Boccaccio's biography of Dante, in which Beatrice is finally transformed into a definitely human Florentine girl.[47]

Why drawing an angel? Dante — it has been said — plays here with a topos of medieval poetry,[48] and at the same time with a medical notion: falling in love is always to deal with an image, painted within the lover's heart.[49] Still, Dante gives new life to the cliché, through a threefold operation: he externalizes the practice of image-production by depicting himself in the material act of painting; the work is not a portrait of Beatrice, but is rather the figure of an angel; the image is drawn, and seems therefore to imply a preliminary nature of the operation, a first sketching for a further and never achieved work of art.

As Didi-Huberman writes, again in relation to Fra Angelico:

> Paintings are often disconcerting because their relative lack of determination, their limited conceptual means — and in particular, their fundamental incapacity, noted by Freud, to represent logical relations in a univocal way — nevertheless make them the fabulous instrument of an overdetermination of meanings and a true exuberance of thought.[50]

Dante's self-representation in the act of painting can therefore allude to the peculiar indeterminacy of visuality, in which 'the archiropoetic dream' of icons not painted by human hands[51] is interwoven with 'the profoundly organic dream' of Christian incarnation, giving birth, as Freud acknowledged, to a 'work of *figurability* that gives to dreams, symptoms, and phantasms their paradoxical visual quality, their dissemblant semblances'. 'These semblances', Didi-Huberman continues, 'are always displaced, inextricably tied up with one another, touched by the great wind of the *Unheimliche*' (p. 8). Through *VN* xxxiv, Dante would therefore explore the limits of figurality and representation, in the same way as in *VN* xxv he had discussed those of literary personifications in poetry: the challenge, in both chapters, is give account of the radical newness of Dante's experience, that of a 'nine' made into flesh that unavoidably forces the borders between image and resemblance, between subject, love and its object, and between 'words' and 'things'. The *objectivity* of Beatrice that marks the fissure between Dante and Cavalcanti situates Dante's major task outside the self-analysis of inner processes from which all exteriority is excluded, and touches the very core of the problem of representation that had been faced by Christian art in confronting the problem of the Incarnation. Dante's skipping of the topos of the 'Lady's beauty' is doubtlessly to be connected to this strategy: in the same way as the representations of Christ should give account of the excess — namely, the divine — shining in his human features, Beatrice cannot merely be an 'image' in the subject's 'mind'/'memory', dependent on the simple rules of mimesis. As Didi-Huberman recalls, Dionysius the Areopagite distinguishes between two kinds of *eikónes*: 'one kind are "fashioned in the resemblance of their object" while the other, on the contrary, "push fiction [...] to the very limits of the implausible and the absurd"'.[52] The latter kind of image is 'a type of painting that [seeks] presence before representation',[53] and is therefore the most apt to represent, as Dionysius states in the *Coelestis hierarchia*, the heavenly beings: 'dissemblance' is the '*ideal, the perfection of figures'*, so that 'it is precisely this dissemblant image that we ought to prefer to any semblance to the divine, any "appropriateness"'; since 'resemblance fools us', attributing an essence to what is 'absolutely *superessential'*.[54] Representing the unrepresentable means therefore to move outside the paradigm of mimesis (that of the image painted in the heart, or of every representation of earthly matters, as the Laura portrayed by Simone Martini will be), and to follow instead that of *vestigium*, namely of the subtle echo of divinity:

> *the art of painting*, inasmuch as its stakes are given as 'devout', transcendent, *does not proceed by means of the image but by means of the vestige*. That is the fundamental and very simple consequence of the fact that God is not, for any painter whatever, 'the Being to be seen'.[55]

Drawing an angel on the first anniversary of Beatrice's death means therefore to actually portray her, but precisely by means of vestige: not by abstraction, but rather in the only way medieval Christian art had conceptualized the possibility of painting the divine, namely via difference and dissemblance. In parallel, Dante's operation of drawing and writing can be seen, not as the production of a set of signifiers standing at the place of the irrecoverable object, but rather as a 'free tropology' in which the multiplicity of human creations reaffirms the centrality of the Incarnation they are claimed to praise:[56] the drawn angel and the double-oriented sonnet encompass Beatrice's circular parabola from time to the eternal and back again to time.

This operation is however imperfect. On the one hand, the act of drawing presupposes a future painting, that the sudden intrusion of the external world prevents Dante from completing. On the other, the oscillation enacted by the two beginnings of the sonnet, that between time and the eternal, is justified by the double perspective that pervades the text, namely that before and after the revelation of *VN* XLII, so to say the time of narration that explains and inscribes within a superior frame the episodes preserved in the book of memory: 'Lo verace giudicio del detto sogno non fue veduto *allora* per alcuno, ma *ora* è manifestissimo a li più semplici' [The true interpretation of the dream I described was not perceived by anyone *then*, but *now* it is very clear to even the least sophisticated] (*VN* III, 15; emphasis mine). We should not however forget that the revelation of *VN* XLII is surely the moment in which writing begins, namely *after* the end of the events to be narrated; but is at the same time, and most of all, the moment in which writing must arrest, that of the 'mirabile visione, ne la quale io vidi cose che mi fecero proporre di non dire più di questa benedetta infino a tanto che io potesse più degnamente trattare di lei' [miraculous vision in which I saw things that made me resolve to say no more about this blessed one until I would be capable of writing about her in a more worthy fashion] (*VN* XLII, 2). It seems therefore that Dante's unachieved figure of the angel and the self-philological operation of the double beginning of 'Era venuta' stand as visible emblems of the liminal and interlocutory nature of the *Vita Nuova* as a whole, a book conceived in the very moment of its self-overcoming, and already preluding to a further resolution of its intimate tensions. Not by chance, all the themes raised by *VN* XXXIV will reappear, deeply metamorphosed, at the end of *Paradiso*, where the problem of the representation of Beatrice is finally resolved into an apparent renunciation:

> Se quanto infino a qui di lei si dice
> fosse conchiuso tutto in una loda,
> poco sarebbe a fornir questa vice.
>   La bellezza ch'io vidi si trasmoda
> non pur di là da noi, ma certo io credo
> che solo il suo fattor tutta la goda.
>   Da questo passo vinto mi concedo [...] (*Par.* xxx, 16–22)[57]

[If all things said of her up to this point | were gathered in a single hymn of praise, | it would be paltry, matched to what is due. | The beauty that I saw transcends all thought of beauty, and I must believe | only its maker may savour it all. | I declare myself defeated at this point [...]]

In parallel, the oscillation between time and eternity that in the *Vita Nuova* was encompassed by the reciprocal circulation between the two beginnings of the sonnet, reverberates in the *Paradiso* through the miraculous metamorphosis of the 'lume in forma di rivera' [light that flows as flows a river] (*Par.* xxx, 61) into the 'candida rosa' [white rose] (*Par.* xxx, 1) of the blessed souls, granted by Dante's new perception: 'mi parve | di sua lunghezza divenuta tonda' [to me it seemed | it had made its length into a circle] (*Par.* xxx, 89–90). These two passages in *Par.* xxx — the final abandonment of the representation of Beatrice, and the line of time transformed into the circle of the eternal — ultimately resolve the aporias of *VN* xxxiv, in the light of a new understanding that goes beyond representation and speech, as peculiarities of such imperfect creatures as humans, in favour of an enjoyment in which all desire is perpetually fulfilled and renewed.[58] In doing this, the language of *Paradiso* takes the place of painting, in accepting the challenge of depicting what cannot be depicted, and forcing the limits of the human tongue: 'every story concerning Christ aims, in every sense, beyond the story', so that 'all tenses must be represented, for the story aims toward memory, toward imminence, and, above all, toward the end of time. [...] *Eternity in painting*' — but, in the case of Dante, eternity in poetry — 'means first of all a double quality, chromatic and luminous: it is a glow, a radiance, an optical shimmering'.[59]

Notes to Chapter 5

1. Ashmolean Museum, Oxford. See Dante Gabriel Rossetti, *The Paintings and Drawings 1828–1882: A Catalogue Raisonné*, ed. by Virginia Surtees, 2 vols (Oxford: Clarendon Press, 1971), I, 22. Unless otherwise specified, all translations in the essay are my own.

2. See the first draft of Boccaccio's biography: 'i suoi parenti [...] ragionarono insieme di volergli dar moglie [...]. E trovata una giovane, quale alla sua condizione era decevole, con quelle ragioni che più loro parvero induttive, la loro intenzione gli scoprirono. E [...] dopo lunga tencione [...] al ragionamento seguì l'effetto: e fu sposato' [his relatives thought together to find a wife for him. When they found a young woman who was suitable for his condition, they revealed their intention to him, by advancing the reasons that they thought to be most persuasive. After long discussions, the event followed, and he was married]. Giovanni Boccaccio, *Vite di Dante*, ed. by Pier Giorgio Ricci (Milan: Mondadori, 2002), pp. 3–62 (p. 14). Rossetti could read this passage quoted in Cesare Balbo's *Vita di Dante*, 2 vols (Turin: Giuseppe Pomba, 1839).

3. See for example Rossetti's narrative poem *Dante at Verona* (1848–52), in which Dante is portrayed reaching his room in the Verona palace, oppressed by the memory of Beatrice: 'At such times, Dante, thou hast set | Thy forehead to the painted pane | Full oft, I know; and if the rain |

Smote it outside, her fingers met | thy brow; and if the sun fell there, | Her breath was on thy face and hair. || Then, weeping, I think certainly | thou hast beheld, past sight of eyne, — | within another room of thine' (lines 187–95). Dante Gabriel Rossetti, *The Collected Works*, ed. by William Michael Rossetti, 2 vols (London: Ellis and Elvey, 1890), I, 1–17 (p. 7).

4. City of Birmingham Museum and Art Gallery. See Rossetti, *The Paintings and Drawings 1828– 1882*, I, 12.

5. Dante Gabriel Rossetti, 'Hand and Soul', in *The Germ: The Literary Magazine of the Pre-Raphaelites* (Oxford: Ashmolean Museum, 1992), pp. 23–33 (p. 25). On *Hand and Soul* and its Dantean sources, see Fabio Camilletti, 'The Golden Veil: Purezza e malinconia in un racconto di Dante Gabriel Rossetti', *Rivista di Studi Vittoriani*, 8.15 (2003), 77–93.

6. Rossetti, 'Hand and Soul', p. 26.

7. For the English translation of the *Vita Nuova* I generally follow Dante, *Vita Nuova*, trans. by Mark Musa (Oxford: Oxford University Press, 1999), amending it occasionally to suit my purposes.

8. See Dante Alighieri, 'The New Life', trans. by Dante Gabriel Rossetti, in Rossetti, *Collected Works*, II, 30–95 (p. 84).

9. Rossetti, 'The New Life', p. 84. See also Joan Rees, *The Poetry of Dante Gabriel Rossetti* (Cambridge: Cambridge University Press, 1981), p. 19.

10. See Michele Cometa, *Parole che dipingono: Letteratura e cultura visuale tra Settecento e Novecento* (Rome: Meltemi, 2004), p. 13.

11. See Federica Mazzara, *Lettere in cornice: Traduzioni artistico-letterarie di Dante Gabriel Rossetti* (Catania and Rome: Bonanno, 2010).

12. Julia Straub, *A Victorian Muse: The Afterlife of Dante's Beatrice in Nineteenth-Century Culture* (London: Continuum, 2009), p. 18.

13. Melchior Missirini, *Dell'amore di Dante Alighieri e del ritratto di Beatrice Portinari* (Florence: Ciardetti, 1832).

14. Guglielmo Gorni, 'La Beatrice di Dante, dal tempo all'eterno', in Dante Alighieri, *Vita Nova*, ed. by Luca Carlo Rossi (Milan: Mondadori, 1999), pp. v–xl (p. ix).

15. See Elisa Bizzotto, *La mano e l'anima: Il ritratto immaginario 'fin de siècle'* (Milan: Monduzzi, 2001).

16. In Robert Browning, *Men and Women and Other Poems*, ed. by Colin Graham (London: J. M. Dent, 1975), pp. 204–09.

17. Alison Milbank, *Dante and the Victorians* (Manchester: Manchester University Press, 1998), p. 255.

18. Jacques Lacan, 'The Youth of Gide or the Letter and Desire', in *Écrits*, trans. by Bruce Fink (New York and London: Norton, 2006), pp. 623–44 (p. 635).

19. Elisabeth Bronfen, *Over her Dead Body: Death, Femininity and the Aesthetic* (Manchester: Manchester University Press, 1992), p. 15. See more specifically the chapter on 'The Dead Beloved As Muse', pp. 360–83.

20. Bronfen, p. 364.

21. This is the major thesis of my monograph *Dante's Book of Youth: The 'Vita Nova' and the Nineteenth Century 1840–1907* (London: IGRS books, forthcoming 2012).

22. Fernando Salsano, 'Camera', in *Enciclopedia Dantesca*, ed. by Umberto Bosco, 6 vols (Rome: Istituto dell'Enciclopedia Italiana, 1970–78), I, 773.

23. Angelo M. Mangini, 'Stanza della scrittura', in *Luoghi della letteratura italiana*, ed. by Gian Mario Anselmi and Gino Ruozzi (Milan: Bruno Mondadori, 2003), pp. 341–51 (p. 342).

24. See Gorni's commentary to the *Vita Nova*, p. 192.

25. The source of English translations from the Bible is *The New American Bible*, online at the site <http://www.vatican.va/archive/ENG0839/_INDEX.HTM> [accessed 28 July 2011].

26. Dante Alighieri, *Rime giovanili e della Vita Nuova*, ed. by Teodolinda Barolini, notes by Manuele Gragnolati (Milan: Rizzoli, 2009), p. 456.

27. Barolini, p. 456.

28. Barolini, p. 459.

29. In the *Vita Nuova*, Beatrice is progressively constructed as a replacement and a fulfilment of the prerogatives originally belonging to 'Amore'. The first operation in this sense is led through the implicit assertion that Beatrice can create Love *ex nihilo*. In the division to the poem 'Ne li occhi porta', Dante writes that 'ne la prima parte dico sì come virtuosamente fae gentile tutto ciò che

vede, e questo è tanto a dire quanto inducere Amore in potenzia là ove non è' [In the first part I tell how she miraculously makes gracious whatever she looks upon, and this is as much as to say that she brings Love into potential existence there where he does not exist] (XXI, 6). Beatrice does not only, therefore, overrule 'Amore', but is invested with a prerogative that is characteristic of God (Domenico De Robertis, in Dante, *Vita Nuova*, ed. by Domenico De Robertis (Milan and Naples: Ricciardi 1980), p. 137n); as Marco Santagata summarizes, 'Beatrice ha poteri divini, è come Dio' [Beatrice has divine power, she is like God]: *Amate e amanti: Figure della lirica amorosa fra Dante e Petrarca* (Bologna: Il Mulino, 1999), p. 44. The final liquidation of the god of Love takes place in *VN* XXIV: ' "E chi volesse sottilmente considerare," ' says Amore in XXIV, 5, ' "quella Beatrice chiamerebbe Amore per molta simiglianza che ha meco" ' [Anyone of subtle discernment would call Beatrice Love, because she so greatly resembles me]; quite interestingly, the association is already present in the corresponding sonnet, 'Io mio senti' svegliar dentro a lo core' (' "e quell'ha nome Amor, sì mi somiglia" ', line 14 [and she who so resembles me is Love]).

30. Gorni, 'La Beatrice di Dante', pp. XV–XVI.

31. See Harald Weinrich, *La memoria di Dante* (Florence: Accademia della Crusca, 1994), pp. 10–11.

32. Federica Pich highlights that these panels are made of wood, but Dante openly echoes the waxen tablets of ancient mnemotechnique and of the medieval commentaries to Aristotle's *De anima*, which intensifies the impression of an ephemeral operation: 'L'immagine *donna della mente* dalle Rime alla *Vita Nova*', in *Le Rime di Dante*, ed. by Claudia Berra and Paolo Borsa, *Quaderni di Acme*, 117 (2010), 345–76. I would like to thank Paolo De Ventura for bringing the problem of the verb 'disegnare' to my attention.

33. See the note in Gorni's edition, pp. 339–40.

34. Guglielmo Gorni, 'Beatrice agli Inferi' in *Omaggio a Beatrice (1290–1990)*, ed. by Rudy Abardo (Florence: Le Lettere, 1998), pp. 143–58 (p. 151).

35. Jacques Lacan, *The Seminar Book VII: The Ethics of Psychoanalysis 1959–1960*, trans. by Dennis Porter (London and New York: Routledge, 1992), p. 150.

36. See for example *DVE* I, ii, 3. On the relationship between desire and language in Dante and the Middle Ages see Alessandro Raffi, *La gloria del volgare: Ontologia e semiotica in Dante dal 'Convivio' al 'De Vulgari Eloquentia'* (Soneria Mannelli: Rubbettino, 2004), and Elena Lombardi, *The Syntax of Desire: Language and Love in Augustine, the Modistae, Dante* (Toronto and London: University of Toronto Press, 2007).

37. Slavoj Žižek, 'Courtly Love, or Woman as Thing', in *The Žižek Reader*, ed. by Elizabeth Wright and Edmond Wright (London: Blackwell, 1989), pp. 148–73 (p. 155).

38. ibid., p. 156.

39. ibid.

40. Georges Didi-Huberman, *Fra Angelico: Dissemblance and Figuration*, trans. by Jane Marie Todd (London: University of Chicago Press, 1995), pp. 23–24. Further references to this book are given after quotations in the text.

41. Giorgio Agamben, *Stanzas: Word and Phantasm in Western Culture*, trans. by Ronald L. Martinez (Minneapolis and London: University of Minnesota Press, 1993), p. 129.

42. See Andrea Torre, *Petrarcheschi segni di memoria: Spie, postille, metafore* (Pisa: Edizioni della Normale, 2007).

43. See Fabio Camilletti, 'Dante's *Vita Nova* and the Victorians: The Hidden Image behind Rossetti's *Giotto Painting the Portrait of Dante*', in *The Victorians and Italy: Literature, Travel, Politics and Art*, ed. by Alessandro Vescovi, Luisa Villa and Paul Vita (Monza: Polimetrica, 2009), pp. 181–92.

44. See Luisa Passerini, *L'Europa e l'amore: Immaginario e politica fra le due guerre* (Milan: Il Saggiatore, 1999), pp. 211–20.

45. Francesco De Sanctis, 'Francesca da Rimini' (1869), in *On Dante*, ed. and trans. by Joseph Rossi and Alfred Galpin (Madison: University of Wisconsin Press, 1957), pp. 33–52 (pp. 38–39).

46. Pich, 'L'immagine', p. 375.

47. Giorgio Agamben, *Ninfe* (Turin: Bollati Boringhieri, 2007), p. 48.

48. See Pich, 'L'immagine', pp. 361–68, for a detailed survey of the topos in Italian medieval poetry and in Dante's *Rime*.

49. Agamben, *Stanzas*, pp. 61–131. See also Lina Bolzoni, *Il cuore di cristallo: Ragionamenti d'amore, poesia e ritratto nel Rinascimento* (Turin: Einaudi, 2010).

50. Didi-Huberman, p. 7.

51. See Pich, 'L'immagine', pp. 359–60. See also Michele Bacci, *Il pennello dell'Evangelista: Storia delle immagini sacre attribuite a San Luca* (Pisa: ETS, 1998), and Eugenio Burgio, *Racconti di immagini: Trentotto capitoli sui poteri della rappresentazione nel Medioevo occidentale* (Alessandria: Edizioni dell'Orso, 2001), pp. 61–131

52. Didi-Huberman, p. 51.

53. Didi-Huberman, p. 10.

54. Didi-Huberman, pp. 51–52.

55. Didi-Huberman, p. 49.

56. Didi-Huberman, p. 62.

57. Translations from the *Commedia* are taken from Dante Alighieri, *The Divine Comedy*, ed. by Robert Hollander and trans. by Robert and Jean Hollander, 3 vols (New York: Doubleday, 2000–07).

58. See Lino Pertile, 'Paradiso: A Drama of Desire', in *Word and Drama in Dante: Essays on the Divina Commedia*, ed. by John C. Barnes and Jennifer Petrie (Dublin: Irish Academy, 1993), pp. 143–80; Caroline Bynum, *The Resurrection of the Body in Western Christianity, 200–1336* (New York: Columbia University Press, 1995); Elena Lombardi, *The Syntax of Desire*, p. 12.

59. Didi-Huberman, p. 61.

PART II

Senses and Intellect

CHAPTER 6

The Call of the Beautiful:
Augustine and the Object of Desire
in *Purgatorio* x

Peter Dent

With its references to Giotto, Cimabue, Franco Bolognese, and Polyclitus, its encounter with the illuminator Oderisi da Gubbio, its image of Arachne, half spider, amongst the shreds of her tapestry, its use of technical craft terms, its ekphraseis of the sculpted panels embedded into wall and floor, and its penitents humbled beneath their stony loads like *mensole*, the Ledge of Pride has always been the most attractive part of Dante's poem for the art historian.[1] The *Commedia* as a whole may be extremely fertile ground for the study of late medieval visual culture, and *Purgatorio* may offer a self-conscious meditation on artistic media, but on the first of the seven terraces these diffuse materials are gathered into the very heart of Dante's treatment of hubris and humility.[2] Here, perhaps more than anywhere, an art historical approach might yield interesting observations but here, perhaps more than anywhere, art and artistry are also woven inextricably into the intricate fabric of the poem. These themes cannot be easily untangled from that fabric: they take their colour from the surrounding text. The Ledge of Pride is poetry first; its relationship to the world beyond the text, the world of sculptors, illuminators and painters, comes after, and this is to say nothing of the scholarship and commentary that lie between the two. At once both familiar and strange, it is difficult territory for the art historian and yet, appropriately enough, an irresistible goad to *curiositas*.[3]

Before Dante-pilgrim engages with any of the images or image makers on the first terrace of Mount Purgatory, art makes an appearance. Once through the gate, a narrow 'cruna' [needle's eye] (*Purg.* x, 16) leads upwards from a break in the rock. Virgil, ever ready with advice, suggests to his companion that 'qui si conviene usare un poco d'arte' [Here we must use a little skill] (*Purg.* x, 10), and the pair begin to climb.[4] The use of 'arte' here at once reminds the reader that the semantic range of the word in the poem still has more in common with its ancient roots than its modern meaning, and that when Dante speaks of art his definition is more about the know-how of any craft.[5] But the word is also embedded in a set of rhymes (parte-arte-parte) repeated in precisely the same location in canto x of *Paradiso*.[6]

This inter-cantical echo marks out one amongst several internal frames within the poem through which the events of cantos X to XII can be interpreted. Once through the needle's eye, and physically exhausted by the lengthy climb, the pilgrim finds himself on a deserted ledge, unsure of where the path now leads. He scans this ledge as far as his eye can 'wing its flight' (*Purg.* x, 25),[7] and with this description of vision another, extra-textual frame is introduced that points to one possible way of reading Dante's concerns at this point in the poem. It is this frame and the vistas that it opens up that form the argument of this paper.

The metaphor draws on a long tradition. The association of sharpness of vision with flight has an ancient pedigree, particularly in relation to the eagle. Indeed, by the medieval period, an etymology had been constructed deriving aquila from acumen. In Isidore of Seville's words, 'Aquila ab acumine oculorum vocata' [the eagle is named after the sharpness of its eyes].[8] However, confronted with this image of an active eye in flight across the landscape of the purgatorial mountain, an art historian might think first of Dante's later compatriot, Alberti, and his adopted emblem, the winged eye. And, in fact, the German art historian, Ulrich Pfisterer has drawn a direct link between Alberti's *imprese* and the line from *Purgatorio* x, situating them both in a tradition that runs back into biblical exegesis of the six days of creation.[9] This tradition is perhaps best illustrated in Ambrose's *Hexaemeron*, where the church father declares:

> Hence man has kinship with the winged flock in that with his vision he aims at what is high. He flies as if 'on the oarage of his wings' by reason of the sagacity of his sublime senses. Hence it was said of him: 'Your youth is renewed like the eagle's,' because he is near what is celestial and is higher than the eagle, as one who can say: 'But our citizenship is in heaven.'[10]

In the dialogue *Anuli*, in which he describes a seal ring containing a winged eye similar in some respects to his *imprese*, Alberti enriches this interpretation:

> There is nothing more powerful, swift, or worthy than the eye. In short, it is the foremost of the body's members, a sort of king or god. Didn't the ancients regard God as similar to the eye, since he surveys all things and reckons them singly? On the one hand, we are enjoined to give glory for all things to God, to rejoice in him, to embrace him with all our mind and vigorous virtue, and to consider him as an ever-present witness to all our thoughts and deeds. On the other hand, we are enjoined to be as vigilant and circumspect as we can, seeking everything which leads to the glory of virtue, and rejoicing whenever by our labor and industry we achieve something noble or divine.[11]

In both Ambrose and Alberti the image of the winged eye draws together man's potential excellence with his desire to pursue what is good, both appropriate aspirations for souls on the first terrace of the purgatorial mountain as they embark on a process of purification and perfection in pursuit of their ultimate desire, the *summum bonum*, God.

The imagery of wings, however, recurs frequently in the *Commedia* and has its own internal significance, worth bearing in mind because Dante, as will become clear, chooses it rather deliberately here in this expression of visual acuity. Across the poem as a whole, the metaphor of flight is ambivalent.[12] In some cases it corresponds to the positive sense of ascent found in Ambrose and Alberti, for example in *Purgatorio* IV, 27–29, where Dante declares 'here one must fly [...] with the swift wings and the pinions of great desire'.[13] As Shankland and Pertile have demonstrated, this is a commonplace of literature on spiritual ascent to the divine, 'a serial metaphor for the maturing process whereby the loving mind raises itself to the level of God.'[14] Elsewhere, however, the metaphor arises where the intellect overreaches, as when Ulysses and his companions 'make wings of their oars for the mad flight' (*Inf.* XXVI, 125).[15] These positive and negative connotations go to the heart of Dante's own aspirations and anxieties in writing the *Commedia*.[16] Moreover, as Shankland has argued, the imagery of wings, *ali*, may also have had personal significance for the poet, on the basis that his name can potentially be linked to the Virgilian adjective, *aliger*, wing-bearing.[17] This association may well be active here because naming is amongst the explicit themes of the Ledge of Pride and *nome* is the 'keyword of the canto'.[18] In the famous *terzina*, 'Così ha tolto l'uno a l'altro Guido | la gloria de la lingua; e forse è nato | chi l'uno e l'altro caccerà del nido' [Just so, one Guido has taken from the other the glory of our language, and perhaps he is born who will drive both of them from the nest] (*Purg.* XI, 97–99), Dante stops short of naming himself, but the avian metaphor is one of the signs that reveal his identity.[19] It is without doubt significant that Dante reactivates this rich imagery of flight here, just over a major threshold in the poem.

It is also possible to interpret the metaphor in more literal terms. The image conjured of eyesight physically extended in rapid motion through space calls to mind the optical model of extramission. Dante had explicitly rejected the Platonic theory of visual rays in *Convivio* III, IX in favour of Aristotelian intromission.[20] But elsewhere, even within that same work, he makes vivid use of imagery based on the belief that the eye emits a force that may act at a distance.[21] Indeed, following earlier tradition, he often draws on such metaphors in order to underpin the passive and active roles of lover and beloved.[22] There is, I would argue, a sense in which this paradigm is at work here. Indeed optics, subjectivity, and spiritual ascent as flight are drawn together on the Ledge of Pride in order to articulate an important stage in the pilgrim's desire to return to his maker. Before suggesting how this might be the case, however, I would like to argue — with these general indications in mind — that there is another pedigree for Dante's turn of phrase, a textual source that is rich, if not entirely unexpected: Book 10 of Augustine's *Confessions*.

It seems to me that line 25 of *Purgatorio* X, 'e quanto l'occhio mio potea trar d'ale' [and as far as my eye could wing its flight], recapitulates in the vernacular a line of Augustine's Latin, 'quousque potui mittere nuntios radios oculorum meorum' [as far as I could send the rays of my eyes as messengers].[23] The phrasing is similar if not identical. Although this could be coincidental, there is no need to demonstrate that Dante was a close reader of the *Confessions* or that the work was significant for the composition of the *Commedia*, even if the nature and extent of this significance remain open to dispute and were perhaps concealed by the poet himself.[24] There are, probably, structural reasons why Dante might have had Book 10 of the *Confessions* in mind while drafting this canto, the first over the threshold of Purgatory when movement towards God begins in earnest. Book 10 marks a similar shift in gear in the *Confessions* from the personal account in Books 1 to 9 of the road to conversion towards a meditation on God's relationship with his creation with extensive discussions of memory, time, and eternity.[25] It may, moreover, be significant that of the three times Augustine is named in the *Commedia*, the first two come from cantos X and XII of *Paradiso*, the corresponding section of the final *cantica*.[26] More importantly, however, the immediate context of Augustine's line generates an interesting commentary when set alongside the action of the Ledge of Pride.[27]

The line itself comes midway through section 6.9 in modern editions, which is immediately preceded by Augustine's doubts about the virtues of recounting his personal experience of conversion — a theme of obvious interest to Dante — and immediately followed by an extensive discussion of the nature of memory.[28] At this point, Augustine, his heart, as he puts it, pierced by God's word, demands of his Creator: 'But when I love you, what do I love?'[29] In pursuit of answers he interrogates the external world. The power of sight, for Augustine as for others the noblest sense and the one most closely connected to the intellect, represents his best efforts to seek God in nature, before turning inwards to search the vast storehouses of the mind.[30] As he summarizes later in the Book: 'To the best of my powers of sense-perception, I travelled through the external world.'[31] For Augustine, vision here operates by extramission, its worth lying in its superlative ability to grasp things quickly and clearly at a distance.[32] Dante's decision to substitute Augustine's ocular rays for the metaphor of flight shifts the balance away from any particular theory of vision towards the range of associations already indicated that such wing imagery invokes. This perhaps reflects his own allegiance to intromission but, more importantly, it aligns Augustine's phrasing with his own poetics of spiritual ascent.

I would like to concentrate on two of several aspects of Augustine's pursuit of God in this section that are of interest for the Ledge of Pride. First, the passage is rich with references to the Mosaic commandment against worshipping graven images. The first things that Virgil and the pilgrim encounter in Purgatory are precisely that: graven images, marble reliefs carved into the mountainside. Although these objects are God's work, that means they lie on the same ontological plane as nature itself and the possibility remains, as Dante implies, that the viewer may misunderstand their message and value them for their own sake and not for their maker.[33] The lure of potential idolatry hovers about them. Secondly, Augustine's interrogation of the natural world in search of the object of his desire rests on an ancient model of aesthetics in which beauty and voice are conflated. This has interesting implications for Dante's description of the reliefs as visible speech and for the nature of the pilgrim's aesthetic experience in front of these images.

I will take the second of these points first and return to the question of idolatry shortly. Augustine begins his search in the following manner: 'And what is the object of my love? I asked the earth and it said: "it is not I."'[34] He puts the same question to the sea, to living creatures, to the elements, to the sun, moon and stars and they cry out with a great voice, 'We are not your God, look beyond us [...] He made us.'[35] The interrogation complete, he concludes with these words: 'My question was the attention I gave to them, and their response was their beauty.'[36] Shortly afterwards he reinforces this by stating that created things have a voice —

a voice, he clarifies, which is their beauty.[37] In making this connection between beauty and voice, Augustine is drawing on an interpretation of the meaning of beauty, appearing first in the Platonic dialogue, the *Cratylus*, with its roots in ancient Greek etymology.[38] This interpretation linked the beautiful, *kallo*, with the verb to call, *kaleo*. The beautiful thing calls forth. The association of the two is semantically rich because the verb encompasses both the act of naming and, by extension, of calling into existence, and the noun links the beautiful to the good. Once bound to the Judaeo-Christian tradition of the Word, the ramifications of the relationship between beauty, voice and being were teased out in all their rich potential, as Jean-Louis Chrétien has demonstrated.[39] These various associations are all at play when Augustine revisits his interrogation of nature in Book 11, stating: 'See, heaven and earth exist, they cry aloud that they are made [...]. And the voice with which they speak is self-evidence. You, Lord, who are beautiful, made them for they are beautiful. You are good, for they are good. You are, for they are.'[40]

The association of voice with beauty, creation and goodness is so self-evident and inherently apt for his purposes that Augustine never offers the etymological key and of course the Latin word he uses is '*species*', which has a wider semantic range than beauty.[41] It is quite possible, however, that Dante had encountered it elsewhere. It appears in a number of theological works and commentaries. The most important source for the late medieval period would have been *The Divine Names* by Pseudo-Dionysius, where one of the names of God is beauty and 'beauty calls and gathers in all things to itself, whence it is called beauty.'[42] Dante's thought is fretted with Dionysian themes and Dionysius is named in *Paradiso* XXVIII and present in *Paradiso* X, perhaps another significant parallel to *Purgatorio* X. But there is still some disagreement about whether Dante's knowledge of the Dionysian corpus was unmediated.[43] The impact of Dionysian thought was diffuse in the work of thirteenth-century theologians like Aquinas and Bonaventura.[44] Recent work by Diego Sbacchi has demonstrated, definitively it would seem, that Dante approached the *Celestial Hierarchy* through Albert the Great's commentary.[45] Albert also glossed the *Divine Names* where he discusses and explains this Greek etymology of beauty.[46]

Whatever the case, the call of the beautiful offers an alternative way of approaching Dante's description of the reliefs on the Ledge of Pride as 'visibile parlare' [visible speech] (*Purg.* X, 95). This term has plausibly been linked to Augustine's 'verba visibilia' [visible words], a phrase found in several of his texts, that broadly designates non-verbal signs including the sacraments through which one person communicates their intentions to another.[47] Set within the framework of beauty as voice, these 'verba visibilia' on the Ledge of Pride are an act of communication whose nature is to attract attention to itself — to be desirable — in order, however, to signify beyond itself. As Elena Lombardi observes in more general terms: 'the signs of *Purgatorio* enjoy the double status of both being, and pointing to, a higher reality [...]. Within the fictional plan of the poem, they must be physically surpassed in order to continue the ascent'.[48] The reliefs are superlative works of art, superior in skill to nature and Polyclitus. This beauty calls out and captures the attention of the pilgrim. The question is whether this attraction will overpower, or issue in understanding and onward motion to the ultimate object of desire, God.

Indeed, it has been argued that the ekphrasis of the reliefs in canto X is innovative in the extent of its concentration on the unfolding experience of the beholder. The pilgrim is fascinated by the first carving, then prompted forwards by Virgil. His growing absorption in the images is registered in the rising number of lines devoted to the description of each relief in turn.[49] Above all, the miraculous mimesis of the representations confounds the evidence of his senses of sight, hearing, and smell. In other words, the nature of his attention, once captured, is as much at issue as the description of the images themselves. Although this is in part a response to Aeneas's tears before the temple images in Book 1 of the *Aeneid*, it reads just as much like a dramatization of Augustine's description of attention in Book 10.6.9 of the *Confessions*: 'All physical evidence is reported to the mind which presides and judges of the responses of heaven and earth and all things in them, as they say "We are not God" and "He made us".'[50] The mind presiding and judging over the evidence of the senses is central to Augustine and he immediately expands on it further:

> Surely this beauty should be self-evident to all who are of sound mind. Then why does it not speak to everyone in the same way? Animals both small and large see it, but they cannot put a question about it. In them reason does not sit in judgement upon the deliverance of the senses. But human beings can put a question so that 'the invisible things of God are understood and seen through the things which are made' (Rom. 1. 20).[51]

The pilgrim's attention is just such a question. The evidence of his senses is judged, his mind is sound and he hears the voice of beauty correctly, acknowledging, once beyond the reliefs, that their invisible author, the true object of his desire, is 'he in whose sight nothing is new.'[52]

It is important, however, in the *Confessions* and the *Commedia* that created things can be both revelation and veil. Augustine, for example, continues in the following vein:

> Yet by love of created things they [human beings] are subdued by them, and being thus made subject become incapable of exercising judgement. Moreover, created things do not answer those who question them if power to judge is lost. There is no alteration in the voice which is their beauty. If one person sees while another sees and questions, it is not that they appear one way to the first and another way to the second. It is rather that the created order speaks to all, but is understood by those who hear its outward voice and compare it with the truth within themselves.[53]

There is always the danger that the beauty of created things will mistakenly be pursued as desirable for itself, a mistake that Augustine characteristically confesses later in Book 10:

> and in my unlovely state I plunged into those lovely created things which you made. [...] The lovely things kept me far from you, though if they did not have their existence in you, they had no existence at all. You called and cried out loud and shattered my deafness.[54]

In both Augustine and Dante this danger of being distracted by intermediate goals is elsewhere discussed in terms of a pilgrimage, in which, to paraphrase Augustine, the soul risks perversely enjoying things that it should be using.[55] We know that the pilgrim in canto x has avoided this pitfall with his recognition after seeing the reliefs that they are precious to behold because of their maker.[56] But the possibility of failure was certainly present. The pilgrim verges on being subdued by love of the artistry itself. It is not until Virgil's intervention — 'Non tener pur ad un loco la mente' [Do not fix your mind on one place alone] (*Purg.* x, 46) — that he moves forward out of momentary stasis in front of the *Annunciation* relief, setting off a condensed Aristotelian account of cognition, in which sensory perception, followed by judgment, leads to motion before and beyond the images.

But why stage the pilgrim's first experience in Purgatory as an encounter between art work and beholder? Art and artistry are central to Dante's handling of the sin of pride on this terrace, but they also serve to intensify the drama of correctly directed desire and motion. Ekphrasis tends to exaggerate the tension between the temporal succession of words and the spatial extension of images, the narrative momentum of the first being partially arrested in descriptive attention to the second.[57] Recent work in this area indicates that passages of such description are motivated by both competition and desire: competition between the representational powers of each art form, and the desire of the one to possess and encompass the effects of the other. This desire can be refigured in gendered terms, of male word and female image, and it would be both apt and legitimate to see this at work in canto x across a sequence of images that deliberately pair male and female but in which the first *exemplum* complicates the model by showing the active male Word encompassed by its passive female image, Mary.

However, Dante intensifies the encounter even further by selecting sculpture as the medium for this drama of desire and motion. More than any other object, sculpture carries associations of idolatry, and here Dante may have been encouraged in part by Augustine. As mentioned earlier, the passage in Book 10 of the *Confessions* where Augustine interrogates nature is rich with allusions to the commandment against worshipping graven images.[58] This underlines the danger that man might mistake created thing for Creator. In fact, in a recently rediscovered sermon, Augustine addresses an idol in exactly the same fashion that he addresses the created world in the *Confessions*:

> You have made, for example, a wooden god [...]. Why should I not question it? Notice; it is not a voice interrogating a soul, but eyes a shape. My glance is interrogating the appearance and material of that piece of wood [...]. Under all these interrogations it answers me that it is wood, this thing that you say is a god.[59]

The subtext here is set out in *De doctrina christiana*, where Augustine establishes a parallel between Jews enslaved to the word and pagans enslaved in idolatry.[60] The first fail to discern the truth beneath the surface of scripture, the second fail to see the Creator behind creation.[61] The pilgrim faces just such a threat. As already argued, his attention to the reliefs is his interrogation and this interrogation initially fails to move beyond the first image until Virgil intervenes. This I would argue is an understated example of a trope that enjoys considerable popularity in subsequent literature. In looking at the miraculously animated work of art the pilgrim is astonished, turned to stone. The flesh-and-blood viewer risks exchanging places with the lifeless piece of sculpture and ceasing motion absolutely. Stony metaphors of this sort had been extensively used by Dante in the *Rime petrose* where desire leads to various forms of petrification.

For Augustine, this turning away from created things to their Creator begins with a movement from exterior to interior. Immediately after admitting that he has searched through the world 'as far as I could send the rays of my eyes as messengers', he declares: 'What is inward is superior.'[62] In the following sentence — 'All physical evidence is reported to the mind which presides and judges of the responses of heaven and earth and all things in them, as they say "We are not God" and "He made us"' — this turn inwards is underscored by a set of repetitions and inversions in the Latin.[63] On the Ledge of Pride, Dante is operating with different poetic and optical possibilities and the move from exterior to interior is more elaborate. I would like to draw attention to one feature of it here. The process opens with the extramissive gaze borrowed directly from Augustine, but this is inverted at the third relief in the phrase, 'mi biancheggiava' [shone white for me] (*Purg.* x, 72), the only occurrence of the verb in this form in the *Commedia*.[64] This intromissive moment is to be understood here, I would suggest, as the emanation of divine light through creation.[65] This shift from action to passion is one indicator of the passage from pride to humility that is accomplished by penance and instruction on this terrace. The light that falls on the pilgrim from God's beautiful art now penetrates his body through the eyes.[66] However, rather than opening out into a meditation on the storehouse of memory as in the *Confessions*, this move inwards comes to fruition as an interior transformation whose external expression the pilgrim only discovers when he feels his forehead at the end of the terrace and finds that one of the seven marks of sin has been removed.[67]

So the call of the beautiful is ambivalent. The nature of the attention it elicits is crucial. I have attempted to indicate where the relationship between Book 10 of the *Confessions* and canto x of *Purgatorio* might lead. Reading the second text through the first reframes the Ledge of Pride in a way that may permit greater coordination of its various parts, in particular the layering of different types of words, utterances and speech acts. The reliefs — beginning, of course, with an *Annunciation* — re-present and refigure both the 'Word' that brings forth and sustains creation and the 'Word' incarnate within creation.[68] And beyond this, the 'call of the beautiful' ultimately elicits a response which in turn is also a call. The following canto opens with Dante's version of the Lord's Prayer, the words Christ taught humankind to use when addressing God.

It is also worth observing that a visual metaphor in Dante, the winged eye, leads back to a verbal one in Augustine, beauty as voice. The *Commedia* is a poem rich with vision in all its many forms and meanings with its ultimate goal as *visio dei* but, as Elena Lombardi has recently argued, the movement through Hell, Purgatory and Paradise is also a progression from sound, to sign, to pure meaning.[69] Indeed, she describes the middle realm as 'a single sign, one gigantic act of pointing'.[70] With this in mind, the fusion of the verbal and the visual at the threshold of Purgatory proper is particularly effective. It is captured in Dante's 'visible speech' and in the rhymed juxtaposition of 'parlare' and 'guardare'.[71] It is intrinsic to the ekphrastic mode and, above all, it is caught in the paradox of the *Annunciation*, in which the Word is incarnate but not yet representable. In other words, *Purgatorio* x brings the visual and the verbal into a particularly intricate relationship through a rather special type of sign at the point where the mediation of signs takes on an enhanced role within the poem.

In April 1336, another poet found himself on another mountain and turned, supposedly by chance, to Book 10 of the *Confessions*: Petrarch during his (fictional) ascent of Mont Ventoux.[72] The general parallels between the two landscapes have been noted before, but it is tempting to believe that there may be deeper resonances with the Ledge of Pride in *Purgatorio*.[73] As well as quoting directly from Book 10, Petrarch's letter contains elaborate echoes of Augustine's Latin, no doubt for the (imaginary) delight of his (deceased) correspondent, an Augustinian friar. As he stares out from the summit, his vision running on towards distant Italy, Augustine's 'radios oculorum' [rays of (my) eyes] from the passage rephrased by Dante reappear once more.[74] Shortly after, Petrarch's thoughts move from the external world towards the inner realm of his mind. As with Dante, the process remains tied to a visual metaphor: 'I turned my inner eyes within'.[75] Unlike the pilgrim on the purgatorial terrace, however, this inward turn is not accomplished through the contemplation of God's beauty shining and shouting from his works of art. Here it is a passage from a book, from Augustine's text itself that intervenes: 'And they go to admire the summits of mountains and the vast billows of the sea and the broadest rivers and the expanses of the ocean and the revolutions of the stars and they overlook themselves.'[76] In the light of what has gone before, it is, perhaps, a revealing difference. For Petrarch, the created world and the works of humankind, including images, 'possess a silent pleasure' but only books 'speak with us'.[77]

Notes to Chapter 6

1. The bibliography is rich. Two recent and interesting art historical responses to the Ledge of Pride are Ulrich Pfisterer, *Donatello und die Entdeckung der Stile 1430–1445* (Munich: Hirmer Verlag GmbH, 2002), pp. 233–68, and Patricia Lee Rubin, *Images and Identity in Fifteenth-Century Florence* (New Haven, CT, and London: Yale University Press, 2007), pp. 135–73.

2. For *Purgatorio* and the 'fine arts', see Karlheinz Stierle, *Ästhetische Rationalität: Kunstwerk und Werkbegriff* (Munich: Wilhelm Fink, 1997), pp. 389–416. The classic and fundamental discussion of the roles played by art on this terrace is Teodolinda Barolini, 'Re-presenting what God Presented: The Arachnean Art of the Terrace of Pride', in Teodolinda Barolini, *The Undivine Comedy: Detheologizing Dante* (Princeton, NJ: Princeton University Press, 1992), pp. 122–42.

3. Barbara J. Watts, 'Artistic Competition, Hubris, and Humility: Sandro Botticelli's Response to "Visibile Parlare"', *Dante Studies*, 114 (1996), 41–78 (p. 52): 'When I decided that the paper that I would present to the Dante Society of America would address pictorial responses to *Purgatorio* x–xii during the Renaissance, I did not realise the enormity of the sin of pride I had just committed. I do now.'

4. All translations from the *Commedia* are taken from *The Divine Comedy of Dante Alighieri*, ed. and trans. by Robert Durling and Ronald Martinez, 3 vols (Oxford and New York: Oxford University Press, 1996–2011).

5. For art and artistry in the *Commedia*, see Simon A. Gilson, 'Divine and Natural Artistry in Dante's *Commedia*', in *Art and Nature in Dante*, ed. by John C. Barnes (Dublin: Four Courts Press, forthcoming). I am grateful to Professor Gilson for allowing me to read a copy of this essay in advance of publication.

6. For this and other repetitions of 'arte' and its rhyme words (including *Inf.* x, 47–51) that serve to guide the reader backwards and forwards in the text, see Paul Spillenger, 'Dante's *Arte* and the Ambivalence of Retrospection', *Stanford Italian Review*, 10 (1991), 241–68 (pp. 249–50).

7. 'e quanto l'occhio mio potea trar d'ale' (*Purg.* x, 25).

8. *Etymologies* XII, vii, 10–11. Cited from *Isidori Hispalensis Episcopi Etymologiarvm sive originvm libri XX*, ed. by Wallace Martin Lindsay, 2 vols (Oxford and New York: Oxford University Press, 1985).

9. Ulrich Pfisterer, ' "Soweit die Flügel meines Auges tragen": Leon Battista Albertis Imprese und Selbstbildnis', *Mitteilungen des Kunsthistorisches Institutes in Florenz*, 42 (1998), 205–51 (p. 217). Pfisterer also relates the image to a number of classical texts, including Lucian's *Icaromennipus*, for example. For Alberti's *imprese* see also: Horst Bredekamp, 'Albertis Flug- und Flammenauge', in *Die Beschwörung des Kosmos: Europäische Bronzen der Renaissance*, ed. by Christoph Brockhaus (Duisburg: Wilhelm Lehmbruck Museum, 1994), pp. 297–302; and Renée Watkins, 'L. B. Alberti's Emblem, the Winged Eye, and his Name, Leo', *Mitteilungen des Kunsthistorisches Institutes in Florenz*, 9 (1960), 256–58.

10. Ambrose, *Hexaemeron*, VI, 9 'Recte autem non plures, sed duo sunt homini pedes; quaterni enim pedes feris ac belluis sunt, bini avibus. Et ideo unus quasi de volatilibus est homo, quia alta visu petat, et quodam remigio volitet sublimium sagacitate sensum. Et ideo de eo dictum est, Renovabitur sicut aquilae juventus tua [Ps. CII. 5]; eo quod propior sit coelestibus, et sublimior aquilis, qui possit dicere: Nostra autem conversatio in coelis est [Phil. 3. 20].' See Pfisterer, 'Soweit', p. 239, n. 56. Translation from Saint Ambrose, *Hexameron, Paradise, and Cain and Abel*, trans. by John J. Savage (Washington, DC: Catholic University of America Press, 1961), p. 281.

11. From the dialogue 'Anuli'. See Watkins, 'L. B. Alberti's Emblem', pp. 256–57. 'Corona et laetitiae et gloriae insigne est: oculo potentius nihil, volocius nihil, dignus nihil; quid multa? Ejusmodi est ut inter membra primus, praecipuus, et res, et quasi deus sit. Quid quod deum veteres interpretantur esse quidpiam oculi simile, universa spectantem, singulaque dinumerantem? Hinc igitur admonemur, rerum omnium gloriam a nobis esse reddendam Deo; in eo laetandum totoque animo virtute florido et virenti amplectendum praesentemque, videntemque nostra Omnia et gesta et cogitate existimandum. Tum et alia ex parte admonemur pervigiles, circumspectosque esse oportere, quantum nostra ferat animi vis, indagando res omnes quae ad virtutis gloriam pertineant, in eoque laetandum si quid labore et industria bonarum divinarumque rerum simus assecuti.' Translation from Leon Battista Alberti, *Dinner Pieces: A Translation of the 'Intercenales'*, trans. by David Marsh (Binghamton: Medieval and Renaissance Texts and Studies, 1987), pp. 213–14.

12. For the use of this metaphor in the *Commedia,* see Lino Pertile, *La punta del disio: Semantica del desiderio nella 'Commedia'* (Fiesole: Edizioni Cadmo, 2005), pp. 115–35, and p. 106, n. 61, Hugh Shankland, 'Dante *Aliger* and Ulysses', *Italian Studies*, 32 (1977), 21–40, and Hugh Shankland, 'Dante "Aliger" ', *Modern Language Review*, 70.4 (1975), 764–85. It is worth noting that in his 1977 article (p. 24, n. 7), Shankland makes the same connection in passing between Dante's metaphor in general and Alberti's *imprese* as pursued at greater length by Pfisterer.

13. 'ma qui convien ch'om voli; | dico con l'ale snelle e con le piume | del gran disio' (*Purg.* IV, 27–29).

14. The quotation is from Shankland, 'Dante "Aliger" ', p. 766.

15. 'de' remi facemmo ali al folle volo' (*Inf.* XXVI, 125). Shankland, 'Dante *Aliger* and Ulysses', p. 29, points out that the 'noun *volo* is qualified by an adjective three times in the *Commedia*: as 'folle volo' it typifies, in Ulysses's own words, his 'crazy' voyage beyond the Pillars of Hercules (*Inf.* XXVI, 125); as 'alto volo' it characterizes, on two occasions, Dante's exceptional flight to participation in the experience of the elect (*Par.* XV, 54 and XXV, 50).'

16. See Teodolinda Barolini, 'Re-presenting', pp. 132–33, and 'Ulysses, Geryon, and the Aeronautics of Narrative Transition', in *Undivine Comedy*, pp. 48–73.

17. See both Shankland, 'Dante "Aliger" ', and Shankland 'Dante *Aliger* and Ulysses'.

18. Howard Marks, 'Hollowed Names: *Vox* and *Vanitas* in the *Purgatorio*', *Dante Studies*, 110 (1992), 135–78 (p. 142). See also Barolini, 'Re-presenting', pp. 134–40, Anthony Oldcorn, 'Gone with the Wind: A Reading of *Purgatorio* XI', in *Da Dante a Montale: Studi di filologia e critica letteraria in onore di Emilio Pasquini*, ed. by Gian Mario Anselmi and Emilio Pasquini (Bologna: Gedit Edizioni, 2005), pp. 35–63 (esp. pp. 43–48).

19. As Marks observes, Dante's ancestor Cacciaguida, whom he encounters in *Paradiso* XV and with whom he discusses his patronymic, is another. Through this ancestral name, Dante is revealed as the one who will chase Guido ('caccia Guido') from the nest. Marks, 'Hollowed Names', p. 153. See also Guglielmo Gorni, 'Guittone e Dante', in *Dante prima della 'Commedia'* (Fiesole: Cadmo, 2001), 15–42 (pp. 35–36) for the same points made independently.

20. For Dante's knowledge of late medieval models of vision and the associated texts, see Simon A. Gilson, 'Dante and the Science of "Perspective": A Reappraisal', *Dante Studies*, 115 (1997), 185–219, and *Medieval Optics and Theories of Light in the Works of Dante* (Lewiston, NY: Edwin Mellen Press, 2000). For medieval discussions of optics, see David C. Lindberg, *Theories of Vision from al-Kindī to Kepler* (Chicago, IL: Chicago University Press, 1976).

21. For deployment of optical theory by Dante and other late medieval writers, see both Suzanne Conklin Akbari, *Seeing through the Veil: Optical Theory and Medieval Allegory* (Toronto and London: University of Toronto Press, 2004), pp. 114–77 (for Dante), and Dana E. Stewart, *The Arrow of Love: Optics, Gender, and Subjectivity in Medieval Love Poetry* (Lewisburg, PA: Bucknell University Press, 2003), pp. 102–23 (for Dante).

22. See Akbari, *Seeing through the Veil*, Stewart, *Arrow of Love*, and the essay by Robert Sturges in this volume.

23. Augustine, *Confessiones*, 10.6.9. All quotations are taken from the electronic edition of Augustine, *Confessions*, ed. with commentary by James J. O'Donnell, 3 vols (Oxford: Clarendon Press, 1992), available at: <http://www.stoa.org/hippo/>. All translations from Saint Augustine, *Confessions*, ed. and trans. by Henry Chadwick (Oxford: Oxford University Press, 1991), p. 184.

24. Robert Hollander, 'Dante's Reluctant Allegiance to St. Augustine in the *Commedia*', *L'Alighieri*, 32 (2008), 5–16, provides a brief summary of Dante's indebtedness to Augustine (p. 15). He offers a useful bibliography (p. 7, n. 8) and a list of twenty-seven points in the *Commedia* where Dante appears to be responding to Augustine's Latin, but notes there are many more. Seven of these are drawn from the *Confessions*. The convergence suggested here between *Purgatorio* X and *Confessions* 10 is not listed and, as far as I am aware, has not previously been noted. It is as close to Augustine as any example given by Hollander. It is not the only echo of Augustine in this canto. Lines 124–25 ('non v'accorgete voi che noi siam vermi | nati a formar l'angelica farfalla' [do you not perceive that we are worms born to form the angelic butterfly]) are drawn from *In Iohannis Euangelium Tractatus*, 1.13: 'Nam omnes homines de carne nascentes, quid sunt nisi vermes? et de vermibus Angelos facit'. See Massimiliano Chiamenti, *Dante Alighieri traduttore* (Florence: Le Lettere, 1995), p. 178. For the importance of the *Confessions* to the *Commedia* as a model of spiritual biography, see John Freccero, 'Dante's Prologue Scene', in *Dante: The Poetics of Conversion*, ed. by Rachel Jacoff (Cambridge, MA: Harvard University Press, 1986), pp. 1–28, with Caron Ann Cioffi, 'St. Augustine Revisited: On "Conversion" in the *Commedia*', *Lectura Dantis Virginiana*, 5 (1989), 68–80 less positive. See also Shirley J. Paolini, *Confessions of Sin and Love in the Middle Ages: Dante's 'Commedia' and St. Augustine's 'Confessions'* (Washington, DC: University Press of America, 1982), and John Took, 'Dante and the *Confessions* of St. Augustine', *Annali d'Italianistica*, 8 (1990), 360–83. Marchesi argues that Dante's work suggests a new or renewed interest in Augustine between the *Convivio* and the *Commedia*, see Simone Marchesi, *Dante and Augustine: Linguistics, Poetics, Hermeneutics* (Toronto, Buffalo and London: University of Toronto Press, 2011), p. 11 (see also the useful bibliography at p. 197, n. 2).

25. While there is no explicit structural marker in the text to divide it in this fashion, the turn away from the narrative of conversion is clear. See O'Donnell's 'Prolegomena' to the electronic edition of the *Confessions*, under the heading 'A Reading of the *Confessions*', and the opening remarks in his commentary to Book 10.

26. The third naming occurs at *Par.* XXXII, 35. See Hollander, 'Dante's Reluctant Allegiance', p. 9.

27. In other words, this essay discusses Augustine for what Marchesi would call a traditional analysis of textual meaning. The 'metapoetic' issues that concern him certainly arise in this context, but cannot be pursued in sufficient depth here. See Marchesi, *Dante and Augustine*, p. 18.

28. Whatever text Dante saw would not have been subdivided to this extent. Medieval manuscript copies mark off the thirteen books, but further subdivision was introduced only in early printed editions. See Henry Chadwick, 'Introduction' in Augustine, *Confessions*, p. XXVI.

29. 'quid autem amo, cum te amo?', Augustine, *Confessiones*, 10.6.8.

30. For Augustine's views on the senses, see Eugene Vance, 'Seeing God: Augustine, Sensation, and the Mind's Eye', in *Rethinking the Medieval Senses: Heritage, Fascinations, Frames*, ed. by Stephen G. Nichols, Andreas Kablitz and Alison Calhoun (Baltimore, MD: Johns Hopkins University Press, 2008), pp. 13–29.

31. 'lustraui mundum foris sensu quo potui'. Augustine, *Confessiones*, 10.40.65.

32. Augustine certainly adhered to a version of the doctrine of extramission: 'per oculos enim corporis corpora uidemus quia radios, qui per eos emicant et quidquid cernimus tangunt', *Corpus Augustinianum Gissense*, ed. by Cornelius Mayer (Basel: Schwabe, 1995), *De Trinitate*, 9.3. Accessed via Intelex Past Masters <http://library.nlx.com/xtf/search?browse-collections=true>.

33. For a rigorous discussion of the ontological status of the reliefs, see Andreas Kablitz, 'Jenseitige Kunst oder Gott als Bildhauer: Die Reliefs in Dantes *Purgatorio* (*Purg.* X–XII)', in *Mimesis und Simulation*, ed. by Andreas Kablitz and Gerhard Neumann (Freiburg im Breisgau: Rombach, 1998), pp. 309–56.

34. 'interrogavi terram, et dixit, "non sum."' Augustine, *Confessiones*, 10.6.9.

35. '"non sumus deus tuus; quaere super nos." [...] et exclamaverunt voce magna, "ipse fecit nos."' Augustine, *Confessiones*, 10.6.9.

36. 'interrogatio mea intentio mea et responsio eorum species eorum.' Augustine, *Confessiones*, 10.6.9.

37. 'nec vocem suam mutant, id est speciem suam', Augustine, *Confessiones*, 10.6.10.

38. For the origin and evolution of this tradition, see Jean-Louis Chrétien, *The Call and the Response*, trans. by Anne A. Davenport (New York: Fordham University Press, 2004), pp. 5–43.

39. Chrétien, pp. 5–43.

40. 'ecce sunt caelum et terra! clamant quod facta sint [...] et vox dicentium est ipsa evidentia. tu ergo, domine, fecisti ea, qui pulcher es (pulchra sunt enim), qui bonus es (bona sunt enim), qui es (sunt enim).' Augustine, *Confessiones*, 11.4.6.

41. This point is made specifically in relation to this passage by R. A. Markus, *Signs and Meanings: World and Text in Ancient Christianity* (Liverpool: Liverpool University Press, 1996), p. 27, n. 74. For some of the ramifications of this vocabulary in relation to the idea of beauty in both Augustine and Dante, see Joseph Anthony Mazzeo, 'The Augustinian Conception of Beauty and Dante's Convivio', *The Journal of Aesthetics and Art Criticism*, 15.4 (1957), 435–48.

42. The original Greek can be found in Pseudo-Dionysius Areopagita, *De Divinis Nominibus*, ed. by Beate Regina Suchla (Berlin and New York: Walter de Gruyter, 1990), p. 151 (IV.6.7; 701C–D). Translation from Pseudo-Dionysius, *The Complete Works*, trans. by Colm Luibheid and ed. by Paul Rorem (New York and Mahwah, NJ: Paulist Press, 1987), p. 76. It is not known which Latin translations may have been accessible to Dante. The three most likely give: 'et velut omnia ad se ipsum uocans, inde et pulchrum dicitur, et uelut tota in totis se congregans' (Johannes Scottus Eiriugena, *c.* 867); 'et sicut omnia ad se ipsum uocans, unde et callos dicitur, et sicut tota in totis congregans' (Johannes Sarracenus, *c.* 1167); 'et ut omnia ad se ipsum uocans, unde et pulchritude dicitur, et ut tota in totis in idem congregans' (Robert Grosseteste, *c.* 1235). There is also the paraphrase by Thomas Gallus, abbot of Vercelli, dating to 1238: 'et quasi omnia ad se ipsum vocat, et kallos id est pulchritudo, dicitur, sicut omnia in omnibus ad idem congregans.' See *Dionysiaca: Recueil donnant l'ensemble des traductions latines des ouvrages attribués au Denys de l'Aréopage*, 2 vols (Bruges: Desclée de Brouwer, 1937), I, 180 and 683.

43. Gilson, *Medieval Optics*, pp. 239–45, for example, doubts that the evidence supports direct knowledge of the Dionysian corpus.

44. Gilson, *Medieval Optics*, pp. 245 and Diego Sbacchi, *La presenza di Dionigi Areopagita nel Paradiso di Dante* (Florence: Olschki, 2006), pp. XV–XVIII.

45. Sbacchi, *Dionigi*, pp. 1–20. The argument in favour of Dante's direct knowledge of Dionysian texts has grown considerably in strength over recent years. See, for example, Marco Ariani, '"e sí come di lei bevve la gronda | de le palpebre mie" (*Par.* XXX, 88): Dante e lo Pseudo Dionigi Areopagita', in *Leggere Dante*, ed. by Lucia Battaglia Ricci (Ravenna: Longo, 2003), pp. 131–52; Stefano Prandi, 'Dante e lo Pseudo-Dionigi: Una nuova proposta per l'immagine finale della *Commedia*,' *Lettere Italiane*, 61.1 (2009), 3–29; Diego Sbacchi, 'Il linguaggio superlativo e gerarchico del *Paradiso*', *L'Alighieri*, 31 (2008), 5–22; and Antonio Rossini, *Il Dante sapienziale: Dionigi e la bellezza di Beatrice* (Pisa and Rome: Fabrizio Serra, 2009). Rossini discusses the

significance of the idea of beauty as a call for the *Commedia* and for Beatrice in particular at pp. 43–73.

46. 'Deinde ponit tertiam condicionem; et primo ponit eam, secundo probat per significationem nominis apud Graecos, ibi: *unde et kallos etc.* Dicit ergo, quod *supersubstantiale bonum et,* idest etiam, *dicitur pulchritudo, sicut evocans omnia ad seipsum;* pulchritudo enim rapit omnia ad desiderium sui. *Unde et* pulchrum apud Graecos *dicitur "kallos",* quasi "vocans"'. Albertus Magnus, *Super Dionysium De Divinis Nominibus,* ed. by Paulus Simon (Aschendorff: Monasterii Westfalorum, 1972), chapter 4, 77 (p. 186). Aquinas comments as follows: '*sicut uocans omnia ad seipsum,* inquantum convertit omnia ad seipsum sicut ad finem, ut supra dictum est et propter hoc pulchritudo in graeco *cállos dicitur* quod est a vocando sumptum'. Thomas Aquinas, *In librum beati Dionysii de Divinis Nominibus expositio,* ed. by Ceslai Pera (Turin and Rome: Marietti, 1950), p. 113 (C. IV, I. v, 340).

47. The best summary of the potential links is Marco Collareta, 'Visibile parlare', *Prospettiva,* 87–88 (1997), 102–04, although this lacks any reference to the earlier literature that had already made this connection.

48. Elena Lombardi, *The Syntax of Desire: The Language of Love in Augustine, the Modistae, Dante* (Toronto and London: University of Toronto Press, 2007), p. 153.

49. A point made by Barolini, 'Re-presenting', p. 123.

50. 'ei quippe renuntiabant omnes nuntii corporales, praesidenti et iudicanti de responsionibus caeli et terrae et omnium quae in eis sunt dicentium, "non sumus deus" et, "ipse fecit nos."' Augustine, *Confessiones,* 10.6.9. For this passage as ekphrasis, see most recently Matthew Treherne, 'Ekphrasis and Eucharist: The Poetics of Seeing God's Art in *Purgatorio* X', *The Italianist,* 26 (2006) 177–96, with earlier bibliography. For the relationship with the *Aeneid,* see Marianne Shapiro, 'Ecphrasis in Virgil and Dante', *Comparative Literature,* 62.2 (1990), 97–115.

51. 'nonne omnibus quibus integer sensus est apparet haec species? cur non omnibus eadem loquitur? animalia pusilla et magna vident eam, sed interrogare nequeunt, non enim praeposita est in eis nuntiantibus sensibus iudex ratio. homines autem possunt interrogare, ut invisibilia dei per ea quae facta sunt intellecta conspiciant': Augustine, *Confessiones,* 10.6.10.

52. 'Colui che mai non vide cosa nova' (*Purg.* X, 94).

53. 'sed amore subduntur eis et subditi iudicare non possunt. nec respondent ista interrogantibus nisi iudicantibus, nec vocem suam mutant, id est speciem suam, si alius tantum videat, alius autem videns interroget, ut aliter illi appareat, aliter huic, sed eodem modo utrique apparens illi muta est, huic loquitur: immo vero omnibus loquitur, sed illi intellegunt qui eius vocem acceptam foris intus cum veritate conferunt.' Augustine, *Confessiones,* 10.6.10.

54. 'et in ista formosa quae fecisti deformis inruebam [...] ea me tenebant longe a te, quae si in te non essent, non essent. vocasti et clamasti et rupisti surditatem meam.' Augustine, *Confessiones,* 10.27.38.

55. For the *uti/frui* distinction as it relates to the image of the pilgrimage, see Augustine, *De doctrina christiana,* 1.3–4. For Dante's recapitulation of this metaphor see *Convivio,* IV, xii, 14–15. Barolini describes *Purgatorio* as 'the most Augustinian of Dante's three canticles' because its plot 'hinges on an Augustinian view of temporal goods'. As she puts it, 'the tension between the legitimacy of the object of desire on the one hand and the need to relinquish it on the other is the tension that sustains the second canticle'. Teodolinda Barolini, 'Purgatory as Paradigm: Traveling the New and Never-Before-Traveled Path of this Life/Poem', in *Undivine Comedy,* pp. 99–121 (pp. 101–02 for quotes). This is certainly true of the reliefs.

56. 'e per lo fabbro loro a veder care' [precious to see also because of their maker], *Purg.* 10.99.

57. For this passage in particular, see Treherne, 'Ekphrasis and Eucharist', and more generally across this tradition with relation to these points about gender, competition, space and time, James A. W. Heffernan, *Museum of Words: The Poetics of Ekphrasis from Homer to Ashbery* (Chicago, IL, and London: University of Chicago Press, 1993), pp. 1–45.

58. Exodus 21. 4: 'non facies tibi sculptile neque omnem similitudinem quae est in caelo desuper et quae in terra deorsum nec eorum quae sunt in aquis sub terra.' See O'Donnell's commentary to Augustine, *Confessiones,* 10.6.10.

59. 'Deum fecisti, uerbi gratia ligneum [...] quid si [Dolbeau: quidni] interrogarem eum? — uide: non interrogat uox animam, sed oculi formam. Speciem ligni illius atque materiam interrogat

aspectus meus [...] In omnibus istis interrogationibus repondet se mihi lignum esse, quod tu dicis deum'. From a sermon on Psalm 81 (82): Deus stetit in synagoga deorum. Augustine, *Vingt-six sermons au peuple d'Afrique: Retrouvés à Mayence*, ed. by François Dolbeau (Paris: Institut d'Études Augustiniennes, 1996), pp. 88–106. Translation from Augustine, *The Works of Saint Augustine*, ed. by Boniface Ramsey, 50 vols (Hyde Park, NY: New City Press, 1990), vol. III (newly discovered sermons), sermon 23B (Dolbeau 6, Mainz 13), p. 39. It is unlikely that Dante knew of this sermon.

60. See *De doctrina christiana*, III.5.9–7.11. The connection between the Mainz sermon, *Confessions* 10.6.9–10 and enslavement to signs is set out in Markus, *Signs*, pp. 22–29.

61. For the significance of this theme throughout the *Commedia*, see John Freccero, 'Medusa: The Letter and the Spirit', in *Dante and the Poetics of Conversion*, pp. 119–35.

62. 'quid horum est unde quaerere debui deum meum, quem iam quaesiveram per corpus a terra usque ad caelum, quousque potui mittere nuntios radios oculorum meorum? sed melius quod interius.' Augustine, *Confessiones*, 10.6.9.

63. 'ei quippe renuntiabant omnes nuntii corporales, praesidenti et iudicanti de responsionibus caeli et terrae et omnium quae in eis sunt dicentium, "non sumus deus" et, "ipse fecit nos".' Augustine, *Confessiones*, 10.6.9. Note 'renuntiabant', 'nuntii' picking up 'nuntios' and 'caeli et terrae' reversing 'terra usque ad caelum'.

64. 'I' mossi i piè del loco dov' io stava, | per avvisar da presso un'altra istoria, | che di dietro a Micòl mi biancheggiava' [I moved my feet from the place where I was standing, so as to see up close another story that shone white for me from behind Michal] (*Purg.* X, 70–72).

65. For a brief summary of the essentials of this metaphysics of light, see Christian Moevs, *The Metaphysics of Dante's 'Comedy'* (Oxford and New York: Oxford University Press, 2005), pp. 19–21 and 27–28.

66. For the body penetrated by light, see Monica Rutledge, 'Dante, the Body and Light', *Dante Studies*, 113 (1995), 151–65.

67. There are some interesting intersections between the pilgrim's whole interaction with the sculptures and elements of Dante's use of the term 'aspetto' [aspect] as analysed by Fortuna and Gragnolati, particularly if the 'visible speech' of the reliefs is understood as a form of prosopopeia. See Sara Fortuna and Manuele Gragnolati, 'Dante after Wittgenstein: "Aspetto", Language, and Subjectivity from *Convivio* to *Paradiso*', in *Dante's Plurilingualism: Authority, Knowledge, Subjectivity*, ed. by Sara Fortuna, Manuele Gragnolati, and Jürgen Trabant (Oxford: Legenda, 2010), pp. 223–47.

68. The wider significance of this 're-presentation' is dealt with by Barolini in 'Re-presenting'.

69. Lombardi, *Syntax*, pp. 17, 145.

70. Lombardi, *Syntax*, p. 153.

71. For the rhyme, see Nancy J. Vickers, 'Claudel's Delectation in Dante', *Claudel Studies*, 8.1 (1981), 28–41 (p. 35). This is the only occurrence of this rhyme-pair.

72. *Familiares*, 4.1. Out of the extensive bibliography see, for example, Albert Russell Ascoli, 'Petrarch's Middle Age: Memory, Imagination, History, and the "Ascent of Mount Ventoux"', *Stanford Italian Review*, 10.1 (1991), 5–43.

73. See Ascoli, 'Petrarch's Middle Age', pp. 10–12 with earlier bibliography and recently Theodore J. Cachey, Jr., 'Petrarchan Cartographic Writing', in *Medieval and Renaissance Humanism: Rhetoric, Representation and Reform*, ed. by Stephen Gersh and Bert Roerst (Leiden: Brill, 2003), pp. 88–91. For Petrarch's complicated response to Dante, see now *Petrarch & Dante: Anti-Dantism, Metaphysics, Tradition*, ed. by Zygmunt G. Barański and Theodore J. Cachey, Jr. (Notre Dame, IN: University of Notre Dame Press, 2009). For the two in relation to Augustine, see Italo Sciuto, 'Agostino fra Dante e Petrarca', in *Verità e responsabilità: Studi in onore di Aniceto Molinaro*, ed. by Leonardo Messinese and Christian Göbel (Rome: Centro Studi S. Anselmo, 2006), pp. 381–89.

74. 'Dirigo dehinc oculorum radios ad partes italicas, quo magis inclinat animus.' [I then directed my sight toward Italy where my heart always inclines.] Francesco Petrarca, *Le Familiari libri I–IV*, ed. and Italian trans. by Ugo Dotti (Urbino: Argalìa, 1970), p. 491. Translations from Francesco Petrarca, *Rerum familiarium libri I–VIII*, trans. by Aldo S. Bernardo (Albany, NY: SUNY Press, 1975).

75. 'Tunc vero montem satis vidisse contentus, in me ipsum interiores oculos reflexi'. Petrarca, *Familiari*, p. 497.

76. Petrarca, *Familiari*, p. 497. From *Confessiones*, 10.8.15: 'Et eunt homines admirari alta montium et ingentes fluctus maris et latissimos lapsus fluminum et oceani ambitum et giros siderum, et relinquunt se ipsos'.

77. 'aurum, argentums, gemme, purpurea vestis, marmorea domus, cultus ager, picte tabule, phaleratur sonipes, ceteraque id genus, mutam habent et superficiarum voluptatem; libri medullitus delectant, colloquuntur'. Petrarca, *Familiari*, 443–45 (III. 18). See Maurizio Bettini, *Francesco Petrarca sulle arti figurative: Tra Plinio e sant'Agostino* (Città di Castello: Sillabe, 2002), p. 14.

CHAPTER 7

Desire and Devotion,
Vision and Touch in the *Vita Nuova*

Robert S. Sturges

Vision, touch, and desire are closely related in the literary and philosophical imagination. Modern authors regularly depict the desiring gaze as a tactile one, in which, for example, the desire for knowledge of another person may be represented visually: 'His little eyes were like tentacles thrown out to catch the floating intimations [...]'.[1] Indeed, erotic longing itself may be similarly described: 'Beal's eyes strike the tall woman's back like rocks pitched hard'.[2] Wittgenstein even theorized the psychology (though not the physical reality) of vision in similar terms: 'We don't see the human eye as a receiver; it seems, not to let something in, but to send out. [...] With the eye one may terrify, not with the ear or the nose.'[3] Such descriptions of the gaze as terrifying tentacles or hurled missile suggest that the ancient extramissive theory of optics, in which the eye touches its object of vision, perhaps violently, retains its power even in the modern cultural imaginary.

In this paper, I would like to start synthesizing some recent work, including my own, on medieval desire and vision, and to locate the *Vita Nuova* in the medieval traditions of desire, simultaneously erotic and spiritual, that this recent scholarship has been exploring. With luck such a synthesis may also enable some speculation on the nature of the obscure links between medieval desire and the modern master narrative of psychoanalysis, or at least with the master narrative's prehistory. In a recent essay entitled 'Visual Pleasure and *La Vita nuova*', I have suggested that whether or not psychoanalysis can help us understand Dante, Dante and the traditions of medieval visuality, and their relationship with desire that he instantiates, may well help us understand the underpinnings of psychoanalysis, especially those theories of the gaze enunciated by Jacques Lacan and Laura Mulvey (and their critics).[4] In the present essay I would like to explore both the medieval traditions and their relevance to the master narrative in further detail.

I will start with the physical senses of vision and touch, which, as Richard Newhauser suggests in the same recent issue of *The Senses and Society*, are more closely related in medieval theory than we might expect.[5] It is not uncommon to distinguish between two different pre-modern visual theories. In this view, an earlier medieval understanding of vision is extramission, in which the eye of the beholder emits rays, which, strengthened by ambient light as they pass through the atmosphere, touch the object of their vision and return to the eye with the resulting impression: thus they take on the form of their object and return it to the eye.[6] From this perspective, which dates back to Plato and the Neoplatonists, and was transmitted to the medieval period by St Augustine, among others,[7] the senses of sight and of touch are closely related: to see something is to touch it with the rays emitted from the observer's eyes. The later scholastics would disagree; their suggestion — made by Aquinas, for instance — is that sight is the most 'spiritual' and least material sense.[8] According to what is sometimes thought of as the later, alternative model of vision, called intromission, however, light is emitted by the object and transmitted across the atmosphere by the multiplication of *species*, a kind of image or representation, to the eye of the beholder. These *species* may weaken and even deform the object of vision, but they also make it present to the observer, however imperfectly.[9] Forms of intromission were proposed in antiquity, and, most influentially for the later Middle Ages, were central to the optical theory of the eleventh-century Islamic natural philosopher Alhacen, whose work influenced the Perspectivist optics of such thinkers as Roger Bacon.[10]

Newhauser, in his essay on the late thirteenth-century *Tractatus moralis de oculo* by Peter of Limoges (a text that uses Perspectivist optics allegorically, as an exercise in moralizing theology), points out that Peter cites Claudius Ptolemy's first-century theory of vision as an authority for his own. Ptolemy was an early exponent of the extramissionist theory of vision, and perhaps the thinker most influential in linking the senses of vision and touch.[11] As David C. Lindberg explains it, for Ptolemy, in a formulation that goes back in some ways to Plato's *Timaeus*, vision can be attributed to 'the action of a visual flux issuing conically from the observer's eye', but Ptolemy additionally 'gave the visual radiation a physical interpretation'[12] that marks him as a follower of Plato's notion that the visual current or fire issuing from the eye coalesces with daylight and thus 'passes on the motions of anything it comes in contact with or that comes into contact with it, throughout the whole body, to the soul, and thus causes the sensation we call seeing'.[13] Newhauser thus finds that, in spite of their intromissionist position, something of this extramissionist concept of vision as touch remains in the Perspectivist philosophers like Alhacen and Roger Bacon, on whom Peter of Limoges relies in the *Tractatus*, and that Peter of Limoges in turn passes this view on to his own wide readership: 'Sight [...] is closely related to touch in its operation for Ptolemy, and an element of the sense of touch in understanding vision remained with the Perspectivists as well [...]. But Peter emphasizes far more than is found in the work of other Perspectivists the active participation of the viewer in the process of perception'.[14] Extramission and intromission, then, cannot be so easily separated either in time or in their theoretical implications, and some of the most significant thinkers employ both. Specifically, both may link the senses of vision and of touch.

It should be emphasized here that Peter of Limoges was writing in the last third of the thirteenth century — Newhauser dates his treatise to between 1275 and 1289[15] — which is to say that his work slightly predates the composition of the *Vita Nuova*, typically assigned to the period 1292–94. Peter's *Tractatus* was a medieval best seller: it survives in 220 manuscripts, with evidence of more than 40 others that have been lost, according to Newhauser.[16] Peter's views were thus widely disseminated, as were the Perspectivist optics he moralized and popularized. Whether or not Dante was aware of Peter of Limoges, he was certainly aware of the theories of vision found in his text: Dante's interest in optics and vision, including contemporary theoretical speculation on them, is well known and heavily documented, for instance by Patrick Boyde. Indeed, the older view that Dante was an original thinker in the science of optics[17] has been largely displaced by one that situates Dante's theories well within those that would have been widely available. It is not uncommon to suggest that, like his contemporary Peter of Limoges, Dante deployed a combination of extramissionist and intromissionist theories of vision, depending on the specific visual effect he was attempting to produce in any given passage. Thus Boyde finds that while Dante explicitly rejects extramission in favour of intromission in the *Convivio*, he also 'fully understood the psychological truth of Plato's theory'.[18]

In the *Convivio*, Dante does indeed condemn an extramissionist position that he describes as Platonic:

> Veramente Plato e altri filosofi dissero che 'l nostro vedere non era perché lo visibile venisse all'occhio, ma perché la virtù visiva andava fuori al visibile: e questa oppinione è riprovata per falsa dal Filosofo in quello del Senso e Sensato. (*Conv.* III, ix, 10)[19]

> [In truth Plato and other philosophers state that we see not because that which is seen comes to the eye, but because the visual power moves out to that which is seen. And this opinion is proven false by the Philosopher in his work *On Sense and Sensibilia*.]

His own description of how vision works in the *Convivio* can more easily be described as intromissionist, though it takes a bit of deciphering:

> Queste cose visibili [...] vengono dentro all'occhio — no dico *le cose*, ma *le forme* loro — per lo mezzo diafano, non realmente ma intenzionalmente, sì quasi come in vetro trasparente. [...] Di questa pupilla lo spirito visivo, che si continua da essa alla parte del cerebro dinanzi dov'è la sensibile vertude sì come in principio fontale, [quivi] subitamente sanza tempo la ripresenta, e così vedemo. (*Conv.* III, ix, 7–8)

> [The objects of vision [...] pass into the eye — not the *things themselves* but their *forms* — through the diaphanous medium, not really but intentionally, almost as if into transparent glass. [...] From the pupil, the optic spirit, which remains in contact with it, to the anterior portion of the brain — where the power of sensation lies as the originating principle — immediately, in no time, presents it again, and this is how we see.]

This convoluted sentence suggests that the *species*, or what Dante calls '*le forme*' as opposed to the things themselves, '*le cose*', pass through the transparent medium of air or daylight and alight on the eye, but not '*realmente*'. The 'optic spirit', in contact with the pupil, immediately re-transmits the image to the front portion of the brain, where the seat of sensation is located. Here, as in the *Convivio* passage I cited previously, Dante insists on distancing himself from an extramissionist position: the visible things themselves are carefully distinguished from their forms or *species*, and only the latter pass into the eye; even having made this distinction, he again insists that this process is 'intentional' rather than 'real'. Simon A. Gilson points out that 'Averroës uses *intentio* to denote the type of non-corporeal impression that light makes in the medium' and that Albert the Great and Aquinas, whom Dante follows, both 'describe sense objects in the medium as having *esse intentionale*' as opposed to the Perspectivists' argument 'that likenesses are transmitted to the eye corporeally'.[20]

This very insistence, however, perhaps indicates some awareness of just how easily the merely intentional can come to seem real, and indeed how easily the *species* could be mistaken for the objects of vision themselves. This impression of potential confusion is reinforced by the imagery Dante uses to describe the process as a whole: whereas the Perspectivists write of the *species* as representations being multiplied across space, each *species* derived from the one before, Dante, as Boyde points out, represents the 'forms' as if they were moving objects passing through the air and into the eye, where they are stopped by the physical boundary of the 'acqua ch'è nella pupilla dell'occhio' [water that is in the pupil of the eye].[21] Here too, as Gilson suggests, Dante may be following Albert and Aquinas, who both use 'the example of the ball rebounding in order to explain how forms are brought to a halt in the eye'.[22] It is difficult not to understand Dante as continuing to think in metaphors of tangibility even as he disclaims the tangible reality of the 'forms'.[23]

This impression may be borne out with reference to Dante's poetic representations of vision, as distinct from the theoretical ones presented in the *Convivio*. We have already seen that, for Patrick Boyde, Dante may believe in the scientific truth of intromission and yet still make use of the psychological implications of extramission. Dallas G. Denery II, too, in his work on optics and theology in the later Middle Ages, agrees that Dante 'accepted the truth of intromissionist theories of vision and yet, when imagining the effect that the beloved's glance has on her lover or how God is present to the beatified in heaven, he was more than happy to deploy more traditional extramissionist models of vision.'[24] We might look to the *Vita Nuova*, then, for a complex rendering of the spiritual and erotic intentions and effects of vision, one in line with the combination of intromissive and extramissive theories evident in contemporary thinkers like Peter of Limoges and those cited by Gilson.[25] As Gilson notes, the attempt to identify specific sources for Dante's thought 'is less valid for a poetic work as richly complex as the *Comedy*',[26] and the same might be said of the *Vita Nuova*, though Gilson's book devotes only two paragraphs to it.

Thus, in the recent essay I cited earlier, I attempt to think about the libidinal and spiritual implications of these different models of vision and how they come into play in the *Vita Nuova*. Briefly, I suggest that Dante's exploration of his desire for Beatrice and all she represents can be understood as conditioned by both models at once, and that both have interesting consequences for a prehistory of psychoanalysis.

It is tempting to observe the two tendencies of the male gaze identified by Laura Mulvey in her influential essay 'Visual Pleasure and Narrative Cinema', namely scopophilia, or pleasure in looking, and identification with the heterosexual male gaze, in the two complementary aspects of Dante's text, the poems and the prose narrative surrounding them, but this tidy division can be applied only loosely and provisionally.[27] Nevertheless, the poet's prose discussions of his poems do underscore the formal perfection of the poetry, with their comments on the poems' elaborate structural features along with their suggestions about the manner in which these 'divisions' direct the poem's interpretation. This perfection of form, as Mulvey influentially suggests about cinematic form, does regularly seem to interpellate the reader as male and heterosexual and to invite his scopophilic, pleasurable looking, because the body of Beatrice appears as a perfect but passive image inviting the male poet's and readers' gaze. The famous 'eaten heart' poem in *VN* III, 'A ciascun'alma presa' ['To every captured soul'] is a good example. While the image as a whole does eventually come to life in this particular poem, as the God of Love feeds Beatrice the heart, the body of Beatrice itself remains a passive object of vision. This passivity becomes pure stasis, with Beatrice again functioning as the object of male vision, upon her death:

> Era venuta ne la mente mia
> la gentil donna che per suo valore
> fu posta da l'altissimo signore
> nel ciel de l'umilitate, ov'è Maria. (*VN* XLII, 7)

> [There came into my mind
> the gentle lady who by her worth
> was sent by the highest lord
> into the heaven of humility, where Mary is.]

Beatrice here is nothing but a mental image: this unfinished sonnet turns her into a pure object of the male poet's mental vision, in turn passed on to the scopophilic male reader. The process is completed in the final poem in the *Vita Nuova*, in which Beatrice literally shines forth as the explicit object of Dante's desiring gaze, his sigh:

> Quand'elli è giunto là dove disira,
> vede una donna, che riceve onore,
> e luce sì, che per lo suo splendore
> lo peregrino spirito la mira. (*VN* XLI, 11)

> [When it was arrived there where it desired
> it saw a lady, who received honour,
> and shone herself, so that by the light of her splendour
> the pilgrim spirit gazed at her.]

The scopophilia implied earlier is thus eventually made explicit: Beatrice in heaven is the luminous but passive object of the male gaze. As Mulvey's theories would suggest, the poem's formal perfection does indeed construct her as static. In this case that perfection of form is announced ahead of time by the 'divisions' that precede the poem rather than, as is more typically the case, coming after: this commentary directs the reader's view of Beatrice ahead of time, before he even reads the poem. Scopophilia is thus achieved precisely through the formal mastery over the objectified female body that Mulvey insists on. It disavows the potential imperfection of a real woman's body by sublimation: the poem, and the visual pleasure it induces in the male reader, literally makes her sublime.[28]

Just as the poet-narrator gains dominance, through sublimating poetic language, over Beatrice's body, the reader, interpellated as male and heterosexual, may also claim a share in that mastery by means of an identification with the narrator made possible in the diegetic prose sections. This prose narration typically describes the poetic visions before they are re-presented in the poems, which is why any neat distinction between prose and poetry in these terms must remain only provisional. The narrative sections offer only the poet-narrator's own point of view for this identification; while the reader is subjected to that perspective, he has access to Mulvey's second mode of visual pleasure, identification, along with the first, scopophilia. The narrator claims in section xv that 'sì tosto com'io imagino la sua mirabile bellezza, sì tosto mi giugne uno desiderio di vederla, lo quale è di tanta vertude, che uccide e distrugge ne la mia memoria ciò che contra lui si potesse levare' [as soon as I imagine her miraculous beauty, there comes to me a desire to see her, which is so powerful that it destroys and kills from my memory whatever could rise up against it] (*VN* xv, 2). Given such direct contact with the narrator's consciousness as the reader is regularly allowed, the latter is enticed to identify with the former's fantasy of mastery, in which he is able to 'kill and destroy' — erase from his consciousness — whatever resists this sovereign pleasure in seeing and the desire that accompanies it. Here the narrator's desire to see is specifically fantasized as aggressively and overpoweringly phallic, and the (heterosexual, male) reader is encouraged to take part in his pleasure in visual dominion. The desire to see, though confined to the narrator's memory, extramissively attacks what stands between it and its desired object.

However, in this same passage, and throughout the *Vita Nuova*, the claim that the narrative voice, if it provides a source of identification, also provides an ego-ideal for the heterosexual male reader would be difficult to maintain. Instead of a pathway to mastery over the silent and passive female body, the desire to see, and indeed the experience of vision itself, often emasculate the narrator, and allow the sight of Beatrice to dominate him in turn. If the desire to see in the passage quoted above erases, in the narrator's imagination, all opposition, that fantasy may be understood, as we have seen, as an extramissive one: Dante's narrator, in this reading, imagines his gaze as phallic, one in which his tactile vision extramissively breaks down the barriers that keep him from Beatrice almost in a physical sense, and even, as in the language examined earlier in the *Convivio* and Peter of Limoges, touches her very body, visually gaining control over it and bringing it within the poet's own consciousness. But such an understanding of the desire to see as phallic, extramissively conforming that which opposes it to its own will, remains no more than a fantasy. In the passage just cited, for example, the obstacle that the narrator must destroy is his own memory of having been emasculated by the sight of Beatrice: his desire is masterful in this way only on the condition that 'io non perdessi le mie vertudi' [I did not lose my powers] when he 'saw her' (*VN* xv, 2); it is the consciousness of his previous malfunctions of 'virtú' in her presence that have to be eliminated.

In fact, throughout the *Vita Nuova*, or at any rate while Beatrice remains alive, the sight of her strips the narrator of his masculine power. In his description of the moment at which she first 'appeared' ('apparve'):

> lo spirito della vita, lo quale dimora ne la secretissima camera de lo core, cominciò a tremare sì fortemente, che apparia ne li menimi polsi orribilmente; e tremando disse queste parole: 'Ecce Deus fortior me, qui veniens dominabitur mihi'. [...] Lo spirito animale, lo quale dimora ne l'alta camera, ne la quale tutti li spiriti sensitivi portano le lore percezioni, si cominciò a maravigliare molto, e parlando spezialmene a li spiriti del viso, sì disse queste parole: 'Apparuit iam beatitudo vestra'. [...] Lo spirito naturale, lo quale dimora in quella parte ove si ministra lo nutrimento nostro, cominciò a piangere [...]. (*VN* II, 4–6)

> [the vital spirit, which inhabits the most secret chamber of the heart, started trembling so violently that I felt it horribly in even my slightest pulses; and trembling spoke these words: *Behold a god more powerful than I who comes to dominate me.* [...] The animal spirit, which inhabits the high chamber to which all the sensitive spirits carry their perceptions, began to marvel greatly and, speaking particularly to the spirits of vision, uttered these words: *Your source of blessedness appears.* [...] The natural spirit, which inhabits that part where our nutrition is administered, began to weep [...].]

This passage foreshadows later visual exchanges between the poet–narrator and Beatrice.[29] Rather than the fantasy of overmastering vision quoted above, this exchange is one in which the narrator is visually subjugated: Beatrice is a vision of blessedness which is at one and the same time a vision of the narrator's abjection. This dual vision has tangible consequences that once again suggest a continuity between the senses of sight and touch, but in this case the experience of vision seems more intromissionist than extramissionist: here the observer is rendered powerless, and it is the object of vision that touches the observer. As I observe in my earlier essay, 'the dissolution of the narrator's sense of self as a coherent body runs precisely counter to the early Lacanian model of the mirror stage employed by Mulvey: rather than acquiring a sense of coherence and mastery through identification with the narrator's male gaze, the reader who identifies with the narrator must experience a dizzying abjection.'[30]

The notion of the object of vision as an intruder has recently been formulated helpfully by Heather Webb, in *The Medieval Heart*. She places Dante's use of the trope within a poetic tradition that also includes such poems as Cavalcanti's sonnet, 'Voi che per li occhi mi passaste 'l core', in which '[t]he spirits flowing from the woman's eyes strike with such force that the soul is shaken from its dwelling and turns back to see that dwelling destroyed, or in other words to see the heart dead.'[31] And as she points out of *Vita Nuova* VII and XV, '[t]he spirits that radiate from Beatrice's eyes penetrate to the poet's heart before he has time to lift his eyes and see her. [...] The crucial first component of the poetic analysis of romantic love is a spiritual invasion of the poet's body'.[32] Here, too, the perceiver loses bodily coherence: pleasure now lies precisely in the denial of mastery — in being subjugated to the other's visual touch. This emphasis on the narrator seeing Beatrice's gaze is a good example of the manner in which the interplay between extramission and intromission may also be understood as the interplay been activity and passivity, or, in tactile terms, between touching and being touched. The gaze is 'something active that is perceived by other gazes'.[33]

Mulvey has been criticized for her attachment to Lacan's early works, and indeed some of Lacan's later writings resonate more fully with this aspect of the *Vita Nuova*. Here we may find that the (male) gaze, as Todd McGowan suggests, actually 'marks the point in the image at which the subject is completely subjected to it'; according to McGowan, 'the gaze triggers the subject's desire because it appears to hold the key not to the subject's achievement of self-completion or wholeness but to the disappearance of self in the experience of enjoyment.'[34] Lacan himself suggests that 'what the subject is looking for is not, as one says, the phallus — but precisely its absence';[35] 'the libidinal captation has an irremediably fatal significance for the individual'.[36] Henry Staten links this aspect of Lacan's thought to the Platonic/Augustinian tradition mentioned above: 'Only the journey to the absolute core of destructiveness can issue in the final beyond that is "limitless love", the love whose name in the tradition is agape [...]'.[37] Fortuna and Gragnolati have examined the dissolution of the self in this active/passive interplay of gazes as it appears in the *Paradiso*;[38] in the earlier *Vita Nuova*, the pleasure of this interplay seems more distinctly sadomasochistic.

The stealthy *jouissance* in the abject failure of phallic domination finds more support in the *Vita Nuova* than Mulvey's commitment to the mirror stage. Dante's union of visual pleasure and passive abjection, on being touched by the other's gaze as well as, or instead of, touching with one's own gaze, is articulated in his own culture's visual terms, but those terms themselves may enable a historicization of the master-narrative of psychoanalysis.

One route that such a historicization might take would lead through the recent work on the visuality of the spiritual life in the later Middle Ages,[39] and this is also a tradition in which I would like to situate the Dante of the *Vita Nuova*: specifically in the tradition of late medieval, post-Augustinian devotional vision, of which Dante may considered an early exemplar. Staten explores this tradition from a psychoanalytical perspective, but several medievalist scholars have recently noted that late medieval devotional writers also drew on Augustinian visual theory, especially as elaborated in Augustine's *De Trinitate*, to describe an inner-directed vision that, through desire, imprinted an image of God in the desiring soul, thus rendering them similar.

Specifically, Jennifer Bryan, in her 2008 study of late medieval English devotional literature, *Looking Inward*, points out that Augustine's work on spiritual vision in *De Trinitate*, chapter 11, was informed by the extramissive model, which Bryan, like Dante, identifies as Platonic or Neoplatonic.[40] Literary and art historians may not employ the philosophical vocabulary of extramission and intromission, but in the words of the art historian Margaret Miles, '[t]he visual ray, the strongest concentration of the body's animating fire, is projected from the eye to touch its object. In the act of vision, viewer and image are connected in a dynamic communication';[41] or, as Bryan puts it, '[s]ubject and object touch only momentarily, but the cumulative effect of such moments was a lasting impression'.[42] Augustine, of course, Christianizes this model, finding in the tripartite structure of vision (the object of vision, vision itself, and the mind's attention to the object) one of his interior models of the Trinity (*De Trinitate* 11.2.2).[43] Furthermore, Bryan makes an observation for late medieval devotional literature that we have already found in commentators on Dante: that even as this model was discredited as a physical phenomenon, 'it became even more ubiquitous and influential as a way of understanding the operation of the spiritual eye'.[44]

The way this spiritual understanding works, as distinct from physical vision, however, also has something in common with an intromissive model, because it involves the influence of the object of contemplation upon the self. The viewer both touches and is touched: 'the soul [...] could be transformed by what it reflected, and by what it reflected upon. The darkened image of God could be reimprinted as a better likeness; the soul could reflect more accurately by seeing more intensely.'[45] This imprint in the soul comes about through the deployment of the will and desire. As Augustine himself suggests, 'the will possesses such power [...] that it moves the sense to be formed to that thing which is seen, and keeps it fixed on it when it has been formed. And if it is so violent that it can be called love, or desire, or passion, it likewise exerts a powerful influence on the rest of the body of this living being.'[46] For Augustine and his followers, desire is thus a violent form of the will, which directs the senses, and indeed the living being itself, to conform to what is seen: the divine visual object captured by the seeing self also causes the self to conform to the object. As I suggested earlier, extramission cannot be separated from intromission, even for an earlier and Neoplatonic thinker like Augustine: the Augustinian spiritual gaze may move out and touch the objects of desire, but only so that the object, God, may re-form the soul. Visual activity leads ultimately to a desired passivity before the divine touch. This is the function of late medieval devotional writing, for literary historians like Bryan, and of visual imagery as well, for art historians like Miles: it encourages the contemplation of the divine object of desire, focusing the desiring will on God and thereby reforming the self in his image.

Bryan's particular concern is with late medieval English religious texts, and Miles's with Italian church paintings, both early and late medieval; together their work suggests a widespread phenomenon in which the combination of extramission and intromission that I have been describing affects the production and perception of numerous medieval cultural artefacts. Such an impression is borne out by other recent scholars whose focus is somewhat narrower. Jessica Brantley, for example, limits herself to the exploration of Carthusian devotion in England in her book *Reading in the Wilderness*; indeed, her study focuses on a single famous fifteenth-century English Carthusian manuscript, British Library MS Additional 37049, with its elaborate combination of image and text providing material for an internal devotional performance. In terms of contemplative vision, Brantley suggests that, like Beatrice, the 'image of Christ in the book "looks back," for devotional performances in the cell always have an audience in the person of an omniscient, omnipresent, divine spectator. Through [...] the thorough-going conflation of subject and object that result, this book "acts" on its reader, as surely as the reader acts on it'.[47] According to Brantley, this kind of visual reciprocity is anticipated in one of the letters of St Bruno, the eleventh-century founder of the Carthusian order: withdrawn from the world, Bruno claims, men 'can acquire that eye that with its clear look wounds the divine spouse with love, and that, because of its purity, is granted the sight of God.'[48] The divine spouse is, like Beatrice — and like the female objects of the male gaze cited at the beginning of this essay — touched, even wounded, by the phallic extramissive gaze, but at the same time he actively grants himself as a vision to the passive beholder.

Turning to late medieval Italian culture, Elizabeth Bailey in a recent article finds that a middle-class, late medieval Florentine, too, naturally used physical contemplation to cross the boundary into the world of spirit. Giovanni Morelli, with the help of visual images of the Passion, was able to 'expand the image and extend the narrative. Thus, inspired by the figure of Christ in his panel, Morelli pictured Christ's death in his mind';[49] Morelli's faith 'allowed him to move easily from exterior sight to interior vision and from meditation on Christ's humanity to contemplation of his divinity.'[50]

Bailey draws a link between Morelli and Dante, pointing out that Morelli owned writings by Dante and describing Morelli's visions as 'Dantesque'. She also suggests a link between Dante's visuality and the function of vision taken for granted by Morelli.[51] I would like to close by suggesting some further connections between the *Vita Nuova* and these post-Augustinian theories of spiritual vision that combine extramissive and intromissive models, as well as a further consideration of how these medieval models may underpin psychoanalytic theories of the gaze — as well as those modern literary representations of the desiring gaze with which we began.

Rather than continuing to think in terms of intromission and extramission, it may be more helpful to move away from those terms and distinctions in favour of more nuanced understandings of medieval visuality, and to acknowledge that a flexible combination of the two, emphasizing reciprocity, may provide a more useful model. In the *Vita Nuova*, at any rate, as I have been suggesting, Dante's extramissive, phallic gaze disguises a desire for abjection before the object of vision and desire, a reformation of the self in which the self is lost in contemplation of the other. In spiritual terms, the physical vision of Beatrice ultimately gives way to the contemplation of the divine object.

This contemplation is also associated with death. For McGowan, the death of the observing subject must also be implicated in the gaze: 'Even when a manifestation of the gaze does not make death evident directly [...] it nonetheless carries the association insofar as the gaze itself marks the point in the image at which the subject is completely subjected to it.'[52] *The New Life* must thus end with death: 'E poi piaccia a colui che è sire de la cortesia, che la mia anima se ne possa gire a vedere la gloria de la sua donna, cioè di quella benedetta Beatrice, la quale gloriosamente mira ne la faccia di colui *qui est per omnia secula benedictus*' [And then it may please Him who is the lord of courtesy that my soul may be able to go to behold the glory of its lady, that is, of the blessed Beatrice, who gloriously looks upon the face of him *who is blessed through all ages*] (*VN* XLII, 5). The ultimate self-dissolution in death is thus simultaneously the perfect fulfilment of desire in an eternal gaze at the beloved object that is also an unending 'disappearance of self in the experience of enjoyment'. This kind of psychoanalytic thought is thus prefigured in Dante and his contemporaries, and indeed one might claim that it is not properly comprehensible without reference to them.

Notes to Chapter 7

1. Edith Wharton, *The House of Mirth* (1905); (repr. New York: Collier, 1987), p. 289.
2. Carolyn Chute, *The Beans of Egypt, Maine* (New York: Ticknor and Fields, 1985), p. 104.
3. Ludwig Wittgenstein, *Remarks on the Philosophy of Psychology* (Oxford: Blackwell, 1980), p. 192, cited in Sara Fortuna and Manuele Gragnolati, 'Dante After Wittgenstein: "Aspetto", Language, and Subjectivity from *Convivio* to *Paradiso*', in *Dante's Plurilingualism: Authority, Knowledge, Subjectivity*, ed. by Sara Fortuna, Manuele Gragnolati, and Jürgen Trabant (Oxford: Legenda, 2010), pp. 223–48 (p. 229).
4. Robert S. Sturges, 'Visual Pleasure and *La Vita nuova*: Lacan, Mulvey, and Dante', in *Pleasure and Danger in Perception: The Five Senses in the Middle Ages and the Renaissance*, ed. by Corine Schleif and Richard G. Newhauser, special issue of *The Senses and Society*, 5.1 (March 2010), 93–105. For a related interrogation of the usefulness of psychoanalysis in reading medieval texts, and the *Vita Nuova* in particular, see Fabio Camilletti's essay in the present volume.
5. Richard G. Newhauser, 'Peter of Limoges, Optics, and the Science of the Senses', in Schleif and Newhauser, eds, *Pleasure and Danger*, pp. 28–44.
6. See, for example, Michael Camille, 'Before the Gaze: The Internal Senses and Late Medieval Practices of Seeing', in *Visuality Before and Beyond the Renaissance: Seeing as Others Saw*, ed. by Robert S. Nelson (Cambridge: Cambridge University Press, 2000), pp. 197–223 (pp. 204–05); Cynthia Hahn, '*Visio dei*: Changes in Medieval Visuality', in Nelson, ed., as previous, pp. 169–96 (pp. 174–75); Christopher M. Woolgar, *The Senses in Late Medieval England* (New Haven, CT: Yale University Press, 2006), p. 21.
7. See, for example, Augustine's contention that in normal vision (here contrasted with blindness), the mind will 'direct the sense of the body outwardly towards a body, and unite with it in order to see it, and fix its gaze upon it when it is seen', *The Trinity*, trans. by Stephen McKenna (Washington, DC: Catholic University of America Press, 1963), 11.2.2, p. 318; '[...] et eius intentio luminibus amissis non habeat quidem sensum corporis quem uidendo extrinsecus corpori adiungat atque in eo uiso figat aspectum,' *De trinitate libri xv*, ed. by W. J. Mountain, 2 vols, Corpus Chritsianorum 50–50A (Turnhout: Brepols, 1968), I, 335. On Augustine's influence on optical theory, see Woolgar, *Senses*, p. 21; Dallas G. Denery II, *Seeing and Being Seen in the Later Medieval World: Optics, Theology, and Religious Life* (Cambridge: Cambridge University Press, 2005), p. 83; Eugene Vance, 'Seeing God: Augustine, Sensation, and the Mind's Eye', in *Rethinking the Medieval Senses: Heritage / Fascinations / Frames*, ed. by Stephen G. Nichols, Andreas Kablitz, and Alison Calhoun (Baltimore, MD: Johns Hopkins University Press, 2008), pp. 13–29 (pp. 23–24).
8. 'Visus autem, quia est absque immutatione naturali et organi et obiecti, est maxime spiritualis, et perfectior iner omnes sensus, et communior' [Now, the sight, which is without natural immutation either in its organ or in its object, is the most spiritual, the most perfect, and the most universal of all the senses], St Thomas Aquinas, *Summa theologiae* (1888–1906; rev. edn Rome: Editiones Paulinae, 1962), Pt. I, Q. 78, Art. 3, p. 372; English translation from: *Summa theologica*, trans. by Fathers of the English Dominican Province, 5 vols (New York: Benziger Brothers, 1948), I, 393.
9. See Camille, 'Before the Gaze', pp. 205–06; Denery, *Seeing*, pp. 82–100; Woolgar, *Senses*, pp. 21–22.
10. Denery, *Seeing*, pp. 82–83.
11. Newhauser, 'Peter of Limoges', p. 36. On Peter, see also Denery, *Seeing*, pp. 75–115.
12. David C. Lindberg, *Theories of Vision from Al-Kindi to Kepler* (Chicago, IL: University of Chicago Press, 1976), p. 15.
13. Plato, *Timaeus* 45d, trans. by Francis F. Cornford, *Plato's Cosmology: The Timaeus of Plato* (London, 1937), cited in Lindberg, *Theories*, p. 5
14. Newhauser, 'Peter of Limoges', p. 36.
15. Newhauser, 'Peter of Limoges', p. 31.
16. Newhauser, 'Peter of Limoges', p. 31.
17. See, for example, the large claims made for Dante's originality in the *Convivio* made by Gino Ricchi, 'Il meccanismo della visione seconda Dante Alighieri', *Giornale dantesco*, 10 (1902), 177–

79, as well as Alessandro Parronchi's classic *Studi su la dolce prospettiva* (Milan: Aldo Martello, 1964).

18. Patrick Boyde, *Perception and Passion in Dante's 'Comedy'* (Cambridge: Cambridge University Press, 1993), p. 106. A thorough discussion of contemporary developments in optical theory and Dante's awareness of them in his early career can be found in the first two chapters of Simon A. Gilson, *Medieval Optics and Theories of Light in the Works of Dante* (Lewiston, NY, Queenston, and Lampeter: Edwin Mellen, 2000), pp. 7–73. Gilson demonstrates that Dante's optics lacked the Perspectivists' 'technical sophistication' and that his ideas were 'readily available in a wide variety of general sources' (p. 72) — including vernacular poetry like Guinizzelli's and Cavalcanti's, and preaching handbooks like that of Peter of Limoges (pp. 32–37). For a more specific comparison of Dante's use of visual theory with Cavalcanti's, see Massimiliano Chiamenti, 'The Representation of the Psyche in Cavalcanti, Dante and Petrarch: The *Spiriti*', *Neophilologus*, 82 (1998), 71–81.

19. Translations of Dante's works are my own.

20. Gilson, *Medieval Optics*, pp. 63–64.

21. Boyde, *Perception*, pp. 70–71.

22. Gilson, *Medieval Optics*, p. 68.

23. On Dante's indirect indebtedness to Plato, see also Margherita de Bonfils Templer, 'La prima visione della *Vita Nuova* e la dottrina dei tre spiriti', *La Rassegna della letteratura italiana*, 76 (1972), 303–16.

24. Denery, *Seeing*, p. 171. On the medieval debate over whether vision should be considered active or passive, see also Monica Rutledge, 'Dante, the Body and Light', *Dante Studies*, 113 (1995), 151–65 (p. 157). For this debate's influence on Dante, see pp. 157–59.

25. Gilson, *Medieval Optics*, briefly discusses the *Vita Nuova* in terms of medieval optical theory, pp. 40–42.

26. Gilson, *Medieval Optics*, p. 73.

27. Laura Mulvey, 'Visual Pleasure and Narrative Cinema' (1975), repr. in her *Visual and Other Pleasures*, 2nd edn (Basingstoke and New York: Palgrave, 2009), pp. 14–27; for a discussion of this essay's possible relevance to a reading of the *Vita Nuova*, see Sturges, 'Visual Pleasure', pp. 94–97. My discussion of the *Vita Nuova* in the following five paragraphs is derived from this essay's argument.

28. On sublimation, and on 'Era venuta' in particular, see also Camilletti.

29. A discussion of the medical doctrine of spirits and their relation to visuality lies beyond the scope of this essay. See Sturges, 'Visual Pleasure', pp. 99–100; Chiamenti, 'Representation'; de Bonfils Templer, 'La prima visione'; James Bono, 'Medical Spirits and the Medieval Language of Life', *Traditio*, 40 (1984), pp. 91–130.

30. Sturges, 'Visual Pleasure', p. 100. See Jacques Lacan, 'The Mirror Stage as Formative of the Function of the I as Revealed in Psychoanalytic Experience' (1949), reprinted in his *Écrits: A Selection*, trans. by Alan Sheridan (New York: Norton, 1977), pp. 1–7.

31. Heather Webb, *The Medieval Heart* (New Haven, CT: Yale University Press, 2010), p. 160. See Guido Cavalcanti, 'Voi che per li occhi mi passaste 'l core', in his *Complete Poems*, ed. and trans. by Marc Cirigliano (New York: Italica Press, 1992), p. 30. On passivity before the gaze in Cavalcanti, see also Dana E. Stewart, *The Arrow of Love: Optics, Gender, and Subjectivity in Medieval Love-Poetry* (Lewisburg, PA: Bucknell University Press, 2003), pp. 81–101. Stewart discusses Dante's *Rime* in similar terms, pp. 102–21.

32. Webb, *Medieval Heart*, p. 69. Cf. Chiamenti, 'Representation': '[I]n Dante and Cavalcanti the *spiriti* are chiefly employed to show an interior distress', p. 78.

33. Fortuna and Gragnolati, 'Dante after Wittgenstein', p. 234.

34. Todd McGowan, *The Real Gaze: Film Theory after Lacan* (Albany: State University of New York Press: 2007), p. 7.

35. Jacques Lacan, *The Four Fundamental Concepts of Psycho-Analysis* (1973), ed. by Jacques-Alain Miller, trans. by Alan Sheridan (New York: Norton, 1978), p. 182.

36. Jacques Lacan, *The Seminar of Jacques Lacan, Book I: Freud's Papers on Technique* (1975), trans. by John Forrester (New York: Norton, 1988), p. 148.

37. Henry Staten, *Eros in Mourning: Homer to Lacan* (Baltimore, MD: Johns Hopkins University Press: 1995), p. 184.

38. Fortuna and Gragnolati, 'Dante after Wittgenstein', pp. 234–43.

39. For an art-historical overview of the problem in terms of activity and passivity, see Katherine H. Tachau, 'Seeing as Action and Passion in the Thirteenth and Fourteenth Centuries', in *The Mind's Eye: Art and Theological Argument in the Middle Ages*, ed. by Jeffrey F. Hamburger and Anne-Marie Bouché (Princeton, NJ: Princeton University Department of Art and Archaeology in Association with Princeton University Press, 2006), pp. 336–59.

40. Jennifer Bryan, *Looking Inward: Devotional Reading and the Private Self in Late Medieval England* (Philadelphia: University of Pennsylvania Press, 2008), pp. 65–68, pp. 78–80, pp. 123–24.

41. Margaret Miles, *Image as Insight: Visual Understanding in Western Christianity and Secular Culture* (Eugene, OR: Wipf and Stock, 1985), p. 45.

42. Bryan, *Looking*, p. 123.

43. St Augustine, *De Trinitate*, ed. by Mountain, 11.2.2, I, p. 334; *The Trinity*, trans. by Stephen McKenna, p. 316.

44. Bryan, *Looking*, p. 123. On the 'eyes of the spirit' in the *Vita Nuova*, see also Camilletti.

45. Bryan, *Looking*, p. 124.

46. *The Trinity*, trans. by McKenna, 11.2.5, p. 321; 'Voluntas autem tantam habet uim [...] ut et sensum formandum admoueat ei rei quae cernitur et in ea formatum teneat. Et si tam uiolenta est ut possit uocari amor aut cupiditas aut libido, etiam ceterum corpus animantis uehementer afficit', St. Augustine, *De Trinitate*, ed. by Mountain, I, p. 339.

47. Jessica Brantley, *Reading in the Wilderness: Private Devotion and Public Performance in Late Medieval England* (Chicago, IL: University of Chicago Press, 2007), p. 21.

48. St Bruno, 'Ad Radulphem, cognomento Viridem, Remensem praepositum', *Lettres des premiers Chartreux* (Paris: Les Éditions du Cerf, 1962), p. 70, quoted in Brantley, *Reading*, p. 338, n. 12, trans. on p. 34.

49. Elizabeth Bailey, 'Raising the Mind to God: The Sensual Journey of Giovanni Morelli (1371–1444)', *Speculum*, 84 (2009), 984–1008 (p. 995).

50. Bailey, 'Raising', p. 996.

51. Bailey, 'Raising', p. 1006.

52. McGowan, *Real Gaze*, p. 7.

CHAPTER 8

Intellectual Memory and Desire in Augustine and Dante's *Paradiso*

Paola Ureni

In the famous *incipit* of T. S. Eliot's *The Burial of the Dead*, the terms 'memory' and 'desire' appear as a sort of oxymoron, next to each other in the text but pertaining to two separate spheres: 'April is the cruellest month, breeding | Lilacs out of the dead land, mixing | Memory and desire, stirring | Dull roots with spring rain.'[1] The verb 'mixing' signals the connection between two entities otherwise naturally unrelated because they refer to two different dimensions: memory concerns the lost past, and desire the soul's reaching for something unattainable.

The reader of Dante's *Paradiso* also encounters a separation between 'desire' and 'memory' at the very beginning of canto I: 'e vidi cose che ridire | né sa né può chi di là sù discende; | perché appressando sé al suo disire, | nostro intelletto si profonda tanto, | che dietro la memoria non può ire' [and have seen things which whosoever descends from up there has neither the knowledge nor the power to relate, because, as it draws near to its desire, our intellect enters so deep that memory cannot go back upon the track] (*Par.* I, 5–9).[2] These lines seem to indicate a relationship of non-correspondence between the poet's limited memory and the pilgrim's desire that will be fulfilled in the heavenly experience. There is an important conceptual distance between 'intelletto' and 'disire' on the one hand, and 'memoria' on the other hand. In his essay 'Perchè "dietro la memoria non può ire" (*Paradiso* I, 9)',[3] Bruno Nardi analyses these lines in order to prove that memory is a faculty separated from intellect and incapable of the deepest intellectual experience. According to Nardi, the limits of memory, as declared in line 9, refer to the Aristotelian localization of memory in the sensitive part of the soul. Hence, according to Nardi's interpretation, the pilgrim's Aristotelian memory is confined to a sensitive existence, and is therefore separated from the intellectual dimension of his highest desire, that is to experience the divine. However, Nardi refers both memory and intellect to Dante as protagonist in the poem. While Dante here certainly expresses the inadequacy of memory, he attributes this inadequacy not to the pilgrim but rather to the poet.[4]

In this essay I would like to suggest the existence in Dante's *Paradiso* of a different notion of memory in the character of Dante the traveller, a purely intellectual memory, which participates in the pilgrim's ascent through the heavenly spheres toward the beatific vision. If memory participates in the anagogical journey of Dante's *Paradiso*, then it certainly shares the intellectual dimension which defines the pilgrim's 'desire' as it is expressed in *Par.* I, 7. The gap between desire and memory posited at the beginning of *Paradiso* is bridged by the correspondence between memory and desire. The same intellectual dimension therefore encompasses both desire and memory. I will argue that intellectual notions of memory and desire go along with the pilgrim's intellectual path toward knowledge of the heavenly spheres (and ultimately of the Empyrean). Lino Pertile has shown that desire is the dynamic principle driving the whole *cantica*. Pertile considers desire mainly in two ways, the desire for knowledge and the desire for God.[5] While investigating the pattern of both types of desire, Pertile shows how the pilgrim's desire to know becomes integrated in the search for God, which is the ultimate goal and the sustaining force of the *Paradiso* as a whole.[6] Speaking specifically about the desire for God, Pertile writes: 'Quando giunge in cielo, l'anima non viene appagata una volta per sempre, il suo desiderio spento per l'eternità; nel momento in cui conosce il sommo bene, desiderio e appagamento raggiungono in lei un equilibrio, un'uguaglianza, che dura per sempre' [When the soul reaches heaven, it is not satisfied once and for all, nor is its desire extinguished for eternity; when the soul knows the supreme good, desire and fulfillment reach a balance, an equivalence which lasts forever].[7] In this dynamic of constantly renewed fulfillment, the soul enjoys its beatitude and the presence of God in a non-static, active condition. The faculties which participate in such a heavenly condition define the highest intellectual activity of the soul itself.

This essay investigates the possible existence and activity of memory as a faculty of the soul in its intellectual dimension; whence it follows that memory, besides being a sensitive power dependent upon sense perception, imagination, and the passing of time, can act as a purely intellectual power, in a condition of independence from any sensitive process and temporal sequence. In order to trace this type of memory in Dante's poem, I will explore the Augustinian notion of memory. Augustine defines his notion of memory across texts such as *Confessions* and *de Trinitate*, adding each time nuances that span from a definition of memory as a faculty related to the process of the formation of images, which derives from sense perception, right through to its definition as an entirely inward mental activity separated from any sensitive dimension. The *de Trinitate* is crucial for its treatment of the highest intellectual stage of the soul's epistemological path toward God. Furthermore, I will briefly show how, in Augustine, the activity of the Trinitarian structure of the soul is deeply intertwined with the dynamic principle of desire, which, as in Dante's *Paradiso*, is the moving force behind the soul's path toward knowledge and toward God. The Trinitarian structure impressed on the human soul bears the relationship of likeness between the human soul and God. The self-reflective activity of the trinity establishes a further correspondence between God and the soul, between the path of knowledge which leads to God and a path of self-knowledge which leads the soul towards its origin, its most intimate and perfect being. Finally, I will suggest a twofold reading of Dante's text, a philosophical approach through Augustine, which underscores the capacity of memory to partake in a broader intellectual ascent beyond the human condition, and a rhetorical approach, through the notion of *transsumptio* that focuses on the linguistic implications for the expression of such transcendent concepts in human terms.

In works such as the *Confessions* and *de Trinitate*, Augustine consistently locates memory in the rational soul. Augustinian memory, an essential part of the 'inner man', therefore contains, in its magnitude, everything known to the soul and, by an act of will, enables the soul to access truths not directly perceived by thought. The act of recollection is completely intellectual; it can have an image as its object, but need not. Functioning in the rational dimension, memory can contribute to direct knowledge. In his study *Augustine's Philosophy of Mind*, Gerard O'Daly considers Augustine's treatment of memory in the *Confessions*, distinguishing between, on the one hand, an empirical memory 'such as that of objects perceived by the five senses' and, on the other, 'a memory that does not deal in images of the things remembered'.[8] Interestingly, O'Daly's analysis of the *Confessions* links memory with the 'quest for a happy or a blessed life, which he [Augustine] identifies with a quest for God. It is, he believes, a universal desire.' O'Daly underscores how Augustine does not place desire for happiness in the empirical memory, since such desire 'is not a corporeal condition', but rather speaks of 'a concept of happiness in our memory'.[9] Along the lines of a memory independent of imagination and sensitive activity, O'Daly points out how 'Augustine's use of "memoria", in *Confessions* x extends the connotations of the word beyond any normal usage, so that it becomes practically equivalent to the sum total of one's conscious and unconscious awareness.'[10] As O'Daly indicates, this extended usage of *memoria* is also witnessed in Book XIV of *de Trinitate*, where memory becomes aligned with the soul's self-knowledge, according to the equation 'to remember oneself' equals 'to be present to oneself'. A close reading of the *de Trinitate* underscores how the emergence of such a non-empirical, rational memory is linked to the epistemological ascent of the soul's potencies toward an increasingly intellectual condition, right through to the Beatific vision. This *iter* of the soul signifies both the journey toward knowledge, which ultimately leads to God, and the reflective act of self-knowledge through which the soul regains its original likeness with God, both of which pertain to the anagogical course of the soul. Both Augustine's *de Trinitate* and Dante's *Comedy* present an anagogical journey based on the growth of the soul's potencies, a journey that parallels the intellectual growth and deepening of the soul's desire. As the soul's powers gradually increase until they become purely intellectual and completely independent of any sensitive knowledge, so does the soul's desire proceed toward real fulfillment in its highest object, God. In order to explore, through the presence of a purely rational memory, the possible link between the anagogical *iter* of the soul in the *de Trinitate*, and the similarly anagogical journey conveyed in Dante's *Comedy*, I will underscore the rise of memory as a rational power, as inseparable from intelligence and will in the trinity of the spirit (which mirrors the divine Trinity). Memory therefore partakes in a condition independent of human cognitive parameters, beyond human notions of space and time; a condition in which the creature returns to its perfect correspondence with the Creator.[11]

The ability to overcome sensory notions of space and time is what distinguishes the activity of the soul's faculties in the trinity of the spirit from the lower trinities of the soul. While in the lower trinities there is a distance between the formation of a memory and the deliberate act of recollection (which has the effect of linking memory to human time and hence to human frailty), the human spirit is, on the contrary, aware of itself through the simultaneous and constant activity of all three of its elements in a continuous presence. The spirit's constant self awareness and the simultaneous activity of its three elements are such that Augustine explains how 'it is always difficult to distinguish in [the mind] the memory of itself from the understanding of itself. For it would almost seem as if they were not two things, but two different names for one and the same thing, since they are so closely united in the mind that the one does not precede the other in time' (de Trinitate x, 12: 'difficile in ea [mente] dignoscitur memoria sui, et intelligentia sui. Quasi non sint haec duo, sed unum duobus vocalibus appelletur, sic apparet in ea re ubi valde ista conjuncta sunt, et aliud alio nullo praeceditur tempore').[12] The trinity of the spirit, being the highest form of the soul's epistemological ascent, is deeply linked to the process of fulfillment of the soul's highest desire for ultimate knowledge. Hence, memory and desire are no longer separated, but rather share the same intellectual dimension. Further examples of this are found in Book xv. Speaking of the trinity of the spirit which mirrors the divine Trinity, Augustine says:

> Quae tria in sua mente naturaliter diuinitus instituta quisquis uiuaciter perspicit et quam magnum sit in ea unde potest etiam sempiterna immutabilisque natura recoli, conspici, concupisci (reminiscitur per memoriam, intuetur per intellegentiam, amplectitur per dilectionem), profecto reperit illius summae trinitatis imaginem. (de Trinitate, xv, 20. 39)

> [But anyone who intelligently perceives that these three things are by nature divinely established in his own mind, and how great a thing is in it, where even an eternal and unchangeable nature can be recalled, beheld, and desired — remembers it by memory, contemplates it by his understanding, and embraces it by his love; certainly such a one discovers the image of the highest trinity.] [13]

In order to trace the presence of a memory-intelligence in Dante's *Comedy*, in particular the *Paradiso*, I will begin by examining Dante's reference to the Trinitarian structure of the human soul, and the three elements of memory, intelligence, and will. To this end, cantos xxiv and xxv of the *Purgatorio* become fundamental. In the latter canto, Statius's digression on the generation of the embryo and the formation of the fictive body in the afterlife provides certain evidence of Dante's awareness of the medical and theological debates of his time. Less obvious, but perhaps more important, is the relevance of this technical exposition to Dante's poetics. The long scientific digression clarifies the centrality of the ongoing analogy between procreation and poetic creation, appearing within the six cantos dedicated precisely to a discussion of poetry, to the definition of the 'dolce stil novo' [sweet new style], and to the crucial encounters between the pilgrim and Bonagiunta da Lucca, Guido Guinizzelli and Arnaut Daniel.

John Freccero has underscored a correspondence between the generation of the embryo and what might be called the generation of the poetic word in the act of writing.[14] According to this interpretation, the specific moment of the infusion of the rational soul by God in *Purg.* xxv corresponds to the divine inspiration of the poet's inner word in *Purg.* XXIV ('I' mi son un che, quando | Amor mi spira, noto ed a quel modo | ch'e' ditta dentro vo significando' [I am one who, when Love inspires me, takes note, and goes setting it forth after the fashion which he dictates within me] (*Purg.* XXIV, 52–54)). As God directly inspires ('spira') the rational soul into the embryo, so does *Amor* directly inspire (again, 'spira') the poet. The account of the infusion of the rational soul in *Purg.* XXV therefore becomes central to the meaning of both the single canto and the poem as a whole:

> lo motor primo a lui si volge lieto
> sovra tant'arte di natura, e spira
> spirito novo, di vertù repleto,
>   che ciò che trova attivo qui, tira
> in sua sustanzia, e fassi un'alma sola,
> che vive e sente e sé in sé rigira'. (*Purg.* XXV, 70–75)

> [the First Mover turns to it with joy over such art of nature, and breathes into it a new spirit replete with virtue, which absorbs that which is active there into its own substance, and makes one single soul which lives and feels and circles on itself.]

In the rational soul, the direct connection between man and God is the 'spirito novo', created directly by God and independent of anything outside of God. Christian Moevs clarifies the relationship of likeness between the intellectual soul and the divine dimension: 'Thus this soul not only "lives and feels" (*vive e sente*), through the powers of nutrition and sensation it has subsumed; it also "turns itself upon itself" (*sè in sè rigira*): like the angels, and the ultimate ontological principle itself, it is a power of self-awareness or consciousness or self-knowledge, a power to know all things as itself, and to know itself as (one with) the ground of all things.'[15] The same dynamics define poetic inspiration in *Purgatorio* XXIV. According to Freccero, the embryology of Statius's speech is assimilated to what Dante takes to be the unitary source of spiritual inspiration of both the soul of the foetus and the spirit of the text. In *Purgatorio* XXV, Statius discusses the separation of the soul from the body that occurs immediately after death as the moment in which the intellectual faculties are distinguished from the sensitive powers. In lines 82–84 Statius defines the rational soul as a coming together of memory, intellect, and will: 'l'altre potenze tutte quante mute; | memoria, intelligenza e volontade | in atto molto più che prima agute' [the other faculties all of them mute, but memory, intellect, and will far more acute in action than before] (*Purg.* XXV, 82–84). This definition immediately precedes the description of the formation of the aerial body, made of thin air, and again underscores the separation of the intellective faculties of the soul from the body.[16] Dante's quotation from the *de Trinitate* identifies the rational soul with the trinity of the Spirit, comprised of memory and will. Memory and will, according to Augustine, are characteristic of the highest part of the soul, where intelligence proceeds from memory, and will, as the third person of the Trinity, binds together both intelligence and memory.

The correspondence between the Augustinian trinity of the Spirit and the inner inspiration of the poet clarifies the role of intellectual memory in the *Comedy*. Retroactively, we may read canto XXV of the *Purgatorio* as an authorization to investigate of the presence of the Augustinian notion of memory in Dante's poem, specifically the third *cantica* of the *Paradiso*. Moreover, the connection with *Purgatorio* XXIV suggests that inner, rational memory participates in the process of poetic creation at the moment of inspiration. The faculty of memory, as part of the trinity of the Spirit, shares in the nature of the inner word as dictated, or rather breathed into, the poet by *Amore*.

Purgatorio XXIV and XXV illuminate the presence of intellectual memory in the *Comedy*, and, at the same time, allow us to relate it to the inspiration necessary for writing to take place. Memory must be separate from and independent of the sensitive activities of the soul in order to be consistent with the intellectual dimension of the pilgrim's journey in the *Paradiso*. In the fictive worlds of Hell and Purgatory, memory is linked to the sensitive soul. In the *Paradiso*, however, where the subject of the poem is the process of transcending the human realm ('trasumanare'), Dante represents the constant presence of purely intellectual time.

The ascent narrated in the *Paradiso* aims for direct intellectual vision and unmediated knowledge of the divine essence, such as that of which the pure angelic intelligences are capable. In this final *cantica*, the pilgrim's mind aspires to overcome its human limits and to reach perfect beatitude and ultimate knowledge in the contemplation of the Divine. This knowledge comes through only at the end, as Barański points out: 'Il carattere simbolico del Paradiso dantesco è il correlativo formale di quella struttura del "desiderio" che sostiene l'ultima cantica, di modo che il *Paradiso* resta permanentemente solo un "preludio" alla vera visione divina' [The symbolic character of Dante's *Paradiso* is the formal correlative of that structure of desire which sustains the last *cantica*; in this way the *Paradiso* remains simply a 'prelude' to the real divine vision].[17] The pilgrim reaches the 'vera visione divina' only in the final image of the *Comedy*, when his individual soul's desire will be fulfilled and will coincide perfectly with the desire of the universe, constantly fulfilled as it revolves around God. Freccero has solved the crux of this final image of the celestial wheel, and has shown the 'double' fulfillment of the soul that takes place in it. This fulfillment comes with the soul's inner rotation and with its participation in the rotation of the universe, and is diversified into 'disio' and 'velle', where 'disio' refers to the individual intellectual desire's satisfaction and 'velle' to the fulfillment of the universe in the enjoyment of God. Both movements participate in the single movement of the celestial wheel.[18] The gradual ascent of the mind, engendered by intellectual desire and made possible by divine Grace, is therefore best understood as a gradual strengthening of the human faculties, necessary in order for the pilgrim to be able to withstand the heavenly experience and the increasing proximity to the divine essence. This process of refinement, being purely intellectual, includes the Augustinian notion of rational memory.

Although the intimate connection between intellectual memory and will that is posited in *Purgatorio* XXV with an explicit reference to Augustine, does not appear elsewhere in the Dantean text, the subject and the language of the *Paradiso* imply an intellectual dimension which goes beyond human cognitive parameters. The blessed souls and the angels partake completely in the transcendent condition, while the pilgrim's journey is intended to show the gradations that mark the distance between the human and angelic conditions. The heavenly *iter* is a constant forward motion and, at the same time, an inward movement of self-knowledge which raises the soul to its highest intellectual potential. The strengthening of the intellectual powers breaks the link between the soul and its sensitive activity, therefore its human, earthly condition. Once the soul overcomes the human ('trasumanare'), it rediscovers the trace of its likeness to God in the deepest, most intimate recesses of itself, where, according to Augustine and Dante/Statius, memory, intellect, and will are found. Memory therefore actively participates in the journey, which is a recovery of the soul's original likeness to God.[19]

How does intellectual memory manifest itself in the pilgrim's experience as well as in the poetic text of the *Paradiso*? In other words, is there space for rational memory in the content as well as in the language of the *Paradiso*? Is there a rhetorical anagogical movement of the text, which parallels the anagogical movement of the soul through the heavens as well as within its own depths? Dante scholars have discussed extensively this problem of the poet's declared inability to convey the plenitude of the heavenly dimension, and the presence of the actual text of the *Paradiso* as a metaphor for the pilgrim's experience of that ineffable reality.[20] Freccero has argued that 'the representation points to no reality, however fictive, beyond itself. The structure of the *cantica* depends not upon a principle of *mimesis*, but rather upon metaphor: the creation of a totally new reality out of elements so disparate as to seem contradictory by any logic other than that of poetry.'[21] The written text of the third *cantica* therefore stands as a metaphor for the reality of Paradise. The principle of metaphor must therefore guide a reading of the *Paradiso*, as it links the poem's structural level and content to the level of its rhetorical search for the most appropriate expression of its transcendent subject. Poetry, in the *Paradiso*, demands the expression in human terms of the divine reality, which by definition goes beyond both the human condition and language.

Both philosophical and rhetorical concerns substantiate the medieval speculation on the problem of expressing the divine in human terms. As indicated by William Purcell in his essay, '*Transsumptio*: A Rhetorical Doctrine of the Thirteenth Century', the metaphorical principle of substitution is included in the much broader rhetorical tradition of *transsumptio*. Purcell defines the trope of *transsumptio* in medieval speculation (distinguishing it from metaphor)[22] through the analysis of the acceptable modes of expression in the discourse about the divine in Alexander of Hales and Thomas Aquinas. Through Alexander's *Summa theologica*, Purcell establishes a link between theology and *transsumptio*, positing *transsumptio* as the connection between the tropological and theological levels. Alexander designates both poetry and theology as transumptive (here in opposition to scientific modes of expression) thereby establishing a direct relationship between *transsumptio* and theology through poetic language.[23] *Transsumptio* becomes a way of expressing the divine, namely a rhetorical instrument capable of expressing subjects for which ordinary language is not sufficient. Focusing on the analysis of the main medieval rhetorical treatises,[24] Purcell shows how the notion of *transsumptio*, derived from classical trope in Quintilian, later expanded to encompass a dimension much broader than a simple equation with metaphor. He points out that, according to thirteenth-century rhetorical tradition, the trope of *transsumptio* subsumes several other tropes, among which are metaphor, allegory, antonomasia, onomatopoeia, synecdoche, and catachresis. Interestingly, *transsumptio* relies upon a syllogistic mode of reasoning, what Purcell calls 'a syllogistic pattern which connects expressions through intermediate terms'.[25] This syllogistic principle already signifies a rhetorical *iter* that develops from the connection of three or more linguistic elements and is finalized in figurative speech: 'In [Geoffrey of Vinsauf's] *Poetria nova*, *transsumptio* subsumes the tropes of metaphor, allegory, antonomasia, and onomatopoeia. The term "transsumptio" seems to refer to a syllogistic method of connecting words for figurative use.'[26] Moreover, syllogistic movement proper of *transsumptio* is gradual, so that, through the link provided by its intermediate terms, this trope allows progressive passage from one word to another not directly connected to the first. Furthermore, Purcell shows that the significance of *transsumptio* in medieval thought, specifically in John of Garland's work, goes beyond the role of a trope, overcoming the strictly stylistic dimension in order to be more directly connected with the creative act: 'It is significant that John includes *transsumptio* as a category of *inventio* rather than style. As in *Poetria nova* and in [Gervasius of Melkey's] *Ars poetica*, *transsumptio* appears to be a construct much broader than a trope.'[27]

In her analysis of the canzone 'Donne ch'avete intellecto d'amore' and other moments of the *Vita Nuova*, Maria Luisa Ardizzone shows that transumptive modes are fundamental in connecting human and divine realities. In Ardizzone's argument, *transsumptio* becomes the rhetorical mode through which Dante translates in alphabetical terms the mental language proper to the angelic intelligences. By investing Beatrice with the language of *transsumptio*, Dante transfers onto an earthly creature the rhetorical modes proper to the praise of the divine.[28] Ardizzone investigates the usage of *transsumptio* by Boncompagno da Signa in the *Rhetorica Novissima*, demonstrating that Boncompagno uses *transsumptio* in its broader sense. Like the authors of the *poetrie* mentioned by Purcell, Boncompagno sees *transsumptio* as inclusive of other tropes such as allegory or metaphor. Through *transsumptio* something is said and something else is understood; more specifically, 'transsumptio est queddam natural velamen sub quo rerum secreta occultius et secretius proferentur' [*Transsumptio* is a certain natural veil, behind which the secrets of things are more secretly pronounced].[29] Ardizzone underscores how, according to Boncompagno, *transsumptio* can establish a relation between the human and celestial conditions, in that it is the necessary mode of expression for subjects that are beyond human comprehension and language.[30] *Transsumptio* was, in fact, invented directly by the Creator, in the perfect state of the Earthly Paradise.[31] According to Boncompagno, therefore, *transsumptio* belongs to the dimension in which God created man in His own image, the dimension of the perfect original likeness, of which a trace is found in the most intimate depths of the human soul. According to the Augustinian tradition, this is precisely the place in which memory is one and the same with intelligence and will, and where the inner word is born. Since it expresses itself in mental images, *transsumptio* becomes an appropriate expressive mode for subjects that precede the formation of language.

In the last part of my essay, I would like to trace the possible presence of both of these philosophical and rhetorical tracks, namely the Augustinian theories of memory and the tradition of *transsumptio*, in the text of the *Paradiso*. At present, this is still work in progress. If, as I have argued, memory, intelligence, and will are the defining powers of the rational soul, then the several references in Dante's *Paradiso* to the strengthening of the pilgrim's rational powers become central to an interpretation of the third *cantica*. At the same time, the actual text of this *cantica* can be thought of as a transumptive mode of expression for the divine content of Paradise. The presence of specific tropes, subsumed under the broader notion of *transsumptio*, therefore reveals Dante's use of transumptive modes in order to express one thing and to understand (*intelligere*) something else, something deeper. This is the precise project of the language of the *Paradiso*.

In order to introduce what I believe is the most significant example of possible transumptive language in the *Paradiso*, I would like to first briefly reiterate the philosophical identification between memory and mind/intellect. While there are more explicit references to the term 'memory' or to the action of remembering in the text, the identification of memory and mind/intellect require us to broaden our search to the entire semantic field related to mind, intellect or vision (clearly intended as intellectual vision). The text of the third *cantica* substantiates the link which medieval tradition establishes between vision and knowledge.[32] The angelic intelligences and the blessed souls satisfy their desire for God (which corresponds to their highest satisfaction) in the direct, unchangeable vision of the divine. The 'face to face' beatific vision, through which God is known, is inaccessible from within human parameters which remain linked to the sensitive activities of the soul. The gradual heavenly ascent increases the pilgrim's intellectual powers and knowledge through his ability to see, sustain, and enjoy heavenly visions. The linguistic references to the experience of heavenly visions become therefore important indicators of the pilgrim's intellectual strengthening. As a matter of fact, in *Paradiso* I, the poet conveys the highest heavenly experience with the verb 'vidi' [I saw];[33] and throughout the poem the numerous repetitions of the verb 'vidi' (as well as the use of synonymous terms such as 'mirare' [to gaze/look upon]), often introduce heavenly visions and imply the idea the pilgrim's ascent toward intellectual knowledge.[34] Alongside references to the failures of the mind's potencies, there are passages expressing the higher degree of purely intellectual power reached by the pilgrim, which manifests itself as a higher ability to sustain and understand the heavenly visions. Central, among others, are the passages from canto XXX. In the following verses, Dante first describes the disorientation of his sight:

> Come subito lampo che discetti
> li spiriti visivi, sì che priva
> da l'atto l'occhio di più forti obietti,
>   così mi circumfulse luce viva;
> e lasciommi fasciato di tal velo
> del suo fulgor, che nulla m'appariva. (*Paradiso* XXX, 46–51)

[As a sudden flash of lighting which scatters the visual spirits so that it robs the eye of the sight of the clearest objects, so round about me there shone a vivid light and left me so swathed in the veil of its effulgence that nothing was visible to me.]

A few lines later, the poet points out the strengthening of the pilgrim's faculties as he becomes closer to the experience of the Divine:

> Non fur più tosto dentro a me venute
> queste parole brievi, ch'io compresi
> me sormontar di sopr'a mia virtute;
>   e di novella vista mi raccesi
> tale, che nulla luce è tanto mera,
> che li occhi miei non si fosser difesi. (*Par.* xxx, 55–60)

[No sooner had these brief words come within me than I comprehended that I was surmounting beyond my own power, and such new vision was kindled in me that there is no light so bright that my eyes could not have withstood it.]

The lexical choice of the verb 'kindled' ('riaccendersi'/'mi raccesi'), which here renews the pilgrim's ability to see transforming his visual faculty into a higher intellectual power, recalls the terminology proper to the continuous rekindling of intellectual desire through the heavenly ascent. In the last canto of the *Paradiso*, the triad mind-vision-kindling is employed again in a more directly transumptive mode. The pilgrim's 'mente' [mind], strengthened in its intellective powers beyond the human condition, is continuously rekindled as it stretches towards the experience of the Divine, which will constitute the fulfillment of its highest intellectual desire: 'Così la mente mia, tutta sospesa, | mirava fissa, immobile e attenta, | e sempre di mirar faceasi accesa' [Thus my mind, all rapt, was gazing, fixed, motionless and intent, ever enkindled by its gazing] (*Par.* xxxiii, 97–99). The increasing proximity to the Divine denotes an increasing proximity to the desired perfect knowledge which transcends human limits and becomes immediate understanding and beatitude in the direct vision of God. This knot of intellectual relations comprehends the specific notion of rational memory, and allows for the equivalence of rational memory with unmediated knowledge of the heavenly dimension. The rhetorical structure of the *terzina* recalls the syllogistic character of transumptive language. If this is the case, Dante uses this transumptive figurative mode precisely in order to express the interplay between the increase in the pilgrim's intellectual powers and his desire, caught in its constant motion of fulfillment and rekindling. Lines 97–99 of *Paradiso* xxxiii express the continuous rekindling of the mind stretching toward the beatific vision. Line 97 introduces the word 'mente' [mind], that knot of intellective powers (which includes the rational memory) strengthened beyond the human dimension in order to be able to sustain the vision/experience of the Divine. Line 99 then closes the *terzina* with the adjective 'accesa', which is referred to the mind, and figuratively expresses the constant renewal of the mind's desire for the heavenly vision. The connection between the first element, that is the mind, and the last, that is the adjective 'accesa', passes through the verb 'mirava', which defines both the act of the mind, at line 98, and the object of the mind's desire at line 99. The action of 'mirare' functions therefore as an intermediate term between the opening element of the *terzina*, 'mente', and its closing adjective 'accesa.' In this way, the poet not only rhetorically connects two elements through a third term; he also renders the image of the heavenly mental *itinerarium* using the language of *transsumptio*. The result is a rhetorical pattern which overcomes an exclusively stylistic dimension in order to partake of the level of the *inventio*, and functions as a linguistic compromise between the transcendent content of the *Paradiso* and its human expression.

Notes to Chapter 8

1. T. S. Eliot, 'The Burial of the Dead', from *The Waste Land*, in *The Annotated Waste Land with Eliot's Contemporary Prose* (New Haven, CT: Yale University Press, 2005), p. 57.

2. Translations of the *Commedia* are from Dante Alighieri, *The Divine Comedy*, trans. and with a commentary by Charles S. Singleton, 3 vols (Princeton, NJ: Princeton University Press, 1970–75).

3. See Bruno Nardi, 'Perchè "dietro la memoria non può ire" (*Paradiso* I, 9)', in Bruno Nardi, *'Lecturae' e altri studi danteschi*, ed. by Rudy Abardo (Florence: Le Lettere, 1990), pp. 267–76.

4. Robert Hollander, in his commentary to the *Paradiso*, refers to Nardi's essay, and follows Nardi's definition of 'memoria' at line 9 as the Aristotelian faculty excluded from the transcendent condition of *Paradiso*. See Dante Alighieri, *Paradiso*, trans. by Robert and Jean Hollander, intro. and notes by Robert Hollander (New York: Doubleday, 2007). In order to support Nardi's position, Hollander cites the *Epistle to Cangrande* where the explanation of *Par*. I, 5–9 starts with these words: 'Et reddit causam dicens: "quod intellectus in tantum profundat se" in ipsum "desiderium suum", quod est Deus, "quod memoria sequi non potest" [And he explains the reason saying: 'because the intellect enters so deeply' into 'its own desire', which is God, 'that memory cannot follow the same path'] (*Epistola* XIII, 78, in Dante Alighieri, *Opere minori*, 2 vols (Milan and Naples: Riccardo Ricciardi Editore, 1979), II). This quotation from the *Epistola* introduces the question of the limitations of memory, but the real explanation of the lines follows immediately after: 'Ad que intelligenda sciendum est quod intellectus humanus in hac vita, propter connaturaliter et affinitatem quam habet ad substantiam intellectualem separatam, quando elevator, in tantum elevator, ut memoria post reditum deficit propter trascendisse humanum modum' [In order to understand those things, one needs to know that the human intellect, in this life, because of the likeness it has with the separate substance, when it [the intellect] ascends, it ascends so much that, upon return, memory loses some of its power since it has transcended the human condition] (*Epistola* XIII, 78). The words from the *Epistola* are clear: 'post reditum' refers 'memoria' not to the intellectual experience of the pilgrim in *Paradiso*, but rather to the experience of the poet who, back on earth, can no longer recuperate that heavenly dimension.

5. Elena Lombardi underscores how, in the *Convivio*, 'Dante describes desire as a pyramidal structure, where the base is the ultimate desire (for God) and the tip the minimal desire'. Lombardi also designates knowledge and God as 'the main tracks of desire in Dante's poem'. See Elena Lombardi, *The Syntax of Desire: Language and Love in Augustine, the Modistae, Dante* (Toronto, ON, and London: University of Toronto Press, 2007), p. 161.

6. With this aim, Pertile analyses the lines from *Par*. IV, 124–26, about the mind's desire for truth and knowledge, which lead to God: 'Io veggio già che giammai non si sazia | nostro intelletto, se 'l ver non lo illustra | di fuor dal qual nessun vero si spazia. | Posasi in esso come fera in lustra, | tosto che giunto l'ha; e giugner puollo: | se non, ciascun disio sarebbe *frustra*' [Well do I see that never can our intellect be wholly satisfied unless that Truth shine on it, beyond which no truth has range. Therein it rests, as a wild beast in his lair, so soon as it has reached it; and reach it can, else every desire would be *in vain*]. Pertile concludes his analysis of these lines, and of the notion of the desire to know, stating: 'In realtà, anche il desiderio di sapere è parte integrale della ricerca di Dio che sostiene tutta la terza cantica e, come ogni dubbio ritarda strategicamente la perfetta felicità che verrà alla fine, così ogni acquisto di conoscenza in parte l'anticipa e assicura' [In reality, even the desire to know is an integral part of the search for God which sustains the whole third canticle and, as any doubt strategically delays the perfect beatitude which will come at the end, so every achievement of knowledge partly anticipates and guarantees it]: Lino Pertile, *La punta del disio: Semantica del desiderio nella 'Commedia'* (Fiesole: Cadmo, 2005), p. 152. Translation is my own.

7. Pertile, *La punta del disio*, p. 145. Translation is my own.

8. Gerard O'Daly, *Augustine's Philosophy of Mind* (Berkeley and Los Angeles: University of California Press, 1987), p. 202. On Augustinian speculation about memory, especially with reference to the *Confessions*, see also the commentary to the *Confessions* by James O'Donnell: Augustine, *Confessions*, with a commentary by James Joseph O'Donnell, 3 vols (Oxford: Clarendon Press, 1992). On memory as part of the trinity of the spirit, see also Lewis Ayres, *Augustine and the Trinity* (Cambridge: Cambridge University Press, 2010). For another important recent study of Augustine, see Brian Stock, *Augustine's Inner Dialogue: The Philosophical Soliloquy in Late Antiquity* (Cambridge: Cambridge University Press, 2010). On the specific relationship between Augustine and Dante, see Simone Marchesi's recent *Dante and Augustine: Linguistics, Poetics, Hermeneutics* (Toronto: University of Toronto Press, 2011).

9. O'Daly, *Augustine's Philosophy of Mind*, p. 203.

10. O'Daly, *Augustine's Philosophy of Mind*, p. 204.

11. In Book XIV of the *de Trinitate*, referring to human notions of space, Augustine speaks of the spirit that turns inwardly not through spatial movement but rather through that which he refers to as 'conversion': 'It remains, therefore, that its sight is something belonging to its nature, and the mind is recalled to it when it thinks of itself, not as it were by a movement in space, but by an incorporeal conversion' (*de Trinitate* XIV, 6: 'Proinde restat ut aluquid pertinens ad ejus naturam sit conspectus ejus, et in eam, quando se cogitate, non quasi per loci spatium, sed incorporeal conversion revocetur').

12. Furthermore, in Book XIV, Augustine writes: 'Wherefore, as in past things, that is called memory which makes it possible for them to be recalled and remembered, so in a present thing, which the mind is to itself, that is not unreasonably to be called memory, by which the mind is present to itself, so that it can be understood by its own thought, and both can be joined together by the love of itself' (*de Trinitate* XIV, 11: 'Quapropter sicut in rebus praeteritis ea memoria dicitur, qua fit ut valeant recoli et recordari: sic in re praesenti quod sibi est mens, memoria sine absurditate dicenda est, qua sibi praesto est ut sua cogitatione posit intelligi, et utrumque sui amore conjungi'). Translations are from Augustine, *On the Trinity. Books 8–15*, ed. by Gareth B. Matthews, trans. by Stephen McKenna (Cambridge: Cambridge University Press, 2002).

13. It is here necessary to pay specific attention to Augustinian terminology. While the same adjective *immutabilis* guarantees again the transcendental condition to which the soul approximates itself under the trinity of the spirit, the verb 'desired' expresses the activity of the third person of that trinity, *voluntas*: the Latin term is *concupisci*, which often alludes to physical rather than intellectual desire, and therefore negatively connotes desire itself. The Augustinian vocabulary of desire is interestingly fluid (see Lombardi, *The Syntax of Desire*, p. 26), and the philosopher reverses the more typical use of terms such as *concupiscere* from a physical, hence sense-related meaning, in favour of an intellectual one which is independent of the senses. In the *Enarrationes in Psalmos*, Augustine distinguishes *laudabilis concupiscentia* from *damnabilis concupiscentia*: depending on its object, *concupiscentia* can even conduct the soul towards God's kingdom: 'concupiscentia sapientiae conducit ad regnum'. See *Enarratio in Psalmum* CXVIII, sermo VIII (*Patrologia Latina*, 35).

14. John Freccero, 'Manfred's Wounds and the Poetics of the *Purgatorio*', in *Dante: The Poetics of Conversion*, ed. by Rachel Jacoff (Cambridge, MA: Harvard University Press, 1986), pp. 195–208. Recent contributions to the analysis of Statius's digression include: Manuele Gragnolati, *Experiencing the Afterlife: Soul and Body in Dante and Medieval Culture* (Notre Dame, IN: University of Notre Dame Press, 2005); Zygmunt Barański, '"Per *similitudine* di abito scientifico": Dante, Cavalcanti and the Sources of Medieval "Philosophical" Poetry', in *Science and Literature in Italian Culture*, ed. by Pierpaolo Antonello and Simon A. Gilson (Oxford: Legenda, 2004), pp. 14–52; Vittorio Bartoli and Paola Ureni, 'Controversie medico-biologiche in tema di generazione umana nel XXV del Purgatorio', *Studi danteschi*, 68 (2003), 83–111, and 'La dottrina di Galeno in "sangue perfetto" (*Purg.* XXV 37)', *Studi danteschi*, 70 (2005), 335–44; Jennifer Fraser, 'Dante/ *Fante*: Embryology in Purgatory and Paradise', in *Dante and the Unorthodox: The Aesthetics of Transgression*, ed. by James Miller (Waterloo, ON: Wilfrid Laurier University Press, 2005), pp. 290–309; Simon A. Gilson, 'The Anatomy and Physiology of the Human Body in the *Commedia*', in *Dante and the Human Body: Eight Essays*, ed. by John C. Barnes and Jennifer Petrie

(Dublin: Four Courts Press, 2007), pp. 11–42; Joseph Ziegler, 'The Scientific Context of Dante's Embryology', in *Dante and the Human Body*, as previous, pp. 61–88.

15. Christian Moevs, *The Metaphysics of Dante's* Comedy (Oxford: Oxford University Press, 2005), p. 127.

16. Manuele Gragnolati has given a thorough and significant analysis of the formation of the fictive body in his *Experiencing the Afterlife*.

17. Zygmunt Barański, *Dante e i segni: Saggi per una storia intellettuale di Dante Alighieri* (Naples: Liguori, 2000), p. 73. Translation is my own.

18. See John Freccero, 'The Final Image: *Paradiso* XXXIII, 144', in *Dante: The Poetics of Conversion*, pp. 245–57. On the different interpretations of the final image of the celestial wheel, see Pertile, 'L'ultima immagine', in *La punta del disio*, pp. 265–81.

19. The intimate connection between the heavenly journey to the Empyrean and the inner journey of knowledge of the self constitutes the paradisiacal experience. On the act of self-consciousness of the soul in the heavenly dimension, Christian Moevs has written: 'Un'intelligenza creata raggiunge l'Empireo quando capisce che l'unica realtà ad esistere in senso assoluto è la pura coscienza, che dà essere a ciò che vede' [A created intelligence reaches the Empyrean when it understands that the only reality which exists in an absolute sense is pure consciousness, which gives 'being' to what it sees] (translation is my own). Furthermore, Moevs links the self-reflective act of consciousness with the creative act, and writes the following on the final section of Paradiso XXIX: 'Questa è la funzione di *Paradiso* XXIX, con il discorso finale sulla creazione, che tratta appunto di come il mondo nasce dall'amore, dalla riflessività della coscienza' [This is the function of *Paradiso* XXIX, with the final discourse on creation, which deals with the birth of the world from love, from the reflexivity of consciousness]. See Christian Moevs, '"Al divino dall'umano": *Paradiso* XXVII–XXVIII–XXIX', in *Esperimenti danteschi: 'Paradiso' 2010*, ed. by Tommaso Montorfano (Genoa: Marietti, 2010), p. 279. (Translations are mine.) The self-reflective act of consciousness as a creative act, and the relationship of likeness between the most intimate, highest part of the intellective soul and God, find their analogue in the Trinity. As the act of self-consciousness of the Godhead, the Trinity is the source of all creation, as we see in the opening of *Paradiso* X: 'Guardando nel suo Figlio con l'Amore | Che l'uno e l'altro etternalmente spira, | lo primo e ineffabile Valore, | quanto per mente e per loco si gira, | con tant'ordine fè, ch'esser non puote | sanza gustar di lui chi ciò rimira' [Looking upon His Son with the love which the One and Other eternally breathe forth, the primal and ineffable Power made everything that revolves through the mind or through space with such order that he who contemplates it cannot but taste of Him] (*Par.* X, 1–6). As shown by Augustine in the *de Trinitate*, the image of the divine Trinity is impressed upon the human soul, in accordance with the direct correspondence of memory with the Father, intelligence with the Son, and will with the Holy Spirit. It follows logically that the trinity of the spirit is the act of self-consciousness of its three elements, namely memory, intelligence, and will. Memory is present in the soul's intellectual ascent, which is moved by desire; it is also a rational power of the *anima intellectiva*, that is the *pars animae* which carries the closest image of the original perfect likeness with God. As a rational power of the soul, memory partakes of the divine dimension of creation/inspiration. Just as the divine Trinity creates *ab eterno*, the rational powers of the soul, which Statius defines as memory, intelligence, and will, inspired by God, create the poetic text.

20. See for example Peter Hawkins, *Dante's Testaments: Essays in Scriptural Imagination* (Stanford, CA: Stanford University Press, 1999); Giuseppe Ledda, *La guerra della lingua: Ineffabilità, retorica e narrativa nella 'Commedia' di Dante* (Ravenna: Longo, 2002).

21. Freccero, *Dante: The Poetics of Conversion*, p. 222. Lina Bolzoni reiterates this interpretation while speaking of the structure of the *Paradiso* in her essay 'Dante o della memoria appassionata', *Lettere Italiane*, 60 (2008), 169–93. See also Zygmunt Barański, *Dante e i segni*, p. 72; Lino Pertile, 'Paradiso: A Drama of Desire', in *Word and Drama in Dante: Essays on the 'Divina Commedia'*, ed. by John C. Barnes e Jennifer Petrie (Dublin: Irish Academic Press, 1993) pp. 143–80 (pp. 145–46).

22. See William M. Purcell, '*Transsumptio*: A Rhetorical Doctrine of the Thirteenth Century', *Rhetorica*, 5.4 (1987), 369–411. On the importance of *transsumptio* see also Fiorenzo Forti, 'La transumptio nei dettatori bolognesi e in Dante', in *Dante e Bologna nei tempi di Dante*, ed. by La Facoltà di Lettere e Filosofia dell'Università di Bologna (Bologna: Commissione per i Testi di Lingua, 1967), pp. 127–49.

23. This is the passage by Alexander of Hales, as reported by Purcell: 'Onmis modus poeticus est inartificialis sive non scientialis, quia est modus historicus vel transumptus, qui quidam non competent arti; sed theologicus modus est poeticus vel historicus vel parabolicus; ergo non est artificialis' [No poetic mode of representation is in accordance with the rules of art or science, because poetry is either an historical mode of representation or a transumptive one; neither pertains to art. But the theological mode is poetic, or historical, or parabolic. Therefore, it is not artificial]: Alexander of Hales, *Summa theologica*, ed. by P. Bernardi Klumper (Florence: S. Bonaventure, 1924), 7–8, cited in Purcell, '*Transsumptio*', p. 397.

24. Purcell refers especially to Geoffrey of Vinsauf's *Poetria Nova*, Gervasius of Melkey's *Ars poetica*, John of Garland's *De arte prosayca, metrica, et rhitmica*, and Eberhard the German's *Laborintus*. See Purcell, '*Transsumptio*, p. 375.

25. Purcell, '*Transsumptio*', p. 374.

26. Purcell, '*Transsumptio*', p. 380.

27. Purcell, '*Transsumptio*', p. 391.

28. See Maria Luisa Ardizzone, *Dante, Il paradigma intellettuale: Un'inventio degli anni fiorentini* (Florence: Olschki, 2011), especially chapters I and II.

29. Boncompagno da Signa, *Rhetorica Novissima*, in *Scripta Anecdota Glossatorum*, ed. by A. Gaudenzi (Bologna: 1896), p. 281. Translation is my own.

30. See Ardizzone, *Dante*, pp. 90–91.

31. See Boncompagno, *Rhetorica Novissima*, p. 286.

32. On the relation between vision and knowledge and its broad philosophical background, see Giorgio Stabile, 'Teoria della visione come teoria della conoscenza', *Micrologus*, 5 (1997), 225–46.

33. See *Par.* I, 5–6, which I quoted at the beginning of my essay: 'e vidi cose che ridire | nè sa nè può chi di là sù discende' [and have seen things which whosoever descends from up there has neither the knowledge nor the power to relate].

34. See, for example, *Par.* XXX, 61: 'E vidi lume in forma di rivera | fluvido di fulgore, intra due rive | dipinte di mirabil primavera' [And I saw a light in form of a river glowing tawny between two banks painted with marvelous spring]. In the same canto, 'vidi' again expresses the pilgrim's experience of Beatrice's beauty, which transcends human perception: 'La bellezza ch'io vidi si trasmoda | non pur di là da noi, ma certo io credo | che solo il suo fattor tutta la goda' [The beauty I beheld transcends measure not only beyond our reach, but I truly believe that He alone who made it can enjoy it at all] (*Par.* XXX, 19–21).

CHAPTER 9

Sexualities and Knowledges in *Purgatorio* XXVI and *Inferno* V

Marguerite Waller

In this essay, I will focus on the reconfiguration in *Purgatorio* XXVI of the poetics of eroticism as Dante presents the poets of the Italian lyric tradition themselves confronting this question. I will then use this reading to reread and reconsider what passes for sexual desire within the darkness and tumult of the Second Circle of Hell. In both instances, Dante's question to Francesca concerning how she came to *know* her desire resonates very powerfully. Desiring and knowing, sexualities and knowledges, emerge as so fundamentally interimplicated in both these cantos that the geometry of submitting reason to desire ('la ragion sommettono al talento'; *Inf.* V, 37) (or, for that matter, desire to reason, as the inhabitants of Hell's First Circle appear to have done) becomes untenable, opening the way toward a different metaphysics in which such oppressive binaries do not take shape.

Contexts

Recent scholarship on the nature and status of the human body in Dante's afterlife is unanimous concerning the importance of reading this body contextually. In her magisterial essays on *Inferno* V, Teodolinda Barolini embeds the passion of Paolo and Francesca within the rich intertextual matrix of the Italian lyric tradition and the cruel sociopolitical realities of Romagnolo power politics and dynastic marriages.[1] Manuele Gragnolati emphasizes the fluid *re*contextualizations performed by the poem itself in its different renderings of the relation between body and soul in the Infernal and Purgatorial treatments of gluttony.[2] Writing about the treatment of bodies in the fifteenth-century illuminations of *Paradiso* by Sienese artist Giovanni di Paolo, art historian Benjamin David urges that we read Dante's paradisal poetics and Giovanni's paradisal images in terms of each other in order to appreciate how Giovanni's 'ambivalent intersections' of narrative and simile reopen the plural meanings of Dante's text, while Dante's text assuages concerns, such as those of John Pope-Hennessy, about Giovanni's conflation of narrative and figural images.[3] Gary Cestaro finds the intersection between the history of the figure of Lady Grammar and the 'grammar of the nursing body' crucial to reading not only Dante's images of bodies but also the heterodoxy of the philosophy of language developed in the *Commedia*.[4]

In recent feminist and queer theory the nexus of language and the body has emerged as a particularly productive location from which to investigate the deployment of categories of gender and sexuality in the realms of philosophy, ideology, and social organization. Eve Kosofsky Sedgwick, Elizabeth Spelman, Judith Butler, and other feminist thinkers, have laid out the deep interimplications of heteronormative sexuality and Western epistemology from Plato and Aristotle to the present day. Their work has complicated our relations to representations of sexuality, alerting us to the limits of our assumptions and interpretations.[5] Not surprisingly, a growing company of scholars, including Barolini and Cestaro, have begun reading the *Commedia* in this context as well. Rachel Jacoff, Regina Psaki, Jeffrey Schnapp, and this author, among others, have focused specifically on the poem's presentations of sex, sexuality, sexual desire, and the sexual body.[6] As these discussions continue in the emerging contexts of postcolonial and posthuman theory, a correlative project presents itself. Denotations and connotations that even feminist/queer theory may have taken for granted lose their stability as the epistemological contexts within which they have been understood lose their appearance of cultural and transhistorical universality. What happens epistemologically when the referents of 'sex', or 'sexuality', are themselves called into question?

Despite the many feminist and queer critiques of Western epistemology now available, it remains mysterious how actually to read, to think, and to feel in ways that challenge the very ground of our *sensoria*. I discovered the cultural specificity of my own understanding of sexuality in conversation with a Nigerian-American feminist, Obioma Nnaemeka, who pointed out that what US academic feminist theorists meant by the term 'sex' had no translation in her Igbo culture.[7] Another Nigerian, Oyeronke Oyewumi, corroborates that the same holds true for Yoruba categories. The gender category 'woman', Oyewumi demonstrates, is an artefact of colonialism, particularly the imposition of nineteenth- and twentieth-century British political, economic, and judicial systems.[8] Becoming 'women', she notes, has 'inferiorized' female members of formerly 'corporate' peoples and rendered them economically and judicially 'invisible'[9] — an analysis corroborated by Virginia Woolf in her delineations of the inferiorized position of even the most privileged women in imperial Great Britain.[10]

Sharing this postcolonial feminist optic, pre-Colombian scholar Sylvia Marcos contrasts European binary oppositional constructions of gender and sexuality with 'the feminine-masculine dual unity' fundamental to the creation, regeneration, and sustenance of the cosmos in pre-Colombian Mesoamerican thinking.[11] The Mesoamerican dual genders are entirely relational and conceived of as a continuum rather than as the discontinuous, polarized and hierarchized male–female opposition still current in the cultures of the West. As Marcos notes: '[W]e can never infer any categorizing of one pole as "superior" to the other.'[12] The ideal toward which this cosmos, including its human inhabitants, strives is a kind of balance or equilibrium rather than permanence or stasis. Gender difference and sexual desire are the current of energy, the movement, that animates all the dimensions and modalities of this cosmos; they keep everyone and everything interrelated and in process. Marcos describes the corporeal body within this schema as 'a vortex generated by the dynamic confluence of multiple entities, both material and immaterial and often contradictory that combine and recombine in endless play.'[13] This notion of the porous body underlies the practices, continuing today, of traditional healers or *curanderas*. It is a body that does not lend itself to either medical or sexual objectification.

One more context could be added to these West African and Mesoamerican examples. As a prelude to the following discussion of Dante's figuration of sexualities and sexual bodies in relation to the production of 'intellectual' knowledge, the self-colonization of Europe itself should also be taken into consideration. Marcos notes that the modern-day practices of *curanderas* are the result of a syncretism between indigenous Mexican and early modern European healing knowledges, the latter imported by sixteenth-century Spanish conquistadors.[14] That is, in the New World we find survivals of a non-academic 'folk' culture (whose importance in the *Commedia* I will return to) that was forcibly suppressed, at the cost of the lives of possibly millions of women, during the articulation and consolidation of religious orthodoxies and notions of nation, person, and science that occurred unevenly but relentlessly in Europe, beginning in the fifteenth century.[15] Nation- and empire-building involve the subjugation of the knowledges and sexualities of domestic no less than foreign 'others'.

These contexts support Regina Psaki's critiques of the notions of sex and the body that until relatively recently Dante scholarship has projected onto the *Commedia*. Psaki finds a 'tendency to delimit the medieval within a set of parameters that we will not allow the period to transgress'. Evidence that does not fit our assumptions about how medieval culture differed from our own, she argues, has been distorted, explained away, or discarded altogether.[16] Complementary to the 'othering' tendency, Naomi Schor has alerted us, would be a tendency toward 'saming' in which readers assume that referents for such terms as 'sex', 'body', 'erotic', and 'divine' can be stabilized, either within the *Commedia* or transhistorically.[17] If a growing number of contemporary readers agree that sexual love inhabits the sacred in the poem, does that mean that we 'know' what 'sex' and 'sacred' mean? And what happens to other binary pairs to which this pair is closely linked, pairs such as 'desire and intellect', 'body and soul', 'material and spiritual', 'woman and man'? What happens to binary thinking itself when fundamental oppositions between sex and the sacred, body and soul, become blurred?

Purgatorio XXVI and the 'male body in crisis'

One of the more striking attributes of the ant-like files of figures of *Purgatorio* XXVI, hastening back and forth in opposite directions, briefly kissing, then weeping and shouting out their respective chants, is that they appear composed only of male figures. The contrast with *Inferno* V, whose flocks and files of the lustful are not merely co-ed, but seemingly dominated by females, already presents a puzzle to which we will have to return. What separates the two purgatorial cohorts from one another appears to be a distinction without a difference between males who erotically desired females and males who erotically desired males, although

Prue Shaw reads them more particularly as the 'heterosexual lustful and the homosexuals', making what has come in our own day to be called 'homosexuality' a disordered version, akin to lust, of what has come to be called 'heterosexuality'.[18] In order not to subordinate any sexuality to any other sexuality, for the moment, I would like instead to use Eve Sedgwick's term 'homosocial' to encompass both these groups.[19] This term is just as anachronistic as any others available to us, but Sedgwick's neologism for male–male bonds that are politically, socially, and emotionally primary (regardless of sexual partnering) and which enable men to stabilize hierarchical relationships with one another while collectively dominating women anticipates the intensely political significance that the canto gives to both cohorts.[20] The poem's own complex articulation of the distinction between these two groups quickly leads us into deep waters, where gender categories themselves become fluid and the ontology of the desiring, sexual 'body' uncertain.

The very desire that has gotten Dante's poem underway, sexual desire between male and female, is figured here as singularly 'perverse'. As the pilgrim watches intently, the two groups come together and, after greeting one another by kissing, try to out-shout each other, one group, the first Dante encounters, crying, 'Ne la vacca entra Pasife, | perchè 'l torello a sua lussuria corra!' [Into the cow enters Pasiphaë, so that the bull may run to her lust! (translation mine)] (*Purg.* XXVI, 41–42).[21] As he later learns from the figure of the poet Guido Guinizzelli, his 'native informant' on this terrace, this group consists of males who desired females. But how might a female-desiring male be related to the female sexual transgressor Pasiphaë, who became the mother, via interspecies copulation, of the Minotaur, the hybrid creature that in *Inferno* XII served to introduce the circles of the violent? The recollection of the story of Pasiphaë in the cries of this cohort of lustful souls seems to imply, shockingly, that the articulations of male–female sexual desire by these erotic love poets were not grounded in either biology or gender.[22] That is, in twentieth-century terms, their desire was neither 'natural', nor particularly 'masculine'. It was not politically neutral either. Though this complex figure offers a startlingly literal image of the objectification or reification of the female body, the contorted figure of the queen Pasiphaë, masquerading as a cow, links the objectification of the female sexual body, not with 'men' *per se*, but with power politics. The story arises in multiple ways out of Pasiphaë's ambivalent position as a female member of the ruling family of Crete, which placed her at the mercy of a conflict between her husband Minos and the god Poseidon, but also gave her access to the talents of her husband's craftsman/artist Daedalus, who built the wooden cow that enabled her to have sex with a bull. As we will also see in the case of Francesca, Dante is deeply interested in the paradoxes of gender and class and uses upper class women's contradictory position as privileged and powerless as a point of entry into a complex unfolding of the violence of political and epistemological sovereignty.

The falling out between Poseidon and Minos occurred when the god sent a beautiful white bull to the latter to ratify his kingship, with the understanding that Minos would then sacrifice the bull to him. (This is a perfect example of the homosocial dynamic described by Sedgwick, in which affective relations between male figures are reciprocally stabilizing.)[23] Minos, though, decided to keep the magnificent creature for himself and sacrificed another bull in its place. It was to punish Minos (necessary to the restoration of his temporarily destabilized position) that Poseidon sent Pasiphaë into uncontrollable lust for the animal. In other words, Pasiphaë's self-objectification points back to the conflict 'between men' involving the structure of their respective sovereignties, which, Poseidon's strategy reveals, already instrumentalized her. Pasiphaë's own paradoxical performance of political sovereignty (she can command Daedalus's art) and uncontrollable lust offers a strikingly deglamorized mirror image of her covetous husband's behaviour. It also figures the general congruence or analogy between sovereignty claims ('lust for power') and 'disordered sexuality', described by Rachel Jacoff in her discussion of Dante's Semiramis in *Inferno* v.[24] Jacoff notes perceptively that Dante 'rhymes' Pasiphaë with Semiramis by using the same suggestive *rima equivoca*, 'legge' / 'legge' [law/read] in his descriptions of both figures.[25] In both cases, Dante is, on one level, following the Christian historian and student of St Augustine, Orosius, who makes Semiramis's political power analogous to, and prophetic of, her disordered sexuality.[26] But by allowing the analogy between sovereignty claims and sexual lust to apply not only to female figures (whose desires and political power, regardless of their nature, destabilize patriarchal male sovereignty), but also to male figures — the love poets, and implicitly King Minos — the poem challenges the rules of patriarchy itself. As Jacoff concludes about Semiramis, Pasiphaë, and *Inferno* xxx's Myrrha, whom she also discusses, they 'appear to be icons not only of transgressive female desire, but of the nature of all female desire, and, ultimately, perhaps of desire itself — any desire, that is, which is reluctant to relinquish "specific corporealities".'[27] By acknowledging that their sexuality is related to Pasiphaë's, Guinizzelli's cohort acknowledges first, that they, too, immobilized and encased female sexuality in rigid, artificial constructions masquerading as natural. And second, that, not masculinity per se, but a particular mode of (ultimately patriarchal) domination, grounded in male–male competition — re-enacted here in the purgatorial shouting match — is implicated in this objectification.

Significantly, the poets' own 'male' bodies appear to have fared no better than Pasiphaë's. The story of Pasiphaë's human body, encased in a rigid construct so that she could engage in sex with a bull, also figures what contemporary feminist philosopher Judith Butler refers to as the 'male body in crisis'.[28] In a discussion of the relation between 'materiality' and 'reason' in the history of Western philosophy, Butler argues that the female body is not the only body excluded from Plato's 'domain of the less than rational human'. The 'man' or 'male subject of reason' produced by these exclusions is

> without a childhood; is not a primate and so is relieved of the necessity of eating, defecating, living and dying. [...] This is a figure of disembodiment, but one which is nevertheless a figure of the body, a bodying forth of a masculinized rationality, the figure of a male body which is not a body, a figure in crisis, a figure that enacts a crisis it cannot fully control.[29]

That is, masculinity, as it is related to reason, is figured as a disembodied body, all the bodily functions being displaced onto women, children, slaves, and animals. It follows that sexuality and sexual desire, though they are also fundamental to it, throw this version of the masculine subject into crisis. When the pilgrim encounters Matelda in the Earthly Paradise, after having passed through and beyond the barrier of fire that burns away lust, he experiences his attraction to her in terms of just such a crisis. He first feels the encounter as a catastrophic loss, like the drowning of Leander, of the rape of Proserpine, though he stands to gain everything by it.[30]

In the passage of *Purgatorio* XXVI that we are exploring, the crisis of masculinity is dramatically figured by 'sexual' intercourse between the reified body of Pasiphaë (whose reification is all the more horrifying because she is associated with light: her name means 'all shining', and her father was Helios, the sun god — figuratively linked, therefore, with Dante's multiple uses of the sun's light as reference point)[31] and the body of a male animal (the *torello*). What is performed in this scenario is the consequence of a masculine subject, occupying the position of Judith Butler's disembodied 'male subject of reason' while engaging in the physicality of the sex act. He can occupy this self-contradictory position — he can perform as if he were both embodied and disembodied — without precipitating the crisis that would expose this contradiction, only by recapitulating the mind/body split of Platonic philosophy, which postulates and subordinates a physical body that is different from, and should be governed by, a disembodied intellect that is identified as the real self. But, as the canto's figure of Guido Guinizzelli glosses the story of Pasiphaë, such a disjunction between the subject and its physical body (the mind/body split, which has remained a canonical focus of Western philosophical attention since Plato) at once reifies and bestializes the lover.[32] Pasiphaë, he explains, 's'imbestio nelle 'mbestiate schegge' [made herself a beast within the beast-like timber] (*Purg.* XXVI, 87). That is, in order to engage in sexual activity, the masculine subject, constructed and operating within the politico-philosophical regime that both Butler and Dante appear to be referring to, has to 'feminize' itself in the sense of alienating from itself and objectifying a merely material 'body', which it subordinates to its disembodied, sovereign, intellectual subjectivity. (I place this 'body' in quotes because only under the conditions of what Jacques Derrida and others after him have dubbed 'phallogocentrism' would it be possible to conceive of a body separable in this way from the subject.)[33] In a diabolical parody of achieving the salvific state in which will and intellect are one, the progeny of the chronic crisis of the subject of reason brought about by sexual desire is figured by the bovine head and human torso of the voraciously cannibalistic Minotaur. The Minotaur's bestial intellect, coupled in an ungainly way with a human *soma* is a perfectly chiastic reflection of the binaries and hierarchies of mind and body, male and female that gave birth to it. *Purgatorio* XXVI, by contrast, challenges us to consider how sexuality might be released from these binaries and hierarchies through a purgation and metamorphosis that would configure intellect, body, and 'sexual' desire quite differently.

Guido Guinizzelli's gloss on the cry of the other cohort, the so-called sodomites, has already made hierarchy and binarism central to the canto's analysis of male sexuality. Referencing political power, imperial domination, and militarism, the members of this group are said to have offended by doing that for which 'Cesar, triünfando, | "Regina" contra sé chiamar s'intese' [Caesar, in his triumph, heard 'Queen' called out against himself (translation mine)] (*Purg.* XXVI, 77–78). This circuitous way of naming male–male sexual desire, every bit as oblique and complex as the evocation of Pasiphaë, situates the sodomitical group, not as binary opposites to Guinizzelli's group, but instead as no less caught up than they are in the eroticism of a misogynist, heteronormative philosophico-political system that makes being called *regina* an insult and a threat to the legitimacy of Caesar's rule.[34] Caesar 'trïunfando' is a precise image of the masculine subject of reason we looked at earlier, the triumph being a spectacularized presentation of the bodies of captives (slaves), women, and animals under the command of an imperial male ruler.[35] The fragility of Caesar's position at the apex of the triumphal display is brought home by the homophobic heckling that threatens to cast the triumph as a fake, as a masquerade. Which, of course, it is. It is no accident that the term 'regina' also links these figures to Pasiphaë. Like Pasiphaë's masquerade, the triumph is a performance of and by bodies that is choreographed by temporal political power.

Historically, the purpose of the triumph was to constitute and consolidate as a new material reality the effects of military victory. The category 'materiality' itself, Judith Butler suggests in her argument about male and female bodies, 'designates a certain effect of power or, rather, *is* power in its formative or constituting effects. Insofar as power operates successfully by constituting an object domain, a field of intelligibility, a taken-for-granted ontology, its material *effects* are taken as material data or primary *givens*' (emphases mine).[36] In contrast to the triumph evoked in this passage, the divinely authored triumph of the Church in *Purgatorio* XXIX and XXX is interactive and pedagogical. Initially made up of iconographic representations of Christ, the authors of the Old and New Testament, and the theological and cardinal virtues, and organized around the veiled figure of Beatrice, the procession, by the end of *Purgatorio* XXXII, includes the transformation of the triumphal chariot into a monster, dragged away by a giant, not to be seen again. Rather than *constituting* an ontology, this triumph has enacted a de-ontologizing of the Church. As Beatrice explains to the wondering pilgrim, 'Sappi che 'l vaso che 'l serpente ruppe | fu e non è' [Know that the vessel that the serpent broke was and is no more] (*Purg.* XXXIII, 34–35).

Purging the sin of both groups in *Purgatorio* XXVI, it now seems, might include revealing these masquerades as persuasive, or even intelligible, only within a certain matrix of subject positions and relations that must themselves be read as contingent, temporal, and political. The phallocentric heteronormative matrix itself, in the case of *Purgatorio* XXVI, is presented as 'fittizio', as a text that invites lovers to be readers, a move that, as many commentators have noted, the lovers of *Inferno* V, exemplified by Paolo and Francesca, made in reverse — from reading to sex, rather than from sex to reading.[37] Sex and sexual attraction operate *in potentia* as the undoing of the choreographies that produce polarizing, hierarchizing, and therefore immobilizing binaries like mind and body, male and female, 'heterosexual and homosexual', as Regina Psaki has eloquently argued in her discussion of the *Commedia*'s 'redemptive erotics' and Judith Butler in her deconstruction of 'masculine impenetrability'.[38] By contrast, phallic, patriarchal heteronormativity, or whatever one should call it with reference to Dante, perverts and impedes mutual, intersubjective sexual relations. It is, in effect, a *denial* of sexual difference (as Jacques Lacan, Luce Irigaray,

Judith Butler, and others have argued in our own day) and, therefore, an absence or blockage of transitive, interactive sexual relations, or what Butler refers to as a 'failed model of reciprocity'.[39] To paraphrase Teodolinda Barolini on 'love', what is called 'sex' may not always be sex in the *Commedia*.[40]

We must be careful, furthermore, as I have already indicated, not to assume that the referent of 'sex' is either universal or even knowable. Indeed, as we have begun to see, the *Commedia* actively disturbs any such assumption. In our own day, Eve Sedgwick, in her exposé of the interimplication of sexualities and knowledges in key nineteenth- and twentieth-century Euro-American texts, makes short work of heteronormative categories of sex and sexuality merely by making the decision to take seriously 'the things that can differentiate even people of identical gender, race, nationality, class, and "sexual orientation"'.[41] Her Rabelaisian catalogue of some of the things we 'know' about sexuality, but somehow do not think about, include such everyday observations as:

> — Even identical genital acts mean very different things to different people.
> — To some people, the nimbus of 'the sexual' seems scarcely to extend beyond the boundaries of discrete genital acts; to others, it enfolds them loosely or floats virtually free of them.
> — Sexuality makes up a large share of the self-perceived identity of some people, a small share of others.
> — Some people spend a lot of time thinking about sex, others little.
> — Some people like to have a lot of sex, others little or none.
> — Many people have their richest mental/emotional involvement with sexual acts that they don't do, or even don't *want* to do.
> — For some people, it is important that sex be embedded in contexts resonant with meaning, narrative, and connectedness with other aspects of their life; for other people, it is important that they not be; to others it doesn't occur that they might be.[42]

The list, of course, could go on indefinitely. These characteristics could apply to the same person at different times of his/her life and could flow from one person to another, as well. To the possible epistemological objection that such knowledge depends on a trust in people's self-perception, self-knowledge, or self-report, she responds wryly, 'where would the whole, astonishing and metamorphic Western romance tradition [...] be if people's sexual desire, of all things, were even momentarily assumed to be transparent to themselves? Yet I am even more impressed by the leap of presumptuousness necessary to dismiss such a list of differences than by the leap of faith necessary to entertain it.'[43]

The 'leap' into the serious consideration of difference as *irreducible* (as not subsumable) within a system of binaries, does not destroy knowledge, but opens theoretical spaces in which to deal with 'a large family of things *we know* and need to know about ourselves and each other with which we have [...] so far created for ourselves almost no theoretical room to deal.'[44] The reasons for this foreclosure or exclusion are not hard to find, but Sedgwick delays her punch line until after she has made another important non-exclusionary gesture. In the modern Western context in which sexuality has been made central to identity and knowledge, she carefully proceeds, alienating from anyone, for any reason, the authority to describe their own sexual desire 'may represent the most intimate violence possible'.[45] Since she has just demonstrated that this alienation is, it seems, a general fact of Western sexuality, we can conclude that 'we' (Western subjects) are all subject to this intimate epistemic violence.

The Figure of Arnaut/Ulysses: Fluidity and Intertextuality

As if Sedgwick's catalogue had been animated, the constant movement of the figures in *Purgatorio* XXVI rather strenuously enacts the constant flowing together and apart of categories and figures not polarized as binary opposites. Together the two groups operate more like the fluid duality described by Sylvia Marcos in her work on gender in Mesoamerica, moving on a continuum, in and out of each other's spaces. There are no 'us and them', 'self and other'; there are merely those with whom Dante falls in and 'those who do not come with us'. The groups are fluid within themselves as well, as the image of Guinizzelli disappearing into the fire, 'come per l'acqua il pesce andando al fondo' [as a fish going to the bottom disappears into the water (translation mine)] (*Purg.* XXVI, 135) beautifully exemplifies. Though both the pilgrim and Guinizzelli make attempts to rank the poets of the vernacular lyric tradition, the histories they evoke feature shifting reputations and a pattern of porous literary boundaries, culminating in the becoming permeable of the famously 'closed' style of Arnaut Daniel. Ironically, while Guinizzelli insists that, compared to himself, Arnaut was 'il miglior fabbro del parlar materno' [the better craftsman of the mother tongue] (*Purg.* XXVI, 117), Arnaut, (in a provocative echo of Ulysses' 'folle volo' [mad flight] [*Inf.* XXVI, 125]) dismisses his own poetry as 'folly':

> Ieu sui Arnaut, que plor e vau cantan;
> consiros vei la passada folor,
> e vei jousen lo joi qu'esper denan. (*Purg.* XXVI, 142–44)

[I am Arnaut, who weeps and goes singing; with chagrin I view my past folly, and rejoicing I see ahead the joy I hope for.]

Implicit in this response to his poetic descendant is a disruption and reconceptualization of the grounds for appreciating, evaluating, and historicizing vernacular love poetry. As I have argued elsewhere, Arnaut here abandons his esoteric *trobar clus*, his closed style, in response to the pilgrim's courteous questioning: 'Tan m'abellis vostre cortes deman, | qu'ieu no me puesc ne voill a vos cobrire' [So pleasing to me is your courteous request, that I cannot nor will not hide myself from you] (*Purg.* XXVI, 140–41). But this opening happens in relation to a reader reading. Read intertextually, a move that Dante's text visibly and audibly performs here, Arnaut's poetry joins the universe of allegorical-historical signifiers, neither more nor less valuable than any other signifiers, though perhaps less seductive than some precisely because of Arnaut's attentiveness to the materiality of the language with which he played so inventively.[46] If Dante's Ulysses used language virtuosically for the purpose of seducing himself and his men to make their final 'folle volo' toward absolute notions of virtue and knowledge, Arnaut was perhaps induced by his virtuosic command of the materiality (the body) of the vernacular toward a contrasting, but similarly misguided, lack of faith in its epistemological possibilities. Within this intertextual matrix of readings, linearity and hierarchy give way to a fluid poetics of relation that calls upon readers not to remain within, but to move across and between texts.[47] Likewise the achronological permeability of Guinizzelli to the 'vestigio' [trace] left in him by his encounter with the pilgrim, genealogically his poetic descendant, denaturalizes tree-form genealogical thinking, suggesting the rich possibilities of alternative paradigms of narrativity in which heterogeneous sources open the possibility of historiographical and aesthetic alternatives.[48]

Corpi fittizi and the Fluid Body

The striking contrast that this fluidity presents to the binary oppositional system in terms of which 'male' and 'female' sexuality are more conventionally played out will help us puzzle through another drama enacted when Dante's body arouses the curiosity of the *ombre* he encounters: 'Colui non par corpo fittïzio' [This one does not appear to be a fictive body] (*Purg.* XXVI, 12), they begin to say to each other, as they see how he blocks the sun's rays. The pilgrim, apparently trying to impress them, betrays his own confusion about, and complicity in, the reifications of desire being purged in this canto:

> O anime sicure
> d'aver, quando che sia, di pace stato,
>   non son remase acerbe né mature
> le membra mie di là, ma son qui meco
> col sangue suo e con le sue giunture.
>   Quinci sù vo per non esser più cieco;
> donna è di sopra che m'acquista grazia
> per che 'l mortal per vostro mondo reco. (*Purg.* XXVI, 53–60)

[O, souls certain to have, whenever it will be, a state of peace, my limbs, neither young nor old, do not remain yonder but are here with me with their blood and their joints. I go up here in order to be no longer blind. There is a woman above who gains grace for me so that I may bring my mortal body through your world.] (translation mine)

The split between corporeality (complete with blood and joints) and some other, governing, dimension of subjectivity is conspicuously in evidence here. The pilgrim, furthermore, appears to be rather proud or pleased that he can navigate purgatory in this dissociated condition. He implies, indeed, that his configuration of subjectivity is, in fact, preferable to theirs. The joke, however, is on him as the canto dramatizes in very precise ways the perceptual distortion caused by his 'having' (though notably not 'being') his mortal bodily parts. The word 'membra' reconfigures two of the most powerful and foundational binary oppositions in Western discourse: that between female and male and that between singular and plural.[49] Thinking about the word with the Wittgensteinian attentiveness brought to language by Dante the poet, if not yet by the pilgrim, we might note that it is masculine in the singular [*membro*] and feminine in the plural [*membra*], and, because its plural form retains the form of the Latin neuter [*membrum*] from which it descends, its ending in the plural resembles that of an Italian feminine singular.[50] The term itself, in other words, can be read as 'embodying', not the inert, objectified corporeality the pilgrim is lugging up the mountain (which, significantly, grows lighter as he ascends), but the coming together and moving apart of the agile *corpi fittizi* whose dance of relation I discussed earlier and will return to below.

The pilgrim, though, assumes that his 'membra' have or are something that a 'corpo fittizio' is lacking, and makes a point of calling attention to what he takes to be the plenitude of a 'real' material body, which, given the explicit details of blood and joints, we should probably understand as 'correct', too. Although the word 'membra', meaning limbs or bodily parts collectively, is denotatively distinct from *membro*, referring to the *membro virile*, which has no plural form, 'membra' also does not exclude *membro*, which is, after all, a metaphor based on the image of *membrum* as a limb. It seems unlikely that for the poet Dante, the semantic overlap of the two terms would not have presented itself. The pilgrim, digging himself ever deeper into his phallogocentric reading (or, as feminist theorists put it, 'construction') of the body, addresses these *corpi fittizi* as 'anime' [souls], which tacitly recuperates them to his own mind–body binary and conveniently genders them female.[51] Without their masculine 'mortal', as he inaccurately calls what Christian theology claims is the *im*mortal human body, they seem to him symbolically castrated, not full-fledged 'male subjects of reason', to borrow Judith Butler's useful term. The two-edged simile comparing their astonishment to that of a rustic mountaineer, bewildered ('stupido') when entering a city, nicely captures his inversion of his and their respective positions, (and displays the pilgrim's snobbism or classism as a corollary of his sexism):

> Non altrimenti stupido si turba
> lo montanaro e remirando ammuta,
> quando rozzo e slavatico s'inurba,
> che ciascun' ombra fece in sua paruta. (*Purg.* XVI, 67–70)

> [Not otherwise is the mountain peasant struck with awe and troubled, falling silent as he gazes, when, crude and rustic, he enters the city: than each soul then appeared.]

The pilgrim, of course, is the stupid tourist, a city slicker, climbing their mountain. His disdain for the peasant contrasts with the poem's use of the subjugated knowledges, images, and idioms of rural life. From the simile of the fireflies seen by the peasant that offer a diminutive image of the towering Ulysses in *Inferno* XXVI to the metaphor of the threshing floor which earth resembles from the perspective of the eighth sphere in *Paradiso* XXII, folk culture subtly asserts itself, like sexuality, as a source of alternatives to the epistemologies of wealth and power. Here the pilgrim presents himself, not humbly, as part of a larger universe, but condescendingly as fully present and soon to be, if not already, sovereign. His Butlerian 'disembodied male body', fully in control of its mortal, material parts, ("l mortal [...] reco'), on his way to insight ('non esser più cieco') is vetted, he asserts, by a highly placed lady who will acquire grace for him. His precise wording, though, evocative of court politics and material acquisition, as if *grazia* were a material substance that could be acquired for a third party, immediately ironizes the pilgrim's stance, echoing

Francesca's confused elision of power politics with grace in *Inferno* v, about which I will say more below. Symptomatically, it does not occur to the pilgrim that the astonishment of the people undergoing purgation here is the result, not of admiring his *membra*, but of wondering what on earth, or on the Mountain of Purgatory, this hunk of meat, this objectified flesh, is doing here. They must be shocked to see someone in their midst who still literalizes and objectifies his corporeality. They see a living man who is unable, apparently, to read the contingencies of history and politics in the cultural mapping of his gender and sexuality. As Michel Foucault and others have extensively demonstrated and as the poets in this canto, as well as Adam and Cacciaguida in *Paradiso* and many other figures in the poem, make explicit, the languages, styles, and politics of subjectivity — including gender and sexuality — come and go. Far from being irreducibly material, bodies and their *sensoria* are rich historical texts, allowing the reader to read his or her own desires and bodily knowledges as locally 'situated' and relational, as irreducibly different from those of every other person, and, by virtue of being so, as the salvifically partial (rather than universal) experiences that enable metamorphosis.[52] The pilgrim here fails to read sexual differences as ontologically the 'same' difference, which makes everyone's position partial, contingent, incomplete, and open to the interactive, metamorphic, and hence sexual love that animates the universe, 'che move il sole e l'altre stelle' [moves the sun and the other stars] (*Par.* XXXIII, 145).

In the subsequent interactions among the poets, in which historical moments and movements are invoked and released, and one poet gives place to another, everyone, nevertheless, leaves a trace (*vestigio*) in someone else: Guinizzelli in Dante and, perhaps more surprisingly, Dante in his predecessor Guinizzelli, Arnaut in Guinizzelli and Dante, and they in him. Languages, dialects, and styles, like human sexualities, come and go, appear and disappear, but the nonlinear, nonbinary dance of what Jacques Derrida has called an originary *différance*, which is both linguistic and sexual, is ongoing. If Arnaut gets the last word in *Purgatorio* XXVI, his performance subverts any further attempts at reifying canon formation. Instead, he presents a beautiful, heterolinguistic image of love (which at this point I do not think the poem authorizes us to separate into sexual and spiritual, physical and Platonic). Arnaut's Occitan, his nurturing and sexual 'parlar materno' [mother tongue] (*Purg.* XXVI, 117) becomes 'materially' and semantically penetrable by Dante's Tuscan dialect and Dante's Tuscan to it, each one 'saving' the other from the isolation and closure that so often in the *Commedia* become the seductions of autonomy and authority.[53] Arnaut renounces the esotericizing intention of his *trobar clus* style, opening himself to the kind of rereading that Dante, too, must undergo, two cantos later, before he can interact with Beatrice.[54]

Corpi fittizi and Chaos

Yet another, different, set of interactions is set in motion when the two cohorts of *corpi fittizi* in *Purgatorio* XXVI are likened collectively to cranes, 'grue', flying in opposite directions. Immediately after the cries of the two cohorts — 'Soddoma e Gomorra' (*Purg.* XXVI, 40) and 'Nella vacca entra Pasife' (*Purg.* XXVI, 41), we read:

> Poi, come grue ch'alle montagne Rife
> volasser parte e parte inver l'arene,
> queste del gel, quelle del sole schife:
> l'una gente sen va, l'altra sen vène. (Purg. XXVI, 43–46)

[Then, like cranes, who might fly, some towards the Riphean Mountains, some toward the sands, these avoiding frost, those the sun, so one group goes off, the other comes along.]

The geometry, here, and the commentary on it, take us back to our earlier consideration of polarizing binaries, diagramming and deconstructing the principle of binary opposition, not as a productive dualism between two irreducibly different kinds of movement and creature, but as, in fact, a single movement performed by a homogenous species, who will simply repeat the same pattern until they have purged their alternative, but not dissimilar 'lusts'. It is also worth noting that lust is articulated, at this point, not as a desire *for* sensation, but as a desire to *avoid* sensation: to avoid weather, to be precise, and its sensations of heat and cold. ('Lust', in other words, is not characterized here as either an 'excess' or an 'indulgence' to be brought under control, as it might appear to have been from the perspective of the circle of the lustful in *Inferno* v.)[55] Weather, like sex — if sex is understood, as I have begun doing above, as a transitive, metamorphic, interaction between irreducibly different 'vortexes' (to borrow Marcos's term for human subjects) — is unpredictable and without boundaries. It was the study of weather that led to the creation of the field we now call 'chaos theory', a field that, in contrast to conventional science's emphasis on order and stability, sees the universe in terms of 'fluctuations, instability, multiple choices, and limited predictability at all levels of observation'.[56] Patterns and processes, not entities, become the object of study in chaos theory, and temporality or 'the arrow of time' denied by the universalism of Newtonian physics becomes constitutive. 'The future is no longer determined by the present' and events (like the encounter between Dante and Beatrice as children) bring an element of radical novelty to the description of nature.[57] Could it be something like what we call 'chaos' that the erotic love poets Dante encounters in *Purgatorio* XXVI evaded?

Inferno v and the Figure of Francesca/Dante

To answer this question, let us follow these cranes back to the 'gru' [cranes] (*Inf.* v, 46) to which the lustful are compared in *Inferno* v. The grammatical difference between the feminine 'grue' of *Purgatorio* to which male figures are likened and the masculine 'gru' of *Inferno*, whose first three referents are queens Semiramis, Cleopatra, and Helen, already performs a disjunction between the binary linguistic system of gendering nouns specific to the vernacular and the historical genders of the figures the pilgrim is encountering. The transgendering from male to female, which marks the difference between the lustful in *Inferno* v and the lustful in *Purgatorio* XXVI mirrors the transgendering performed by the cries of both cohorts in *Purgatorio* XXVI. As Jeffrey Schnapp has convincingly demonstrated, it will also characterize Dante's figuration of the crucified Christ and, in reverse, of Beatrice, in *Paradiso*.[58] Given the prominence and pervasiveness of this trope, it becomes pertinent, before turning to a brief reading of Francesca's apparent failure to cross genders, to consider how the binary logic that underwrites the production of European gender operates.

In binary thinking, terms become opposed to one another in pairs such as good/ bad, true/false, white/black, inside/outside, male/female, ruler/ruled, rich/poor. The relational nature of meaning-making is transformed into an essentializing polarization of terms, which excludes any middle ground and causes one term to dominate while its binary opposite appears to threaten its integrity. Thus, the female (or the child, animal, or slave) in Butler's description of masculinity-in-crisis appears threatening to — and from — the standpoint of the male and must constantly be contained, controlled, subordinated. This imperative to maintain order and meaning, though, works conveniently to deepen, legitimate, and reinforce the governing terms of the binary. Further, while binary thinking organizes the phenomenal world we see and try to understand, it also structures moral, ethical, and religious categories. Its most subtle and fundamental consequences may, in fact, lie in the realm of the emotional and the aesthetic. The affect of the binarily organized and located subject who makes decisions and judgments about the (binarily organized) world s/he inhabits constantly compounds, reinforces, and 'naturalizes' the hierarchical, exclusionary binary metaphysical paradigm. This vicious circle, I would argue, is never breached in Francesca's discourse.

In *Inferno* v, notwithstanding, or perhaps consistent with, their collective masculinization in the figure of the *gru*, we find a more classical canon of sexual transgressors than in *Purgatorio* xxvi: Semiramis, Cleopatra, Helen, Dido, Achilles, Paris. With the addition of the romance figure Tristan, though, Dante begins, as Teodolinda Barolini perceptively notes, to reframe the classical figures as romance characters, recursively and anachronistically calling them 'donne antiche e ' cavalieri' [ancient ladies and knights] (*Inf.* v, 71). They usher in a romance paradigm that supersedes the frame of moral responsibility carried over from the virtuous heathen of Canto iv to the beginning of Canto v.[59] In fact, one might be tempted to read this group as a kind of literary counter-canon, constituting a tradition outside and possibly opposed to that enshrining the official culture of empire. Not coincidentally, most of them are female, with the exception of two male characters, Paris and Tristan, better known for their erotic than for their martial exploits, and Achilles, who refused to fight after Agamemnon, the leader of the Greek siege of Troy, appropriated his war prize, the princess Briseis. What they all have in common is their marginalization of and by patriarchal moral authority. But do they, in fact, threaten in any fundamental way that ideology's binary opposition between male and female, domination and subordination, reason ('la ragion' (*Inf.* v, 39)) and desire ('il talento' (*Inf.* v, 39))?

Curiously, the pilgrim seems able to identify with figures in *both Inferno* iv and *Inferno* v. The five great poets of Greece and Rome — Homer, Horace, Ovid, Lucan, and Vergil — pay him the supreme honour of including him as their sixth: 'mi fecer de la loro schiera, | sì ch'io fui sesto tra cotanto senno' [they made me one of their band, so that I was sixth among so much wisdom] (*Inf.* iv, 101–02). Yet within less than 150 lines he finds himself intensely drawn to Francesca, a member of the counter-canon of imperial outcasts. The seamlessness of his attraction to figures whose own values place them in opposition to one another pushes us to seek a level of understanding or a perspective from which they come into focus as complementary rather than contradictory. Teodolinda Barolini's feminist reading of Francesca's attempts to exercise agency and to find pleasure accomplishes just this. She argues that it is crucial to take into consideration the cruel 'realpolitik' of the dynastic marriage system in which Francesca was an insignificant pawn, barely mentioned in pre-*Commedia* chronicles and easily replaced by her husband-murderer with a new dynastic wife.[60] The inexorability and brutality of Romagnolo sexual politics make Dante's psychological treatment of Francesca's desire politically resonant. Although making Francesca's psychology available to the reader does not moot the enigmas of gender, sexuality, desire, and knowledge, or ultimately rescue Francesca from the infernal consequences of thinking and feeling as she does (which would destroy her potency as a character), it does stand, Barolini emphasizes, as a condemnation of the context (one thinks again of the labyrinth, constructed by the artist Daedalus both to sustain and contain the Minotaur) that Francesca was unable to find her way out of.

Another strong and subtle articulation of what is at stake, both politically and epistemologically, in how we read Francesca's sexual desire has been offered by Margaret Ferguson in her foundational work on a later counter canon, which, like Dante, she locates in relation to Dido. In her Prologue to *Dido's Daughters: Literacy, Gender, and Empire in Early Modern England and France*, Ferguson notes that Dido is an anomalous character in Virgil's *Aeneid* because of the manner of her death:

> Dido is the only character in Vergil's epic to die in a way that somehow deceives not only humans but the gods — one of whom, Venus, has cruelly deceived Dido. [...] [D]ying 'neither in the course of fate (*nam quia nec fato*), nor by a death she had earned [in battle]' (*Aen.* IV, 696), Dido manages to escape Fate — however briefly — by dying before her appointed time (*ante diem*) (697). She does so by committing suicide with Aeneas's sword, having led her nurse and her sister into believing she was about to perform a ritual (perhaps a ritual sacrifice) for the Roman god Jupiter who has, along with Venus, played cruelly with Dido's life. For a moment — one decried by her sister Anna as a moment of fraud — Dido surprises the gods and many of Vergil's readers as well. In that moment of surprise, supremely painful for Dido herself (her death is delayed because the gods have not prepared for it), she becomes a brilliant emblem for a human departure from a foreordained historical narrative. Although her fate is, of course, being manipulated by Vergil, in ways that later writers will challenge as well as admire, the poet himself seems to grant to this one character at this one moment an agency that creates a kind of rift in the poem's ideological fabric. The rift is a mystery the poem leaves unexplained.[61]

Virgil's Dido, in other words, is not simply recuperated by the history and hegemony of the Roman Empire. The poet's version of her self-sacrifice, which already contradicts other versions in which Dido and Aeneas never met, dramatizes, Ferguson argues, 'the existence of competing histories in what counts (for some) as the cultural literacy of the West'. Dido becomes a metonym for the subjugation and sacrifice of those other literacies to Roman absolutism.[62] This tear in the narrative does not make the lost ways of reading ontologically or morally superior, but it does allow them to haunt Virgil's imperial historiography, enabling the poem's listener or reader to 'read' its inevitability and universality as, paradoxically, aesthetic, metaphorical, and situated. If Dido by herself cannot impede the master narrative of empire through her action, nevertheless the reader can choose whether or not to pass through the textual rift her action opens up.

Could the enormous ambivalence that readers have felt toward Francesca be due, at least in part, to the congruence between her role in the *Commedia* and that of Dido, as Ferguson frames it for us, in the *Aeneid*? Like Virgil, Dante does not give Francesca's subject position — either her desire ('disiri') or her way of knowing it ('conoscere') — any ontological superiority, but the 'modo' (manner) of her death — both earthly and spiritual — leaves in shreds the ideological fabric she herself was unable to shed.

A close reading of Francesca's literarily overwrought discourse (whose densely layered samplings of the lyric tradition Teodolinda Barolini has so skilfully parsed that the twenty-first-century reader can thoroughly appreciate how *au courant* this young woman was, whatever her ultimate lack of insight into the pathology of the political imaginary within which she was operating), offers a different picture of her relationship to romance from the one she seems to hold herself.[63] In her initial greeting to the pilgrim, Francesca refers to a divinity, 'il re dell'universo' [the king of the universe] (*Inf.* v, 91), to whom she would pray for the pilgrim's peace if she were on better terms with him. She appears, that is, to have projected the political image of a petty tyrant onto the divinity, and, once she has done so, to construe this ruler as not friendly to her. She then implies that her own situation, condemned for all eternity to the second circle, is simply a consequence of this figure's enmity. Such violence and arbitrariness were unquestionably the way Romagnolo politics operated, as Barolini has demonstrated in her account of the murderous Malatesta family.[64] But Francesca appears to accept this political paradigm as absolute and universal, and she reproduces it in the story of her own journey to knowledge.

Referencing Guinizzelli and numerous other vernacular lyric poets including Dante himself,[65] Francesca uses the proper noun 'Amor' to explain how her sexual desire was awakened:

> Amor, ch'al cor gentil ratto s'apprende,
> prese costui de la bella persona
> che mi fu tolta, e 'l modo ancor m'offende.
>   Amor, ch'a nullo amato amar perdona,
> mi prese del costui piacer si forte
> che, come vedi, ancor non m'abbandona.
>   Amore condusse noi ad una morte.
> Caina attende chi a vita ci spense. (*Inf.* v, 100–07)

[Love, which is swiftly kindled in the noble heart, seized this one for the lovely person that was taken from me; and the manner still injures me. Love, which pardons no one loved from loving in return, seized me for his beauty so strongly that, as you see, it still does not abandon me. Love led us on to one death. Caina awaits him who extinguished our life.]

This 'Amor' works suspiciously like the 're dell'universo' she has just invoked as her enemy, although this tyrant seems to have taken a greater interest in her than that one, anticipating the relative positions in her life of the two Malatesta brothers: her husband Gianciotto and her lover Paolo. Hierarchizing and objectifying all that comes within his purview, 'Amor' structurally mirrors rather than threatens the political imaginary Francesca has just invoked — perceptively — as not her friend. The congruity of sovereignties, regardless of whether they seem hostile or friendly, continues in the grammatical ambiguity of Francesca's phrase 'e 'l modo ancor m'offende', which could qualify either the way Paolo was taken with her 'bella persona' or the way in which her 'bella persona' was taken from her by her murderer. This ambiguity invites us to think further about how those two relationships — the dynastic marriage to her husband and her romantic relationship with Paolo — add up to obverse sides of the same coin.

Under the influence of a substantivized 'Amor', Paolo seems to have (mis)taken Francesca for a 'bella persona' — not only a body, but a kind of social mask or masquerade. (By contrast, Beatrice will be veiled when the pilgrim finally comes face to face with her in *Purgatorio* XXXII.) One could as well read the term *persona* as a precise signifier of 'the body' as it was instrumentalized socially and politically in the context of dynastic marriage. Also under the influence of the tyrannical 'Amor', Francesca appears to have found Paolo's attraction to this embodied social self and the elevation of that self to the status of a literary lady, irresistible. Since the social persona of Paolo, the younger brother of Francesca's husband, is no less rooted than hers in dynastic Romagnolo politics, Francesca's reciprocation of his attraction to her can only draw them ever further into the labyrinth of patriarchal sexual desire, typified in *Purgatorio* XXVI by Pasiphaë. Thus, even before the lovers are physically murdered by Francesca's cuckolded husband, they have already cut the ground out from under their own feet by trying to realize their politically transgressive 'disiri' and 'conoscenza' in terms of their socially constructed personae.

In a misguided bid to emancipate themselves from the socio-cultural matrix in which their sex/gender positions are rooted, the two lovers have instead reduced themselves to those positions. Teodolinda Barolini has written compellingly and nonjudgmentally of Francesca's attempt to exercise agency and to assert female sexual desire within a political context that absolutely denied both. Francesca might, in this very precise sense, be considered a female alter-Dante (as she often has been, but in a looser sense). At the poem's outset, the pilgrim's agency and desire also appear to have been blocked, the former by exile and the latter by Beatrice's death. Dante, as a male member of the lesser nobility, though, has more social and geographical mobility than his aristocratic female counterpart. While it is ultimately the inexplicable and unknowable gift of 'grace' that allows the pilgrim radically to revise his understandings of agency and desire, Barolini's feminist analysis of how Francesca deals with her impossible subject position directs us toward, and coheres with, the terrible realization that, had he been born into Francesca's gender and class, Dante's desire might have played out more like hers, and, conversely, had Francesca, the great lover of literature, been born into Dante's, she might have become a great poet. (This is one of many instances in the poem when the spiritual consequences — for better and for worse — of earthly political arrangements are foregrounded with paralysing clarity.) Instead, in her manner of aspiring to be 'liber[a], dritt[a], e san[a]' [free, upright and sound] (*Purg.* XXVII, 140) Francesca has, like Caesar in his triumph, attempted to legitimate and naturalize a contingent, relational subject position rather than to follow her desire beyond the deceptive illusions projected by political sovereignty. To say that 'Amor' brought Paolo and Francesca to one death is, in this sense, quite precise. The personification, or making a persona, of Love, the very term that should signify relational meaning and transitive interaction, has initiated a cascade of literalisms and essentialisms. It is not surprising that by the time Paolo and Francesca are reading the *Lancialotto*, the way they relate to the fictional figures of the text is to essentialize them as well. Paolo and Francesca really never start reading, in the sense of interacting with, a text. They plunge instead into a self-colonizing *identification* with what they (mis)take for more glamorous versions of 'themselves'.

Thus, Francesca did not get to *know* her socially transgressive and potentially salvific desires at all. On the contrary, she remained fixed in her contingent, social persona, cut off from all acquaintance with, and enjoyment of, the unpredictable, transformative 'chaos' of 'Amor'. The pilgrim's identificatory swoon at the canto's close registers the parallel between his situation and hers, which persists, or re-emerges, in *Purgatorio* XXVI: 'E caddi come corpo morte cadde' [And I fell as a dead body falls] (*Inf.* V, 142). The five trochaic thuds of this line, the repetition of emphasis on the first syllable of each word, retards the line and emphasizes, as if from different camera angles, the immobilizing loss of consciousness of the pilgrim — in striking contrast to the fleet-footed *corpi fittizi*, who kiss one another without slowing their pace: 'basciarsi una con una | sanza restar' [to kiss one another without stopping] (*Purg.* XXVI, 32–33). A metaphorical dead body, which is to say a body that has been objectified — rendered separate and material (in Butler's sense), or 'mortal' in the lexicon of *Purgatorio* — is a body that can neither think nor love. In both *Inferno* V and *Purgatorio* XXVI, Dante the love poet implicates himself as rooted in a regime of phallic masculinity that does precisely this, not only to the female body but to the male body as well.

The resurrection of the sexual body from this 'death' has nothing to do with restitching a material body to a transcendent soul. Rather, as the human being metamorphoses from 'vermo' to 'angelica farfalla' (*Purg.* X, 124–25), it no longer makes sense to separate and oppose body and soul, reason and desire, intellect and will. It is the binary oppositional episteme that creates the illusory contradiction between human sexuality and divine love. The project that makes the *Commedia* both deeply indebted to, and dramatically different from, the tradition of love poetry with which Dante (inter)relates it in both the cantos we have been considering is the metamorphosis of the patriarchal, phallogocentric, heteronormative matrix itself.

Notes to Chapter 9

I am deeply grateful to Manuele Gragnolati, Francesca Southerden, Gina Psaki, Stephanie Jed, Sante Matteo, Margaret Brose, Áine O'Healy, Martha Waller, Monica Green, and Chris Castiglia for their many and various contributions to this project.

1. See Teodolinda Barolini, 'Dante and Cavalcanti (On Making Distinctions in Matters of Love): *Inferno* v in its Lyric Context', *Dante Studies*, 116 (1998), 31–63, and 'Dante and Francesca da Rimini: Realpolitik, Romance, Gender', *Speculum*, 75 (2000), 1–28.
2. Manuele Gragnolati has written extensively about the body and its relationships with the soul and with the separated souls of the *Commedia*, commenting in one of his more recent essays on the transformation that his own readings have undergone. See his book *Experiencing the Afterlife: Soul and Body in Dante and Medieval Culture* (Notre Dame, IN: University of Notre Dame Press, 2005) and the following essays: 'Gluttony and the Anthropology of Pain in Dante's *Inferno* and *Purgatorio*', in *History in the Comic Mode: Medieval Communities and the Matter of Person*, ed. by Rachel Fulton and Bruce W. Holsinger (New York: Columbia University Press, 2007), pp. 238–50; 'Nostalgia in Heaven: Embraces, Affection and Identity in the *Commedia*', in *Dante and the Human Body: Eight Essays*, ed. by John C. Barnes and Jennifer Petrie (Dublin: Four Courts Press, 2007), pp. 117–37; '(In-)Corporeality, Language, Performance in Dante's *Vita Nuova* and *Commedia*', in *Dante's Plurilingualism: Authority, Knowledge, Subjectivity*, ed. by Sara Fortuna, Manuele Gragnolati and Jürgen Trabant (Oxford: Legenda, 2010), pp. 211–22.
3. Benjamin David's reading of the sexuality in Giovanni di Paolo's illuminations and Regina Psaki's of sexuality in *Paradiso* have both been influential on my thinking about *Purgatorio* xxvi and *Inferno* v. See David's 'The Paradisal Body in Giovanni di Paolo's Illuminations of the *Commedia*', *Dante Studies*, 122 (2004), 45–69 and Psaki's 'Love for Beatrice: Transcending Contradiction in the *Paradiso*', in *Dante for the New Millennium*, ed. by Teodolinda Barolini and H. Wayne Storey (New York: Fordham University Press, 2003), pp. 115–30.
4. See Gary P. Cestaro, *Dante and the Nursing Body* (Notre Dame, IN: University of Notre Dame Press, 2003).
5. See Eve Kosofsky Sedgwick, *Epistemology of the Closet* (Berkeley and Los Angeles: University of California Press, 1990); Elizabeth V. Spelman, *Inessential Woman: Problems of Exclusion in Feminist Thought* (Boston, MA: Beacon Press, 1988); Judith Butler, *Bodies that Matter: On the Discursive Limits of 'Sex'* (New York and London: Routledge, 1993).
6. See Rachel Jacoff, 'Transgression and Transcendence: Figures of Female Desire in Dante's *Commedia*', in *The New Medievalism*, ed. by Kevin Brownlee, Marina Brownlee, and Stephen Nichols, (Baltimore, MD: Johns Hopkins University Press, 1991), pp. 183–90, and her later essay, '"Our Bodies, Our Selves": The Body in the *Commedia*', in *Sparks and Seeds: Medieval Literature and its Afterlife. Essays in Honor of John Freccero*, ed. by Dana E. Stewart and Alison Cornish (Turnhout: Brepols, 2000), pp. 119–37. Also see Regina Psaki's series of essays on sexuality in the *Commedia*: 'The Sexualized Body in Dante and the Medieval Context', *Annali di storia dell'esegesi*, 13 (1996), 539–50; 'The Sexual Body in Dante's Celestial Paradise', in *Imagining Heaven in the Middle Ages: A Book of Essays*, ed. by Jan Swango Emerson and Hugh Feiss, OSB (New York and London: Garland Publishing, Inc. 2000), pp. 47–61; and her 'Love for Beatrice' cited above. Jeffrey Schnapp explores the terminology of sexuality more abstractly in his 'Dante's Sexual Solecisms: Gender and Genre in the *Commedia*', in Brownlee, ed., *The New Medievalism*, pp. 201–25. My arguments in this essay also build upon my earlier essay on sexuality in the *Commedia*, 'Seduction and Salvation: Sexual Difference in Dante's *Commedia* and the Difference It Makes', in *Donna: Woman in Italian Culture*, ed. by Ada Testaferri (Toronto: Dovehouse Editions, 1989), pp. 225–43.
7. This was a personal communication in the context of a fourteen-week Resident Research Seminar I convened in the fall of 1999 at the University of California Humanities Research Institute in Irvine, California. The focus of the group was the use of difference among feminisms as an epistemological resource, and Professor Nnaemeka was a featured guest interlocutor.
8. See Oyewumi's startling, and now widely accepted, argument concerning the nonexistence of

gender as a category among the Yoruba prior to British colonization in *The Invention of Women: Making an African Sense of Western Gender Discourses* (Minneapolis: University of Minnesota Press, 1997), pp. 121–56.

9. See Oyewumi, pp. 152–53.

10. See Woolf's canonical argument concerning women's lack of access to class privileges in *A Room of One's Own* (New York: Harcourt Brace & Co, 1989).

11. Sylvia Marcos has done extensive work on the way gender categories operate in the cosmology of the pre-Colombian Maya in the region of what is now Central America and Southern Mexico. See her 'Embodied Religious Thought: Gender Categories in Mesoamerica', in *Gender/ Bodies/Religion: Adjunct Proceedings of the XVIIth Congress on the History of Religions*, ed. by Sylvia Marcos (Cuernavaca, Mexico: ALER Publications, 2000), pp. 93–114, and her book *Taken from the Lips: Gender and Eros in Mesoamerican Religions* (Leiden and Boston, MA: Brill, 2006).

12. See Marcos, 'Embodied Religious Thought', p. 96.

13. Marcos, 'Embodied Religious Thought', p. 101.

14. See Marcos, *Taken from the Lips*, pp. 41–61.

15. See David Noble's work on gender, religion, and the roots of enlightenment Western science in *A World without Women: The Christian Clerical Culture of Western Science* (New York and Oxford: Oxford University Press, 1992) and *The Religion of Technology: The Divinity of Man and the Spirit of Invention* (New York: Penguin, 1997).

16. See Psaki, 'Love for Beatrice', p. 117.

17. See Naomi Schor, 'This Essentialism which is Not One', *differences*, 2 (1989), 38–58. I refer here to her discussion of 'saming' on pp. 45–46.

18. Prue Shaw, 'Canto XXVI: The Fires of Lust and Poetry', in *Lectura Dantis: Purgatorio*, ed. by Allen Mandelbaum, Anthony Oldcorn, and Charles Ross (Berkeley, Los Angeles, and London: University of California Press, 2008), pp. 288–302 (p. 290).

19. Sedgwick introduces and unfolds the concept of 'homosociality' in her book *Between Men: English Literature and Male Homosocial Desire* (New York: Columbia University Press, 1985).

20. See Sedgwick, *Between Men*, especially pp. 1–20.

21. Citations from Dante's *Inferno* and *Purgatorio* are from *Dante Alighieri, The Divine Comedy of Dante Alighieri*, ed. and trans. by Robert M. Durling and Ronald L. Martinez, 3 vols (New York and Oxford: Oxford University Press, 1996–2011). Unless otherwise indicated, all translations are from the Durling and Martinez translation.

22. See Barolini, 'Dante and Cavalcanti', for an in-depth survey and analysis of the many different theories of desire broached in this tradition.

23. See Sedgwick, *Between Men*, p. 45.

24. See Jacoff, 'Transgression and Transcendence', pp. 186 and 191.

25. See Jacoff, 'Transgression and Transcendence', p. 191.

26. Jacoff, 'Transgression and Transcendence', p. 186.

27. Jacoff, 'Transgression and Transcendence', p. 195.

28. See Judith Butler, 'Bodies that Matter', in *Bodies that Matter*, pp. 27–55.

29. See Butler, 'Bodies that Matter', pp. 48–49.

30. I characterized the pilgrim's encounter with Matelda in less philosophical terms in 'Seduction and Salvation': '[The pilgrim] is, at last, a mature adult male, permeable to the other. His permeability, of course, is inconsistent with the Ulyssean sense of mastery and command whose last stubborn vestiges must be given up. Fortunately and indicatively, the drowning of these aspects of himself, reenacted metaphorically in the reference to Leander, is not fatal. Dante no longer defends or defines himself in terms of a Ulyssean self-image, and therefore the loss of those vestiges leaves something — everything — left over. Nevertheless, this is his first real sexual experience, and a real sexual encounter can feel, to the uninitiated, like the ravishment alluded to in the reference to Proserpine. Like her, he loses half the world — the female half that suddenly appears as a strange, new, uncharted territory. But as Matelda points out, it is not she or the territory that is new. "Voi siete nuovi", she says to Dante and his companions. What he loses, then, is his sense of being at home in, and central to, half the world, but his is a loss which is tantamount to the saving realization that one is also a stranger, a passer-through, a pilgrim in one's own world' (p. 41).

31. For an extended discussion of Dante's metaphorics of the sun, see Alison Cornish, *Reading Dante's Stars* (New Haven, CT, and London: Yale University Press, 2000).

32. For further feminist commentary on this *locus classicus* of Western thought, see Spelman's *Inessential Woman*.

33. The term 'phallogocentrism' is a neologism coined by Jacques Derrida to refer to the privileging in Western metaphysics of determinateness and stability of meaning ('logocentrism') to produce 'truth', and the gendering of this truth as male ('phallocentrism').

34. For the textual sources of this passage, see Schnapp's 'Dante's Sexual Solecisms: Gender and Genre in the Commedia', in which he specifies that, according to Suetonius, the triumph in question was precisely that celebrating Julius's final victory over the last of the republican forces, making him the uncontested ruler of the empire (p. 208). Schnapp's larger argument concerns Dante's extensive use of gender reversals as a 'powerful tool for reconceptualizing relationships between fathers and sons, ancients and moderns, authorities and subjects, and "major" and "minor" literary genres' (p. 215). My project here has much in common with his, and Cestaro has very successfully elaborated Schnapp's argument concerning the importance of the maternal feminine, but my conclusions concerning the erotic (or sexuality) are distinctly different from Schnapp's. He ultimately sees these reconceptualizations as displacements of the erotic, whereas I see sexuality, not as displaced or sublimated, but as both reconceptualizing and reconceptualized.

35. For a fuller treatment of the triumph motif as deployed by both Dante and Petrarch, see my essay, 'The Spectacle of Society: The Semiotics of Renaissance Pageantry and the Triumphs of Petrarch', in *Petrarch's Triumphs: Allegory and Spectacle*, ed. by Konrad Eisenbichler (Ottawa: Dovehouse Editions, 1990).

36. See Butler, 'Bodies That Matter', pp. 34–35.

37. See, for example, Jacoff, 'Transgression and Transcendence', p. 197.

38. See Psaki, 'Dante's Redeemed Eroticism', *Lectura Dantis*, 18/19 (1996), 12–19, and Butler, 'Bodies that Matter', p. 51.

39. See Judith Butler, 'Prohibition, Psychoanalysis, and the Production of the Heterosexual Matrix', in *Gender Trouble: Feminism and the Subversion of Identity* (New York and London: Routledge, 1990), pp. 35–78; Luce Irigaray, *Speculum of the Other Women*, trans. by Gillian C. Gill (Ithaca, NY: Cornell University Press, 1985), pp. 101–03; Jacques Lacan, 'The Meaning of the Phallus', in *Feminine Sexuality: Jacques Lacan and the École Freudienne*, ed. by Juliet Mitchell and Jacqueline Rose, trans. by Jacqueline Rose (New York: Norton, 1985), pp. 74–85.

40. In her discussion of the diverse lyric contexts of *Inferno* v, especially that of Guido Cavalcanti's philosophy and poetics of love, Barolini writes: 'we learn that what is called love may not always be love, even when enveloped in citations from Guido Guinizzelli and Andreas Capellanus.' Her argument that '[b]y working to make distinctions between different kinds of human impulses popularly grouped together under the general rubric "love", *Inferno* v resists the totalizing effect of Cavalcanti's philosophy' anticipates and is compatible with the argument I am making in this essay about totalizing notions of sex and sexuality. See Barolini, 'Dante and Cavalcanti', p. 42.

41. See Eve Kosovsky Sedgwick, *Epistemology of the Closet*, p. 25.

42. Sedgwick, *Epistemology of the Closet*, p. 25.

43. Sedgwick, *Epistemology of the Closet*, p. 26.

44. Sedgwick, *Epistemology of the Closet*, p. 24.

45. Sedgwick, *Epistemology of the Closet*, p. 26.

46. See Marguerite R. Waller, *Petrarch's Poetics and Literary History* (Amherst: University of Massachusetts Press, 1980), pp. 59–60.

47. Manuele Gragnolati's conclusions regarding Dante's meeting with Casella in *Purgatorio* ii — another instance of the seductions of 'closed' poetry — resonate with this reading of Dante's encounter with Arnaut, although we differ in our understandings of the term 'body', which I argue is undergoing metamorphosis in *Purgatorio*. His brilliant discussion of the meaning of resurrection in *Paradiso* suggests, though, that we are fundamentally on the same trail. See Gragnolati, 'Nostalgia in Heaven', especially pp. 133–37.

48. I borrow the term 'tree-form' thought from the work of Gilles Deleuze and Félix Guattari, particularly their 'Introduction: Rhizome', in *A Thousand Plateaus: Capitalism and Schizophrenia*,

trans. by Brian Massumi (Minneapolis: University of Minnesota Press, 1987), pp. 3–25. My understanding of the 'poetics of relation' comes from postcolonial philosopher Édouard Glissant, *Poetics of Relation*, trans. by Betsy Wing (Ann Arbor: University of Michigan Press, 1997). My position differs from that of Prue Shaw, who suggests that 'through Guinizzelli Dante is imposing his own pattern of meaning on recent literary history'. She sees Guinizzelli as the poet's spokesperson in 'polemically asserting the true line of poetic succession [...] Guinizzelli now speaks with authority from a world beyond the human, putting the seal on a radical and definitive realignment of poetic reputations' (p. 298). I would suggest that Guinizzelli's manifesto be read instead dramatically, as an exemplification of yet another facet of the complicated business of lust that is being foregrounded — visibilized and verbalized — on this terrace, the better to be metamorphosed from a form of bondage to a *via* toward freedom. Dante the pilgrim inaugurated this discussion with a left-handed compliment whose temporal and material limitations Guinizzelli appears not to register: 'Li dolci detti vostri, | Che, quanto durerà l'uso moderno, | Faranno cari ancora i loro incostri' [Your sweet poems, which, as long as modern usage lasts, will make precious their very ink] (*Purg.* XXVI, 112–14). It is in response to this confinement of his work to 'modernity' and its association with the ephemera of ink and paper that Guinizzelli falls into the discourse of literary last judgment. Perhaps this defensiveness and desire for definitiveness are the referents of the 'lust' he is purging on the seventh terrace.

49. Dante uses the word 'membra' many times in the *Commedia*, notably in *Paradiso* I, 19–21, where the poet prays to Apollo to do with him what he did to the presumptuous Marsyas, drawing the latter from the sheath ('vagina') of his limbs ('membra'). Even though 'vagina' was not used during Dante's time for the female anatomy, the sense of the invocation to Apollo is to ask that corporeal markers of sexual difference no longer operate as they did before. The poet is praying for help in inhabiting a male body that is no *less* corporeal than the *corpo* of phallogocentrism, but as *unlike* that *corpo* in structure and capability as the 'angelica farfalla' [angelic butterfly] of *Purgatorio* X is from the 'vermo' [worm] that metamorphoses into it (lines 124–25). Indeed, the image of being drawn from the sheath of the *membra* works as paradisal gloss on *Purgatorio* X's image of the butterfly emerging from the rigid cocoon spun by the caterpillar around itself in order to undergo its metamorphosis. What the butterfly image leaves as yet unarticulated is the operation of grace in this transformation. I am indebted to personal communications from Sante Matteo (30 May 2011), Regina Psaki (4 June 2011), and Monica Green (26 June 2011) concerning the possible semantic fields for Dante of the terms 'membra' and 'vagina'.

50. See Fortuna and Gragnolati, 'After Wittgenstein' for a beautiful aligning of Ludwig Wittgenstein's *Philosophical Investigations* and the poetics of *Paradiso*.

51. One needs to distinguish here between the 'body' for which the figures in *Paradiso* are nostalgic and the 'body' as it is constituted in the pilgrim's pre-resurrection, pre-transhumanized discourse, which, as I have been arguing, has not yet been liberated from the effects of phallogocentrism. Manuele Gragnolati makes a powerful argument in support of the primary importance that corporeality retains throughout *Paradiso* in 'Nostalgia in Heaven', which complements Regina Psaki's focus on sexuality in *Paradiso* (on which, see Psaki, 'Love of Beatrice'). My reading of *Purgatorio* XXVI is deeply compatible with both of these arguments. See also Gragnolati's '(In-) Corporeality', which foregrounds the metamorphoses of the self both between the *Vita Nuova* and the *Commedia* and within the *Commedia* itself, concluding that embodiment is no longer seen as irreducible materiality, but merges with the linguistic performance of subjectivity 'in the revolutionary linguistic operation of *Paradiso*' (p. 220).

52. See Michel Foucault, *The History of Sexuality*, trans. by Robert Hurley, 3 vols (New York and Toronto: Random House, 1970–85).

53. Space does not permit my following the linkages from this passage in *Purgatorio* XXVI to the appearance of the refiner and teacher of 'proper' Tuscan, Brunetto Latini, in *Inferno* XV, but the two sites share a concern with the ways in which linguistic and sexual propriety inform and mirror one another.

54. See Waller, 'Seduction and Salvation', p. 240.

55. Schnapp writes in terms of 'excess' in 'Dante's Sexual Solecisms', p. 207, and Barolini refers to 'indulgence' in 'Dante and Francesca da Rimini', p. 49.

56. See Ilya Prigogine, *The End of Certainty: Time, Chaos, and the New Laws of Nature* (New York: Bantam Books, 1984), p. 4.
57. Prigogine, *The End of Certainty*, pp. 5–6.
58. See Schnapp's brilliant argument, in 'Dante's Sexual Solecisms', pp. 204 and 208–14, concerning Dante's use of the grammatical and sexual monstrous to figure salvation, and, as an aspect of this figuration, to map a fruitful, non-Oedipal relationship between ancient and modern, epic and lyric, and other potential binaries. Schnapp, however, ultimately makes Beatrice a 'middle ground' between binary terms. I am arguing, instead that we consider binary thinking itself as at stake and all of its terms as symptoms of the same phallogocentric construction of the human subject.
59. See Barolini, 'Dante and Francesca da Rimini', p. 9.
60. See Barolini, 'Dante and Francesca da Rimini', pp. 2–5.
61. See Margaret W. Ferguson, *Dido's Daughters: Literacy, Gender, and Empire in Early Modern England and France* (Chicago, IL, and London: University of Chicago Press: 2003), pp. 1–2).
62. See Ferguson, *Dido's Daughters*, pp. 1–2.
63. See Barolini, 'Dante and Cavalcanti'.
64. See Barolini, 'Dante and Francesca da Rimini', pp. 19–20.
65. See Barolini, 'Dante and Cavalcanti', pp. 36–38.

PART 3

Textuality and *Translatio*

CHAPTER 10

Between 'Unio' and Alienation: Expressions of Desire in the Strophic Poems of Hadewijch

Almut Suerbaum

I

In exploring aspects of mystical union with the divine in a lyric mode, the author Hadewijch, active probably in Brabant, and probably around the middle of the thirteenth century, is exceptional.[1] Her *oeuvre* comprises forms which one might expect in religious writing, such as visions and discursive tracts, but it also includes a group of strophic poems which draw on secular literary traditions: they are clearly inspired by northern French courtly love songs, and in some cases directly or indirectly by the Occitan lyric. Although allusions to secular poetry have been posited for other thirteenth-century religious writers, most notably Mechthild of Magdeburg, these are hard to substantiate, and in any case concern only individual motifs; the sustained use of secular lyric forms and motifs is unprecedented. The most plausible explanation for familiarity with such a literary milieu is that Hadewijch was from an aristocratic family, since this would account for her knowledge of French lyric forms as well as acquaintance with contemporary theological debates on issues such as the nature of the trinity. But the most fascinating question is not how she might have come to be familiar with such secular sources, but rather the literary use she makes of them. In her songs, Hadewijch transposes expressions of secular love and love-service into religious forms, oscillating between courtly vocabulary and complex theological concepts in such a way that listeners are often clear about the urgency of the sense of longing expressed long before they can establish whether this is a longing for another human being or for God.

Identifying a literary context for this unusual figure is not entirely straightforward, because we have little by way of firm historical information: the manuscripts in which her works are transmitted are late, without exception from the fourteenth century. Indeed, a recent study has suggested that the courts of fourteenth-century Brussels rather than a thirteenth-century *béguinage* may provide a more plausible place of origin, especially for a familiarity with lyric and musical forms.[2] Nevertheless, given that many of the theological elements of her visions point to concerns that are virulent in the mid-thirteenth century, this is still the most likely setting. Some passages in Hadewijch's letters point to a *béguinage*, i.e. a group of *mulieres religiosae*, often lay women with spiritual interests, rather than an established convent, as the probable social context in which Hadewijch's work originates.[3]

What the manuscript transmission reveals is an *oeuvre* in which prose visions, letters, couplet verse poems and strophic poems are united under the name of Hadewijch as author, and this author is given additional profile by a list of those with whom she is said to have been in correspondence — a list which starts with Jesus, Mary, and St John the Baptist, but also includes contemporary figures, both men and women.[4] Yet what we can trace is not the historical figure, but only the author as manifest in the literary work, through a variety of voices. The range of these is unusual, as is the fact that we have what appears to be a female voice unmediated through collaboration with male confessors, as is the norm in thirteenth-century religious writing by women. What we hear in Hadewijch's songs is a lyric 'I' which, like its secular counterpart in the courtly love lyric, discourages identification with a historical figure outside the literary work; an 'I' furthermore which, like its secular model, articulates desire for an other in terms that are often confident as well as demanding.[5] Yet unlike most of its secular analogues in the poetry of the troubadours and trouvères, this 'I' is, at least at times, identified as female.

Ever since Hadewijch's first editor, the Jesuit van Mierlo, pointed to the importance of love and desire in her work, scholars have attempted to define the cultural context to which these texts belong. Mostly, they have been approached through discussion of the theological ideas expressed, and van Mierlo himself set the trend of seeing expressions of love firmly and exclusively as articulations of a relationship between the human soul and God. What this paper aims to demonstrate instead is the significance of secular contexts, in which the texts move much more freely between the sphere of the secular and that of the religious, and where desire becomes a central concept in which such movement between spheres is articulated.[6]

II

The poetic strategies used in these songs are complex, as an analysis of three main examples will demonstrate. The first of these is Song I, 'Ay, al es nu die winter cout', which opens the collection of strophic poems in all three manuscripts.[7] In terms of metre and structure, it is quite clearly inspired by secular models, using a complex strophic form with a four-line macaronic refrain. This points to northern French models: a similar form is attested in the *oeuvre* of Gautier de Coinci (1177/78–1236), though with a variation in the refrain, but also in the work of German twelfth-century poets such as Heinrich von Morungen and Reinmar.[8] Gautier's song in turn appears to be a contrafacture of a secular love song, indicating that the move between the religious and secular sphere is a feature of late twelfth-century lyric contexts — and one of the areas that would need more detailed investigation is in fact the influence which liturgical lyric forms such as hymns and sequences play within Hadewijch's *oeuvre*.[9] Nevertheless, the courtly love song and its world is a prominent framework of reference for Hadewijch the author as well as for her intended audience.

The signals towards this framework are positioned firmly in the opening section of the song with its nature introduction, invoking the arrival of winter as a point of comparison for the inner state of the lyric 'I' in a manner familiar from twelfth-century secular songs.[10] Where secular songs often operate with a binary juxtaposition of winter and summer, or longing and fulfilment, the topical introduction is here used to create a sense of expectation of imminent change. Winter, lamented in the exclamatory opening, despite its association with night and darkness, in fact heralds a new summer and a new beginning ('dat es in schine | Bi desen nuwen iare' [that can be seen clearly | from the year now beginning anew] (I, 5–6)). As the song performs this turn to new hope, evoking the pleasures of imminent spring by the token of the catkins ('die hasel brinct ons bloemen fine' [the hazel tree brings us beautiful blossom] (I, 7)), this sense of anticipated joy is underlined by the refrain, which calls down a thousandfold blessing on those who hope to be joyful in love. Yet the refrain simultaneously shifts the literary ground: the intercalated two Latin lines are from a sequence in which the apophatic topos is related to the glory of God.[11] Furthermore, there is at least a residual ambiguity about the exact nature of this exclamation — 'vale', if interpreted as 'hail', may simply invoke a blessing, thus underlining the hope of those looking for joy and love; yet the particle 'ay' [alas], more commonly used in valedictions, indicates that this is a hope from which the speaker is taking leave.

In this first strophe, therefore, there are no firm indications that we are dealing with anything other than a secular love song, albeit one creatively playing with some of the conventions of the genre.[12] The song then moves through a variety of voices to present different aspects of the love thus evoked: where the second strophe highlights the strength required of those affected by a love metaphorically associated with a storm, the third identifies the speaker as female with the apostrophe 'alendech wijf' [wretched woman] (I, 25).[13] Again, the metaphors underline the passive nature of those afflicted by this love: the lyric 'I' laments the near-impossible situation in which she finds herself, both unable to love, and to cease loving. Not knowing where to turn, the speaker portrays herself as isolated from all others, while encouraging them to persevere in their own pursuit of love, despite her misfortune. This isolation and sense of alienation is of course common to many secular love songs, in which the (male) lyric 'I' may simultaneously represent his courtly audience and portray himself as set apart from them by unrequited desire. Up to this point, it is difficult to establish who or what the object of this love might be — the focus has been entirely on the strength of the experience and its effects on the subject. Yet in the fifth strophe, in which the singer addresses God, Hadewijch's song turns away from purely secular concerns by introducing vocabulary that firmly situates the love relationship in a religious context. At the same time, this shift of perspective also changes the nature of the lament: while granting God alone the right to judge, the admission of sinful behaviour marks a departure from the conceit of love service as used in the secular songs. If God rather than a human lady is the object of desire, then any obstacle in the path towards a consummation of the relationship is associated not with the object of the singer's desire, but with the singer herself.

Simultaneously, this admission of sinfulness and the concomitant repentance marks out the signer and reinforces the sense of isolation — but now, this is no longer the isolation of the unhappy lover whose desire is unrequited where others are more successful, but rather an isolation comparable to that of Job, who is invoked in an allusion in I, 48.[14] Where others attempt to interfere by offering help in controlling the singer, they in turn reveal their lack of understanding about the exclusive nature of the relationship which is a search for pure truth ('claerre waerheit'). The Platonic vocabulary evoked in this phrase is extended in the following two strophes which draw on the notion that God is both unknowable and radically different, rendering futile any attempt to understand and apprehend him. At the same time, they articulate a confidence that this God who is Love will act as a rejuvenating force, changing the defective human condition and granting 'nuwen sin | ter edelre minnen ende vrie' [a renewed mind for nobler and freer love] (I, 98–99). In its emphatic repetition of the concept of renewal, the final strophe re-contextualises the nature introduction of the first strophe: no longer a contrast of winter and summer, but rather a reference to the circular process of renewal which is an integral part of mystical theology. Indeed, the seventh strophe evokes one of the central metaphors of mystical renewal in its image of ascent achieved by degrees: 'Die ter hogher minnen rade [...] volclemt van grade te grade' [those who ascend to the mystery of perfect love, step by step] (I, 82–84).

The Platonic image of an ascent towards union with the source of all good is one in which the focus is on the attributes of God: his love may in turn be the cause of renewal. In contrasting the frame of mind of the singer with that of friends and foes around her, the exclusivity of her relationship with God is grounded in the insight that such reciprocation is ultimately dependent on God who, like the Lady of the secular love songs, has the power to punish or to reward. The opening song of the collection thus foregrounds a sense of hope precisely through the singer's insight into her own sinfulness.

III

Where the first song presents a concept of desire that is allied not to a directed sense of demand towards an 'other' but rather highlights the cyclical movement of renewal and self-renewal, the conceit of the cycle of the seasons is handled quite differently in the second song, 'Tsaermeer sal in corten tide' (II). It has Occitan as well as northern French analogues and uses a *tornada* — that is, the repetition of an incomplete short strophe at the end of the song, in which metre and rhyme correspond to the end of the preceding complete strophe.[15] This is a feature of the Occitan lyric, though it has been suggested that its occurrence may also be linked to features of liturgical forms, especially the sequence.[16] As in the Romance models, the *tornada* signals closure, and often picks up on central themes or ideas.

Unlike the first song with its prominent first person speaker, the second one is descriptive, starting from general observations which are couched in universal terms, referring to those who love as a collective group. Love, moreover, is expressed in Ovidian terms as an act of warfare, and where a singular form is used, this is marked as grammatically masculine. Love, personified quite conventionally as female and a Lady, is in turn conquered by the steadfast warrior. Later strophes modify the image: what needs to be conquered is not the lady, but the suffering of the lover: 'hi sal verwinnen al sine noet' [he shall conquer all his distress] (II, 38). As in the previous song, the central strophe marks a turning point — it shifts from stating universal truths about the nature of love to a self-reflexive assessment on the nature of poetry. In introducing a lyric 'I', the song focuses on the act of singing while simultaneously introducing a perspective of time: 'Mi sijn mine nuwe sanghe | Intoe in groten wenene bracht' [My new songs have been turned into great lamentations] (II, 46–47). Lament is the response to a sense of distance, in which Love, the object of the singer's desire, has withdrawn herself and can no longer be reached. That the song articulates hope despite this is the result of a paradoxical turn: rejection, which causes the singer to age and wither (II, 63), is finally presented as an opportunity to demonstrate loyalty — a virtue which the singer is confident will ultimately be rewarded. Again, the parallels to secular wooing songs are obvious, yet the final strophes place these conceits in a specific theological context in alluding to the need for self-abandonment. Only the suppression of individual will, the acceptance of powerlessness, allows the possibility of union with the beloved. Here, Hadewijch articulates ideas prominent in pseudo-Dionysian thought which is sometimes referred to as 'negative theology' — 'negative' because of its focus on the unbridgeable difference between God and man, in which God is unknowable and unattainable.[17]

IV

This relationship between will, desire, and acceptance is at the heart of the final example to be discussed here — song XXV 'In allen tiden vanden jare', which introduces a personification of Desire as well as Reason alongside that of Love common to almost all of Hadewijch's songs.[18] Here, in a song that appears to have no direct counterpart in French or Occitan lyric,[19] the opening orchestrates reciprocated love — but only as an imagined hope in the hypothetical cry of the lover who might say: '"Ay ic ben al di; lief, wes al mi, | Alset di behaghe!"' ['O, I am all yours, be mine | if it pleases you'] (XXV, 9–10) — admitting in the second line that this is no symmetrical relationship: the fear of displeasure colouring the hope of acceptance. As in the example discussed above, the song from the start establishes a link between desire and speech or song — 'Begherte en mach niet swighen stille, | Ende rehenne ghevet hare clare den raet' [Desire may not be silent, | and Reason offers her advice] (XXV, 51–52). In fact the articulation of anticipated fulfilment is itself the result of distress experienced for the sake of love. Reason, the adviser who helps the soul towards greater perfection, thereby leading her towards union with the beloved, is however a paradoxical force: in the same strophe in which consummated union is performed in language as an ever-repeated variation of terms in which subject and object of desire become interchangeable grammatically (XXV, 60–71), Reason is also the force which at this moment reminds the soul of its imperfection: 'Ende redene [...] | toent dar onghewassenheit inne, |

Waer redenne ye ghelieve oneffenne wach' [showing the soul's lack of growth, |
because of which Reason judges the loved soul and the Beloved ever unequal]
(xxv, 65–67), thus destroying the moment of equality which had been attained.[20]
Strikingly, though, the focus of the song is not a lament for this lost moment of
union, but rather an acceptance that Reason, the insight into the unbridgeable gap,
is the only source of healing. It is not desire, but the acceptance that desire may
be unrequitable, that will, paradoxically, lead to its fulfilment. It may be possible
to express this in terms of Lacanian psychoanalysis: the phenomenon I have just
described in Hadewijch's song appears to be what Lacan terms an 'ethical' act — that
is, 'an act of obliteration of symbolic Law whose aim is unfathomable, even to the
performer.'[21] The relationship between Lacan and Pseudo-Dionysius would merit
further investigation — if I prefer the terminology of Latin theology here, then it
is in part because this is the framework of reference with which Hadewijch herself,
on the evidence of her letters, was familiar: she quotes from William of Thierry.[22]

Desire and fulfilment are thus usually presented as interrelated, and indeed the
terms 'begherte' [desire] and its antonym 'ghenoechte' [fulfilment] often occur
together.[23] But whereas in the secular love lyric the opposition between these
terms is at times straightforward, juxtaposing unfulfilled longing with the joy of
reciprocated or consummated love, Hadewijch's songs develop a triadic concept of
'begherte' in which joy is seen negatively, as the avoidance of pain, and in which
therefore desire is the necessary stage leading towards its transcendence in a form of
unio described as 'ghebruken', i.e. *fruitio*. In Willaert's view, desire takes on a central
position within Hadewijch's songs: it breaks through the self-centred pleasure of the
lover and is a reminder of the fact that *unio* had not yet been attained, yet is at the
same time a force which drives the human lover towards greater self-perfection and
thus towards perfect *unio*.[24] Whether this move from an antithetical opposition of
desire and fulfilment to a triadic structure is the result of a move from the secular
to the religious sphere, as Willaert suggests, or rather an example of Hadewijch's use
of a tension that is inherent in much secular love lyric as well, is a question I would
like to consider briefly in the final section, assessing the range and impact of some
of the central metaphors for desire used within Hadewijch's songs.

V

Within the group of forty-five strophic songs, certain metaphors for desire occur
with characteristic frequency: images of chivalric conquest, images of journeying
and exile, and finally images of hunger and satiety. While the first of these refers
overtly to the sphere of secular literature on which Hadewijch draws within her
songs, the second and third are more common in a religious context. Indeed,
secular songs, though often prominently concerned with the senses of sight, hearing
and touch, rarely refer to the sense of taste in more than the common metaphor
of sweetness. All three conceptualize desire as paradoxical, incorporating mutually
incompatible opposites.[25] At the same time, all three go beyond a definition of love
through the oxymoron of 'sweet suffering', focusing instead on specific aspects of
love, in particular by highlighting the tension between love and reason.

Ovidian metaphors of love as warfare are common in northern French as well as Occitan and German courtly love songs. As in Ovid, they are often used to highlight the imbalance between lover and beloved object, casting the lover in the role of the victim, conquered while attempting to conquer the beloved. Hadewijch evokes such images, especially where the lyric 'I' is presented as a knight in armour — 'So ridic minen hoghen telt' [then I ride my proud steed] (x, 40) — though one whose military success is so uncertain that he finds himself unhorsed and on foot (x, 45). Indeed, the knight setting out to conquer is often vanquished, so his shield is smashed by blows ('want mi es die scilt so sere dorehouwen' (III, 26)), whereas personified Love uses her own shield to devastating effect ('si can na hare ghetesen | Wel scermen onder den scilt' (xxxix, 52–53)). The extended allegory of siege-warfare, picturing love as the strongest castle ('die alre staercste veste' (XLI, 61)) with the best defences ('die scoenste were' (XLI, 62)), and the highest walls ('die hoechste mure' (XLI, 62)), demonstrates the same turn, since the image culminates not in an apotheosis of love as the mistress of the castle, but rather the prisoner who is unable to escape from this fortress. Thus the poetic force of these conventional images lies in their ability to recast power relationships: not victory, but the willingness to be conquered is presented as the ultimate aim.[26] In focusing on the aspect of love service, Hadewijch therefore uses conventional Ovidian imagery to quite specific effect, especially where knighthood is strongly associated with the willingness to risk adventure.

Journeys are of course not just part of a narrative of chivalry, but also a well-established image in spiritual writing, expressing the tension between the desire for a spiritual home and security, and the precariousness of the path towards such a goal.[27] The combination of such imagery of journeying with that of chivalric fight is less common in secular love poetry, although Guest has pointed to striking parallels in the poetry of Jaufré Rudel and his focus on desire 'de lonh'.[28] Within Hadewijch's strophic poems, the emphasis is on the hardship and precariousness of the journey. Thus, song IX praises the willingness to venture abroad rather than staying at home, and celebrates the acceptance of suffering 'sweet exile'. In similar fashion, song XXXIV focuses on the paradox of love, whose receiving is always giving, and applies the same paradoxical structure to the metaphor of the journey, so that 'wandering lost in love' becomes a source of sweetness. The song culminates in a quotation from the *Song of Songs*, using Cant 2.16, 'You are all mine, Beloved, and I am yours', as a way not just of describing, but of staging mystical union of bride and bridegroom.[29] As in the earlier examples, negatively connoted hardships of travel — the absence from home, the state of exile, the loss of direction — are re-interpreted as positive, and associated with spiritual sweetness. The best known and most striking of these images is that of traversing the wilderness or even desert.[30] Here, the characteristic tone of Hadewijch's song is perceived to emerge most clearly: the insistence on absence and distance rather than on the joy of consummated union.[31]

Hunger and satiety offer a third set of contrasting concepts through which such tension in articulating desire is explored within Hadewijch's songs. Neither hunger nor satiety are expressions of physical experience,[32] and Caroline Walker Bynum has amply demonstrated that their prevalence in the writing of medieval women should not be seen as a result of simple gender stereotypes.[33] Bynum highlights that 'metaphors of eating are usually to Hadewijch not metaphors of engulfing and incorporating but metaphors of emptiness and hunger'.[34] Yet it is striking that the majority of the examples which Bynum discusses are from the (narrative) visions and the more overtly didactic poems in couplets ('Megeldichten'). Here, the emphasis on sensuality has a strong theological grounding, in that it expresses the conviction that God is not just the distant and unknowable, but also human and therefore to be experienced in an encounter which 'engages all our humanity'.[35] The strophic songs share the same theological concern, but they are often much more emphatic about the paradoxical relationship between the antonyms, presenting them not just as 'inseparable satiety and hunger' (XXXIII, 25), but relating both to a form of love which holds out the promise of fulfilment yet usually remains out of reach. As a result, the final strophe desires not satiety, but new hunger 'so vast | That new Love may devour new eternity!' (XXXIII, 55). These lines move beyond the paradoxical opposition of contrasts where both concepts are of equal value; instead, hunger, like suffering, is here re-positioned as positive. As a result joy, like satiety, is an expression of dulled senses, whereas hunger and suffering are the expression of perfect desire which hence paradoxically is closest to achieving the ultimate goal. This structure of paradoxical interdependence can be related directly to elements which are familiar from the courtly love poetry, and it seems that the secular models offer not just a language of desire which can be appropriated as an analogy for the spiritual relationship with God, but rather a mode of experiencing, not describing, desire.

VI

The nature of love in Hadewijch has been the source of controversy from the very start. While early interpretations followed van Mierlo in reading the strophic poems as religious songs, replacing human erotic love with love for God, Paepe had been the first to stress the significance of Occitan concepts of 'fin amors' for Hadewijch, because they present love as a dynamic process in which self-reflection of the lyric subject is as important as the object of desire.[36] They allow her to develop structures which are not linear, and therefore move beyond seeing desire as leading towards a specific goal.[37] Indeed, the frequent use of refrain and *tornada* serve the same purpose in their emphasis of cyclical return. It seems that this is more than just a literary device that was part of a characteristic Occitan style. Rather, the *tornada*, with its repeated re-use of part of a strophe, enacts the constant movement between different stages. Hadewijch thus transforms motifs from the courtly love lyric within the theological framework of her songs. At the same time, the songs articulate a central tension: desire for *unio* is a movement towards transcending the gap between the created world and God, yet the songs simultaneously articulate an awareness that, because of the fundamental difference between the human soul and the divine creator, such desire is inherently unrequitable. It is here that the special significance of secular lyric forms within Hadewijch's *oeuvre* is most evident: in staging desire as a performative act, characterized by a tension between gradual approximation and an awareness of inalienable difference, they articulate a central element of mystical theology by means of the secular discourse on love.

Notes to Chapter 10

1. Hadewijch's songs were first edited by Josef van Mierlo in Hadewijch, *Strophische gedichten, vol. I: Tekst en commentaar, vol. II: Inleiding*, Leuvense studiën en tekstuitgaven, 13 (Antwerp: Standaard-Boekhandel, 1942), on the basis of manuscript C (Gent, Universiteitsbibliotheek, ms 941). They are here quoted from the critical edition, Hadewijch, *Strofische gedichten: Middelnederlandse tekst en moderne bewerking met een inleiding*, ed. by Edward Rombauts and Norbert de Paepe (Zwolle: Tjeenk Willink, 1961). For an edition based on manuscript A (Brussels, Bibliothèque Royale, ms. 2879–80), with commentary and an appendix with melodies, see Hadewijch, *Liederen*, ed. and trans. by Veerle Fraeters and Frank Willaert, with a reconstruction of the melodies by Louis Peter Grijp (Groningen: Historische Uitgeverij, 2009). A somewhat pedestrian English translation is available in Hadewijch, *The Complete Works*, trans. and with an introduction by Mother Columba Hart, and with a preface by Paul Mommaers (Mahwah, NJ: Paulist Press, 1980). On Hadewijch's life and social context, see Frits van Oostrom, *Stemmen op schrift: Geschiedenis van de Nederlandse literatuur vanaf het begin tot 1300* (Amsterdam: M. Bakker, 2006), pp. 419–56; Joris Reynaert, 'Hadewijch: Mystic Poetry and Courtly Love', *Medieval Dutch Literature in its European Context*, ed. by Erik Kooper, Cambridge Studies in Medieval Literature, 2 (Cambridge: Cambridge University Press, 1994), pp. 208–25; Paul Mommaers, 'Hadewijch', *Die deutsche Literatur des Mittelalters: Verfasserlexikon*, 2nd edn, ed. by Kurt Ruh and others, 14 vols (Berlin and New York: de Gruyter, 1981), III, cols 368–78.
2. Frank Willaert, 'Hadewijch und ihr Kreis in den *Visionen*, *Abendländische Mystik im Mittelalter: Symposion Kloster Engelberg 1984*, ed. by Kurt Ruh (Stuttgart: Metzler, 1986), pp. 368–85, considers Hadewijch's works as composed 'für einen kleinen Kreis Gleichgesinnter' (p. 381); Geert Warnar, *Ruusbroec: Literature and Mysticism in the Fourteenth Century* (Leiden: Brill, 2007), pp. 71–73, argues for a dating close to that of the manuscripts in fourteenth-century Brussels, on the basis of identifying her as the heretic attacked by Ruusbroec, chaplain in Brussels before his move to the Groenendaal, though this view has been widely disputed. See for example Volker Mertens, 'Hadewichs Kontrafakturpraxis in den *Strofischen gedichten* und das Datierungsproblem', in *Deutsche Mystik im abendländischen Zusammenhang: Neu erschlossene Texte, neue methodische Ansätze, neue theoretische Konzepte. Kolloquium Kloster Fischingen*, ed. by Walter Haug and Wolfram Schneider-Lastin (Tübingen: Niemeyer, 2000), pp. 680–82; Fraeters and Willaert, pp. 13–17, offer a survey of the debate on the identity of Hadewijch, and conclude that van Mierlo's assumption of 1246 as a *terminus post quem* on the basis of the so-called 'List of the perfect' (discussed in note 4) remains convincing.
3. Fraeters and Willaert, p. 17; see Kurt Ruh, *Geschichte der abendländischen Mystik*, vol. II: *Frauenmystik und Franziskanische Mystik der Frühzeit* (Munich: C. H. Beck, 1993), pp. 159–232.
4. The so-called 'List of the perfect' ('Lijst der volmaakten') is transmitted together with the visions in all three of the oldest manuscripts; see Mommaers, cols 368–69. For an English translation, see H. Rolfon, 'Hadewijch of Antwerp: The List of the Perfect', *Vox Benedictina*, 5 (1988), 277–87. Even if the list is not authorial, it indicates the extent to which literary production was considered an activity within a social network spanning much of Europe. See Anneke Mulder-Bakker, *Lives of the Anchoresses: The Rise of the Urban Recluse in Medieval Europe* (Philadelphia: University of Pennsylvania Press, 2005), p. 157.
5. See van Oostrom, pp. 419–20, who points out that Hadewijch is unique amongst female religious writers of the Middle Ages, because she speaks to us directly and in her own voice — unlike Beatrice of Nazareth, Luitgard von Tongeren, or even Hildegard of Bingen, whose voice is mediated through their (male) confessors and scribes.
6. For a survey of recent scholarship, see Rob Faesen, *Begeerte in het werk van Hadewijch* (Antwerp: Peeters, 2000), pp. 11–23, who offers a detailed analysis of 'begheerte' in Hadewijch's *oeuvre*, but defines desire as an exclusively theological property. While his study is therefore an invaluable

guide to the theological context, tracing the concept from William of Thierry to Bernard of Clairvaux and Richard of St Victor on the one hand, and discussing Hadewijch in the context of vernacular hagiography on the other, it is entirely silent on the tradition of the secular love song.

7. As van Oostrom points out (p. 428), the forty-five songs are treated as an ordered collection in all three manuscripts, so that the sense of authorship concerns not only the composition of individual songs, but also the arrangement of songs within a the collection. Whether this ordering is the work of the same person responsible for the composition of the songs, or of a later redactor, is uncertain and impossible to establish in view of the interdependence of all three main manuscripts: see Fraeters and Willaert, pp. 32–33. Whether they are considered songs or poems depends on how one assesses the significance of the northern French models: none of the manuscripts transmits music, yet the fact that the French models clearly have tunes indicates that Hadewijch's strophes may also have been composed for singing. See Louis Peter Grijp, 'De zingende Hadewijch: Op zoek naar de melodieen van haar Strofische gedichte', in *Een zoet accord: Middeleeuwse lyriek in de Lage Landen*, ed. by Frank Willaert, Nederlandse literatuur en cultuur in de Middeleeuwen, 7 (Amsterdam: Prometheus, 1992), pp. 72–92; Anikó Daróczi, 'Hadewijch's mystiek tussen oraliteit en schriftlijkheid', *De fiere nachtegaal: Het Nederlandse leid in de middeleeuwen*, ed. by Louis Peter Grijp and Frank Willaert (Amsterdam: Amsterdam University Press, 2008), pp. 33–53.

8. See Frank Willaert, *De poetica van Hadewijch in de Strofische Gedichten* (Utrecht: HES Uitgevers, 1984), pp. 240–61 (esp. pp. 246–47), for a detailed analysis of metrical analogues in northern French and Occitan poetry. On Song I, see Frank Willaert, 'Registraliteit en intertextualiteit in Hadewijchs Eerste Strofische Gedicht', *Veertien listen voor de literatuur: Huldeboek aangeboden aan Prof. Dr. Celm Neutjens*, ed. by Luc Herman, Geert Lernout, and Paul Pelckmans (Kapellen: DNB-Pelckmans, 1993), pp. 165–90, who notes the use of images from Job; Faesen, pp. 46–54, reads the poetic 'I' of the song as a representative in whom each member of a spiritual community can see his or her relationship with Christ reflected (p. 54).

9. Anikó Daróczi, *Groet gheruchte van dien wondere: Spreken, zwijgen en zingen bij Hadewijch* (Antwerp: Peeters, 2007), pp. 177–83, offers a brief discussion of Notker Balbulus, whose prologue to his *Liber Hymnorum* explains the sequence as giving words to the otherwise wordless 'Alleluia jubilus' — a creation myth that was to remain powerful, even if modern musicologists consider it unlikely. Song 45 has long been recognized as a contrafacture of the sequence 'Marie preconio'; see Daróczi, pp. 177–83, with reference to Grijp and Margot Fassler, *Gothic Song: Victorine Sequences and Augustinian Reform in the Twelfth-Century Paris* (Cambridge: Cambridge University Press, 1993).

10. See Hans Schottmann, 'Der Natureingang in den Liedern Hadewijchs', *Beiträge zur Geschichte der deutschen Sprache und Literatur (Tübingen)*, 83 (1971), 213–27; Olive Sayce, *The Medieval German Love Lyric 1150–1300: The Development of its Themes and Forms in their European Context* (Oxford: Clarendon Press, 1982), pp. 39–45.

11. See Norbert de Paepe, *Hadewijchs Strofische Gedichten: Een studie von de minne in het kader der 12e en 13e eeuwse mystiek en profane minnelyriek* (Gent and Leuven: Wetenschappelijke uitgeverij en boekhandel, 1967).

12. Early scholarship viewed the strophic songs almost exclusively in terms of their relationship with the trouvères and read them as secular love songs. See Reynaert, pp. 208–09. More recently, the focus has been almost exclusively on Hadewijch as a religious writer, especially on her Visions.

13. Fraeters and Willaert (p. 66) interpret the adjective as an expression of spiritual isolation, pointing to the speaker as one who is exiled from her true home in God. This is plausible if reading from the end of the song, but although 'alendech' can have such connotations, there are no other indications within this strophe which would suggest a religious meaning.

14. Job 19, 13–19. See Hart's translation, p. 128.

15. Willaert (pp. 224–28) lists the songs using the *tornada* or refrain and notes that the frequency with which it is used points strongly towards Romance rather than Middle High German as the dominant source of influence on Hadewijch's songs. For a discussion of the French and Occitan parallels to song II, see p. 248f.; the earliest one in a song by Chrétien de Troyes, but the strophic form appears to have been particularly popular in the first half of the thirteenth century. Fraeters

and Willaert (pp. 392–93) consider Gace Brulé's song 'Qui sert die fausse poire', a popular song judging by the number of surviving manuscripts, the nearest analogue. See Ulrich Mölk, *Trobadorlyrik* (Munich and Zurich: Artemis, 1982), pp. 47–58 (esp. pp. 49–50), on possible links of the *tornada* to liturgical forms.

16. See Mölk. For Hadewijch, the significance of liturgical forms would need further investigation.

17. See Niklas Largier, *Die Kunst des Begehrens: Dekadenz, Sinnlichkeit und Askese* (Munich: C. H. Beck, 2007), p. 50.

18. On the use of 'ghenoechte' as personification and is use either in opposition to 'begerte' or as its complement, see Willaert, p. 149–54.

19. Fraeters and Willaert, p. 402.

20. On the significance of reason ('rede'), see Saskia Murk Jensen, *The Measure of Mystic Thought: A Study of Hadewijch's Mendeldichten* (Göppingen: Kümmerle Verlag, 1991), pp. 78–81, who demonstrates that within Hadewijch's *oeuvre*, it is usually considered subordinated to Minne: 'Reason is primarily a tool to be used in the early stages of sevice to Minne' (p. 78), as documented in a complex allegory in Vision 9 and in Letter 18, which contains a passage from William of St Thierry about the two 'eyes' of spiritual sight. 'Here again the text implies that although *redene* is a necessary part of striving towards God, it is not the highest or the best part' (p. 79). The ultimate source for this subordination of reason to love is Augustine, Confessions IX, ch. x.

21. William Burgwinkle, 'Ethical Acts and Annihilation: Feminine Heroics in "Girart de Roussillon"', in *Women and Medieval Epic: Gender, Genre and the Limits of Epic Masculinity*, ed. by Sara S. Poor and Jana K. Schulman (New York and Basingstoke: Palgrave Macmillan, 2007), pp. 159–82 (p. 164).

22. See Josef van Mierlo, 'Hadewijch en Willem von St. Thierry', *Ons Geestelijk Erf*, 3 (1929), 45–59; Saskia Murk Jensen, *The Measure of Mystic Thought: A Study of Hadewijch's 'Mengeldichten'* (Göppingen: Kümmerle Verlag, 1991), p. 79, suggests knowledge of Pseudo-Dionysius on the part of Hadewijch and discusses her use of William of St Thierry in Letter 18.

23. Willaert, *De poetica*, pp. 149–54, collects the passages in which the two terms occur together, and interprets them as an example of the tendency of mystical texts to express *unio* as the coincidence of opposites, in which the laws of human logic are suspended. He notes a contrast with the secular love lyric: where terms form the semantic field of 'joy' are positively connoted in the courtly love lyric, the change of antonym from the negatively connoted 'ghenoechte' to the more strongly positive term 'ghebruken' leads to a revaluation of 'joy' in Hadewijch.

24. Willaert, *De poetica*, p. 154.

25. On the distinction between contrast and paradox, see Tanis M. Guest, *Some Aspects of Hadewijch's Poetic Form in the 'Strofische gedichten'* (The Hague: Martinus Nijhoff, 1975), pp. 118–19.

26. Guest, in conflating the highly constructed lyric 'I' with the female author Hadewijch, interprets these lines as an expression of 'Hadewijch's sense of utter loneliness in these back moods' (p. 128), misreading the significance of gender role inversions. See Caroline Walker Bynum's introduction to the volume *Gendered Voices: Medieval Saints and their Interpreters*, ed. by Catherine M. Mooney (Philadelphia: University of Philadelphia Press, 1999), for a more differentiated reading of such authorial constructions.

27. For a succinct account of such images of mystical ascent in the context of Pseudo-Dionysian theology, see Walter Haug, 'Wendepunkte in der abendländischen geschichte der Mystik', in *Die Wahrheit der Fiktion. Studien zur weltlichen und geistlichen Literatur der Mittelalters und der frühen* (Tübingen: M. Niemeyer, 2003), pp. 446–63.

28. Guest, pp. 191–92.

29. Such use of the *Song of Songs*, appropriating the dialogue of the biblical text in a performative act, is first seen in vernacular commentaries on the *Song of Songs*, such as the twelfth-century 'St Trudperter Hoheslied', and become a hallmark of religious writing by women: see Almut Suerbaum, 'Die Paradoxie mystischer Lehre im *St. Trudperter Hohenlied* und im *Fließenden Licht der Gottheit*', in *Dichtung und Didaxe: Lehrhaftes Sprechen in der deutschen Literatur des Mittelalters*, ed. by Henrike Lähnemann and Sandra Linden (Berlin: de Gruyter, 2009), pp. 27–40.

30. See for example Song XXXI, 3 (a journey through the desert of love); XII, 5 (a desert created by love in her land); XXXVI, 3 (the wilderness of love). See Paul Dietrich, 'The Wilderness of God in Hadewijch II and Meister Eckhart and His Circle', in *Meister Eckhart and the Beguine Mystics: Hadewijch of Brabant, Mechthild of Magdeburg and Marguerite Porete* (New York: Continuum, 1997), pp. 31–43.

31. Ruh, p. 200, highlights the affinity of such images to Cistercian and Victorine mysticism; see Largier, pp. 139–40, who follows Bernard McGinn, *The Flowering of Mysticism: Men and Women in the New Mysticism (1200–1350)* (New York: Schuster, 1998), p. 220, in seeing this in the context of 'what Gregor of Nyssa called *epektasis*, constant progress in unfulfilled-fulfillment', underlines the characteristic combination of a rhetoric of desire with liturgical elements.

32. Guest, p. 161.

33. Caroline Walker Bynum, 'Hadewijch and Beatrice of Nazareth', in *Holy Feast and Holy Fast: The Religious Significance of Food to Medieval Women* (Berkeley, Los Angeles, and London: University of California Press, 1987), pp. 150–65.

34. Within this context, the affinity of eating with incorporation and pregnancy is nevertheless important; see Bynum, p. 154, Almut Suerbaum, 'O wi gar wundirbar ist dis wibes sterke: Discourses of Sex, Gender, and Desire in Johannes Marienwerder's life of Dorothea von Montau', in *Dorothea von Montau and Johannes Marienwerder: Constructions of Sanctity*, ed. by Almut Suerbaum and Annette Volfing, *Oxford German Studies*, 39.2 (2010), 181–97, and Volfing's 'Ever-Growing Desire' in this volume.

35. Bynum, p. 160.

36. Paepe, pp. 34–35. Mommaers, cols 370–71, dismisses this approach, because it entails an assumption that the object of desire is forever unreachable, which he disputes on theological grounds. This return to a biographical reading of the lyric 'I' consistently underestimates the impact of poetic form and tradition.

37. This debate on whether love in Hadewijch is considered requitable reflects a similar debate about the nature of desire. See Nicolette Zeeman, *Piers Plowman and the Medieval Discourse of Desire* (Cambridge: Cambridge University Press, 2006), p. 33, who contrasts a reading of desire as operating 'within an apparently closed-circuit of sublimation' with that of Freud and Lacan, for whom desire is 'substitutive, metonymic, and for that reason insatiable and intensificatory'.

CHAPTER 11

Desire, Subjectivity, and Lyric Poetry in Dante's *Convivio* and *Commedia*

Tristan Kay

In Chapter xxv of his *Vita Nuova*, Dante, having offered a brief history of the medieval Romance lyric tradition, voices the conviction that any vernacular poet ought to restrict the focus of his writing to the subject of love:

> E questo è contra coloro che rimano sopra altra matera che amorosa, con ciò sia cosa che cotale modo di parlare fosse dal principio trovato per dire d'amore. (*VN* xxv, 6)

> [And I speak against those who write vernacular poetry about any subject other than love, since such poetry was from the beginning intended for the treatment of love.][1]

This seemingly reactionary assertion of the limited horizons available to poetry in the mother tongue in fact becomes the source of some of Dante's most radical decisions as a writer. It is a statement widely seen as reflecting the *libello*'s polemical stance against Dante's dominant Italian forerunner, Guittone d'Arezzo. Guittone's corpus, as crystallized in the famous Laurenziano Rediano 9 manuscript, was rigidly divided between its amatory and ethical phases, between the love poetry of 'Guittone' and the didactic verse of 'Fra Guittone'. Dante's professed loyalty to the 'matera amorosa' points to the *Vita Nuova*'s very conscious departure from his predecessor's austere model of conversion. While Dante similarly jettisons the perceived spiritual recklessness of conventional courtly poetry, he does so without resorting to the arid moralizing which Guittone proposed as its only alternative, conceiving instead of a third way, whereby desire for the *donna* and desire for God improbably emerge as compatible.[2]

As exemplified in the previous essay, numerous medieval writers, both secular and religious, had spliced the semantics of earthly and spiritual desire, often drawing upon the mediating influence of the *Song of Songs*.[3] But what is radical about Dante's approach in the *Vita Nuova* and in the later *Commedia* is the continuity — and not simply the linguistic continuity — between these two forms of desire upon which the author insists. We find no straightforward rejection of erotic desire, but rather an alignment of creature and creator that would have been anathema for medieval theologians. The thorny question this raises is why Dante, a poet so deeply concerned with the ethical and religious purpose and validity of his writing, chooses to make things so difficult for himself. Why does he affirm his ongoing (albeit radically transformative) commitment to the love lyric when moral respectability and cultural authority could have been more straightforwardly attained by following the path of Guittone and unambiguously cutting his ties to the 'matera amorosa'?

In the hope of shedding a little light upon this topic, I shall focus in this essay upon an important shift in Dante's poetics from the abandoned philosophical treatise the *Convivio* (c. 1304–07) to his masterpiece the *Commedia* (c. 1307–20). The relationship between these texts has been the subject of a great deal of critical inquiry, especially concerning their respective philosophical and theological foundations and the diverse intellectual tensions and affinities between them.[4] My aim here, however, is to disengage the two texts' relationship from these dominant critical topics and to foreground instead the very different ways in which they handle the relationship between vernacular lyric poetry, desire, and subjectivity. In so doing, I shall explore, with reference to his lyric predecessors Guittone and Folco of Marseilles, Dante's negotiation of and eventual departure from a dualistic courtly paradigm of desire and conversion and the intriguing importance he attaches to his erotic commitment as a spiritually engaged poet.

Desire and the Mother Tongue

We cannot reflect upon Dante's fidelity to love poetry without first considering his commitment to vernacular language. In contrast with Latin, Dante saw the mother tongue as intimately connected to affectivity and corporeal selfhood, as has been thoroughly demonstrated by Gary Cestaro.[5] The poet describes in the *De vulgari eloquentia* how the vernacular is a form of language both 'rationale [...] et sensuale' (*DVE* I, iii, 2), reflecting man's unique standing as a being bestowed with intellect but weighed down by the mortal flesh. Unlike animals, man may communicate his interior consciousness, and yet, unlike angels, he is impelled to do so corporeally and through the compromised means of the arbitrary and mutable linguistic sign. Dante sees Latin as an attempt to overcome the vernacular's inherent corruptibility, reintroducing a stability lost with the fall of the Tower of Babel. Yet, in so doing, a 'grammatical' language such as Latin dispenses with the uniquely subjective properties that define the mother tongue. These properties are encapsulated in a passage from the *Convivio*:

> Questo mio volgare fu congiungitore de li miei generanti, che con esso parla-vano, sì come 'l fuoco è disponitore del ferro al fabbro che fa lo coltello; per che manifesto è lui essere concorso a la mia generazione, e così essere alcuna cagione del mio essere. (*Conv.* I, xiii, 4)

> [This vernacular of mine, being the language in which my parents spoke, brought them together, functioning like the fire which prepares the iron for the smith to make a knife. It is clear, then, that it helped to bring about my birth, and was, therefore, to an extent the source of my being.]

Dante tells us here how the 'volgare' not only channelled the desire of his parents and brought them together in sexual union, but also how it now resides at the core of his own identity, illustrating the nucleus between language, desire, and (embodied) subjectivity that Dante saw as the essence of the 'parlar materno' [mother tongue] (*Purg.* XXVI, 117).

A fundamental problem facing Dante as a committed vernacular poet, and one who conceived of the vernacular in these terms, was that such language was perceived as of a piece with humankind's fallen condition. As the intersection of corporeality, desire, and the linguistic sign — all markers of man's separation from God — the vernacular closely pertained to the Augustinian 'region of unlikeness'. This was particularly pronounced in the case of lyric poetry, which thematically privileged the very space of unfulfilment. Nonetheless, for all that Latin was the conventional language of theological discourse, Dante identified something uniquely valuable in the vernacular love lyric, as a form of writing that opened windows onto the subjective self and its constitutive desires. To sever vernacular poetry from desire, as 'Fra Guittone' had done in such lapidary fashion, was to sever it from its defining characteristics; it was to render living language — 'natural' language as Dante defines it in the *De vulgari* — lifeless and inert. Thus, in Dante's eyes, for all that Guittone's conversion might have been an example of moral probity, it saw him fail as a poet, and it is no coincidence that in *Purgatorio* XXVI, home to the penitent lustful, we see Dante privilege the erotic verse of Arnaut Daniel and Guido Guinizzelli (the latter is presented as a vernacular lyric 'padre') over the avowedly non-erotic poetics of Guittone and his perceived Occitan counterpart Giraut de Bornelh.[6] We might say that the principal challenge that Dante ultimately sets himself as a vernacular poet is to reformulate the love which fuels poetry in the mother tongue into something spiritually tenable, without extirpating its subjective, corporeal essence and thereby betraying a deeply held conviction.

Desire, Authority, and Subjectivity in the *Convivio*

If the passage from the *Convivio* cited in the previous section can elucidate Dante's commitment to the vernacular and his rejection of a binary model of conversion, it can also distract us from the fact that the *Convivio* itself emerges, in this regard, as a somewhat reactionary work, which adheres far more rigidly to the cultural and ideological norms of the period than do the *Vita Nuova* and the *Commedia*. This conservatism can be attributed to a significant extent to the treatise's well-documented pursuit of *auctoritas*. The work's use of commentary and allegory and its continual recourse to classical authors reflect Dante's attempts to associate his own vernacular compositions with the Latin, exegetical culture of the scholastics — the 'authoritative' literary culture of his time and one inextricably linked to ethics — and to fashion himself as an *auctor*.[7] As well as to the Bible, exegetes in this tradition paid increasing attention to pagan authors, extracting the universal, transhistorical moral truths which the ancients' poetry was seen to contain, while suppressing its morally contentious elements. One such element was earthly love, with plainly erotic classical texts invariably handled by commentators in such a way that their lascivious dimension was altogether ignored, or else artificially moralized.[8]

While these issues would become increasingly nuanced over the course of the thirteenth and fourteenth centuries,[9] we can nonetheless speak of an overarching cultural dichotomy in the later Middle Ages between authority and subjectivity, which was both reflected and reinforced by the linguistic dichotomy between Latin and the vernacular. This was a dichotomy that both the *Vita Nuova* and the *Convivio* in different ways attempted to subvert, in the hope of realizing Dante's ultimate objective of spiritually redeeming and culturally authorizing his activity as a vernacular poet and — as Albert Ascoli has shown — integrating the categories of 'authority' and 'personality'.[10] Yet, for all that the *Convivio* strives to achieve this, in its fusing of vernacular poetry and expository prose, it ultimately immerses itself too fully in the modalities of what we might loosely term 'Latin' culture. While its opening chapters reverberate with Dante's deeply individuated sense of post-exilic injustice, its later pages often read like a Latin treatise that happens to be written in the vernacular, privileging abstract and transhistorical truths and theories over the subjectivity and desire identified as the hallmarks of vernacular textuality.

The *Convivio* is nevertheless a work that meditates extensively (albeit abstractly) upon the topic of desire. We find the first of two particularly important reflections towards the end of Book III:

> Che con ciò sia cosa che ciascuna cosa naturalmente disia la sua perfezione, sanza quella essere non può contento, che è essere beato; ché quantunque l'altre cose avesse, sanza questa rimarebbe in lui desiderio; lo quale essere non può con la beatitudine, acciò che la beatitudine sia perfetta cosa e lo desiderio sia cosa defettiva; ché nullo desidera quello che ha, ma quello che non ha. (*Conv.* III, xv, 2–3)

> [The reason for this is as follows: since every being naturally desires its own perfection, without this perfection man cannot be content, that is, blessed; for however abundantly he might possess other things, without perfection desire would still be present in him, and desire cannot coexist with beatitude, since beatitude is something perfect, while desire is something defective, because no one desires what he has, but what he does not have.]

Dante here expounds the Aristotelian notion that any being naturally desires its own perfection, a perfection which for humankind may be found only in beatitude. Until we reach heaven, our lives are defined by an innate sense of lack, which only in the presence of God — the only legitimate *telos* of desire — will be fulfilled. Thus, desire for Dante, as for numerous medieval Christian thinkers, possesses an ambivalent status, as both a by-product of man's separation from God and the road whereby he may return to his spiritual *patria*. Such a vision of desire had implicitly underpinned the *Vita Nuova*: Dante's love for Beatrice was shown to be an expression of a more profound desire, born out of his separation from God, with which his love for her eventually became reconciled. Yet such a reconciliation is not of interest to Dante in the *Convivio*. The work's lengthiest reflection on desire, from which I cite only an extract, comes in Book IV:

> Onde vedemo li parvuli desiderare massimamente un pomo; e poi, più procedendo, desiderare uno augellino; e poi, più oltre, desiderare bel vestimento; e poi lo cavallo; e poi una donna; e poi ricchezza non grande, e poi

grande, e poi più. E questo incontra perché in nulla di queste cose truova quella che va cercando, e credela trovare più oltre. Per che vedere si può che l'uno desiderabile sta dinanzi all'altro alli occhi della nostra anima per modo quasi piramidale, che 'l minimo li cuopre prima tutti, ed è quasi punta dell'ultimo desiderabile, che è Dio, quasi base di tutti. (*Conv.* IV, xii, 16–17)

[And so we see small children desiring above all else an apple; then, when they are somewhat older, desiring a little bird; then, later still, desiring fine clothes; then a horse; then a woman; then riches in small measure; then riches in greater measure; then even more riches. This happens because people find in none of these things what they are actually seeking, and think that they will find it a little way on. It may be gathered from this that, from the viewpoint of our soul, each desirable object stands in front of another in pyramid form, so that the smallest, coming first, covers all the others, and is the apex of the ultimate desirable object, God, who constitutes the base of all others.]

This passage closely follows Augustine's distinction between *uti* and *frui* — between learning from earthly desires and merely enjoying them.[11] While every Christian *camminatore* possesses a natural desire to return to his Maker, there are two forms of desire between which he must choose: the one, directed only towards God, will lead to fulfilment; the other, directed towards ephemeral goods as ends in themselves, will merely generate further desire. As Teodolinda Barolini has shown, this Augustinian 'anatomy of desire' in many ways foreshadows the *Commedia*, and the *Purgatorio* in particular.[12] Yet it is also transcended in the later work's more radical treatment of eros. Among the worldly objects that can enslave the desiring subject of the *Convivio* — situated between the 'cavallo' and the more sinister 'richezza' in the sequence above — is the 'donna', as earthly love is lumped with avarice in a chain of cupidinous desires.[13] In the *Commedia*, however, eros is afforded a redemptive, as well as a corruptive, capacity, evinced above all in the pivotal role of Beatrice but also hinted at in the strikingly ambivalent, rather than unequivocally censorious, treatment of the love poets in Purgatory. By contrast, the *Convivio* consistently reduces love for the (non-allegorical) *donna* and moral probity to a rigid opposition.

This tendency is apparent in the *Convivio*'s very first chapter, where Dante configures the relationship between the ethical *Convivio* and the amatory *Vita Nuova*:

E se nella presente opera, la quale è Convivio nominata e vo' che sia, più virilmente trattasse che nella Vita Nova, non intendo però a quella in parte alcuna derogare, ma maggiormete giovare per questa quella; veggendo sì come ragionevolemente quella fervida e passionata, questa temperata e virile essere conviene. Ché altro si conviene e dire e operare ad una etade che ad altra; per che certi costumi sono idonei e laudabili ad una etade che sono sconci e biasimevoli ad altra, sì come di sotto, nel quarto trattato di questo libro, sarà propia ragione mostrata. E io in quella dinanzi, all'entrata della mia gioventute parlai, e in questa dipoi, quella già trapassata. (*Conv.* I, i, 16–17)

[If in the present work, which is called *Convivio*, as I wish it to be, the subject is treated more maturely than in the *Vita Nuova*, I do not intend by this in any way to disparage that book but rather more greatly to support it with this one, seeing that it understandably suits that one to be fervid and passionate, and this one to be temperate and mature. For, different actions and words befit different ages; and certain deeds are praiseworthy at one age that are inappropriate at another, as will be explained in Book IV of this work. And the *Vita Nuova* was written only on the cusp of manhood, whereas this work is the product of maturity.]

The carefully calibrated relationship between the two works serves, on the one hand, to harmonize them and to construct an exemplary model of authorial development. Yet while Dante's treatment of the *Vita Nuova* is not straightforwardly palinodic, we certainly sense that the earlier work is belittled. The *Convivio* situates the path to rectitude and maturity as founded squarely in the surpassing of the 'fervid and passionate' love of the *Vita Nuova* and the espousal of more muscular ethical, political, and philosophical themes. Such a description of the *libello* does it a disservice, for its innovation was precisely that it was *not* 'fervid e passionate' and that love and rationality could, in fact, transcend the opposition which Dante believed to have shackled his lyric forerunners.[14] Nevertheless, the earlier *prosimetrum* is confined to the sphere of youthful passion.

Much the same tendency emerges in the *Convivio*'s handling of Dante's pre-existing amatory canzoni 'Voi che 'ntendendo' and 'Amor che ne la mente mi ragiona'. Dante insists that these love poems were written not for a flesh-and-blood woman, but for the allegorical figure of Lady Philosophy, and his exposition of them seeks to rid him of the charges of infidelity to Beatrice which he fears they may otherwise bring: 'Temo la infamia di tanta passione avere seguita, quanta concepe chi legge le sopra nominate canzoni in me avere segnoreggiata' [I fear the infamy of having yielded myself to so great a passion that anyone who reads the canzoni mentioned above must believe once ruled me] (*Conv.* I, ii, 16). In playing down these poems' literal sense (dismissed elsewhere as a 'bella menzogna' [beautiful lie] (*Conv.* II, i, 3)), Dante's language is again strikingly dualistic, establishing a dichotomy between 'passione' and 'vertù' (*Conv.* I, ii. 16), which corresponds to the line drawn between the 'impassioned' *Vita Nuova* and the 'temperate' *Convivio* in the treatise's opening chapter.

Despite being written in the vernacular, that linguistic conduit of desire, we are learning that the temperate *Convivio* in fact endeavours to leave desire to one side. Indeed, in the canzone 'Le dolci rime', commented upon in Book IV, the bond between vernacular poetry and love, previously deemed sacrosanct by Dante, is explicitly severed, replaced by a technically accomplished yet vapid brand of scholastic argumentation:

> Le dolci rime d'amor ch'i' solia
> cercar ne' miei pensieri,
> convien ch'io lasci; non perch'io non speri
> ad esse ritornare,
> ma perché li atti disdegnosi e feri
> che ne la donna mia
> sono appariti m'han chiusa la via
> de l'usato parlare.
> E poi che tempo mi par d'aspettare
> diporrò giù lo mio soave stile,
> ch'i' ho tenuto nel trattar d'amore;

> e dirò del valore,
> per lo qual veramente omo è gentile,
> con rima aspr'e sottile. (*Conv.* IV, lines 1–14)

[The sweet love-poetry I was accustomed to seek out in my thoughts I must now forsake; not that I do not hope to return to it, but the proud hard bearing that in my lady has become apparent has barred the path of my usual speech. And so, since it now seems a time for waiting, I will lay down that sweet style of mine which I held to in writing of love, and I will speak instead concerning the quality by which man is truly noble in harsh and subtle rhymes.]

With the interiority of the lyric subject ('*miei* pensieri') now replaced by the universal theme of *gentilezza* ('per lo qual [...] *omo* è gentile'), 'Le dolci rime' is the poem in Dante's corpus most easily reconciled with the *Convivio*'s broader movement away from individuation towards abstraction. It is also the poem in which Dante comes closest to emulating the Guittonian model he formerly shunned — a model most famously articulated in the Aretine's conversion manifesto 'Ora parrà':

> Ora parrà s'eo saverò cantare
> e s'eo varrò quanto valer già soglio,
> poi che del tutto Amor fug[g]h' e disvoglio,
> e più che cosa mai forte mi spare:
> ch'a om tenuto saggio audo contare
> che trovare — non sa né valer punto
> omo d'Amor non punto;
> ma' che digiunto — da vertà mi pare
> se lo pensare — a lo parlare — sembra,
> ché 'n tutte parte ove distringe Amore
> regge follore — in loco di savere. (VI, lines 1–11)[15]

[Now it will become apparent if I shall know how to sing, and if I am worth as a poet what I was formerly worth, now that I completely flee Love and 'diswant' it, and find it more terrible than any other thing. I have heard it said by a man considered wise that a man not pierced by Love does not know how to write poetry and is worth nothing; but this seems far from the truth to me, if thought and word are in agreement, for wherever Love seizes madness, and not wisdom, reigns.]

Dante's canzone, like Guittone's, is concerned with laying down an amatory subject matter to address weightier, ethical themes. Guittone similarly foregoes (albeit more forcefully) the subjectivity of the lyric to expound upon topics common to the generic *omo*. Each poet closes himself to the external stimuli that had formerly inspired and sustained their verse, proclaiming a virile poetics founded upon an active projection of universal moral truths rather a passive submission to eros. We continue to sense, however, an anti-Guittonian anxiety on Dante's part. It seems telling that in lines 1–4 of 'Le dolci rime', Dante stresses that he abandons love poetry only temporarily ('non perch'io non speri | ad esse ritornare'), in the very same lines that Guittone stresses the permanence of his own rejection of 'Amor' ('poi che del tutto Amor fuggh' e disvoglio'). Dante was surely mindful here of the Aretine's precedent, and sought to distance himself from it. Yet however much Dante protests, this didactic canzone — like the *Convivio* itself — is highly Guittonian in its rigid separation of lyric and ethical concerns. The 'dolci rime' that remain in the *Convivio* — the canzoni of Books II and III — are little more than fossils of a suppressed lyric past; their subjectivity, desire, and vitality extracted by a rigid mode of allegory.

A final example of the *Convivio*'s restrictive treatment of desire comes in the closing chapters of Book IV. Here, Dante maps out the 'four ages of man' and the sort of behaviour befitting each of them, delineating a model of development which continually reinforces an opposition between desire and reason. Significantly, this model is exemplified through the classical figure of Aeneas, who abandoned the siren call of Dido to follow his public and transhistorical vocation of founding Rome:

> E così infrenato mostra Virgilio, lo maggiore nostro poeta, che fosse Enea, nella parte dello Eneida ove questa etade si figura: la qual parte comprende lo quarto, lo quinto e lo sesto libro dello Eneida. E quanto raffrenare fu quello, quando, avendo ricevuto da Dido tanto di piacere [...], e usando con essa tanto di diletazzione, elli si partio, per seguire onesta e laudabile via e fruttosa, come nel quarto dell'Eneida scritto è! (*Conv.* IV, xxvi, 8)

> [Virgil, our greatest poet, shows that Aeneas was temperate in this way in that part of the Aeneid in which this age of life is allegorized, the part comprising the fourth, fifth, and sixth books of the Aeneid. How great was his restraint when, having experienced so much pleasure with Dido [...] and having derived from her so much gratification, he took his departure from her to follow an honourable, praiseworthy and profitable path, as is recorded in the fourth book of the Aeneid!]

The tale of Dido and Aeneas is seen as an emblematic example of the opposition between 'youthful' eros and 'virile' restraint at the heart of the *Convivio*. Indeed, as I have discussed in detail elsewhere, the paradigm of *Aeneid* IV is used as something of a blueprint for Dante's own authorial development as set out in the treatise, with the author's self-presentation in the opening chapters of the work displaying suggestive parallels with the portrayal of Aeneas here.[16] If the author of the *Convivio* may be seen to fashion himself as a temperate Aeneas, it is intriguing that in the *rime petrose*, also belonging to this ideologically anomalous 'middle period' of Dante's career, the poet likens himself to the fervent Dido: 'E m'ha percosso in terra, e stammi sopra | con quella spada ond'elli ancise Dido' [Love has struck me to the ground and stands over me | with that sword with which he slew Dido] (*Rime* 1.35–36). The paths of rectitude and of love are at this time cast as inherently diverging — the former leads to Rome and to public duty; the latter to Carthage, to immoderation and self-destruction, as Dante the love poet and Dante the *cantor rectitudinis* begin to follow separate paths.

The *Commedia* and Dante's Poetics of Integration

Despite staging Dante's return to Beatrice, it would be simplistic to cast the *Commedia* as a 'sequel' to the *Vita Nuova* and a rejection of the abandoned *Convivio*.[17] Far more than this, it is an integration of the two earlier works, as the political, philosophical, and ethical concerns of the earlier treatise are welded to the redeemed erotics of the *libello*, with Beatrice assuming some of the characteristics of the *Convivio*'s Lady

Philosophy.[18] Nonetheless, the *Commedia* and *Vita Nuova* are allied — and at odds with the *Convivio* — not only in their common theological foundations but also in their handling of the relationship between vernacular poetry and desire.[19] As in the *Vita Nuova*, Dante's love for Beatrice in the *Commedia* seeks to transcend dualism, to redeem in some sense the lyric mode. As Regina Psaki in particular has argued, the *Commedia* in fact attempts to do this more forcefully, with the Beatrice of the *Commedia* a more strongly embodied and eroticized presence than the ethereal Beatrice of the later chapters of the *Vita Nuova*.[20] The *Convivio*'s more orthodox, Augustinian notion of desire finds a home in the *Purgatorio*, where earthly desire is redirected towards Heaven above.[21] In the *Paradiso*, however, this notion is problematized anew, as an emphasis is placed not only upon desire for God, but also — as shown by Manuele Gragnolati and Rachel Jacoff — upon the souls' striking desire for the return of their resurrected bodies and the concomitant redemption of a corporeal and relational sense of identity.[22] Scholars such as Moevs and Raffa have persuasively argued that the *Paradiso* — wholly unlike the *Convivio* — is defined by its non-duality, its emphasis on an incarnational form of truth beyond worldly logic.[23] This idea of non-duality relates crucially to the subject of allegory, which is handled in a much more nuanced fashion than in the *Convivio*, where the literal and allegorical senses — and with them 'passione' and 'vertù' — were starkly separated. By contrast, the *Commedia*'s figural representation depicts its characters in a state that distils and fulfils their earthly characteristics, while retaining the historical dimension that distinguishes them from mere allegorical symbols. This dimension is particularly important with respect to Beatrice. As Franke writes, 'debates have stretched over centuries, attempting to resolve the question of [Beatrice's] identity — as either a Florentine girl or an allegory for theology — one way or the other. But considered figurally, her historical reality does not exclude but rather grounds her theological meaning. Her apotheosis as an incarnation of divine revelation — that is as a personal saviour and beatifier, a *figura Christi* for Dante — brings to the highest imaginable consummation his real, historical relation to her as the object of his total love and devotion.'[24] Beatrice's historicity in the *Commedia* becomes ever less explicit, and ostensibly less significant. Yet it is precisely the continuity between the Beatrice of Florence and the Beatrice of Paradise — and between the notionally conflictual forms of desire associated with these incarnations — which allows Dante to simultaneously redeem and eroticize his poetics.

Lest my argument be misconstrued, I should emphasize at this juncture that the *Commedia* is far from permissive when it comes to unalloyed earthly love. In *Inferno* V, *Purgatorio* XXVI, and *Paradiso* IX, eros is damned, purged, and forgotten respectively, while Dante's unique opportunity to overcome the dualism that had hamstrung his vernacular rivals is only possible thanks to the intercession of a woman who, as Dante is at pains to tell us, is a miracle.[25] Yet through Beatrice — carefully constructed upon the fault-line between time and eternity, body and soul, desire and intellect — the conventional dichotomy between erotic and divine love, reinforced in the *Convivio*, is negotiated in radical and transformative ways. My aim in the remaining pages of this essay is to consider the ways in which the *Convivio*'s more restrictive treatment of desire and lyric poetry is viewed from the perspective of the *Commedia*, and to do this I shall turn now to the Heaven of Venus (*Paradiso* VIII–IX).

Questions of Desire in the Heaven of Venus

Located in Venus, the last of three heavens found in the earth's shadow, are those souls who rejected a propensity to carnal love to become passionate servants of God. As always in the *Commedia*, the theme of earthly love is inseparable from the world of love literature, to which the two main speakers in canto IX, Cunizza and Folco, are intimately linked. Cunizza was known for her love affair with the Italian troubadour Sordello, while Folco was a thirteenth-century troubadour, noted for his erotic fervour, who in later life rejected love poetry to become a bishop, penning at least two crusade songs which starkly rejected earthly love. It is upon Folco, a poet often excluded from critical discourse on love and love poetry in the *Commedia*, that I wish to focus here.[26] Critics have often suggested that the former troubadour is, in terms of his moral and ideological *iter*, specular of Dante himself: 'lo specchio più perfetto nel quale Dante può proiettare la sua propria immagine di poeta d'amore' [the most perfect mirror into which Dante can project his own image as a love poet], as Michelangelo Picone puts it.[27] To substantiate this view, they point to Folco's description of how the serene denizens of Venus feel no regret towards their erotic pasts:

> Non però qui si pente, ma si ride,
> non de la colpa, ch'a mente non torna,
> ma del valor ch'ordinò e provide. (*Par.* IX, 103–05)

['Yet here we don't repent, but smile instead; | not at our fault, which comes back not to our mind, | but for the Power which ordered and foresaw.']

These words are often read in conjunction with Cunizza's earlier in canto IX:

> Cunizza fui chiamata, e qui refulgo
> perché mi vinse il lume d'esta stella;
>   ma lietamente a me medesma indulgo
> la cagion di mia sorte, e non mi noia;
> che parria forse forte al vostro vulgo. (*Par.* IX, 32–36)

['Cunizza was my name and, overcome | by this star's splendor, I shine here. | I gladly pardon in myself the reason for my lot, nor does it grieve me — a fact that may | seem strange, perhaps, to those unschooled among you.']

Critics such as Patrick Boyde and Pamela Williams have argued that Cunizza's serenity here points to the constructive role that eros played in her salvation, and that the 'forte' of line 36 refers to the perplexing continuity between eros and *caritas* which our 'common crowd' ('vostro vulgo') cannot comprehend. While the souls in Venus show that 'folle amore' [maddened love] had to be mastered in order to attain salvation, Williams in particular argues that they nonetheless link their propensity to eros to the fervent godliness of their latter years, and present sexual desire as 'somehow dispositive towards divine love'.[28]

To me it would seem mistaken, however, to interpret this serenity as indicative of a continuity between erotic and divine love that foreshadows or mirrors Dante's love for Beatrice. Folco's refusal to repent for his former lust in Heaven does not mean that it is now celebrated; rather, it means that he may acknowledge it with what Jacoff, in another reading of this canto, terms a 'post-palinodic' tranquillity.[29] Following their submergence in the River Lethe, regret is a notion alien to the blessed throughout the third *cantica* — a notion that we mortals may find 'forte'. The ex-troubadour in fact makes it clear that his salvation was attained in spite of his weakness to erotic love, with the caesura 'la colpa, ch'a mente non torna' underlining the schism between his erstwhile commitment to eros and his current beatitude. Folco's decisive movement away from earthly love is also highlighted as he describes how he burned (with lust) like Dido until his hair turned grey:

> che più non arse la figlia di Belo,
> noiando e a Sicheo e a Creusa,
> di me infin che si convenne al pelo. (*Par.* IX, 97–99)

['for the daughter of Belus was no more aflame, | bringing grief to Sichaeus and to Creusa, | than I, until the colour of my hair began to fade.']

The evocation of Dido here is interesting in this context, for she was the figure used by Dante in the *Convivio* to implicitly articulate his own surpassing of erotic love in aligning himself with the figure of Aeneas. Moreover, it shows how Folco draws a stark line between the receptive, feminized sphere of love poetry (one recalls how the morally robust 'Fra Guittone' saw his errant former self as 'd'Amor punto' [pierced by love]) and the masculine sphere of (public) Christian service and moral probity. This gendered opposition is reinforced by the additional comparison that Folco makes between his courtly identity sense and the female figure of Phyllis, taken from Ovid's *Heroides*. The epithet 'Folco' used by the former poet in *Paradiso* IX ('Folco mi disse quella gente a cui | fu noto il nome mio' ['Folco the people called me, if they knew my name'] (*Par.* IX, 94–95) is also significant in this respect, for, as noted by Michelangelo Picone and Paolo Squillacioti, this was the name used in medieval manuscripts when dealing with his episcopal activity, while the more effeminate diminutive 'Folquet' was associated with his career as a love poet.[30] Folco's identity is thus founded upon opposition: between the lyric poet and the crusading bishop, feminized and passive youth and virile maturity, the private and the public spheres. Indeed, this dualism is especially pronounced in the case of a troubadour who not only abandoned love poetry, but also played a central role in the Albigensian Crusades, in which the culture that fostered the poetry of the troubadours was brutally condemned as heretical.

(Anti-)courtly Conversions: Folco, Guittone, Dante

While Folco's corpus is far less extensive, its bipartite nature, divided between amatory and ethical phases, between 'Folquet' and 'Folco', calls to mind not the Dante of the *Vita Nuova* and the *Commedia*, but Guittone. This comparison is by no means superficial, for Folco's own conversion poem 'Chantars mi torna ad afan' displays striking and unremarked similarities to Guittone's 'Ora parrà':

Chantars mi torna ad afan
quan mi soven d'En Barral,
e pois d'amor plus no·m cal,
no sai com ni de que chan;
mas quecs demanda chansso
e no·il cal de la razo:
c'atressi m'es ops la fassa
de nuou, cum los motz e·l so;
e pois forssatz, ses amor
chan per deute de follor,
pro er mos chans cabalos
si non es avols ni bos. (XIV, 1–12)[31]

[Singing for me turns into pain | when I recall Sir Barral, | and since I no longer care for love, | I do not know how nor of what to sing; | but each asks for a song | and doesn't care about the subject: | and so it is necessary for me to invent it [the *razo*], | along with the words and the music; | and since, constrained, without love, | I sing out of debt and from folly, | my song will be worthy, | whether it is good or not.]

While Guittone's conversion was born out of the poet's meditation upon human love upon taking his religious orders, Folco relates his conversion here to the death of his feudal lord Barral. The memory of his departed lord, he tells us, means that his poetry can now describe only pain (*afan*). As seen in lines 3–4, the poet, since he is no longer interested in love, no longer knows how nor of what to sing ('pois d'amor plus no·m cal'). This calls to mind Guittone's canzone, which, in the equivalent lines and using strikingly similar language and syntax ('poi che del tutto Amor fugh'e disvoglio'), announces his own renunciation of love and expresses an anxiety as to the poetic validity of a love-less poetics.

Like Guittone, Folco is eager to underline the novelty of this undertaking. His circumstances, he says in lines 7–8, require that he reassess the parameters of his poetry, in terms of its content, lexis, and sound. His converted praxis, in other words, involves a complete reappraisal of his writing, as he emphasizes the absolute lack of continuity between the old poet and the new. As in 'Ora parrà', however, such concern is swiftly replaced by an assured declaration of intent and a calling into question of conventional courtly values. Whether the poem corresponds to what is conventionally deemed 'good' or 'bad', Folco declares in line 12, no longer concerns him. 'Ora parrà' similarly disputed the wisdom of the 'om tenuto saggio' [the man considered wise]. Guittone's evocation of this figure serves to call into question the conventionally subjective barometer of poetic worth, just as Folco seeks to do here in his prioritizing of what he claims to be 'empirically' important.

These proemial stanzas thus perform precisely the same function: firstly, they announce in very similar terms that the poet is no longer concerned with love; secondly, they show that this abandonment of love contravenes the prevailing ethos of the lyric tradition; finally, they challenge the entrenched courtly maxim that poetry must depend upon the articulation of erotic desire, and postulate instead a new notion of poetic worth, contingent instead upon an unequivocal rejection of love and espousal of virtue.

Folco's second stanza sees the ideological affinities between himself and Guittone become yet more pronounced:

> Amador son d'un semblan
> e·l ric cobe d'atretal,
> c'ades ab dolor coral
> mermon lor joi on mais n'an:
> qu'en luoc de fenestra so
> que merma s'om i apo;
> on plus pren quecs so que cassa
> plus a del segre ochaiso;
> per qu'ieu teng cel per meillo
> que rei ni emperador
> qui celz mals aips vens amdos
> que vensso·l plus dels baros. (xiv, 13–24)

[Lovers are all of the same ilk, | just like the greedy rich, | for always with heartfelt pain | their joys decrease when they have more of them, | for they [joys] are like a window | whose aperture decreases if one adds adornments to it; | for the more one obtains what one pursues | the more motive he has for pursuing it; | for which I believe that one better | than king or emperor | who overcomes both these ills | which overcome most of the barons.]

Not only does Folco's focus shift from lyric subjectivity towards universality (and from the first person to the third) in a manner highly reminiscent of Guittone, but the categories of sinner described — the lustful and the avaricious — are the very ones denounced in the second stanza of Guittone's poem:

> ché grande onor né gran bene no è stato
> acquistato — carnal voglia seguendo,
> ma promente valendo
> e astenendo — a vizi' e a peccato;
> unde 'l sennato — apparecchiato — ognora
> de core tutto e di poder dea stare
> d'avanzare — lo suo stato ad onore
> no schifando labore:
> ché già riccor — non dona altrui posare
> ma 'l fa 'lungiare, — e ben pugnare — onora;
> ma tuttavia lo 'ntenda altri a misora. (vi, 20–30)

[for neither great honour nor great good have been attained by following carnal desire, but instead by living as good men and abstaining from vice and from sin. Therefore the wise man must always be prepared with all his heart and power to advance his state to honour, not shunning labour; since indeed riches do not give anyone peace but in fact distance it, and good striving brings honour, as long as one pursues it with measure.]

Just as Folco dismisses human love without qualification ('Amador son d'un semblan') and relates it to the immoderate pursuit of wealth ('e·l ric cobe d'atretal), so Guittone reduces all 'amore' to 'carnal voglia' and aligns it with avarice ('riccor non dona altrui posare | ma 'l fa lungiare') as a sin of cupidity.

Barolini has expertly shown how 'Ora parrà' serves as an important model for Dante's canzone 'Doglia mi reca' (a lyric which in turn informs the *Commedia*) in its demystification of courtly love and emphasis on the commonality of all sins of desire.[32] 'Chantars', however, constitutes an important precursor to both these Italian canzoni. Indeed, Barolini's description of 'Ora parrà' ('"Ora parrà" indicts courtly love by refusing to segregate it. This move allows the poet first to conflate courtly love with lust and then, even more interestingly, to conflate lust with desire in any form') could just as well apply to Folco's *canso*.[33] It is a poem well represented in medieval Italian troubadour anthologies, and was often included at the end of sequences of Folco's poems, in an attempt to convey the poet's conversion from earthly love.[34] It is therefore more than plausible that Fra Guittone was mindful of Folco's precedent. It is also highly probable that Dante knew the poem, given the *Commedia*'s emphasis upon Folco's episcopal activity and the echoes noted by several commentators between the crusade poems and *Paradiso* IX's invective against the avaricious Church.[35]

Thus, far from foreshadowing the *Vita Nuova*'s handling of earthly and divine love, as critics have often claimed, Folco is much more profitably understood as a Guittone *avant la lettre*, defined by the very dualism that the *Vita Nuova* and *Commedia* so carefully opposed. But what I hope has also become apparent is that both Folco and 'Fra Guittone' display an important ideological kinship with the Dante of the *Convivio*, in their stark delineation of the relationship between *Amor* and rectitude. As implied by his self-comparison to Dido, Folco's conversion is analogous to that mapped out by Dante in the 'four ages of man' of *Convivio* IV — a model to which, as I have shown, Dante in the *Convivio* himself professed to adhere in his self-alignment with Aeneas. By contrast, the Dante of the *Commedia* aligns himself not only with Aeneas, but also with Dido. Upon beholding Beatrice in the Earthly Paradise, he cites (or rather translates) Dido's foreboding words upon falling in love with Aeneas: 'conosco i segni de l'antica fiamma' ['I recognize the signs of the ancient flame'; *Purg.* XXX, 48] — words which signpost the improbable presence (and redemption) of eros at the core of his 'sacred poem'.[36]

In light of the parallels indicated between Folco's treatment of desire and subjectivity and that which we saw in the *Convivio*, it is no coincidence that in this particular Heaven Dante is identified by Charles Martel as the author of the canzone 'Voi ch'intendendo', the first poem allegorized by Dante in the *Convivio*:

> 'Noi ci volgiam coi principi celesti
> d'un giro e d'un girare e d'una sete,
> ai quali tu del mondo già dicesti:
> *Voi che 'ntendendo il terzo ciel movete.*' (*Par.* VIII, 34–37)

['In one orbit we revolve with these celestial Princes | — in one circle, with one circling, and with a single thirst | — to whom, from the world, you addressed these words: | *You who, by understanding, move the third heaven.*']

Several critics have interpreted this autocitation as in some way palinodic in intent. There are various subtle ways in which Dante appears to undermine the canzone. Picone has noted the 'distancing' language used by Charles in describing the poem, which he describes as remote both from heaven and from the present time ('ai quali tu *del mondo già* dicesti').[37] Moreover, Dante corrects the earlier poem on a question of angelology: while in the canzone he claimed that the order of angels governing this heaven were the Thrones, he now learns at first hand that they are, in fact, the Principalities.[38]

Yet there is more at stake here than this particular intellectual misdemeanour. For Jacoff, Dante corrects himself with respect to angelology because he wishes to emphasize that the mysteries of heaven were beyond the reach of an earlier work — the *Convivio* — which relied upon and privileged the powers of reason. 'Voi che 'ntendendo' was the moment when Dante first turned to the 'donna gentile', the moment when he rejected the theologized object of his love poetry, Beatrice, and shifted his attention to the necessarily inferior, worldly end of philosophy, reinventing himself, in Zygmunt Barański's words, as 'a secular thinker, whose attention was focused more on the mysteries of this world than of Heaven.'[39] Jacoff also highlights the dualism of the earlier work, arguing that the 'dead end of the *Convivio* is both philosophical and poetic. In that work Dante keeps separate what he will later unite.'[40] She believes Dante alludes to his former self here in the same spirit as Cunizza ('mi vinse il lume d'esta stella') and Folco ('la colpa ch'a mente non torna').[41] In other words, while the poet's attitude towards the canzone and its accompanying treatise is negative, we find no explicit expression of regret, since Dante — like Folco and Cunizza — beholds his misadventure with a 'post-palinodic' serenity.[42]

I concur with Jacoff's two main points: first, that the citation of 'Voi che 'ntendendo' concerns the poet's regret with respect to the treatise's privileging of philosophy and its failure to achieve synthesis; second, that it would be inappropriate, in the third *cantica*, for this regret to be expressed too forcefully. Yet I diverge from another aspect of her reading. Jacoff argues that Dante's 'antico errore' [ancient error] (*Par.* VIII, 6) was his 'prior allegiance to philosophy'.[43] As we have seen, this allegiance to philosophy in the *Convivio* coincided with Dante's movement away from erotic love. Yet the *colpa* of Folco, Cunizza, and Rahab, by contrast, consisted in their former commitment to 'folle amore' [maddened love] (*Par.* VIII, 2), which they now altogether recant. In short, Dante's trajectory, in moving from the *Convivio* to the *Commedia*, does not adhere to the 'Venusian' model, for it sees him shun the path of the non-amorous *cantor rectitudinis* — the path of Guittone and Folco — in favour of a new, redeemed allegiance to *Amor*. If Charles had cited one of Dante's highly erotic 'rime petrose', we could have more easily interpreted the autocitation in the key that Jacoff proposes: that is, as a post-palinodic recollection of how Dante was once conquered by this planet's venereal 'lume'. But Dante-*poeta* cites not a love poem, but a poem evocative of a juncture at which his verse distanced itself from eros in order to exalt an abstract personification of philosophy. How, then, does 'Voi che 'ntendendo' relate to this particular heaven?

Barolini's excellent analysis of the autocitation sheds light upon this issue.[44] Like Jacoff, she regards the citation of 'Voi che 'ntendendo' as palinodic and believes the dualism of the *Convivio* to be implicated in Dante's veiled critique of the canzone. For Barolini, however, this shortcoming does not mean that 'Voi che 'ntendendo' now constitutes Dante's 'colpa', which he looks upon serenely. Rather, she believes the canzone finds itself cited in this heaven because, like the characters we find there, it is dichotomous. In short, she believes the canzone is cited as a 'poem of conflict', since, at the time of its composition (or at least its inclusion in the *Convivio*), Dante saw his love for philosophy and his love for Beatrice as conflictual:[45]

> [...] the fact that Cunizza and Folquet are converts from *folle amore* is registered not positively but negatively, by the duality of their discourses and by the compensation that dictates their political diatribes. The textual status thus assigned by the poet to the third heaven, conceived as the representation of a stage in which the elements of a prior conflict and duality are still visible although no longer conflicting, accounts for the presence and choice of this particular autocitation.[46]

'Voi che 'ntendendo' points, then, to a limited kind of transcendence, which falls short of the needs of the *Commedia*. Barolini contends that its presence in Venus — like the presence of Folco — is intended to point towards the fusion of love and politics uniquely achieved in the 'poema sacro' (*Par.* XXV, 1) and notes the pervasive dualities of this heaven are transcended in *Paradiso* X, beyond the earth's shadow, where 'Love is newly defined in relation to the dynamics of the Trinity': 'Guardando nel suo Figlio con l'Amore | che l'uno e l'altro etternalmente spira' [Gazing on his Son with the Love | the One and the Other eternally breathe forth] (*Par.* X, 1–2).[47] Like his attitude towards Folco, therefore, Dante's attitude towards 'Voi che 'ntendendo' (and, by extension, the *Convivio*) in the *Paradiso* is seen as somewhat ambivalent, rather than censorious. It is cited in a positive light insofar as it saw Dante open up his poetry to weightier public and political themes, but negatively insofar as it entrenched a dichotomy between ethical and political engagement and a poetics founded in desire.[48]

Barolini's insightful reading of the autocitation in line with her reading of the compromised status of Dante's Venusians helps to buttress, from a different angle, two of my central arguments in this essay: firstly, that Folco's model of conversion crucially differs from Dante's in the *Commedia*; and secondly, that there is a significant ideological affinity between Folco's conversion and Dante's *Convivio*. We might say that the distance between the poetics of the *Commedia* and the poetics of the crusade poet Folco can be measured in terms of the distance between the *Commedia* and the *Convivio* — not in terms of the relationship between philosophy and theology, of course, but in terms of the ways in which they handle, as ethically engaged poets, the relationship between lyric poetry, desire, and subjectivity. 'Voi ch'intendendo' therefore evokes Dante's own 'Venusian' moment, when he — like Folco, Guittone, and Aeneas — established an inviolable line between love and probity. Such a conversion was not morally reprehensible. On the contrary, we learn in Venus that, in renouncing eros, Folco saved himself from damnation. But he also ceased to be a love poet. In separating vernacular poetry from desire in the *Convivio* Dante similarly severed himself from the genealogy of love poets eulogized anew in *Purgatorio* XXVI, whose valuable but hitherto morally flawed enterprise Beatrice had afforded him the unique opportunity to redeem. Dante pursuit of *auctoritas* in the treatise led him to compromise his poetic convictions: rather than reconciling the love lyric with the intellectual achievements of scholastic culture, as it intended, the treatise shoehorned vernacular poems into an ill-fitting context, so that the barriers between love and ethics, subjectivity and authority were unwittingly re-affirmed.

It is no coincidence that at the one instance in the *Commedia* where Dante explicitly defines his praxis, he describes himself as one inspired by love:

> 'I' mi son un che, quando
> Amor mi spira, noto, e a quel modo
> che e' ditta dentro vo significando.' (*Purg.* XXIV, 52–54)

['I am one who, when | Love inspires me, takes note, and as | he dictates deep within me, so I set forth.']

Some critics have emphasized here the echoes of the human authors of Scripture, who in similar terms, wrote of being 'inspired' by the Holy Spirit.[49] This resonance should not, however, be construed as evidence that Dante in the *Commedia* rejects eros or the love lyric, for every bit as much as Pentecostal inspiration, the *terzina* evokes the trope of erotic inspiration found throughout the corpus of the troubadours.[50] Our understanding of this vexed *terzina* ought not to choose between these courtly and scriptural *topoi* in order to understand the *Amor* that Dante describes. It should instead recognize and emphasize their careful conflation. I would suggest in conclusion that the essence of Dante's self-proclaimed victory over his vernacular rivals in the *Commedia* is not simply that he travels to the *Paradiso*, much less that he 'leaves behind' the erotic desire he sees purged from Arnaut and Guinizzelli. After all, plenty of poets — not least Guittone — had done this. Rather, it is that Dante is able to achieve salvation *as a love poet*, so that the opposition between 'Guittone' and 'Fra Guittone', between 'Folquet' and 'Folco', between the 'fervid' *Vita Nuova* and the 'temperate' *Convivio* is overcome. Thus, desire for the *donna*, and with it Dante's undiluted convictions as a vernacular poet, find themselves redeemed.

Notes to Chapter 11

1. Unless otherwise stated, translations of Dante's works are taken (and occasionally adapted) from the following editions: Dante Alighieri, *Vita Nuova*, trans. by Mark Musa (Oxford: Oxford University Press, 1992); Dante Alighieri, *The Banquet*, ed. and trans. by Richard Lansing (New York: Garland, 1998); Dante Alighieri, *The Divine Comedy*, ed. and with a commentary by Robert Hollander, trans. by Robert and Jean Hollander, 3 vols (New York: Doubleday, 2000–07); Dante Alighieri, *Dante's Lyric Poetry*, ed., trans., and with a commentary by Kenelm Foster and Patrick Boyde, 2 vols (Oxford: Oxford University Press, 1967).

2. On the *Vita Nuova*'s anti-*guittonismo* and resistance to a dualistic model of conversion, see Tristan Kay, 'Redefining the "matera amorosa": Dante's *Vita Nova* and Guittone's (anti-)Courtly "canzoniere"', *The Italianist*, 29 (2009), 369–99. On other aspects of Dante and Guittone, see for example: Teodolinda Barolini, *Dante's Poets: Textuality and Truth in the 'Comedy'* (Princeton, NJ: Princeton University Press, 1984), pp. 85–123, and her essays 'Guittone's *Ora parrà*, Dante's *Doglia me reca*, and the *Commedia*'s Anatomy of Desire' and '*Sotto benda*: Gender in the Lyrics of Dante and Guittone d'Arezzo (With a Brief Excursus on Cecco d'Ascoli)', both in *Dante and the Origins of Italian Literary Culture* (New York: Fordham University Press, 2007), pp. 47–69 and pp. 333–59; Giuseppe Bolognese, 'Dante and Guittone Revisited', *Romanic Review*, 70 (1979), 172–84; Nievo Del Sal, 'Guittone (e i guittoniani) nella *Commedia*', *Studi danteschi*, 61 (1989), 109–52; Claire E. Honess, 'Dante and Political Poetry in the Vernacular', in *Dante and his Literary Precursors: Twelve Essays*, ed. by John C. Barnes and Jennifer Petrie (Dublin: Four Courts Press, 2007), pp. 117–51 (pp. 125–35); Michelangelo Picone, 'Guittone, Guinizzelli e Dante', *L'Alighieri: Rassegna dantesca*, 18 (2001), 5–19; Justin Steinberg, *Accounting for Dante: Urban Readers and Writers in Late Medieval Italy* (Notre Dame, IN: University of Notre Dame Press, 2007), pp. 13–60.

3. On the *Song of Songs* in the Middle Ages, see for example: Ann W. Astell, *The Song of Songs in the Middle Ages* (Ithaca, NY, and London: Cornell University Press, 1990); E. Ann Matter, *'The Voice of My Beloved': The Song of Songs in Medieval Christianity* (Philadelphia: University of Pennsylvania Press, 1990); Denys Turner, *Eros and Allegory: Medieval Exegesis of the Song of Songs* (Kalamazoo, MI: Cistercian Publications, 1995). On *The Song of Songs* and secular love poetry, see d'Arco Silvio Avalle, *Ai luoghi di delizia pieni: Saggio sulla lirica italiana del XIII secolo* (Milan and Naples: Ricciardi, 1977); Peter Dronke, 'The Song of Songs and Medieval Love-Lyric', in *The Bible and Medieval Culture*, ed. by W. Lourdaux and D. Verhelst (Leuven: Leuven University Press, 1976), pp. 256–62; Lucia Lazzerini, 'La trasmutazione insensibile: Intertestualità e metamorfismi nella lirica trobadorica dalle origini alla codificazione cortese', *Medioevo Romanzo*, 18 (1993), 153–205 and 313–69; Andrea Pulega, *Amore cortese e modelli teologici: Guglielmo IX, Chrétien de Troyes, Dante* (Milan: Jaca Book, 1995). On the *Song of Songs* and Dante, see Paola Nasti, *Favole d'amore e 'saver profondo': La tradizione salomonica in Dante* (Ravenna: Longo, 2007); Lino Pertile, *La puttana e il gigante: Dal 'Cantico dei cantici' al 'Paradiso terrestre' di Dante* (Ravenna: Longo, 1998).

4. On the relationship between these works, see for example: Maria Corti, *La felicità mentale: Nuove prospettive per Cavalcanti e Dante* (Turin: Einaudi, 1983), and *Dante a un nuovo crocevia* (Florence: Sansoni, 1981); John Freccero, 'Casella's Song: *Purgatorio* II, 112', in *Dante: The Poetics of Conversion*, ed. by Rachel Jacoff (Cambridge, MA: Harvard University Press, 1986), pp. 186–94; Robert Hollander, '*Purgatorio* II: Cato's Rebuke and Dante's *scoglio*', *Italica*, 52 (1975), 348–63; Peter Dronke, *Dante's Second Love: The Originality and Contexts of the 'Convivio'* (Exeter: Society for Italian Studies, 1997), pp. 72–76; Ulrich Leo, 'The Unfinished *Convivio* and Dante's Rereading of the *Aeneid*', *Medieval Studies*, 13 (1951), 41–64; Bruno Nardi, *Dal 'Convivio' alla 'Commedia'* (Rome: Istituto Storico Italiano per il Medio Evo, 1960); John A. Scott, 'The Unfinished *Convivio* as a Pathway to the *Comedy*', *Dante Studies*, 113 (1995), 31–56.

5. See Gary Cestaro, *Dante and the Grammar of the Nursing Body* (Notre Dame, IN: Notre Dame University Press, 2003). On Dante and language, see for example Zygmunt G. Barański, 'Dante's Biblical Linguistics', *Lectura Dantis*, 5 (1989), 105–43; *Dante's Plurilingualism: Authority, Vulgarization, Subjectivity*, ed. by Sara Fortuna, Manuele Gragnolati, and Jürgen Trabant (Oxford: Legenda, 2010); Cecil Grayson, '*Nobilior est vulgaris*: Latin and Vernacular in Dante's Thought', in *Centenary Essays on Dante by Members of the Oxford Dante Society* (Oxford: Oxford University Press, 1965), pp. 54–76; Elena Lombardi, *The Syntax of Desire: Language and Love in Augustine, The Modistae, Dante* (Toronto: University of Toronto Press, 2007), pp. 121–74; Pier Vincenzo Mengaldo, *Linguistica e retorica di Dante* (Pisa: Nistri-Lischi, 1978).

6. Giunta describes *Purgatorio* XXVI as 'una poderosa legittimazione della poesia d'amore laica' [a powerful legitimation of secular love poetry] (p. 57), as Dante 'ritorna alle sorgenti della poetica stilnovistica' [returns to the sources of his stilnovist poetics] (p. 60): Claudio Giunta, *La poesia italiana nell'età di Dante: La linea Bonagiunta-Guinizzelli* (Bologna: Il Mulino, 1998). See also Tristan Kay, 'Dante's Ambivalence towards the Lustful', in *Dante and the Seven Deadly Sins*, ed. by John C. Barnes (Dublin: Four Courts Press, forthcoming).

7. On the medieval commentary tradition and the notion of *auctoritas*, see for example Vincent Gillespie, 'The Study of Classical Authors: From the Twelfth Century to *c*. 1450', in *The Cambridge History of Literary Criticism: Volume II: The Middle Ages*, ed. by Alastair J. Minnis and Ian Johnson (Cambridge: Cambridge University Press, 2005), pp. 145–235; *Medieval Literary Theory and Criticism c. 1100–1375: The Commentary Tradition*, ed. by Alastair J. Minnis and A. B. Scott (Oxford: Oxford University Press, 1998); Alastair J. Minnis, *Medieval Theory of Authorship: Scholastic Literary Attitudes in the Later Middle Ages* (Aldershot: Wildwood house, 1984); Susan Reynolds, *Medieval Reading: Grammar, Rhetoric and the Classical Text* (Cambridge: Cambridge University Press, 1996); Giorgio Stabile, 'Autore' and 'Autorità', in *Enciclopedia dantesca*, ed. by Umberto Bosco, 6 vols (Rome: Istituto dell'Enciclopedia Italiana, 1970–78), I, 454–60. As Dante himself tells us (see *Conv.* IV, vi, 3–5), an *auctor* was not merely one able to write well, but also an ethical guide. In this definition, Dante follows two of the three roots suggested in Hugutio of Pisa's *Magnae Derivationes*: the Greek 'autentin' ('worthy of faith and obedience') and the Latin 'auieo' ('to bind'). Numerous scholars have underlined in recent decades the intimate bond between literature and ethics that defined this branch of medieval literary culture. See especially: Judson Boyce Allen, *The Ethical Poetic of the Later Middle Ages: A Decorum of Convenient*

Distinction (Toronto: University of Toronto Press, 1982), and *The Friar as Critic: Literary Attitudes in the Later Middle Ages* (Nashville, TN: Vanderbilt University Press, 1971); John Dagenais, *The Ethics of Reading in Manuscript Culture: Glossing the 'Libro de buen amor'* (Princeton, NJ: Princeton University Press, 1994).

8. On earthly love in the commentary tradition with particular reference to Dante, see Alastair J. Minnis, '*Amor* and *Auctoritas* in the Self-Commentary of Dante and Francesco da Barberino', *Poetica*, 32 (1990), 25–42.

9. See especially Minnis, *Medieval Theory of Authorship*, but also Allen, *The Friar as Critic*, pp. 2–3; G. R. Evans, 'Exegesis and Authority in the Thirteenth Century', in *'Ad Litteram': Authoritative Texts and Medieval Readers*, ed. by Mark D. Jordan and Kent Emery (Notre Dame, IN: Notre Dame University Press, 1992), pp. 43–111; Nasti, pp. 9–13.

10. See Albert Russell Ascoli, *Dante and the Making of a Modern Author* (Cambridge: Cambridge University Press, 2008).

11. See especially *De doctrina Christiana* I, iv, 4; I, xxii, 20.

12. See Barolini, 'Anatomy of Desire', and 'Purgatory as Paradigm: Traveling the New and Never-Before-Traveled Path of this Life/Poem', in *The Undivine Comedy: Detheologizing Dante* (Princeton, NJ: Princeton University Press, 1992), pp. 99–121.

13. For Barolini, 'Dante implies here that desire for social advancement underpins many of our individual desires, and suggests that it ultimately commodifies them; the objects of desire he lists here are commodities precisely to the degree that their attainment serves to measure our position on the social scale' ('Anatomy of Desire', p. 56). The closing 'poi più' of the list cited, meanwhile, is seen to adumbrate the endless craving of the *Commedia*'s she-wolf (ibid.).

14. The *Vita Nuova*, of course, had described a love which flourished in harmony with 'lo fedele consiglio della Ragione' ['the faithful counsel of reason'] (*Vita Nuova* I, 10).

15. Cited from *Poeti del Duecento*, ed. by Gianfranco Contini, 2 vols (Milan and Naples: Ricciardi, 1960). The translation is my own.

16. On the ways in which Dante uses Aeneid IV and the figures of Dido and Aeneas to frame and reflect upon the oscillations in his own poetics and notion of desire, from the minor works to the *Commedia*, see Tristan Kay 'Dido, Aeneas, and the Evolution of Dante's Poetics', *Dante Studies*, 129 (forthcoming 2012).

17. See especially Zygmunt G. Barański, 'The "New Life" of "Comedy": The *Commedia* and the *Vita Nuova*', *Dante Studies*, 113 (1995), 1–29. For a more sanguine reading of the relationship between the two works, see Michelangelo Picone, 'La *Vita nova* nella prospettiva della *Commedia*', *Letture Classensi*, 38 (2008), 7–15.

18. 'La Beatrice della *Commedia* [...] è il risultato della fusione dell'*auctoritas* lirica del libello giovanile con quella filosofica del trattato dell'esilio' [The Beatrice of the *Commedia* is a product of the fusion of the lyric *auctoritas* of the *libello* and the philosophical *auctoritas* of the post-exilic treatise]: Picone, 'La *Vita nova* nella prospettiva della *Commedia*', pp. 11–12. On the continuities between Lady Philosophy and the Beatrice of the *Commedia*, see Olivia Holmes, *Dante's Two Beloveds: Ethics and Erotics in the 'Divine Comedy'* (New Haven, CT: Yale University Press, 2008).

19. This privileging of the *Vita Nuova* over the *Convivio* in the *Commedia* is reflected especially in Dante's citations of his canzoni 'Amor che ne la mente mi ragiona' and 'Donne ch'avete intelletto d'Amore' in *Purgatorio* II and XXIV respectively. While critics typically see the former as cited palinodically, the latter is presented as something of a blueprint for the *Commedia*'s poetics. For an excellent exposition of Dante's three autocitations in the *Commedia*, see Barolini, *Dante's Poets*, pp. 3–84, for whom the *Vita Nuova* is, in terms of the *Commedia*'s 'inner poetic itinerary [...] an advancement over the *Convivio*' (p. 37).

20. See F. Regina Psaki, 'Love for Beatrice: Transcending Contradiction in the *Paradiso*', in *Dante for the New Millennium*, ed. by Teodolinda Barolini and H. Wayne Storey (New York: Fordham University Press, 2003) pp. 115–30. See also Holmes, pp. 1–34.

21. Barolini writes that '[the] "plot" [of the *Purgatorio*] hinges on an Augustinian view of temporal goods as inherently dissatisfying because of their mortality, as necessarily dissatisfying even when they are (in Augustine's words) "things perfectly legitimate in themselves, which cannot be relinquished without regret"' ('Purgatory as Paradigm', p. 102).

22. See Manuele Gragnolati, 'Nostalgia in Heaven: Embraces, Affection and Identity in the

Commedia', in *Dante and the Human Body: Eight Essays*, ed. by John C. Barnes and Jennifer Petrie (Dublin: Four Courts Press, 2007), pp. 117–37; Rachel Jacoff, '"Our Bodies, Our Selves": The Body in the *Commedia*', in *Sparks and Seeds: Medieval Literature and its Afterlife: Essays in Honour of John Freccero*, ed. by Dana E. Stewart and Alison Cornish (Turnhout: Brepols, 2000), pp. 119–37.

23. See Sara Fortuna and Manuele Gragnolati, 'Dante after Wittgenstein: "Aspetto", Language, and Subjectivity from *Convivio* to *Paradiso*', in Fortuna, Gragnolati and Trabant, eds, *Dante's Plurilingualism*, pp. 223–48; Christian Moevs, *The Metaphysics of Dante's 'Comedy'* (Oxford: Oxford University Press, 2005); Guy Raffa, *Divine Dialectic: Dante's Incarnational Poetry* (Toronto: University of Toronto Press, 2000).

24. William Franke, 'Figuralism', in *The Dante Encyclopedia*, ed. by Richard Lansing (New York: Garland, 2000), pp. 375–79 (p. 378). See also J. Ferrante, 'Beatrice', in ibid, pp. 89–95 (p. 93): 'medieval exegesis demands the reality of a *figura*, the literal level of a sacred allegory, if we can only get over the fact that she is not a recognized saint but a secular woman.' Robert Pogue Harrison states, albeit with reference to *Vita Nuova*, that 'Nothing could be more antithetical to allegory than Beatrice, whose body is indissociable from the phenomenal guises through which she gives herself to perception and poetic figuration.' *The Body of Beatrice* (Baltimore, MD: Johns Hopkins University Press, 1988), p. 60.

25. On the ways in which the *Commedia* ascribes a limited role to eros, see Lino Pertile, 'Dimenticare Beatrice', in *La punta del disio: Semantica del desiderio nella 'Commedia'* (Florence: Cadmo, 2005), pp. 235–46. While Pertile's essay includes many valid and important points, I find reductive its conclusion that by the end of the *Paradiso* '"l'amore che move il sole e l'altre stelle" non ha più niente in comune con "l'amore che a nullo amato amar perdona"' [the 'love that moves the heaven and the other stars' no longer has anything in common with the 'love which absolves no-one beloved from loving'] (p. 246). For an opposing reading, see Psaki: 'I cannot conclude that for Dante ideal erotic love is desexualized, purged of the corporeal, superseded by a generalized and purely mental communion. The individual matters; the relationship with Beatrice powers the entire journey; and Dante insists too heavily on the return of the body for his experience of Beatrice to remain aphysical' (p. 119).

26. On Dante and Folco, see Stefano Asperti, 'Dante, i trovatori, la poesia', in *Le culture di Dante: Studi in onore di R. Hollander. Atti del quarto Seminario dantesco internazionale*, ed. by Michelangelo Picone, Theodore J. Cachey Jr, and Margherita Mesirca (Florence: Cesati, 2003), pp. 61–92; Pietro Beltrami, 'Arnaut e la "bella scola" dei trovatori di Dante', in ibid, pp. 29–59; Barolini, *Dante's Poets*, pp. 114–22; Michelangelo Picone, '*Paradiso* IX: Dante, Folchetto e la diaspora trobadorica', *Medioevo romanzo*, 8 (1981–83), 47–89; Alberto L. Rossi, '"E pos d'amor plus no·m cal": Ovidian Exemplarity and Folco's Rhetoric of Love in *Paradiso* IX', *Tenso: Bulletin of the Société Guilhem IX*, 5 (1989), 49–102; Paolo Squillacioti, 'Folchetto di Marsiglia "Trovatore di Dante": *Tant m'abellis l'amoros pessamens*', in *Rivista di letteratura italiana*, 11 (1993), 583–607; Franco Suitner, 'Due trovatori nella *Commedia*: Bertran de Born e Folchetto di Marsiglia', *Atti della Accademia nazionale dei lincei: Memorie: Classe di scienze morali, storiche e filologiche*, 24 (1980), 579–643; Nicola Zingarelli, *La personalità storica di Folchetto di Marsiglia nella 'Commedia' di Dante* (Bologna: Zanichelli, 1898).

27. Picone, '*Paradiso* IX', p. 71.

28. Pamela Williams, *Through Human Love to God: Essays on Dante and Petrarch* (Leicester: Troubador, 2007), p. 46. Williams sees both Cunizza and Folco as 'positive about the goodness of their sexuality' (p. 41), while Boyde writes that Folquet here 'makes a bold and universal statement about the goodness of the sexual appetite in human beings': Patrick Boyde, *Perception and Passion in Dante's Comedy* (Cambridge: Cambridge University Press, 2006), p. 287.

29. See Rachel Jacoff, 'The Post-Palinodic Smile: *Paradiso* VIII and IX', *Dante Studies*, 98 (1980), 111–22.

30. See Picone, '*Paradiso* IX', pp. 80–82.

31. Cited from Folchetto di Marsiglia, *Le poesie di Folchetto di Marsiglia*, ed. by Paolo Squillacioti (Pisa: Pacini, 1999). Translations of Folco's poetry are my own.

32. See Barolini, 'Anatomy of Desire'. She writes: 'When, in "Doglia mi reca", Dante makes the logical leap from the bad lover to the miser, welding together eros and avarice, he creates a node

of enormous significance for his future, no less than an adumbration of that she-wolf whose cupidity subtends both the lust of Paolo and Francesca and the political corruption of Florence' (p. 66).

33. Barolini, 'Anatomy of Desire', p. 49.

34. See Suitner, pp. 632–33.

35. See Paola Allegretti, 'Canto IX', in *Lectura Dantis Turicensis: Paradiso*, ed. by Georges Güntert and Michelangelo Picone (Florence: Cesati, 2002), pp. 133–44 (p. 138); Barolini, *Dante's Poets*, pp. 117–18; Picone, 'Paradiso IX', p. 86–89; Suitner, pp. 632–33. As well as to the crusade poetry, Suitner (p. 636) links Folco's lines '[...] il maladetto fiore | c'ha disviate le pecore e li agni, | però che fatto ha lupo del pastore' [[...] the accursèd flower | that has led astray both sheep and lambs, | for it has made a wolf out of its shepherd] (*Par.* IX, 131–32) in the *Commedia* to the line 'lupi erant heritici, oves cristiani', found in one of his sermons.

36. See Peter Hawkins, 'Dido, Beatrice, and the Signs of Ancient Love', in *The Poetry of Allusion*, ed. by Rachel Jacoff and Jeffrey Schnapp (Stanford, CA: Stanford University Press, 1991), pp. 113–30; Kay, 'Dido, Aeneas, and the Evolution of Dante's Poetics'.

37. See M. Picone, 'Canto VIII', in *Lectura Dantis Turicensis: Paradiso*, ed. by Güntert and Picone, pp. 119–32 (p. 123).

38. See Barolini, *Dante's Poets*, pp. 70–75.

39. Barański, 'Dante's Biblical Linguistics', p. 126.

40. Jacoff, 'Post-Palinodic', p. 115. She continues: 'The limits [of the *Convivio*] are precisely the *raison d'être* of its successor' (p. 118).

41. Jacoff, 'Post-Palinodic', p. 115.

42. 'In *Paradiso* VIII, Dante's relationship to his earlier work is palinodic in intent, but post-palinodic in emotion. Dante relates to his earlier work here, as the souls of Folco [and] Cunizza [...] relate to their sinful or erroneous lives. The smile of these souls implies a way of looking at the past equally free of guilt and of nostalgia': Jacoff, 'Post-Palinodic', p. 120.

43. Jacoff, 'Post-Palinodic', p. 115.

44. Barolini, *Dante's Poets*, pp. 57–84.

45. '"Voi che 'ntendendo" is a poem about conflict, the conflict experienced by the poet between his love for Beatrice — his mystical, spiritual and poetical interests — and the other chief interests of his life': Barolini, *Dante's Poets*, p. 69.

46. Barolini, *Dante's Poets*, pp. 68–69.

47. Barolini, *Dante's Poets*, p. 68.

48. 'The status of "Voi che 'ntendendo" in the *Comedy* hinges on the fact that the canzone marks a turning point, a crucial watershed, in Dante's career. Its position in Dante's canon is in fact analogous to that of the *Convivio*. From the perspective of the *Comedy*, the *Convivio* is both an erring text that has been eclipsed by the return to Beatrice as a primary source of signification, and also, paradoxically, the text that makes the *Comedy* possible' (Barolini, *Dante's Poets*, p. 78). As Barolini points out (see pp. 80–84), this conflict is, in fact, much more explicit in the non-allegorical 'Le dolci rime', where, as we saw, Dante temporarily rejected the 'matera amorosa'. Barolini believes that Dante opts to cite 'Voi che 'ntendendo' instead, however, because it shares its stilnovist lexis and intellective stress ('Voi che *'ntendendo*') with the two canzoni cited in the *Purgatorio*.

49. See for example Lino Pertile, 'Le penne e il volo', in *La punta del disio*, pp. 115–35 (pp. 124–25).

50. For example, as noted by Barolini, it closely recalls, syntactically as well as lexically, a self-definition by Arnaut Daniel, the *Commedia*'s paradigmatic poet of erotic love: 'Fas, que Amors m'o comanda, | breu chanzo de raiso lonia | cui gen m'aduz de las ars de sa scola' ['I shall write, since Love commands me | A song that's brief, but long in theme, | For nobly Love has trained me in the arts of his school'] (XVI, 3–5). Barolini writes that Arnaut's words here 'proleptically combine the "fabbro" metaphor of *Purgatorio* XXVI with [Dante's] credo of *Purgatorio* XXIV' (*Dante's Poets*, p. 113). Arnaut's poem is cited from *Le canzoni di Arnaut Daniel*, ed. by M. Perugi (Milan and Naples: Ricciardi, 1978).

❖

Desire as a Dead Letter:
A Reading of Petrarch's *RVF* 125

Francesca Southerden

Petrarch's *canzone* 125, 'Se 'l pensier che mi strugge' ['If the thought wasting me'], has often been identified as a crucial text for understanding his experience of desire as it comes to be articulated in the *Rerum vulgarium fragmenta* [henceforth *RVF*].[1] As the first of a series of *canzoni* (125–29) predominantly set in Vaucluse,[2] it revisits the coordinates of that desiring landscape (understood as part geographical locus, part topos of the imagination/memory) to which Petrarch so often returns in search of his beloved Laura, or some trace of her presence there before. As an extended meditation on Laura's elusiveness as the referent of poetic discourse, Petrarch's poem also carries that mark of self-reflexivity that is a distinguishing feature of his poetic universe, with Laura arguably only the pre-text to the 'I''s almost tyrannically subjective meditation on its own status as a desiring subject.[3] Rather less studied than its companion poem, *RVF* 126 ('Chiare, fresche et dolci acque' ['Clear waters, cool and sweet']), however, *RVF* 125 continues to present certain unresolved questions. These include the precise nature of Petrarch's debt to Dante and Augustine — both present in different ways in the autobiographical equation Petrarch establishes in the poem between desire, language, and subjectivity — and the degree to which the resulting poetry is positive or negative in the ends that it achieves.

This paper explores some of those issues in further depth. It extends the intertextual dialogue from Dante (mainly as the author of the *rime petrose*, but also of the *Commedia* and *Convivio*) to Petrarch himself (especially in *RVF* 23, 'Nel dolce tempo de la prima etade' ['There was a sweet time in my earlier years']) and argues that an important dimension of 'Se 'l pensier' resides in the poet's problematic treatment of signs as instruments of knowledge as they are carried, through memory, from one text into another. As Petrarch rewrites aspects of Dante's texts, and incorporates them at key points of tension within his own experience of desire, he simultaneously revisits what in Augustine's theory of language binds word, desire, and knowledge together in the soul's relationship to itself and God, and redefines it on his own terms, culminating in the state of dissolution and fracture common to Petrarch's experience of desire from the *RVF* to the *Trionfi*. By analysing what I will term Petrarch's semantics of desire, which resides in the complex interplay between the self, textuality, and signification, and fails in the case of *RVF* 125 to deliver up the unity or meaning the poet seeks, I will show

how Petrarch's experience of desire-in-language (desire *as* language) pivots upon a 'dead letter' (*lettre morte*) that, like Augustine's fractured and fallen word 'conceived by wanting and born by getting' ('cupiendo concipitur, adipiscendo nascitur'),[4] or the reified language of the melancholic, can neither be fully revivified in the text nor wholly incorporated within signification.[5]

Pivotal to this process is Petrarch's redefinition of the 'metaphysics of language', going back through Dante to Augustine, the fundamentals of which are worth reiterating here since they are intrinsic to the way in which the poetic and desiring subject of *RVF* 125 takes shape. For Augustine and Dante, desire and language unfold as a meaningful teleology of signs and things connecting the soul to its innermost reality in God, and capable — if properly followed — of bridging the distance between the (fallen, time-bound) human world and the (eternal, redeeming) Being of the divinity.[6] Petrarch, by contrast, perceives more the irreducible difference dividing the self from God and from the pristine unity of soul, language, and knowledge. As Petrarch repeatedly 'identifies himself with the stream [of individual thought, memories, desires] and not with the consciousness in which it arises [i.e. God]', he misplaces himself and dissolves or disavows that metaphysical unity which, rooted in the Trinity 'and its Augustinian interior reflection as will, memory, and intellect', had found its supreme embodiment in the linguistic and desiring journey of Dante's *Commedia*.[7]

The importance of this kind of semantic complex for Petrarch, which depends upon the shifting arrangement of the self, language, and signification, is evident from the beginning of *RVF* 125.[8] Already in line 1, the thought of desire ('il pensier che mi strugge') threatens to consume the subject by rehearsing that dispersal (Augustinian *distensio*) of selfhood that will only be exacerbated by the drama of the poem, and especially the anxiety to find a correlation between the experience of desire and the language available to express it.[9] Emphasis immediately falls upon the antagonistic and alienating elements of the poet's psyche, which contribute to a form of semantic impasse, as well as to the bereft state of the subject as he registers the impossibility of breaking out of the negative cycle of his own frustrated desire, caused by Laura's frigidity and absence. As the poem develops, so does the sense of frustration as the 'I' strains to articulate the contradiction between an outer emptiness, both linguistic and erotic ('mi spoglia' [strips me], l. 15), and an inner fullness ('natural vertude' [natural potency], l. 19), neither of which can be put into words. Later, the erotic-linguistic struggle culminates first with the retreat into an infantile state of speechlessness and non-cognition of a desiring subject 'che *dir non sa*' [who *cannot speak*] (l. 42), and then into a wholly adult self-delusion, which paradoxically, however, allows for some illusory pleasure to be found in the imagined proximity with the beloved in the space of the garden. While modelled on Vaucluse, the latter is also a kind of utopia and, as such, has no existence outside of the stanza of the poem in which it appears and with which it eventually fuses and dissolves.

Notwithstanding the series of references (pleas) made to the external landscape, Petrarch's poem essentially moves through a series of interiors, desperately trying to externalize them but largely failing to do so. From the landscape of the poet's mind presented in stanza 1, we enter the enclosure of the lover's heart in stanzas 2 and 3, which leads (in stanza 4) into the interior domain of a frustrated speech, which mirrors the frustrations of desire. There we effectively remain until the apparent breakthrough of stanzas 5 and 6, in which the speaking subject finally manages to project something of itself and its desire outward. However, this too ends up as a somewhat delusory moment as the poetic 'I''s newly retrieved powers of expression, even at their height, fail to fully deliver up their desired referent. Despite what the poet hopes, the 'signs' of Laura's passage through the landscape do not, in this poem, yield any meaning beyond their own, frozen, status. They end up as repositories of a desire that was once full, but is now empty, and can only be partially re-animated in the materiality of the surrounding world. This creates a breach between matter and spirit, and between word and feeling, but also holds them problematically together. It indicates a crucial point of tension that is present throughout the poem and culminates in the wondrous but disconcerting revelation of the undecidability of the Other in the space of the garden/phantasm: 'Spirto beato, quale | se' quando altrui fai tale?' [What are you, blessèd spirit | if you have such effects?] (ll. 77–78).

This occurrence in Petrarch of a desiring impetus that goes against progression or (self-)knowledge, in order to take shelter instead in what Mazzotta terms an 'illusory garden of the mind', is reinforced in Petrarch's dialogue with Dante's *Purgatorio* xxx, and his *rime petrose*.[10] As Petrarch's text conjures the memory, albeit distorted, of the pilgrim's reunion with Beatrice in the Earthly Paradise, it evokes as its antitype the miraculous scene of redemption of the Dantean subject and his past at the summit of Mount Purgatory. However, where Dante surrenders the phantasmata that have led the soul astray to embrace the resurrected presence of Beatrice, Petrarch chooses to 'abbracciar l'ombre' [embrace shadows] (*RVF* 212. 2) as he pursues only the ghost of Laura's absence.

This process of recasting begins in stanza 1 with Petrarch's rewriting, as monologue, the words uttered by Dante-pilgrim to Virgil on their encountering the resurrected Beatrice in the Earthly Paradise, 'men che *dramma* | di sangue m'è rimaso che non tremi | *conosco i segni* dell'antica *fiamma*' [Not a single *drop* of blood | remains in me that does not tremble — | *I know the signs* of the ancient *flame*] (*Purg.* xxx, 46–48):[11]

> Se 'l pensier che mi strugge,
> com'è pungente et saldo,
> così vestisse d'un color conforme,
> forse tal m'arde et fugge,
> ch'avria parte del caldo,
> et desteriasi Amor là dov'or dorme;
> men solitario l'orme
> fôran de' miei pie' lassi
> per campagne et per colli,
> men gli occhi ad ognor molli,
> *ardendo* lei che come un ghiaccio stassi,
> et non lascia in me *dramma*
> che non sia foco et *fiamma*. (ll. 1–13)

[If the thought wasting me | could clothe itself in words | as piercing and as hard as that thought is, | she who burns me and flees | perhaps would feel the heat | and Love would waken there where now he sleeps. | The steps would be less lonely | of my exhausted feet | over the fields and hills, | my eyes not so wet always, | if she *burned* who is like a block of ice | but leaves no *drop* of me | that is not fire and *flame*.]

The decisive line for Petrarch, *Purg.* xxx, 48, is of course already mediated in Dante, since it is 'the [...] translation of Dido's words of foreboding when she first sees Aeneas', which evoke both Dido's memory of desire for her dead husband, and the prefiguration of her own death.[12] However, whereas in the *Commedia* Dante uses the citation to upturn the association in Virgil's text between desire and death, Petrarch's text arguably reinstates it. Moreover, in his poem, the subject is emptied of everything except the most frustrated of burnings, and he is so by the force of Laura's absence rather than her presence or, rather, by the dis-/mis-recognition of the 'signs of the ancient flame' that would signify her existence or return.

Petrarch consequently uses elements of Dante's Edenic recognition scene in order to construct a completely new semantics of desire. In the first stanza, he takes the flame that was the source of knowledge in Dante and reduces it to something purely physical: an *ardendo* [burning], divorced from, or counter to, a [ri]*conoscere* [knowing/recognizing]. In *RVF* 125, it is precisely the *(antica) fiamma* that has been misplaced and, for Petrarch, there are no signs to be interpreted or understood since any change in the status quo depends on finding a lost idiom that cannot in fact be found.[13] Bearing in mind that in the (Dantean-)Augustinian register of language and desire, there exists a systematic relationship between what is known and what is loved, willed, and desired (to be known) — so that it is a case of what has been known before determining that which is sought out and can be recognized[14] — that act of *conoscenza* is precisely what Petrarch repudiates; ultimately the discourse of his poem is not a moment of recognition or even the reaffirmation of a meaningful memory (of desire), but the imagination of a new one, equally vain (which could conceal, rather than transform, an original lack).

The rhyme on 'dramma/fiamma' (ll. 12–13) that Petrarch also borrows from Dante is similarly revealing within its new context in *RVF* 125. In Dante, both words form part of that 'ancient' and miraculous nexus of love which communicates with the rational part of the pilgrim's soul to identify the beloved Beatrice even though she is still veiled to him from view. The 'segni' that Dante-pilgrim identifies in himself, as he trembles in Beatrice's presence, allow him both to identify her as the Beatrice he knew and loved on earth, and to recognize the strength of his desire for her beyond death. To this extent, Beatrice's declaration when it comes: 'Ben *son*, ben *son* Beatrice...' [I am, I truly am Beatrice] (*Purg.* xxx, 73) is merely the affirmation of what the pilgrim already senses, or knows, to be true. The emphasis consequently falls more on the verb *essere*, which confirms Beatrice's continued existence as a resurrected presence, her being what she always is/was, now manifest in the eternal glory of her second life:

> così dentro una nuvola di fiori
> che da le mani angeliche saliva
> e ricadeva in giù dentro e di fori,

> sovra candido vel cinta d'uliva
> donna m'apparve, sotto verde manto
> vestita di color di fiamma viva.
>   E lo spirito mio, che già cotanto
> tempo era stato ch'a la sua presenza
> non era di stupor, tremando, affranto,
>   sanza de li occhi aver più conoscenza,
> per occulta virtù che da lei mosse,
> d'antico amor sentì la gran potenza. (*Purg.* XXX, 28–39)

[thus, within that cloud of blossoms | rising from angelic hands and fluttering | back down into the chariot and around it, | olive-crowned above a veil of white | appeared to me a lady, beneath a green mantle, | dressed in the color of living flame. | And in my spirit, which for so long a time | had not been overcome with awe | that used to make me tremble in her presence — | even though I could not see her with my eyes — | through the hidden force that came from her I felt | the overwhelming power of that ancient love.]

As will be true for Petrarch as well, a text refers to another text (here: *Commedia* to *Vita Nuova*), but whereas Dante evokes those earlier emotions and those 'signs' to move beyond them, Petrarch's goal is the resurrection of the signs themselves, though as his poem later reveals they can only be present as already past (see line 55: 'come quel dì che *già* segnata fosti' [as that by which you were imprinted *once*], referring to the landscape conjured out of the memory-phantasm).[15] To this extent, Petrarch's retroping of Dante's '*vestita* di color di *fiamma* viva' (*Purg.* XXX, 33, said of Beatrice) as referring to the poem itself in a hypothetical future time when a less disjunctive poetic style might be found ('*vestisse* d'un *color* conforme') and his *donna* might again burn with (erotic) desire for him, is suggestive not only of his heightened consciousness of the relationship between desire and textuality but also of the extent to which desire in Petrarch depends on (his control of) the text, at times seeming to follow on from it rather than to precede it.

This is clearly a backward turn, made all the clearer in that Petrarch's desire to move from the 'rime aspre' [harsh verse] to the 'dolci rime leggiadre | che nel primiero assalto | d'Amor usai' [sweet and stylish poems | that I used at the first | assault of Love, ll. 27–29] reverses the trajectory in play in Dante's, 'Le dolci rime d'amor ch'io solia cercar' ['The sweet love-poetry I was accustomed to seek out'], a *rima* which in the *Convivio* stands for the author's desire to break with the earlier love poetry (of the *Vita Nuova*) and embrace instead the 'rima aspra e sottile' [harsh and subtle rhymes], as a sign of a growing poetic maturity and the attainment of new (here philosophical) ground. While Petrarch is unlikely to have had direct knowledge of the poem in the context of the *Convivio* itself, it seems significant that he evokes as the antithesis of his own poem a *rima* whose development deals with precisely that movement *beyond*, and mastering of an earlier (poetic) self, that are closed off to him.[16] Moreover, unlike Dante, Petrarch does not suggest that the earlier mode of writing is being put aside to be recovered later. Instead it is lost, and urgently rued as such, which prompts the retreat only further into memory and out of (temporal or physical) unity.

Harshness, though inevitable for Petrarch in this poem, is thus not so much cultivated, as imposed on him by the destitution of desire, something which leads him simultaneously to revisit the legacy of Dante *petroso*. As Peter Hainsworth argues, *canzone* 125 constitutes 'Petrarch's major encounter with the harsh mode as developed in the *rime petrose* by Dante, who, elaborating on his model, Arnaut Daniel, had posited a circular equation between linguistic harshness, sexual obsession and irreducible resistance in the beloved.'[17] But if, in the *petrose*, Dante had found a way of matching form and content, Petrarch's struggle in *RVF* 125 is with the irreconcilable nature of (the underlying) sweetness and (the extant) hardness, animate desire and linguistic petrification or stone-like death, and the need to find another means of (self-)expression.

Of the four *rime petrose*, 'Al poco giorno' ['To the short day'] and 'Così nel mio parlar voglio esser aspro' [I want to be harsh in my speech] seem to have been the most decisive for the development of 'Se 'l pensier', probably because of the poets' common concern with the destitute quality of the self as it struggles to master the resistance in the lady, and its insufficiency to communicate that experience outwardly, either to move the lady to pity or to widen the circle of the 'I''s own frustrated erotic and linguistic encounter.[18] In his dialogue with Dante's 'Così nel mio parlar', Petrarch emphasizes most the disjunction between inside fullness and outside bareness, and between harshness and sweetness (dialectically present in both, though not to the same degree, with Petrarch characteristically privileging the latter over the former in terms of both form and content).

As Durling and Martinez have argued, 'the structure of "Così nel mio parlar" is demarcated by the development of the dominant metaphor of combat and by the antithesis between the lover's inner experience and his relation with the outside world'; it is consequently 'based on the problematic of inner and outer, in a sense the problematic of language and representation itself.'[19] As the *pondus amoris* (Augustinian in nature — see *Confessions* XIII, ix, 10)[20] causes the speaker to sink under the weight of an earthly, death-oriented desire, the poem maps the stifled and stifling counter-movements that occur in the depths of the soul of the speaker, who would seek to express outwardly the internal pressure exerted upon him. In anticipation of Petrarch's own blocked status in *RVF* 125, the attempts at vocalization initially culminate only in the soundless screams and inner shouts that occur in the speaker's mind. Yet by the end of the poem, even if only projected into a hypothetical future time, Dante has seemingly been able to transform the experience of katabasis (that has seen the speaker descend ever further into the self as a means of countering, and taking shelter from, the *donna*'s hostility and resistance) into a kind of journey beyond any previously known limits of the discourse of desire (even of the other *rime petrose*),[21] almost to the point of being able to sublimate the impasse of a frustrated desire and project it into linguistic, if not physical, violence:

> Canzon, vattene dritto a quella donna
> che m'ha ferito il core e che m'invola
> quello ond'io ho più gola,
> e dàlle per lo cor d'una saetta:
> ché bell'onor s'acquista in far vendetta. (ll. 79–83)

[Song, go straight to that woman who has wounded my heart and robs me of what I most hunger for, and drive an arrow through her heart: for great honour is gained through taking revenge.]

Although potentially only imagined, the fact that Dante's poem ends with at least the possibility of redressing the balance and regaining something of what has been lost to the 'I', allows the poetic subject, in the final moments of the poem, to rechannel the language of desire, or the desire for language, towards a fuller expression. This contrasts with Petrarch's own much more tentative, almost disavowed, relation to his own poem as somehow unable, even in its last hour, to rise to the challenge set it by desire ('come se' rozza' [how unrefined you are]), and painfully conscious (like the poet) of its own inadequacy in both linguistic and desiring terms.

This is where Petrarch's dialogue with his own poetic past, and the memory of *RVF* 23, intervenes to complicate the linguistic and desiring schema already at play in the poem.[22] We should remember that *RVF* 23 identifies desire as a moment of prohibition on looking and speaking; it prepares for a number of structural parallels that will be decisive for *RVF* 125 in the way that desire operates with respect to the voice, and especially the nexus between estrangement, loss of voice, and petrification of the letter of meaning. In particular, *RVF* 125 retropes the subject's earlier linguistic and desiring position at the 'primiero assalto' [first assault] of love and its effects, recalling especially the following lines from *RVF* 23:

> Né meno anchor m'agghiaccia
> l'esser coverto poi di bianche piume
> allor che folminato et morto giacque
> il mio sperar che tropp'alto montava:
> ché perch'io non sapea dove né quando
> me 'l ritrovasse, solo lagrimando
> là 've tolto mi fu, dì et nocte andava,
> ricercando dallato, et dentro a l'acque;
> et già mai poi la mia lingua non tacque
> mentre poteo del suo cader maligno:
> ond'io presi col suon color d'un cigno.
>
> Così lungo l'amate rive andai,
> che volendo parlar, cantava sempre
> mercé chiamando *con estrania voce*;
> né mai in sì dolci o in sì soave tempre
> risonar seppi gli amorosi guai,
> che 'l cor s'umilïasse aspro et feroce. (ll. 50–66)

[And I freeze still with terror | to think how next white feathers coated me, | after my hope that mounted up too high, | was struck by a lightning bolt and fell dead. | And since I had no notion where or when | I might recover it, alone and tearful, | I walked on day and night where I had lost it, | searching beside the waters and beneath them. | And then my tongue, as long as it was able, | was never still about that dismal fall. | So I took on a swan's voice and its color. || I went like this along the banks I loved, | for, though I wished to speak, I always sang, | calling for pity *in an alien voice*, | but never once did I make music of | the pains of love in such sweet or soft tones | that her harsh, savage heart would stoop to me.]

As alluded to earlier, Petrarch claims in *RVF* 125 that he wants to retrieve the idiom that he used 'nel primier assalto d'Amor' [at the first | assault of love], but if we actually look at those early expressions of desire in 'Nel dolce tempo de la *prima* etade' [The was a sweet time in my *earlier* years] we find that the only time he could sing freely was before love held him, since once it did (as Peter Kuon notes) the poem — always already in the posthumous realm of desire — can only map the progressive loss of the poet's powers of expression and the increasing interiorization of the subject's state:

> Riconsiderando la successione delle trasformazioni, si osserva un movimento che va dalla perdita dell'identità alla perdita di ogni possibilità espressiva. [...] Le trasformazioni successive ('sasso' — 'fontana' — 'selce' — 'cervo') sembrano marcare le tappe di un processo di *interiorizzazione*, diretto a cancellare l'espressione del desiderio dalla parola, dalla scrittura, dalla voce e dallo sguardo. In realtà, a dispetto delle numerose indicazioni temporali, non si tratta di una progressione narrativa, ma della reiterazione di un'unica situazione di base; articolazione del desiderio amoroso, metamorfosi e perdita della facoltà espressive, liberazione e ricaduta.[23]

> [Looking again at the succession of transformations, the reader observes a movement that proceeds from the loss of identity to the loss of every possibility of expression. [...] The successive transformations ('stone' — 'fountain' — 'flint' — 'deer') seem to mark the stages of a process of *interiorization*, directed toward cancelling out the ability to express desire from the word, from writing, from the voice and the gaze. In reality, notwithstanding the numerous temporal indicators in the poem, it is not narrative progression that is at stake, but the repetition of a single foundational situation: the articulation of desire, metamorphosis and the loss of the faculties of expression, freeing oneself only to fall a second time.]

In *RVF* 23, that event is heralded by the swan's song (l. 60), which indicates the lament of the love poet trapped without the ability to properly express or articulate his desire. The voice represented in, but also producing, the poem is thus cast as an 'estrania voce' or 'alien voice': it is 'estrania' perhaps in the sense of wonderful, but also estranging, insofar as it derives its sound from something extraneous to the 'I' (here, the animal; later, the fountain and the stone).[24] In particular, and foreshadowing the concern in *RVF* 125 with the dressing up of thought, the estrangement of speech is literally enacted in the covering of the subject with the feathers of the swan, which simultaneously alter his make up as speaker.

Petrarch speaks with an 'estrania voce' in *RVF* 125 too: an 'alien voice' that is intrinsic to his experience of language and desire. However, whereas in *RVF* 23, the subject is divided between the memory of an interior fullness (already lost at the start and rued as so) and the resulting bareness of the external shell ('ch'e' [un pensier] ten di me quel d'entro e io la scorza' [It owns the inner me, and I the shell, l. 20]), in *RVF* 125 what matters most is what lies beneath and the impossibility of externalizing it in a way that is satisfactory. As a consequence, the 'I' identifies most with the subject's earlier position as the tortured captive of a kind of dead materiality, an inanimate discourse of desire nevertheless 'uttered' by the text:

> Morte *mi* s'era intorno al cor avolta,
> né tacendo potea di sua man trarlo,
> o dar soccorso a le vertuti afflitte;
> *le vive voci m'erano interditte;*
> *ond'io gridai con carta et con incostro:*
> Non son mio, no. S'io moro il danno è vostro.
>
> (*RVF* 23, 95–100)

[Death now had wrapped itself around *my* heart; | I could not prize his grip free while not speaking, | or give aid to my battered vital powers, | *since all live speeches were forgiven me.* | *So I gave out an ink-and-paper cry,* | 'I'm not mine, no. If I die, it's your loss.']

Desire is here a literal dead letter, as well as one that in a Pauline sense might 'kill'.[25] Writing is the product of the death of the voice, which everywhere 'cries out' in material things and not words. The subject loses all agency, mostly objectified (made an object) and subject ('*io gridai*') only of an aphasic alphabet of 'parole morte', as in *RVF* 18: '*Tacito* vo, ché *le parole morte* | farian pianger la gente; | et i' desio che le lagrime mie si spargan sole' [I go *silent*; for my *dead words* would make people weep, and I desire my tears to be shed in solitude].[26] Desire declares itself a movement within, something which the poet can neither silence nor speak, but only write — which is an action that also spells out his death. If his voice *is* later restored to him, 'così scossa | voce rimasi de l'antiche some | chiamando Morte e lei sola per nome' [and I was left | as a mere voice, wrenched from my former form, | calling for death, and just for her by name] (*RVF* 23. 139–40), it is only a dead voice, or a voice of death that speaks for him extraneously; literally petrified, it tells only of the 'I''s frozen state and its being divorced from its proper place ('l'antiche some', i.e. his body): a sign of the melancholy lover's 'subversion of his reason by somatic processes'.[27] The forest into which the poem has led him transforms into a hellish space reminiscent of the suicide wood of Dante's *Inferno* XIII (itself an extended meditation on the violence done to language through sin), with the Petrarchan subject's body however returned to him so that he might suffer his pain more fully in corporeal form (ll. 145–46).[28]

I would argue that *RVF* 23 and *RVF* 125 thus form a kind of diptych, insofar as the latter is just another 'ink-and-paper cry' that pivots upon an axis of interior-exterior word, voice and body. *RVF* 125 looks back not so much to a preceding moment of experience, than to a previous attempt at symbolization (and an earlier moment of prohibition). As Mazzotta recognizes, what Petrarch is trying to recover in this poem is not so much Laura, or even the image of her, as the original moment at which desire came to be, of which the subject has no memory, since it is always still being activated and experienced as the very condition of writing: 'The inadequacy of language is not merely a topos of authorial modesty, as the canons of rhetoric explain it; it suggests, rather, the poet's ironic awareness that there is not a proper name for desire.'[29] Bearing a striking resemblance to what modern psychoanalytic theory would call an 'original fantasy', Petrarch's poem consequently (re)enacts the play of loss and hallucinatory compensation that rests at the very foundation of language and the advent of the sign:

> The origin of fantasy would lie in the hallucinatory satisfaction of desire; in the absence of the real object, the infant reproduces the experience of the original satisfaction in a hallucinated form. In this view the most fundamental fantasies would be those which tend to recover the hallucinated objects linked with the very earliest experiences of the rise and the resolution of desire. [...] It is an analytic 'construction' or fantasy, which tries to cover the moment of separation between before and after, whilst still containing both: a mythical moment of disjunction between the pacification of need (Befriedigung) and the fulfilment of desire (Wunscherfüllung), between the two stages represented by real experience and its hallucinatory revival, between the object that satisfies it and the sign which describes both the object and its absence: a mythical moment at which hunger and sexuality meet in a common origin.[30]

We could say that Petrarch's entire poem enacts just such a mythical moment of disjunction and that what the text registers, or rather performs, is precisely that analytic construction or fantasy that seeks to cloak the perception of a real and foundational loss with the trappings of what could be made to look like a temporary dearth — in other words, to transform the dilemma of the subject from one of substance into style. But, whether consciously or not, the poem quickly moves beyond the surface of discourse to bare its complex inner arrangement, which in temporal terms transports the subject as far forward as the unreal future time when he might speak with a unified voice that could perfectly mirror his intentions, and as far back as the origins of speech(lessness — *infans*), in which that voice is nothing if not a locus of estrangement and the subordination of the will to another force (here desire), 'Come fanciul ch' a pena | volge la lingua et snoda, | che dir non sa ma 'l più tacer gli è noia, | così il desir mi mena | a dire' [Like a baby who almost | articulates his babble, | who cannot speak but cannot bear to hush, | so my desire drives me | to speak. ll. 40–44]. In ontological terms, it marks the fracture between willing, desire, and knowing that is to be decisive for the Petrarchan subject's progressive alienation from itself, and ultimately from God.

What is at stake, in *RVF* 23 and 125, is thus a doubly estranged discourse, at once incapable of truly reflecting the inner turmoil of the self or of translating the aporia of its own condition into meaningful speech. The 'sweet rhymes' are essentially prior to any experience that can be directly spoken of in this poem, or any other, and so belong to a pre-linguistic space that is now present only as a (textual) memory. One 'text' recalls the other but precisely because the same fantasy is at play or, better, the same structure repeats itself despite each attempt to overcome it. As the mythical moment in *RVF* 125 reveals itself to be only the recollection of another text (*RVF* 23), equally impenetrable, and still needing to be deciphered, the subject confronts the impossibility of ever truly recovering its earlier position.

Thus although it may be true that through his dialogue with the *petrose*, Petrarch 'brings sweetness and harshness together in a way that undermines the implications of either mode in their Dantesque forms',[31] by introducing the memory of his own *RVF* 23 within the same poem, Petrarch reinforces rather the fact that in whatever mode the subject 'speaks' there remains some aspect of its experience that remains irreducible to language. Or, rather, it cannot rest in any single (linguistic, or desiring) position but instead moves in and out of the language/non-language of an emotional-corporeal selfhood in disarray.

In fact, as the poem stages a voice and a body stripped bare by the despotic effects of desire, which still contain a 'natural potency' (l. 19) that in a Hamletian way 'passes show', it also posits an ambiguous kind of (body-)language characteristically, for Petrarch, somewhere between weeping and speaking.[32]

Stanza 2 is emblematic in this respect. Marked by the deprivation of the voice, it explores the tension between exterior harshness and bitterness (as contained in the harsh rhymes modelled on Dante's *petrose*: 'sforza'; 'spoglia'; 'scorza'; 'scaltro') and interior, natural virtue (hidden, full, but inexpressible). The poet's heart is closed up and encloses precisely what is not, or cannot be, expressed (in tears or lament): the lost 'dolcezza'; the absent 'dolce soccorso', which leave the 'I' not just deprived but specifically abandoned ('di dolcezza *ignude*'; 'così *m'è scorso*'). The problem is less the harshness of the rhymes in themselves than the extent to which the harshness reinforces the bereft state of the 'I' on two levels: *donna*/poetry; desire/language. His tears 'speak' and his laments flow, but neither constitutes a wholly articulate speech. Both cause harm, either to the self or to Laura; each remains in a raw and unpolished state, almost too dense to be transformed into text:

> Se 'l dolor che si sgombra
> aven che 'n pianto o in lamentar trabocchi,
> l'un a me nòce et l'altro
> altrui, ch'io non lo scaltro. (ll. 23–26)

[If the pain seeking outlet | does overflow in tears or in complaints, | the first hurt me, the second | her, since they show no art.]

If the 'I' can partly disavow the pain, he seems unable to separate himself from it, recalling the melancholy subject of modern, psychoanalytic theory, who feels himself deserted by, but cannot relinquish, what he has lost. As the next stanza of Petrarch's poem makes clear, the subject does not have sufficient agency in the *traboccar* (l. 24) for it to truly liberate him, and at any rate in stanza 3 we find out that the *sgombrar* too cannot have been enough since the subject still expresses the wish to *sfogarsi* [find release], l. 32. In turn, the outflow of pain in tears or complaints seems to happen almost independently of the 'cor', which continues to enclose its mysteries and its suffering. In the end, we too are put into an undecidable position in the poem linguistically speaking, since what is released either does not speak of the object of the gaze (so reinstating and extending the *dolor* rather than relieving it), or it may be closest to the inexpressible essence of it and of the 'I'. If the latter, what matters most may be its status as a not-yet speech, a kind of pre-or proto-language, that as a carrier of something like a Kristevan semiotic *signifiance* rather than symbolic *signification*, can be said to have some intangible meaning without meaning anything in symbolic terms at all.[33]

In the end, what Petrarch faces is a radical blockage leading to an expressive inadequacy, which prevents either the proper release of pain and grief, or the externalization of the lady's true nature, which always remains beyond expression. Like the Augustinian desire for meaning and knowledge that remains in suspense until its desired object is found, Petrarch's desire as *appetitus* is caught between the pull of the object, whose uncertain status is itself a catalyst to desire, and the frustration and impossibility of the desire to possess it. These things are represented in the poem by the pervading sense of lack that underscores even the most positive articulations of the search for the beloved, and the ultimate revelation of her non-presence and non-identity beyond the realm of the phantasmata.

In fact the closure and disjunction specified by lines 34–35, which designate the cherished but despotic space inhabited within by 'un che Madonna sempre | depinge e de lei parla' [one who depicts her | always and speaks of her], with whom the 'I' can neither completely identify nor silence, could almost be an expression of the fracture between interior and exterior word in Augustine's theory of language and desire. When the word of the heart — conceived in love — falls victim to 'covetousness' (*cupiditas*, related to the love of the creature) and is alienated from the true goal of its desire as 'charity' (*caritas*, referred only to the Creator), 'it does not help you in your use of it, but corrupts you in your enjoyment of it' (*The Trinity* IX, 2.13). Augustine goes on to clarify that the word conceived in love can only be equal to the word that is born when 'the will rests in the act itself of knowing, which happens in the love of spiritual things'; otherwise: 'in the love of temporal and material things the conception of the word is one thing and its birth another, as it is with the breeding of animals. In this case the word is conceived by wanting and born by getting [...] yet as a matter of fact none of these things satisfies even when you get it' (*The Trinity* IX, 2.13).

The tyrannical inner voice of Petrarch's 125, which however appears not to belong to him, seems to mark the fracture between the conception and birth of the word, just as it marks the eternalization of desire as lack and not fulfilment. Petrarch's 'cor' does not permit any true knowledge into its bounds, nor can it communicate outwardly, either with the beloved on whom it is fixated, nor with the deprived subject. Speaking only of the idolatrous and unattainable 'madonna', the voice inside spells out the distortion of that pristine channel connecting the soul to God, foreclosing knowledge of the Divinity (since it cannot transcend its own fallen state of desire-as-loss) and by extension the self (since it too finds no place in that equation which only alienates it from God and from itself), 'increasing its entropy and deforming and debasing the *imago dei*'.[34]

While it is true that there appears to be a breakthrough at the end of the fourth stanza, when the subject turns to the landscape to speak for him, it is not so much the retrieval of an articulate speech as that of a body language of sighs that the landscape amplifies. Drawing a comparison between the linguistically forlorn (literally tongue-tied, 'a pena volge la lingua e *snode*') subject, 'che dir *non sa*', and the infant caught in a state of speechlessness, Petrarch again underscores the absence of a knowledge that can be communicated outwardly, or the regression to a state of a less logical or rational understanding. Giorgio Agamben discusses this kind of infantile position in Pauline terms as marking the phase of development in which 'understanding is "unfruitful"' precisely because it cannot be understood by any but the child, who has no means of expressing it.[35] In modern theory, on the other hand, it potentially corresponds to what Kristeva terms the semiotic phase of linguistic development, replete with the possibility of meaning (still maternally governed and contained in the symbolically un-ordered drives of *significance*) but awaiting symbolic elaboration in order to signify; if that symbolic elaboration never occurs, the buried meaning can never be translated into language and consequently remains anchored at the very heart of the subject like a kind of corpse:

> What we call meaning is the ability of the *infans* to record the signifier of parental desire and include itself therein in his own fashion; he does so by displaying the semiotic abilities he is endowed with at the moment of his development and which allow him a mastery, on the level of primary processes, of a 'not yet other' (of the Thing) included in the erotogenic zones of such a semiotizing *infans*. Nevertheless, the omnipotent meaning remains a 'dead letter' if it is not invested in signification.[36]

To bring the argument back to the medieval context, it is possible to make some comparison (as Marion Wells does) between the destructive effects of love-melancholy, as they were viewed in the Middle Ages, and the unmediated or 'unreferred' nature of this kind of melancholy desire when it does not succeed in being articulated outwardly, 'for obsessive love, love that derives its relentlessness from the inscription of the phantasm within the imaginative power of the mind is now understood as what Freud calls in "On Transience" a revolt against mourning', i.e. the refusal to relinquish the lost or failed object even knowing that it is dead, or never existed in the first place.[37] But in Petrarch's case, as the soul becomes riveted to the phantasmata and unable to transcend its alienated status among the things of the world, it simultaneously resists that teleology which, in Augustine's view, permits the exiled soul to eventually return to its Maker, reconciling itself to itself through the miraculous experience of the Other.

Returning to Augustine's 'syntax of the word', we can say that Petrarch consequently becomes trapped in the 'realm of unreferred desire'[38]: unreferred to the extent that it is not referred to any higher order or Meaning but ends prematurely in itself (constituting, in John Freccero's terminology, Petrarch's idolatry).[39] At the same time, if poetic experience forecloses knowledge, it simultaneously opens up the imaginative counter-realm for the subjective figuration of desire. The resistance of the discourse to semantic comprehension is a sign of what Brenkman terms (in *RVF* 23) 'a mind whose relation to wisdom has been made radically eccentric by desire', but one that also embraces the ambivalence of its exilic status.[40] If, for Augustine, love is the will to know, for Petrarch in *RVF* 125, desire is the will not to know.

Thus while Mazzotta speaks of 'self-mystification' in Petrarch's poem,[41] there is in fact a more radical alienation both from the possibilities of self-knowledge and from knowledge of the world, which brings Petrarch close to recreating the error of the soul of which Augustine speaks in *The Trinity* x, 3.8–11 when it identifies with what is without, rather than within, so denying its own nature (and the *imago Dei*). According to Augustine, 'when the mind thinks of itself like that, it thinks it is a body': as the soul roots itself not within the ground of its inner truth but instead looks for meaning in the deceitful forms of the material world it so avidly desires, so it becomes confused and estranged from itself; as it internalizes what is extraneous to it, it too falls under the aegis of a mortal desire, it becomes a phantasm.[42]

Petrarch's poem is replete with metaphors that suggest that was is in play is a mind that thinks it is a body, or at the very least a mind that becomes trapped in materiality to the detriment of its own spiritual evolution or progression. As has been noted,[43] the references to clothing and to body in this poem refer primarily to the well-established medieval tradition of equating both material objects with the veil of allegory. However, what has been rightly termed the 'problem of interpretation' or the question of 'the very intelligibility of discourse',[44] and thus of the knowledge articulated through it, extends to the 'I''s relationship to itself as thinking and desiring subject, alternately conscious and denying of its double nature as both spirit and flesh.

Beginning in stanza 1, the poetic subject declares that it would 'dress up thought' like a body, in order to flesh out both his desire, and the poem, and to bolster his own phantasmatic presence as lover (*'men solitarie* l'orme'; *'non lascia* in me'). In line 15, speaking of its divestment of knowledge, the 'I' then registers that lack in psycho-physical terms, 'e di *saver* mi *spoglia*' [and *strips* me of my *skill*]. Finally, in lines 56–58, the tormented subject desires to exchange its hidden thoughts and cares with the river bank through a kind of perverse splitting or alienation, again reminiscent of *Inf.* XIII: 'onde 'l cor lasso riede | col tormentoso fianco | a partir teco i lor pensier nascosti' [and hence my weary heart | drags back my tortured body | to share with you the thoughts they conceal]. If, according to Augustine, the soul must retrieve itself from among the phantasmata in order to think on itself alone, and so to reopen the channel to God, Petrarch's soul is riven from itself and from its Maker as it identifies solely with the phantasms around it.[45]

As Lombardi states, 'signs (words) [for Augustine] are mere sound when disconnected from signification and are therefore not bearers of knowledge'. In the *Confessions*, 'signs and things cannot be transcended in the first section because the order of love is misused (things that should only be used are instead enjoyed)'.[46] This kind of enjoyment over use is radically present in Petrarch's fifth and sixth stanzas and leads to the foreclosure of the signifying chain and the fall into non-meaning or obscurity. At the same time, however, the poem posits a series of 'signs'/non-signs that can be semantically empty, but imaginatively full. The *cogitatio* that Petrarch denies on one level is one that he must achieve by other means: imagination and not thought.[47]

By stanza five, the subject has in fact travelled far enough into nothingness to allow for some stasis of the imaginary in the no-place of the mind's isolation, which radiates out from the 'dead point' of landscape, rooted in the pervading lack of a living sign of Laura, to reanimate some aspect of the landscape that in its emptiness still allows for a ghost of fullness:

> Ben sai che sì bel piede
> non tocchò terra unquancho
> come quel di che *già segnata fosti*,
> onde 'l cor lasso riede
> col tormentoso fianco
> a partir teco i lor pensier nascosti.
> Così avestù risposti
> de' be' vestigi sparsi
> anchor *tra' fior et l'erba*,
> che la mia vita acerba,

> lagrimando, trovasse ove acquetarsi!
> Ma come po s'appaga
> l'alma dubbiosa et vaga.

[You know so fair a foot | has never touched the earth | as that by which you were imprinted once: | and hence my weary heart | drags back my tortured body | to share with you the thoughts that they conceal. | If only you retained | some lovely traces scattered | *amongst the flowers and grass* | so that my bitter life | could find a spot where it could rest and weep! | But my scared, changeful soul | finds what relief it can.]

Yet although the 'segni' of Dantean derivation, absent in stanza 1, do return here, resurfacing in the phrase 'già segnata fosti', referring not to Laura directly but to the landscape inscribed with some memory or dream of her passage through it, they are definitely not a 'viva voce' (cf. *RVF* 23), and only a dead letter of desire at best able to recollect the seal of what occurred in the past (come *quel dì...*), but not the event itself.

Unlike in Dante's Eden, there is only repetition and not rebirth of the landscape. Even though, in the final moments of the poem, the wood can 'flower', it has only truly 'flowered' (*fiorito*) in the past. In reality, it is an 'herba o fior' *'qualunque'* (any: it doesn't matter which), growing on the surface, disconnected from the beloved and needing to be grafted onto the landscape of the mind, which substitutes for but does not replace the loss of her:

> Ovunque gli occhi volgo
> trovo un dolce sereno
> pensando: Qui percosse il vago lume.
> Qualunque herba o fior colgo
> credo che nel terreno
> aggia radice, ov'ella ebbe in costume
> gir *fra le piagge e 'l fiume,*
> et talor farsi un seggio
> fresco, fiorito et verde.
> *Così nulla se 'n perde,*
> et più certezza averne fôra il peggio.
> Spirto beato, quale
> se', quando altrui fai tale?
>
> O poverella mia, come se' rozza!
> Credo che tel conoschi:
> rimanti in questi boschi.

[In every place I look | I find a gentle calm, | when I think, 'Here that dancing light has glanced.' | Any grass or flower I pluck | has roots, I believe, | in ground where once it was her way to walk | *between the hills and river* | and sometimes make herself | a cool, green, flowery seat. | *Thus nought is really lost,* | and a more certain knowledge would be worse. | What are you, blessèd spirit, | if you have such effects? || O my poor song, how unrefined you are! | I think yourself you know it: | hide away in these woods.]

The poetic voice retreats into the voiceless landscape of the vision and poetic language betrays its status as a paradoxically silent, but indefatigable and ever present, interlocutor. As anticipated by the weighty emptiness of stanza 5, the 'signs' that now return are less words than objects, almost pictograms (or hieroglyphs) of desire.[48] The interchangeability of the signs out of which the chain of meaning is created (*anywhere, any* grass *or* flower), in no logical or substantial relationship to one another beyond their likeness to the deceptive images of memory, betrays the fact that in Petrarch's case, unlike Dante's, there is no universal core of meaning in desire or language, only an original void or lack, which allows for the very conditions of displacement and substitution through which desire makes itself felt. In the line 'qui percosse il vago lume' (l. 68), the distance between 'qui' as a deictic and 'percosse' as a past definite (did once, but no longer) marks the ontological as well as linguistic abyss between memory and desire, object and phantasm. Petrarch can perhaps recuperate something of space, but not time, which remains disjunctive and ultimately unbridgeable. What is created from the whole is only a presence problematically tied to the past ('*ebbe* in costume [...] gir et farsi') and a 'spirto beato', which, unnamable, is never fully disclosed and can be defined only in relation to an unknowable other (Other, otherness) — 'altrui'.

Hence the reason why Petrarch's *congedo* is frozen in the present continuous space of 'these woods', where the poem must stay and stay forever: an extension of the desiring self in its perennial quest for meaning that leads nowhere but back inside. As Durling and Martinez state of the similar predicament of the speaker in Dante's 'Così nel mio parlar':

> The final danger in the *petrose* [...] is not so much the death of the lover or the persisting inflexibility of the lady, but the self-enclosure of the poet in his own vision, his own private universe — his own monologism. The status is dead because it cannot speak: Pygmalion's ivory girl is *froide, sourde et mue*; the *petra* must be forced, in the speaker's fantasy, to cry out for him ("perché non latra per me...").[49]

But Petrarch's *petra* (part Laura, part landscape) says nothing, and there comes no answer.

Again, in anticipation of modern psychoanalytic theory, what appears to be at stake in Petrarch's poem is a failure of projection and an excess of introjection, which soon transforms into a fantasy of incorporation. If, as Wells indicates, 'Ferenczi maintains that in "introjection" there exists an "extension of autoerotic instincts" onto external objects, which are then included within the ego', incorporation occurs instead when the object (lost as opposed to present) does not fulfil its role as a mediator of desire because the desires that would be introjected through it are not activated in the proper way and never succeed in transforming (in being sublimated) into something else. As a result, the ego becomes a slave to a set of desires that 'never receive "a name and the right to exist [...] in an objectal sphere"' but instead circulate endlessly around a nameless and unnameable abyss within the subject that cannot be transcended, as per the *congedo* of Dante's 'Io son venuto', or stanza 2 of 'Così nel mio parlar'.[50] The woods into which Petrarch's poem leads are a 'selva oscura' [dark wood] of this kind: they represent the space in which desire loses direction, veers off course, and consequently turns in upon itself instead of forward to the ultimate goal in which it could find release.

And so the Augustinian itinerary of the *vestigium trinitatis* (imprint of the Trinity) that would, if properly ordered, lead the mind of the soul back to God, is transformed by Petrarch into the disordered space of *cupiditas*, in his case marked by the refusal of any itinerary at all amid the chaotic, interstitial pursuit of the 'vestigi sparsi' of Laura's footprints 'tra' fiori et l'erba' (125. 61) and 'fra le piagge e 'l fiume' (125. 72), the recurring space of the fall that extends from the *RVF* right into the *Trionfi*.[51] What seems to be at stake is a misuse in the order of love, similar to that charted in the opening chapters of Augustine's *Confessions* (and embodied, as Mazzotta notes, in the passage on Dido in Chapter 1), in which Petrarch treats signs and things *intransitively* rather than transitively, seeking to enjoy (*frui*) what should only be *used* on the path toward true fulfilment.[52] The model of poetry (and speech) that Petrarch puts forward is one that works against the principles of articulated discourse on several levels: from the resistance to speaking; through the resistance to moving; to the final stasis of the vision itself which suspends everything in a kind of languageless dream.

This is the place in which, as critics have noted, Petrarch diverges from Augustine's theory of language or, better, rewrites Augustine's 'semiology of desire' on his own terms (typically in the key of his idolatry, and as going against any impetus toward true 'conversion').[53] A case in point is Petrarch's use of the phrase 'nulla s'en perde', which potentially reworks both Augustine's 'non perdes aliquid' [you will lose nothing] (which refers to the 'place' of God which can never be lacking or in doubt, *Confessions* IV, xi, 16) and Dante's *Par.* XV, in which Petrarch arguably seeks to retrope that miraculous combination of presence and eternal simultaneity (*totum simul*)[54] implied in Cacciaguida's comparison with a star:

> Quale per li seren tranquilli e puri
> discorre ad ora ad or sùbito foco,
> movendo li occhi che stavan sicuri,
>   e pare stella che tramuti loco,
> se non che da la parte ond' e' s'accende
> *nulla sen perde*, ed esso dura poco:
>   tale dal corno che 'n destro si stende
> a piè di quella croce corse un astro
> de la costellazion che lì resplende; (*Par.* XV, 13–21)

[As through the clear and tranquil evening sky | from time to time a sudden fire will shoot, | drawing the eyes that just before had calmly gazed, | and seems a star escaping from its place — | except from where it first was kindled | *no star is missing* and it lasts but a brief while — | so from the arm of that great cross | extending on the right a star raced to the foot | of the resplendent constellation there.]

Petrarch rewrites the Augustinian and Dantean trajectories of desire, which culminate in divine unity, as a desire that aims for a phantasmatic totality capable of mimicking that miraculous, paradisiacal oneness that the soul enjoys in communion with God. Petrarch tries to construct an equivalent, secular and erotic dwelling place in *RVF* 125 but of course where he puts (the phantasm of) Laura, and not God, at the centre, he cannot enjoy the same sense of eternity, unity or fixity, only the illusion of it, which is nothing at all:

Noli esse vana, anima mea, et obsurdescere in aure cordis, tumultu vanitatis tuæ. audi et tu: verbum ipsum clamat ut redeas; et *ibi* est locus quietis imperturbabilis, *ubi non deseritur amor, si ipse non deserat*. [...] numquid ego aliquo discedo? ait verbum dei. ibi fige mansionem tuam; ibi commenda quidquid inde habes, anima mea, saltem fatigata fallaciis. veritati commenda quidquid tibi est a veritate, et *non perdes aliquid*; et reflorescent putria tua, et sanabuntur omnes languores tui, et fluxa tua reformabuntur, et renovabuntur, et constringentur ad te [...]. (*Confessions* IV, xi, 16)[55]

[Do not be vain, my soul. Do not deafen your heart's ear with the tumult of your vanity. Even you have to listen. The Word himself cries to you to return. *There* is the place of the undisturbed quietness *where love is not deserted if it does not itself depart*. [...] 'Surely I shall never go anywhere else', says the word of God. *Fix your dwelling there*. Put in trust there whatever you have from him, my soul, at least now that you are wearied of deceptions. Entrust to the truth whatever has come from the truth. *You will lose nothing*. The decayed parts of you will receive a new flowering, and all your sickness will be healed [Matt. 4. 23; Ps. 102. 3]. All that is ebbing away from you will be given fresh form and renewed, bound tightly to you.]

Augustine's 'numquid' and 'aliquid' are both potentially echoed in Petrarch's 'unquanco' and 'nulla' as he turns the locus of an infallible desire rooted in the identity of the ever-present One into the stasis of a desire fixated on the unattainability of its object. In that 'place', Petrarch's soul does not undergo any kind of 'new flowering' or any conversion away from its fallen state. Instead, it moves further into the realm of deception, and ever more into itself.

And so Petrarch returns to the troubadours' concept of the *amor de lonh*, an 'anti-Augustinian model of desire' that posits a 'love that never passes into knowledge' or what Agamben terms an *amar ipsa incognita* that 'can never be translated into the logical experience of signification'.[56] That unknowable desire is represented by the line that Petrarch repeatedly walks between the designation of the beloved in/as text (through the syllabic word-play on the letters and sounds of her name)[57] and her ultimate irreducibility to language, together with the 'I''s scattering between and among the signs of her, as in *RVF* 125's repeated designation of the phantasmatic no-place 'between' flower and grass which nevertheless provides the primary dynamism of the vision (ll. 69–74).

If for Augustine, 'the process of navigating through things according to the rules of love in order to reach the longed-for homeland results in an orderly interpretation of a map of signs (indeed ... an articulated discourse) with the aim of approaching the absolute signified', we could say that Petrarch's map of signs represents a disorderly configuration of the vestiges of passion (*ardendo*) whose absolute signified is unattainable but paradoxically desired as such.[58] The subject delights in that disorder and deferral precisely because it allows him to suspend the linearity inherent in the traditional semiology of desire that drives the soul forward to the supreme destination (in which it would find completion). In Augustinian terms, this can only occur at the expense of the soul's attachment to all lesser things in which it has delighted along the way;[59] Petrarch, unwilling to relinquish his desire for them, creates instead a circular itinerary in which the space of delight is illusorily present in each single object and so denies the awareness that the ultimate Object is not in fact contained in them.

A close reading of Petrarch's *RVF* 125 consequently reveals a much more extensive network of intertexts than has been traditionally conceived, one that extends from Dante, to Augustine, to Petrarch himself. However, in lacking the spirit of conversion common to both Dante and Augustine, upon which the possibility of finding meaning within the single individual pivots, Petrarch is denied the possibility of achieving a wholly meaningful text on either level (either the self, or its relationship to the Other, with which it hopes eventually to be joined).[60]

Suspended somewhere between desire and fulfilment in his pursuit of his object, Petrarch is never able to close the sentence of Laura, or his personal history, not even in the short term. We note how the penultimate stanza of his poem ends with a question to which, implicitly, there is no answer, only the repeated attempts to formulate the problem in different ways. The final identity of the beloved (Other) remains a mystery ('quale se'?); enclosed by the landscape, it nevertheless eludes the language of the poem. At best, in *RVF* 125, the subject might return to his state at the end of *RVF* 23, with his heart fixated only on Laura's beauty to the detriment of all other possible experiences:

> ma *fui* ben *fiamma* ch' un bel guardo accense,
> et fui l'uccel che più per l'aere poggia,
> alzando lei che ne' miei detti honoro:
> né per nova figura il primo alloro
> seppi lassar, ché per la sua dolce ombra
> ogni men bel piacer del *cor mi sgombra*. (ll. 164–69)

[But, yes, *I was the flame* that one look lit, | and was the bird that soars most through the air, | uplifting her I honor in my poems. | But I could not abandon the first laurel | for any novel shape. Its sweet shade still | *clears* any lesser beauty *from my heart*.]

With his use of 'fui', Petrarch recalls the voice of the dead souls in Dante's *Commedia*, particularly the damned of the *Inferno* with whom he shares the fate of eternally repeating the same sin that has been the source of his damnation in the first place, and even masochistically takes pleasure in it.[61] As the poet declares himself trapped in the posthumous realm of his own fallen subjectivity, which is paradoxically, however, the source of all experience both present and past, he literally inscribes a dead letter of desire at the very heart of the self. *RVF* 125, still written in the shadow of this masochistic sweetness, which is the true ground of desire for Petrarch, merely re-enacts another refusal to move on from the memory of the first laurel, which every poem in different ways recasts.

Notes to Chapter 12

1. All quotations from Petrarch are taken from Francesco Petrarca, *Canzoniere*, ed. by Marco Santagata, rev. edn (Milan: Mondadori, 1989); translations are by Peter Hainsworth, in *The Essential Petrarch*, ed. and trans. by Peter Hainsworth (Indianapolis, IN, and Cambridge, MA: Hackett, 2010) unless otherwise stated. All emphasis in quotations is mine unless otherwise stated.

2. The overtly political canzone, *RVF* 128, 'Italia mia' ['My Italy'], is the exception as the subject declares himself to be sitting sorrowful and sad on the banks of the Po, 'piacemi almen che' miei sospiri sian quali | spera 'l Tevero et l'Arno | e 'l Po, dove doglioso et grave or seggio' (ll. 4–6). However, as several critics have noted, the placement of this *canzone* within an erotic sequence is undoubtedly problematic and there are in fact several elements that are carried from the erotic into the political sphere, not least the construction of Italy as a gendered space, whose landscape carries the mark of its post-lapsarian status and is the vehicle for the poet's impassioned call for political renewal and rebirth.

3. See Peter Hainsworth, *Petrarch the Poet: An Introduction to the 'Rerum vulgarium fragmenta'* (London: Routledge, 1988), which concludes that in *RVF* 125, 'subjectivity finds pleasure in itself, if at the risk of fetishising elements in the landscape because of their presumed contact with the beloved' (p. 128); and Giuseppe Mazzotta's view in *The Worlds of Petrarch* (Durham, NC: Duke University Press, 1993), that this is a poem where 'Petrarch grounds his notion of the self and its elusiveness within the larger questions of language and desire' (pp. 69–70).

4. Augustine, *The Trinity* IX, 2.14. Quotations come from Saint Augustine, *The Trinity (De Trinitate)*, ed. by John E. Rotelle, trans. by Edmund Hill (New York: New City Press, 1991). See also Elena Lombardi, *The Syntax of Desire: Language and Love in Augustine, the Modistae, Dante* (Toronto: University of Toronto Press, 2007), p. 71.

5. I take the notion of a dead letter ('lettre morte') of desire from Julia Kristeva's study of melancholy subjectivity in, *Soleil noir: Dépression et mélancolie* (Paris: Gallimard, 1987), p. 73. Available in English as, *Black Sun: Depression and Melancholia*, trans. by Leon S. Roudiez (New York: Columbia University Press, 1989).

6. On this 'syntax of desire' in Augustine and Dante, and its relationship to the 'metaphysics of language', see Lombardi, *The Syntax of Desire*.

7. Christian Moevs, 'Subjectivity and Conversion in Dante and Petrarch', in *Petrarch & Dante: Anti-Dantism, Metaphysics, Tradition*, ed. by Zygmunt G. Barański and Theodore Cachey Jr. (Notre Dame, IN: University of Notre Dame Press, 2010), pp. 226–59 (p. 244; p. 236).

8. Marianne Shapiro, in *Hieroglyph of Time: The Petrarchan Sestina* (Minneapolis: University of Minnesota Press, 1980), speaks of a 'semantic complex' in regard to the 'dislocation-identification' of the *donna petra* in Dante's *rima petrosa*, 'Al poco giorno' ['To the short day'], centred, like Petrarch's vision of desire in *RVF* 125, on a 'selva' [wood], p. 97.

9. Augustine, *Confessions* XI, xxvi, 33. The edition from which I cite is: Saint Augustine, *Confessions*, trans. by Henry Chadwick (Oxford: Oxford University Press, 1992).

10. Mazzotta, p. 73.

11. Quotations from the *Commedia* are from Dante Alighieri, *'La Commedia' secondo l'antica vulgata*, ed. by Giorgio Petrocchi, Società Dantesca Italiana, Edizione Nazionale, 2nd rev. edn, 4 vols (Florence: Le Lettere, 1994). Translations are from Dante Alighieri, *Comedy*, trans. by Robert Hollander and Jean Hollander, 3 vols (New York: Doubleday, 2000–07).

12. Cf. 'Agnosco veteris flammae vestigia', *Aen.* IV, 23. On this moment, and its significance in Dante as correcting the 'Virgilian mis-reading of death', see John Freccero, 'Manfred's Wounds and the Poetics of the *Purgatorio*', in John Freccero, *Dante: The Poetics of Conversion*, ed. by Rachel Jacoff (Cambridge, MA: Harvard University Press, 1986), pp. 195–208 (pp. 207–08).

13. If there are any signs at all, they come after. They do not so much give birth to desire (as Augustine would have it), but are posthumous to it.

14. See Augustine, *The Trinity* X, 1.2, 'The more therefore the thing is known without being fully known, the more does the intelligence desire to know what remains; if it only knew that there was a vocal sound like this and did not know that it was the sign of something, it would not look further for anything else, having already perceived as much as it could about a sensible object by sensation.'

15. See *VN* II, 3–4 (Dante's first sighting of Beatrice), for several details that recur in this passage in *Purg.* XXX.

16. On the extent of Petrarch's knowledge of the *Convivio*, the *canzoni* contained in which he is likely to have read as free-standing *rime* without framing prose commentary, see Justin Steinberg, 'Dante *Estravagante*, Petrarca *Disperso*, and the Spectre of the Other Woman', in Barański and Cachey, eds, *Petrarch & Dante*, pp. 263–89 (especially pp. 264–69).

17. Hainsworth, *Petrarch the Poet*, p. 126.

18. I quote the *petrose*, including English translations, from *Dante's Lyric Poems*, ed. and trans. by Kenelm Foster and Patrick Boyde, 2 vols (Oxford: Clarendon Press, 1967), I: *The Poems: Text and Translation*.

19. Robert M. Durling and Ronald L. Martinez, *Time and the Crystal: Studies in Dante's 'Rime petrose'* (Berkeley and Oxford: University of California Press, 1990), p. 171; p. 166.

20. 'A body by its weight tends to move towards its proper place. The weight's movement is not necessarily downwards, but to its appropriate position: fire tends to move upwards, a stone downwards. They are acted upon by their respective weights, they seek their own place. [...] My weight is my love. Wherever I am carried, my love is carrying me.'

21. While it has not been possible to establish a precise chronology for the series of poems that make up the *rime petrose*, Durling and Martinez argue that in poetic and desiring terms at least, 'Così nel mio parlar' seems to exceed the levels reached elsewhere in the sequence, and its difference from them (especially with regard to the extreme force employed to break out of the dominant circle of negativity and frustration) could be a sign of 'a symptom of a crisis in the poetics of the *petrose* themselves'. See Durling's and Martinez's introduction to the poem, in *Time and the Crystal*, pp. 165–66 (p. 165).

22. While it is difficult to provide an exact chronology of Petrarch's texts, as Santagata indicates in his commentary to each poem, it is very likely that the first *stesura* of *RVF* 23 dates to the poet's youthful period — not least since Petrarch himself stated that 'est de primis inventionibus nostris' — so somewhere between 1327–34 (with the poem revised subsequently in two stages: lines 1–89 in *c.* 1336–37, and the remainder *c.* 1350). *RVF* 125, clearly written as a 'sister' poem to *RVF* 126, most likely dates to Petrarch's first or second stay in Vaucluse, so to late 1341/ early 1342, or 1343. The protracted editorial arc of *RVF* 23 thus allows for the possibility of an intratextual dialogue of the kind I am proposing, though even if the poem had been written later than *RVF* 125, the ordering of the texts within the *Canzoniere* itself, and especially the dual revisitation of the 'decisive moment' in the story of the subject's birth of desire for Laura, would still suggest a significant correlation. On the chronology of both poems, see Santagata, p. 101 and pp. 579–80.

23. Peter Kuon, *L'aura dantesca: Metamorfosi intertestuali nel 'Rerum vulgarium fragmenta' di Francesco Petrarca* (Florence: Cesati, 2004), pp. 151–52 (my translation).

24. In fact 'estrania' has tended to be interpreted in two ways: (i) as emphasizing the novelty and 'strangeness' (in the sense of *peregrino*) of a voice unheard of before now: a voice fused with the sweet strains of the swan; and (ii) a voice, like the subject himself, drawn from its proper image: a hybrid, 'strange' voice, not fully human (because swan-like). See in particular, the commentary by Ludovico Castelvetro in Francesco Petrarca, *Le rime*, con note letterali e critiche del Castelvetro (Florence: Ciardetti, 1832).

25. Cf. II Corinthians 3. 6, 'He has made us competent as ministers of a new covenant — not of the letter but of the spirit, for the letter kills but the spirit gives life.' On this point, see also John Freccero, 'Medusa: The Letter and the Spirit', *Yearbook of Italian Studies* (1972), 1–18.

26. The translation here comes from *Petrarch's Lyric Poems: The 'Rime sparse' and Other Lyrics*, ed. and trans. by Robert M. Durling (Cambridge, MA, and London: Harvard University Press, 1976).

27. Marion A. Wells, *The Secret Wound: Love-Melancholy and Early Modern Romance* (Stanford, CA: Stanford University Press, 2007), p. 88.

28. On *Inferno* XIII, see at least Leo Spitzer, 'Speech and Language in *Inferno* XIII', *Italica*, 19.3 (Sept. 1942), 81–104 and, Lombardi, *The Syntax of Desire*, pp. 147–48.

29. Mazzotta, p. 76.

30. Jean Laplanche and J. B. Pontalis, 'Fantasy and the Origins of Sexuality', in *Formations of Fantasy*, ed. by Victor Burgin, James Donald and Kara Caplan (London and New York: Methuen, 1986), pp. 5–34 (pp. 24–25).

31. See Hainsworth, *Petrarch the Poet*, p. 128.

32. See William Shakespeare, *Hamlet*, I. 2. 72–86, 'Seems, madam? nay, it is, I know not "seems." | 'Tis not alone my inky cloak, good mother [...] Together with all forms, moods, shapes of grief, | That can denote me truly. These indeed seem, | For they are actions that a man might play; | But I have that within which *passes show*, | These but the trappings and the suits of woe.'

Cited from *Hamlet*, ed. by Harold Jenkins (London: Arden Shakespeare, 1982).

33. These notions are expanded upon at length in Julia Kristeva's *La Révolution du langage poétique: L'Avant-garde à la fin du XIXe siècle: Lautréamont et Mallarmé* (Paris: Éditions du Seuil, 1974).

34. Lombardi, *The Syntax of Desire*, p. 71.

35. See 1 Corinthians 14, '[19] Yet in the church I had rather speak five words with my understanding, that by my voice I might teach others also, than ten thousand words in an unknown tongue. [20] Brethren, be not children in understanding: howbeit in malice be ye children, but in understanding be men.' See Giorgio Agamben, 'Pascoli and the Thought of the Voice', in *The End of the Poem: Studies in Poetics*, trans. by Daniel Heller-Roazen (Stanford, CA: Stanford University Press, 1999), pp. 62–75 (p. 66). Though it should be said that in Petrarch's case, there is a tension between this unfruitfulness and the 'natural vertude' [virtù] concealed at the level of the marrow of the branch, or the inner core of the subject.

36. Kristeva, *Black Sun*, pp. 62–63.

37. Wells, pp. 78–79.

38. Lombardi, *The Syntax of Desire*, p. 44, 'It is commonplace in Augustine's scholarship to interpret the "region of unlikeness," the narrative of the exterior man contained in Books 1–7, as a realm of loose signs that is not yet referred and compared to the inner truth, as well as a realm of unreferred desire. The famous passage on language learning — which could be summarized as "I want (lack), therefore I speak" — sets the stage for a process of education that consists of a constitutional misuse of the orders of language and desire. The persistence of the *imago dei* within the individual, although vanishing, much veiled and weighted down by sin, makes of the *perversio* in the first chapters the specular opposite of *conversio* — a "disorderly order" of signs and things.'

39. See John Freccero, 'The Fig Tree and the Laurel: Petrarch's Poetics', *Diacritics*, 5.1 (Spring 1995), 34–40.

40. John Brenkman, 'Writing, Desire, Dialectic in Petrarch's "Rime 23"', *Pacific Coast Philology*, 9 (April 1974), 12–19 (p. 13).

41. Mazzotta, p. 72.

42. 'But the mind is mistaken when it joins itself to these images with such extravagant love that it even comes to think it is itself something of the same sort. [...] *When the mind thinks of itself like that, it thinks it is a body.* [...] Hence arises its shameful mistake, that it cannot make itself out among the images of the things it has perceived with the senses, and see itself alone; they are all stuck astonishingly fast together with the glue of love. And this is its impurity, that while it attempts to think of itself alone, it supposes itself to be that without which it is unable to think of itself. So when it is bidden to know itself, it should not start looking for itself as though it had drawn off from itself, but should draw off what it has added to itself' [i.e. earthly/temporal things; death] (*The Trinity* x, 3.8–11).

43. See e.g. Mazzotta, p. 76, '[...] We can perhaps grasp the reasons for the presence of technical metaphors drawn from the repertory of the language of allegory. The thrust of "Se 'l pensier che mi strugge" is to find a language that "vestisse d'un color conforme" (l. 3) the lover's inner thoughts.'

44. See Brenkman, p. 12, in which, in commenting upon a passage from the *Familiares* (1. 9) where Petrarch discusses the relationship of the soul to speech (*sermo*), he gives the following gloss: 'if the soul is disordered because of internal discord of its desires, the discourse it produces will likewise be misshapen. This does not mean, however, that the disordered discourse will adequately reflect the contours of the soul's disorder. Petrarch says instead that the contradictory desires produce a contraction between the speaker's inner character and the words of the spoken discourse. What is threatened, therefore, is the very intelligibility of discourse.'

45. Cf. also Augustine, *The Trinity* XII, 3.16, 'And how could we travel this long way from the heights to the depths except through the half-way level of self? If you neglect to hold dear in charity the wisdom which always remains the same, and hanker after knowledge through experience of changeable, temporal things, this knowledge puffs up instead of building up.'

46. Lombardi, *The Syntax of Desire*, p. 15; p. 44.

47. See also *RVF* 257 for another example of this.

48. Cf. Giorgio Bertone on Maestro Adamo's punishment in *Inferno* XXX which operates in a similar

way: 'L'immagine incisa nella carne, dalla carne si proietta davanti al soggetto che parla in un fotogramma fisso per l'eternità, che è la figura sinestetica di una fissazione psicologica e morale. In quel corpo dilatato il paesaggio nasce cinesteticamente da una dolorosa assenza non colmabile e si fissa al volto' [The image carved into the flesh, of the flesh, is projected in front of the subject who speaks in a photogram fixed for all eternity, which becomes the synaesthesic symbol of a psychological and moral fixation. In that distended body, the landscape is born kinaesthetically from a painful absence that cannot be filled and fixes itself on the face]. In Giorgio Bertone, *Lo sguardo escluso: L'idea del paesaggio nella letteratura occidentale* (Novara: Interlinea, 2000), p. 92 (my translation).

49. Durling and Martinez, *Time and the Crystal*, p. 197.

50. The definitions of introjection and incorporation here draw on Wells's excellent discussion in *The Secret Wound*, pp. 78–79.

51. For the repetition of these motifs, see e.g. Francesco Petrarca, *Triumphus Cupidinis I*, 90; and *Triumphus Cupidinis III*, 157, in which the serpent lies 'tra' fiori ascoso' [hidden among the flowers], in Francesco Petrarca, *Trionfi, rime estravaganti, codice degli abbozzi*, ed. by Vinicio Pacca and Laura Paolino, intro. by Marco Santagata (Milan: Mondadori, 1996).

52. See *Confessions* I, xiii, 21 and Wells's identification of Petrarch as a 'wounded Dido in his analysis of his deadly *atra voluptas* in the Secretum' (p. 73).

53. Again, see Freccero on this in 'The Fig Tree and the Laurel'; Teodolinda Barolini, 'The Making of a Lyric Sequence: Time and Narrative in Petrarch's *Rerum vulgarium fragmenta*', *MLN*, 104.1, Italian issue (Jan. 1989), 1–38, and Moevs, 'Subjectivity and Conversion'.

54. cf. Barolini, 'The Making of a Lyric Sequence', p. 250.

55. Latin text sourced from: Augustine, *Confessiones*, <http://www9.georgetown.edu/faculty/jod/latinconf/4.html> [accessed 13 August 2011].

56. Agamben, p. 64.

57. A prime example of this is of course *RVF* 5, in which, as Mazzotta notes, 'the property of the name is threatened by the duplication of the name "Laureta" into "Laurea"', which 'endangers the unity of the proper name and subverts the possibility that the voice of love is bound to a univocal, stable sign' (p. 78).

58. Lombardi, p. 36.

59. On the importance of this Augustinian paradigm for Dante's *Purgatorio*, see Barolini 'Purgatory as Paradigm: Traveling the New and Never-Before-Traveled Path of this Life/Poem', in *The Undivine 'Comedy': Detheologizing Dante* (Princeton, NJ: Princeton University Press, 1992), pp. 99–120.

60. On these notions in Dante and Augustine, see Lombardi's excellent discussion in *The Syntax of Desire*.

61. On the pain of Hell as consisting in the damned souls' perpetual repetition of their own corrupt essence, see Manuele Gragnolati, 'Gluttony and the Anthropology of Pain in Dante's *Inferno* and *Purgatorio*', in *History in the Comic Mode: Medieval Communities and the Matter of Person*, ed. by Rachel Fulton and Bruce W. Holsinger (New York: Columbia University Press, 2007), pp. 238–50. On desire in Dante's *Inferno* as masochistic, see Elena Lombardi, 'Plurilingualism *sub specie aeternitatis* and the Strategies of a Minor Author', in *Dante's Plurilingualism: Authority, Knowledge, Subjectivity*, ed. by Sara Fortuna, Manuele Gragnolati, and Jürgen Trabant (Oxford: Legenda, 2010), pp. 133–48.

CHAPTER 13

Queer Metaphors and Queerer Reproduction in Alain de Lille's *De planctu naturae* and Jean de Meun's *Roman de la rose*

Jonathan Morton

Is all literature deviant? Insofar as literary works must depart from established models to be original and not merely copies, all such texts must deviate from existing works to a greater or a lesser extent. But it is surely going too far to say that the very act of literary creation is deviant and queer. Or is it? When writing and sculpting are used as metaphors for the depiction of sexual acts, both straight and queer, questions of the straightness or queerness of artistic creation are opened up alongside questions about the possibility or impossibility of successfully writing either licit or illicit sex. To muddy the waters further, the occasion for these questions — the metaphor — itself becomes subject to question. Is metaphor queer?[1]

Starting with the use of writing as a metaphor for sexual activity, queer or straight, I want to consider how figurative language itself, in its slippages and in the impossibility of its maintaining clear distinctions, can be seen as queer in order to investigate the subject of originality in art. If writing and poetry are used to understand sexual reproduction and illicit sexual acts, how in turn can sexual intercourse be used to understand the processes and meaning of poetic creation?

I will examine two texts, one Alain de Lille's twelfth-century Latin prosimetrum *De planctu naturae* [*The Plaint of Nature*] and the other Jean de Meun's continuation of the *Roman de la rose* [*The Romance of the Rose*], written in French in the second half of the thirteenth century. In both texts an allegorical figure named Genius descends from above and, dressed in clerical robes, attempts to preserve sexual orthodoxy and to remove sodomy. In both cases sodomy is described metaphorically as incorrect or deviant writing. To modern ears, genius has inescapable associations with exceptional individual creativity or intelligence, yet here Genius is rather a figure that represents the unindividuated natural drive to procreate. It is against the backdrop of the tension between these two principles, between individual innovation and the faithful, unreflecting transmission of the biological or textual legacy, that the processes of literature are to be investigated.

Before dealing with 'genius', it is important to ask what 'queer' might mean. Taking my cue from the literary depictions of deviant sex in these medieval texts, I use the term here to refer not only to acts and actors that might fall under medieval or modern understandings of sodomy or to modern non-heterosexual identifications, but also to the nonlinear nature of polysemous figurative language and the deviation involved in human cultural production. Queerness is inextricably intertwined with innovation and artistic originality. In its etymology, as both Eve Kosofsky Sedgwick and Gary Cestaro have remarked,[2] the 'queer' involves a departure from the straight line (as, in fact, does 'trope', of which metaphor is a category, deriving from the Greek 'τρόπος' — a turn). It is something that deviates from, or that transverses, the wholly straight norm (or rather the *fantasy* of a wholly straight norm). I use the word 'transverse' deliberately: the queer transverses the straight fantasy in that it intersects with this norm, it acts against it, and works to overturn it.[3] 'Transverse' also contains within it another punning meaning, which is the transposition or translation of an earlier text into verse,[4] a meaning that is wholly imbricated in the notion of a queer genealogy of poetic production that will be introduced towards the end of this article. Queerness stems from a failed or failing natural teleology. It is born in sexual acts rooted in the pursuit of pleasure, acts that exclude the putative natural (and thus divinely appointed) end of sex, that is reproduction and the continuation of the species. This lack of end thus gives rise to a troubling infinity (*infinitus* = endless) that destabilizes the whole order of creation and the imaginary fantasy of the ordered workings of a world that would otherwise be wholly natural or perfectly divine.

It is this queer infinity (encompassing both the lack of a natural end or purpose and eternal, senseless repetition) which renders sodomy irrational, like a journey without a destination. Sodomy (or rather, the unspeakable things that sodomy attempts, and fails, to denote), in its opposition to the ordering rationale of nature and reproduction, disrupts linearity, progression, and logic, on which meaning appears to depend. Sodomy's queer circularity of repetition and its promise of continuous access to *jouissance* undermine what Lee Edelman has called 'futurism', the idealized fantasies of the future — dependent on reproduction — which are also the idealized fantasies of the past.

> Futurism [...] generates generational succession, temporality, and narrative sequence, not toward the end of enabling change, but, instead, of perpetuating sameness, of turning back time to assure repetition — or to assure a logic of resemblance (more precisely: a logic of metaphoricity) in the service of representation and, by extension, of desire.[5]

The eternal repetition of reproduction and the production of meaning that constitutes this straight imaginary are parodied in the spectre of the queer, infinite repetition of *jouissance* and the production of meaninglessness occasioned by sodomy. The attempt to fix a name onto this meaninglessness, to save it and to bring it into language, does not manage to iron out the kink. Rather, it leads to the multiplication of the queer and its destabilization of the symbolic order. As Bill Burgwinkle points out,

> The mere evocation of sodomy seems to stain all that surrounds it such that

distinctions between the sodomitical and normal, between me and it, masculine and feminine, the lawful and unlawful, the symbolic and the imaginary, become impossible to sustain.[6]

Language repeatedly attempts and fails to suture the gap in meaning occasioned by sodomy that cannot be articulated except through imperfect metaphors, and which, through metaphor, spreads, and threatens to cause the whole system of meaning to start unravelling. However, new meanings are generated through a trope's failure to name solely what it wants to mean and thus figurative language, which cannot be made 'to signify monolithically',[7] which always means something other than it intends to, undoes the repetitive linearity of any putative straightness. The plural meanings of tropes make impossible the predetermined conclusions that necessarily derive from the univocal language of logic. On the one hand, then, queerness takes its meaning from that which goes against the established order; it is negative and goes against the continuation of life. On the other, the aspect of queerness that is a departure from the wholly natural leads to originality and novelty. While futurism, despite its apparent imperative towards creation, aims merely at reproduction and entails 'a will to preserve identity',[8] the queer leads, through polyvalent language, to a perverse (transverse?) generation of new meanings. The pitfalls and potentialities of deviation and the relationship between the natural and the unnatural are all at stake in questions about Genius.

At the end of the *De planctu*, Genius, dressed as a bishop, appears in the narrator's dream and pronounces an excommunication of all sinners, foremost among them anyone who 'legitimum Veneris obliquat incessum' [blocks the lawful path of Venus] (*DPN* XVIII, 146; p. 220);[9] this seems to mean those who carry out queer sex-acts, who disrupt the linearity of reproduction and the continuation of the species. The *De planctu* is a dream-vision in which a first-person narrator begins by lamenting mankind's aberrant sexual practices and how they are corrupting humanity, especially the male half, as unrestrained sexual desire (Venus) turns men into women:

> Cum Venus in Venerem pugnans illos facit illas
> Cumque sui magica deuirat arte uiros. (*DPN* I, 5–6)

[When Venus wars with Venus and changes 'hes' into 'shes' and with her witchcraft unmans man.] (p. 67)

The narrator goes on to lament of man that that '[a]rs magice Veneris hermafroditat eum' [Venus's witchcraft has turned man into a hermaphrodite] (*DPN* I, 18; p. 68). The *De planctu*, despite being an extended attack on sodomy, is never much more explicit than this in its description of its subject matter. It can only talk about sexual desire and sexual crime through a veil of metaphor, with the result that we never know exactly what is being discussed. Maybe this should not entirely surprise us given the history of tactical metaphor surrounding sodomy. The euphemism 'peccatum' [sin] or 'nefas contra naturam' [crime against nature] used for (avoiding) describing sodomy is found in legal codes dating back to the mid-sixth century,[10] and was still in use for the sanctions outlined for homosex in the Third Lateran Council of 1179.[11] Sodomy itself, as catachresis, is a forced metaphor used to make up for a linguistic lacuna on the part of an author or speaker:[12] the acts, which cannot be outlined explicitly in literal language, can only be represented as those performed by the inhabitants of Sodom (acts of fornication 'sodomitico more' [in the Sodomitic manner]).[13] What are these acts? The lack of a common definition in straight, clear language makes it impossible to say for sure what sodomy is (although male–male anal sex seems pretty inescapably included in the category). Mark Jordan points out that while there are some definitions of sodomy in penitentials, or confession guides, such frank descriptions are few and far between, and do not seem to offer a clear, universally shared understanding of what is being described.[14] Indeed, Alain de Lille, in his guide to confession, the *Liber Poenitentialis*, exhorts the confessor to avoid specific questions about sexual crime (including the sin *contra naturam*) 'ne peccati incogniti inquisitio det peccandi occasionem' [in case asking about a sin previously unknown leads to the sin taking place] (I, 4).[15] 'Sodomy', then, is a metaphor used to avoid the corrupting specifics of deviant sexuality that cannot be openly discussed and, these specifics remaining to an extent unknown, it becomes a signifier without a stable signified. Its meaning, then, can only be intimated through the context of its enunciation.[16] Metaphor here, and in fact anywhere, is far from stable and it is the uncertainty and deviation present in figurative language that sees it opposed to controlled and wholesome philosophical expression. Over the course of the goddess Natura's complaint we see further metaphorical portrayals of sex, which are every bit as queer as the unnameable practices the text seems to be banning.

After Natura has introduced herself to the ignorant narrator, who does not at first recognize her, she starts to explain how mankind's sins against nature have brought her down from the heavens to the brothels. She recounts how all creatures behave according to the law of nature except humans and she adds her own lament to the narrator's complaint, bewailing that

> [s]olus homo, mee modulationis citharam aspernatus, sub delirantis Orphei lira delirat. Humanum namque genus, a sua generositate degenerans, in constructione generum barbarizans, Venereas regulas inuertendo nimis irregulari metaplasmo. (*DPN* VIII, 54–57)

> [Man alone turns with scorn from the modulated strains of my cithern and runs deranged to the notes of mad Orpheus' lyre. For the human race, fallen from its high estate, adopts a highly irregular [grammatical] change when it inverts the rules of Venus by introducing barbarisms in its arrangements of genders.] (p. 133)

Overwhelming desire, awakened by irrational, even anti-rational, music (or, more generally, art) has caused deviation, and, as we shall see later, irrational and queer desire can itself lead to the production of art. The use of language as a metaphor for sex continues with Natura's narrative but the metaphor of gender in grammar becomes exchanged for that of writing. The deviation of Venus from the correct path is described allegorically as *falsigraphia*, 'pseudography', or false writing, a term used by Natura in an allegorical explanation of human sexuality:

> Ad officium etiam scripture calamum prepotentem eidem fueram elargita, ut in competentibus cedulis eiusdem calami scripturam poscentibus quarum mee

largitionis beneficio fuerat conpotita iuxta mee orthographie normulam rerum genera figuraret, ne a proprie descriptionis semita in falsigraphie deuia eundem deuagari minime sustineret. (*DPN* x, 30–35)

[I had also bestowed on her [Venus] an unusually powerful writing-pen for her work so that she might trace the classes of things, according to the rules of my orthography, on suitable pages which called for writing by this same pen and which through my kind gift she had in her possession, so that she might not suffer the same pen to wander in the smallest degree from the path of proper delineation into the byways of pseudography.] (p. 156)

Correct writing, then, faithful transmission of the given, natural model, stands for procreative sex. *Falsigraphia* stands for sodomitical sex, any sex that has deviated, that is queer.[17] In Natura's narrative, Venus, in her idleness, began to weary of the daily toil of the continuation of the species and turns against her husband, Hymenaeus, committing adulterous fornication with Antigenius, and as this confused allegory continues we are told that 'malleos ab incudum exheredans consortio adulterinis dampnauit incudibus' [she dispossessed the hammers of fellowship with their anvils and sentenced them to counterfeit anvils] (*DPN* x, 135–36; p. 164). The hammers — the tools that Natura gave Venus for the continuation of the human species — could be penises, the intended anvils then presumably vaginas and the counterfeit anvils anuses to which the male tools are now attracted. The metaphor is not quite as straightforward as we might think, however. Natura has already complained about how youths have, for the sake of money, converted Venus's hammers to the functions of anvils, a truly bizarre image if the metaphor is to hold.[18] Which it really cannot. There is a problem here, of which Alain de Lille is hyper-self-conscious, caused by the fact that metaphorical language allows, even necessitates, slippage from straight writing and straight meaning, a point to which we will return.

To the burgeoning list of metaphors that Natura uses to describe sex, we should also add the imagery of rhetorical and logical proof. Man and woman are compared to a syllogism in which the man is the major term (for example, all men are mortal), the predicate, and the woman is the minor term (Socrates is a man), the subject.[19] They join '[i]n assumptione uero relatiuorum osculorum reciprocis impressionibus' [by the adoption of mutual and reciprocal kisses], and 'in conclusione expressissime inherentie uinculo ueriori subiecti predicatique carnalis celebretur connexio' [finally in the conclusion the carnal connection of subject and predicate is to be solemnized by the bonds of very close intercourse] (*DPN* x, 95–98; pp. 160–61). Thus male and female join to result in a purely logical ordered conclusion (therefore Socrates is mortal) and correct sexual reproduction is a mechanical, necessary process. In the metaphor, the most natural, ordered progression of language and argument, the way that clear meaning is guaranteed, is when a thing is what it says it is. Socrates is Socrates and (perhaps particularly pertinently) a man is a man, and there is no confusion in getting from premise to conclusion. It should not be wholly surprising, then, that in this metaphor, Natura, drawing on classical rhetorical theory, outlaws the indirect and unstable speech that is figurative language:

Sicut autem quasdam gramatice dialeticeque obseruantias inimicantissime hostilitatis incursus uolui a Veneris anathematizare gignasiis, sic methonomicas

rethorum positiones, quas in sue amplitudinis gremio rethorica mater
amplectans, multis suas orationes afflat honoribus, Cypridis artificiis interdixi,
ne si nimis dure translationis excursu a suo reclamante subiecto predicatum
alienet in aliud, in facinus facetia, in rusticitatem urbanitas, tropus in uicium,
in decolorationem color nimius conuertatur. (*DPN* x, 108–14)

[Just as I decided to excommunicate from the schools of Venus certain practices
of Grammar and Dialectic as inroads of the most ill-disposed enemy, so too
I banned from the Cyprian's workshop the use of words by the rhetors in
metonymy which mother Rhetoric clasps to her ample bosom and breathes
great beauty on her orations, in case she, digressing most cruelly, transfer the
predicate from its loudly protesting subject to something else, in which case
cleverness would turn into a blemish, refinement into boorishness, a trope into
a defect (or vice) and excessive embellishment into disfigurement.] (p. 162)[20]

Metonymy is a kind of trope that involves the substitution of one name for another
with which it has some connection. One example might be to describe sexual
desire as Venus, as Alain does. Invention, tropes and their attendant pleasure, it
is suggested in this trope, can be too seductive and might lead the predicate, the
male part of the union, into homosexual sin and away from the less alluring female
subject.[21] There is a fear here that runs throughout the *De planctu* that sodomy is
more pleasurable and desirable than heterosex, just as poetry gives more pleasure
than scholastic logic. Venus rebels against her mother, 'magis appetens ociis
effeminari sterilibus quam fructuosis exerceri laboribus' [desiring to live the soft
life of barren ease rather than be harassed by fruitful labour] (*DPN* x, 124–25; p.
163). From this male perspective, heterosexual vaginal penetration is seen as a chore,
and it is deviation (a soft life of barren ease) that is truly attractive. The enactment
of figurative language (of sodomy?) is shown here as a conscious desire to create
beautiful and original expressions risking the result that the pleasure arising from
such deviations will undermine natural, unreflective reproduction.

The text seems to go out of its way to undermine its condemnations. The poetic
images that Alain de Lille uses to illustrate his arguments against sodomy, even as he
condemns such images, self-consciously defeat themselves in their apparent attempt
to present a straight argument. (This is maybe not entirely surprising given that the
rhetorical trope/sodomy has been explicitly opposed to the rational argument of
logical formulae.) The merger of genders that takes place in the opening meter of
the *De planctu* is a perfect example:

> Virginis in labiis cur basia tant quiescunt,
> Cum reditus in eis sumere nemo uelit?
> Que michi pressa semel mellirent oscula succo,
> Que mellita darent mellis in ore fauum. (*DPN* i, 43–46)

[Why do so many kisses lie fallow on maidens' lips while no one wishes to
harvest a crop from them? If these kisses were but once planted on me, they
would grow honey-sweet with moisture, and grown honey-sweet, they would
form a honeycomb in my mouth.] (pp. 70–71)

The male speaker, it seems, has been inseminated and impregnated by female kisses,
which swell, grow and come to term within him as honeycomb. The metaphor

has succeeded in turning the male subject into a female, the very crime for which sodomitical Venus is attacked some fifty lines before.[22]

What, then, is the point of the *De planctu*, a text so clearly shot through with self-defeating metaphor? I suggest that Alain de Lille, or his narrator, is attempting an act of translation. He is attempting to carry the subject matter of sodomy from an unspeakable, obscene sphere into a licit space, where, avoiding the corruption of the ignorant through the explicit obscenity that he warns against in his *De arte praedicatoria*, he can demonstrate the dangers posed by unregulated desire to the very fabric of nature, truth, and language. Natura tells Alain's narrator that:

> quia rebus de quibus loquimur cognatos oportet esse sermones, rerum informitati locutionis debet deformitas conformari.

> [since the language of our discourse should be related to the matters about which we speak, there should be at times an ugliness of style to conform to the deformity of the subject-matter.]

However, she goes on to explain that:

> ne locutionis cacephaton lectorum offendat auditum uel in ore uirginali locum collocet turpitudo, predictis uiciorum monstris euphonia orationis uolo pallium elargiri. (*DPN* VIII, 191–95)

> [it is my intention to contribute a mantle of fair-sounding words to the monsters of vice I mentioned earlier so as to prevent cacemphaton from offending the ears of readers or anything foul finding a place on a maiden's lips.] (pp. 143–44)

There is a tension here in attempting to articulate cleanly and appropriately the dangers of an evil which is to be avoided, an evil whose details are always unfit for human hearing and yet if they are not known, cannot be avoided.[23] Jacques Derrida's investigation of translation, *Qu'est ce qu'est une traduction 'relevante'?*, is helpful here:

> La traduction est toujours une tentative d'appropriation qui vise à transporter chez soi, dans sa langue, le plus proprement possible, de la façon la plus relevante possible le sens le plus propre de l'original, même si c'est le sens propre d'une figure, d'une métaphore, d'une métonymie, d'une catachrèse ou d'une indécidable impropriété.

> [Translation is always an attempt at appropriation that aims to transport home, in its language, in the most appropriate way possible, in the most relevant way possible, the most proper meaning of the original text, even if this is the proper meaning of a figure, metaphor, metonymy, catachresis, or undecidable impropriety.][24]

Alain is translating sodomy into language, and sodomy is absolutely an 'indécidable impropriété', not to mention a figure of speech — for anal sex or whatever. Alain, translating 'le plus proprement possible', seems to be demonstrating that the multiform, twisting potentialities of sodomy — as it mutates incessantly, transverses the norm and changes men into hermaphrodites or women — can best be translated into written language through metaphor that is irrational, confused and unnatural, that twists itself up in knots and undermines every point that it attempts to make. The *De planctu* is a text with an agenda concerning how language should be used to discuss sex just as it has an agenda concerning the acts themselves. The problem it has, though, is that it is almost too successful in its enunciation of the queer language of desire. Once sodomy has been raised, it cannot be banished through language.

This is all a little bit unsettling and at the end of the text there is an attempt to banish the corruption of sodomy. After further complaints from the talkative Natura and the introduction of several other allegorical figures such as Hymenaeus, Truth and Generosity, we see Genius, Natura's other self, who 'in sacerdotali ancillatur officio' [serves [her] in a priestly office] (DPN xviii, 145; p. 206). He arrives and solemnly dons priestly clothes before ruling that everyone who blocks the lawful path of Nature or deviates in other ways from the perfect, idealized norm be excommunicated or 'naturalium rerum uniformi concilio segregetur' [set apart from the harmonious council of the things of Nature] (DPN xviii, 145; p. 220). Then the narrator wakes up and the text ends. At first glance, this appears to provide a reassuring sense of stability and reassertion of the correct, straight, natural order of things. Genius, in these texts, is a concept that seems to represent a principle of masculinity and procreation. It is understandable for him to oppose sodomy, which is sex that avoids procreation and, what is more, which undermines masculinity, as is signalled at the beginning of the De planctu. Yet he, like every other character in the text, cannot escape falling into sodomitical traps. As mentioned earlier, Alain uses the writing process as a metaphor for sex when describing the powerful pen that Natura gave to Venus to ensure the preservation of the species. An analogous reed-pen, a calamus, is held in the right hand of Genius when he approaches at the end of the De planctu to deliver his excommunication. In his left hand he holds the skin of a dead animal

> in qua stili obsequentis subsidio imagines rerum ab umbra picture ad ueritatem sue essentie transmigrantes, uita sui generis munerabat. (DPN xviii, 71–72)

> [on which, with the help of the obedient pen, he endowed with the life of their species images of things that kept changing from the shadowy outline of a picture to the realism of their actual being.] (p. 216)

Genius, Natura's son and father of Truth, writes creatures into being, just as Natura herself does in the second prose of the De planctu (DPN iv, 3–6). The pen could represent genitals and writing could be procreative sex (although by now, we should be fairly wary of trusting Alain's metaphors). However, when Genius's right hand becomes tired then we hear about the other hand,

> [q]ue ab orthographe semita falsigraphie claudicatione recedens, rerum figuras immo figurarum laruas umbratiles, semiplena picturatione creabat. (DPN xviii, 84–85)

> [which, limpingly withdrawing from the field of orthography to pseudography, produced in a half-completed picture outlines of things or rather the shadowy ghosts of outlines.] (p. 216, translation emended)

Falsigraphia, deviation from the ordered path, has been used to stand in for sodomy in Natura's description of Venus, as we saw. This depiction of Genius, a wholly natural, undeviating principle, seems, however, to naturalize sodomy, which now seems to happen when natural male sexuality becomes tired from the hard labour of heterosexual reproduction and then writes 'rerum figuras immo figurarum laruas umbratiles'. If this *falsigraphia* is sodomy, it is still nevertheless productive; it presents images, shady imitations even, of natural things in an identical manner to art — 'simia naturae' — that creates parodic reproductions of natural creatures.[25] This is a queer parody of natural reproduction, just as the infinite aspect of queer sex is a parody of the reproductive ideal of futurism. Like the tropes of the rhetoricians, art is ostensibly made to give pleasure, and is associated with queer sexuality, which seems to be made natural here. It is no wonder Alain quickly draws his work to a close, still unresolved. The prosimetrum, which in the author's lifetime only circulated in a very close circle of associates, seems to expose some of the inherent contradictions in medieval conceptions of natural sexuality, and conceives of poetic invention as a transgressive yet paradoxically natural act.

The Genius of the *De planctu naturae* finds its translated reincarnation in the French verse of Jean de Meun's section of the *Roman de la rose* (composed between 1270 and 1278). As with metaphor, however, all translation necessarily sees some slippage in meaning in its departure from an original, primary sense.[26] Jean's Genius flaunts the impossibility of a totally faithful translation and Jean seems to delight in overtaking the model he has inherited from Alain.[27]

In the first part of the *Rose*, written in the second half of the 1230s, a young narrator dreams that he has entered a garden in which allegorical figures representing courtly virtues, such as Biauté (Beauty) and Largesse (Generosity) are present, although this dreamscape is also home to allegorical figures less welcoming of amorous adventures, such as Jalousie (Jealousy) and Male Bouche (Evil Mouth, representing gossip and slander). The narrator is pierced by arrows fired by Amor (Love or Cupid) and becomes enamoured of the most beautiful rosebud in the garden, after which the impetus that drives the plot is the dreaming Lover's desire to touch, kiss and pluck the rosebud. Guillaume de Lorris's version ends, uncompleted, with the Rose locked inside Jalousie's apparently impenetrable castle with Amant (the narrating Lover) disconsolate and alone. Jean de Meun's continuation (around 17,500 lines added to Guillaume's 4,500), in which different allegorical characters discuss an encyclopaedic range of topics at length, changes the focus of the earlier text so that his version is as concerned with the pursuit of knowledge as it is with projects of sexual conquest and desire. After the diverse speeches, which often contradict each other, the poem finishes with a less than noble Lover penetrating Jalousie's castle in order to pluck the rose in an unashamedly obscene allegory. Then, as in Alain's *De planctu naturae*, the Lover wakes up and the text ends.

One of the earliest critics of the *Rose*, Ernest Langlois, claimed that of Jean de Meun's 17,500 lines of poetry, he had identified around 12,000 that had been taken from earlier sources.[28] It is tempting to see Jean, then, primarily as an omnivorous, encyclopaedic translator who reorders his material in interesting ways, creating a new text by juxtaposing a cornucopia of literary sources. This view is far too simplistic, though; Jean's translation can certainly not be said to be faithful in any modern sense of the term. Rather than translate *verbum pro verbo*, word for word, as Cicero and Jerome — and the medieval theorists they influenced — described literal translation, Jean's is a rhetorical, interpretative translation that reproduces Alain's text in a new form.[29] This practice, characterized by Rita Copeland as 'secondary translation', sees the earlier text/s providing the source material for an appropriative translation that uses rhetorical models of invention.[30] Copeland defines the Classical rhetorical mode of translation, inherited from Cicero in the following way:

> The aim of translation is to reinvent the source, so that, as in rhetorical theory, attention is focused on the active production of a new text endowed with its own affective powers and suited to the particular historical circumstances of its reception.[31]

According to this model, the translator does not merely pass down an inherited textual body, but refashions a new text from existing material. Jean de Meun brings to the fore inconsistencies in the *De planctu naturae* and he skews the focus of inquiry so that rather than primarily using images of tropes and of writing to think about sodomy, he starts with sodomy and disordered sexuality and uses it as a way of reflecting on artistic creation and poetic creation. In both texts, rhetoric and queer sex are used to reflect — and to reflect on — the other, but whereas Alain's prosimetrum attempts to show a hopeless, inescapable loop of sodomy, the *Rose* offers a productive chain of creation that stems from the queerness of deviant sexuality and deviant writing. Having considered the use of figurative language to investigate sexual desire and actions, I now want to look at how sexual desire, queer or otherwise, can be used to understand poetic invention and artistic creation.

Genius descends to earth in Jean's poem, on Nature's orders, in order to preach to Amor's army of allegorical figures who have gathered to help the dreaming narrator enter the castle in which Jalousie keeps the Rose. He gives a speech in which he condemns all those who spurn procreation and goes on to yell hysterically for their castration. He will go on to preach of a bizarrely carnal heaven, the entry to which is largely predicated on having as much procreative sex as possible, but first he pronounces the following anathema:

> saient tuit esconmenié
> li delleal, li renié,
> et condampné san nul respit,
> qui les euvres ont en despit,
> soit de grant gent soit de menue,
> par cui Nature est sustenue. (*RR* 19497–15502)

> [Let them all be excommunicated, those disloyal ones, those renegades, and let them be condemned without reprieve, those who, whether of high or low rank, hold in scorn the works by which Nature is sustained.][32]

This looks similar to the excommunication pronounced by Genius at the end of Alain's text, although it is far from being a literal translation, with a shift of focus (there is, for example, no discussion of non-sexual sins), a reordering of the original material, and the inclusion of new factors (the emphasis on procreation rather than on the sexual act itself). The sexual content and the inherent slippage in metaphor gives occasion for Jean to carry out a sustained reflection on the inherent queerness of art. Starting with the alteration of one apparently innocuous word in Jean's translation it is possible to discern how translation is as unstable and gets caught up in the same web of sodomitical deviation as metaphor and poetry.

Alain's Genius in his condemnation says elliptically: 'Qui a regula Veneris exceptionem facit anomalam, Veneris priuetur sigillo' [Let him who makes an irregular exception to the rule of Venus be deprived of the seal of Venus] (*DPN* XVIII, 150–51; pp. 220–21). Scanlon notes that while the seal of Venus could mean genitalia so that Genius is calling for castration, an alternative meaning is very present:

> If we take *Veneris sigillum* as 'seal of Venus,' then Genius's sanction would mean that these sinners were to be deprived of offspring, since the metaphor of sealing has been used throughout *De planctu Naturae* to mean generation.[33]

Jean excludes this possibility, changing 'seal' for 'sign' and throwing in some extra metaphor for good measure as his Genius declares:

> cil qui tel metresse despisent
> quant a rebours ses regles lisent,
> et qui, por le droit san antandre,
> par le bon chief nes veulent prandre,
> ainz pervertissent l'escriture
> quant il vienent a la lecture:
> o tout l'esconmeniemant
> qui touz les mete a dampnemant,
> puis que la se veulent aherdre,
> ainz qu'il muirent, *puissent il perdre*
> *et l'aumosniere et les estalles*
> *don il ont signe d'estre malles!*
> Perte leur viegne des pandanz
> a quoi l'aumosniere est pandanz!
> Les marteaus dedanz estachiez
> puissent il avoir arrachiez! (*RR* 19627–42)

> [those who scorn such a mistress [Nature] when they read her rules backwards, and who do not want to work for the correct end by understanding the correct meaning, thus pervert the writing when they come to the reading, along with excommunication which damns them all, since they want to stick to their behaviour, *let them*, before they die, *lose the purses and the torches, which are the signs of their masculinity!* May they lose the bits by which the purse hangs! May the hammers within be ripped out!]

There can be (almost) no doubt that what is being described is castration. Where Alain has compulsively made his metaphors ambiguous or paradoxical, Jean provides an example of how ambiguous metaphors can be appropriated by an unscrupulous reader and how slippage can occur in the rewriting of existing texts. The loss of the seal of Venus, the *sigillum Veneris*, could mean the loss of genitals or it could mean the loss of reproduction, the end-point and thus the seal of the sexual act. In the French it is rendered a *signe d'estre malles* [a 'sign of masculinity'], the loss of which is much more likely to mean castration, especially when used in conjunction with so many metaphors that unambiguously refer to male sexual organs. In fact, Genius in the *Rose* makes repeated and insistent use of metaphors of tools — hammers, anvils, pens, tablets, ploughs — for genitals in a way that is far less ambiguous than Alain, though not free from the queerness and deviation with which metaphor is inextricably bound.

The translation into French also sees a switch in tone. The measured and elegant condemnation found in the Latin source has now come to be a hysterical and repetitive screaming. This Genius, far from being any figure of genuine authority is shown to be quite unbalanced, so preoccupied is he with the preservation of the human race, not to mention fetishistically obsessed with genitalia. His clothing as a bishop is shown to be a travesty, as becomes fully clear later on in his rambling sermon, which, in contrast to the very short speech of Alain's Genius, goes on for some 2000 lines. The French Genius preaches an insane gospel in which heaven is described as a park. Its occupants are witless sheep whose chief pleasure is eating to their hearts' content, and in order to gain entrance to the park, these sheep must have as much procreative sex as possible. This monomaniac vision of a world revolving around the hysterical preservation of heterosex is a provocative reading of Alain's arguably unbalanced take on human sexuality and it also picks up on the self-contradictory nature of the *De plantu naturae*'s unstable message. Just as Alain is translating the 'indécidable impropriété' of sodomy into language, so Jean de Meun is translating not simply the literal content of Alain's text but also the unspoken and inappropriate self-contradiction of Alain's impossible exclusion of the queer. After calling for castration, Genius soon goes onto to say that '[g]ranz pechiez est d'ome escoillier' [it is a great sin to castrate a man] (*RR* 20020), when discussing Jupiter's forcible removal of his father Saturn's testicles. Self-contradiction is taken furthest in Genius's metaphor of reading and writing for sex (as outlined in the passage quoted above), which is a deliberately perverse poetic translation, a deliberately falsifying *falsigraphia*. Taking Alain's metaphor of Venus writing and miswriting, Jean rewrites and twists the original model to create a text that bears some resemblance to its predecessor but which has deviated and carries with it new meanings, just as the artistic productions drawn with the left hand of Alain's Genius are shadowy perversions of their natural models. The *Roman de la rose* itself does more literally what Genius says that sodomites do metaphorically. They 'pervertissent l'escriture | quant il vienent a la lecture' [pervert the writing when they come to the reading] (*RR* 19631–32). Jean de Meun has, in his reading of the *De planctu*, changed the words and the sense of the received text and his new production has deviated from the French Genius's ideal of a faithful, direct reproduction. However, Genius himself is not aware that he himself is a perverse figure appearing in a perverse text. He demands faithful logical transmission of texts (or straight, strictly procreational sex) following Alain's Natura. In the *De planctu* Natura tells us that she banned rhetorical devices and imagery from Venus's workshop when tasking her with the work of reproduction. Instead, as we saw earlier, the optimal model is that of the syllogism, standing in metaphorically for straight sex, an undeviating and controlled logical process of reproduction that excludes pleasure and deviation. True heterosexual reproduction, like straight writing or a perfect, lossless translation, does not embellish or seek originality, but rather is the faithful recopying of the original model, the transmission of a scribe rather than that of an author.

This heteronormative fantasy, both of controlled reproductive sexuality and of the controlled transmission of ideas without slippage, is in both texts shown to be impossible and self-defeating. There is always a deviation, a degree of loss (and, in fact, gain) in metaphor and in translation, and especially in rhetorical or poetic translation. If writing is being used as a metaphor for the practices and regulation of sexual desire, the conclusion to be drawn then is that the imperative issued by both Geniuses to be totally straight is as impossible as a perfect translation.

Figures of writing make it possible to explore sexual desire and drive in otherwise impossible ways. But how might the sexual drive help to understand processes of writing? Giorgio Agamben's concept of Genius, as in the *Roman de la rose* and the *De planctu naturae*, is an unindividuated and universal force, a common natural drive or series of drives, and his analysis is useful in thinking about the relationship between desire and artistic production. For Agamben:

> Genius non è solo spiritualità, non riguarda soltanto le cose che siamo abituati a considerare piú nobili e alte. Tutto l'impersonale in noi è geniale, geniale è innanzitutto la forza che spinge il sangue nelle nostre vene o ci fa sprofondare nel sonno, l'ignota potenza che nel nostro corpo regola e distribuisce cosí soavemente il tepore e scioglie o contrae le fibre dei nostri muscoli. È Genius che oscuramente presentiamo nell'intimità della nostra vita fisiologica, là dove il piú proprio è il piú estraneo e impersonale, il piú vicino è il piú remoto e impadroneggiabile. Se non ci abbandonassimo a Genius, se fossimo soltanto Io e coscienza, non potremmo nemmeno orinare. Vivere con Genius significa, in questo senso, vivere nell'intimità di un essere estraneo, tenersi costantemente in relazione con una zona di non-conoscenza.

> [Genius is not merely spirituality and is not just concerned with the things that we customarily regard as higher and more noble. Everything in us that is impersonal is genial. The force that pushes the blood through our veins or that plunges us into sleep, the unknown power in our body that gently regulates and distributes its warmth or that relaxes or contracts the fibers of our muscles — that too is genial. It is Genius that we obscurely sense in the intimacy of our physiological life, in which what is most one's own is also strange and impersonal, and in which what is nearest somehow remains distant and escapes mastery. If we did not abandon ourselves to Genius, if we were only ego and consciousness, we would not even be able to urinate. Living with Genius means, in this sense, living in the intimacy of a strange being, remaining constantly in relation to a zone of nonconsciousness.][34]

Genius, then, is the a-rational, physiological mechanism that preserves life. It is everything about our bodies that is outside of our control. Yet Genius is meaningless unless it is put into contact with an individual, just as for Aristotle matter can have no sense unless combined with form. Each individual is a combination of ego, the conscious, thinking, deciding part, the part where our identity is lodged, and Genius, the system of physiological existence and unconscious movement. How does this link to writing and artistic creation?

> Qual è, allora, per Io, il modo migliore di testimoniare di Genius? Supponiamo che Io voglia scrivere. Scrivere non questa o quell'opera, soltanto scrivere, e basta. Questo desiderio significa: Io sento che da qualche parte Genius esiste, che vi è in me una potenza impersonale che spinge alla scrittura. Ma l'ultima

cosa di cui Genius ha bisogno è un'opera, lui che non ha mai preso in mano una penna (e tanto meno un computer). Si scrive per diventare impersonali, per diventare geniali e, tuttavia, scrivendo, ci individuiamo come autori di questa o quell'opera, ci allontaniamo da Genius, che non può mai avere la forma di un Io, e tanto meno di un autore.

[What, then, is the best way for Ego to testify to Genius? Suppose the ego wants to write — not to write this or that work, but simply to write, period. This desire means: I (Ego) feel that somewhere Genius exists, that there is in me an impersonal power that presses toward writing. But this Genius, who has never taken up a pen (much less a computer) — has no inclination to produce a work. One writes in order to become impersonal, to become genial, and yet, in writing, we individuate ourselves as authors of this or that work; we move away from Genius, who can never have the form of an ego, much less that of an author.][35]

It is impossible to create to even the smallest degree without some conscious decision, without individuation, without ego. The ego is both the condition for and necessary cause of originality and of deviation from the unindividuated, physical and uniform drive, which it nevertheless seeks to appease in writing. Neither the Natura of the *De planctu* nor the Genius of the *Rose*, both abstract concepts of physics or physiology that have bizarrely been given speaking voices, grasp the concept of the ego and individuation. Writing, painting, say, or sculpting, requires the combination of the impersonal drive of Genius and the personal choices of the ego. These personal choices result in deviation from the given model, a translation that cannot be truly faithful, that strays from the wholly natural path and that results in the queerness at the heart of all artistic creation.

Questions of sexuality, as we have seen, are inextricably interwoven with ideas of writing and artistic creation. This is nowhere more clear than in the person of Orpheus, the Classical figure who narrates a large part of Ovid's *Metamorphoses* and who, apart from his foray into the Underworld, is known for two things. He is a symbol of artistic creation, thanks to the amazing power of his music, and he is a symbol for sodomy, thanks to his preference for young boys as his sexual companions and his rejection of the female sex that led to his death. As mentioned earlier, in the *De planctu*, Natura describes the descent into sodomy in metaphorical terms as mankind being crazed into sexual deviancy by the power of Orpheus's lyre and the separating line there between seductive art and alluring sexual licentiousness is so thin as to be barely discernible. Orpheus makes only one appearance in the *Rose*, but Sylvia Huot is undoubtedly right to detect his ghost haunting the whole poetic enterprise.[36] Jean de Meun alludes to Natura's description of the following of Orpheus when he has his Genius condemn sodomites who

> Orpheüs veulent ansivre,
> qui ne sot arer ne escrivre
> ne forgier en la droite forge
> (panduz soit il par mi la gorge!) (*RR* 19621–24)

[want to follow Orpheus, who did not know how to plough nor to write, nor to hammer at the correct forge (may he be hanged from the neck!)]

Orpheus's importance as a symbol of artistic creation is left unspoken but present, hanging over the condemnation of those who write against Nature, those who have sex for pleasure, who write for pleasure, who commit acts *contra naturam*. It is not, though, until we come to the figure of Pygmalion that the contradictions of Orpheus are fully brought to life and the productive power of sodomy is brought to the fore.

In Book x of *Metamorphoses*, Orpheus himself sings of Pygmalion who scorns women (the predicate fleeing the subject, to follow the *De planctu naturae*'s metaphor of the syllogism) and so through his art fashions a beautiful female sculpture for which he ends up lusting to the point of madness. The interaction of ego and Genius identified by Agamben is at work in harnessing the artistic drive which is inextricable from the sexual urge. Pygmalion ends up praying to the gods to bring the artificial object of his unnatural love to life, a prayer granted by Venus.

Jean de Meun's telling of the story takes place just after Genius's sermon and immediately before the final penetrative sex scene that finishes the Rose. In this French version, Pygmalion, racked by the passion of his unnatural desire, which 'est si horrible | qu'el ne vient mie de Nature' [is so horrible that it cannot come from Nature'] (*RR* 20832–33), prays to Venus through the playing of all sorts of musical instruments in an attempt to animate the inanimate object.

> et tabor et fleüste et tymbre,
> et tabore et fleüste et tymbre;
> et cythole et tronpe et chevrie,
> et cythole et tronpe et chevrie;
> et psalterion et vïele,
> et psalterion et vïele. (*RR* 21015–20)

[and he drummed, fluted and played a timbrel; and played a citole and trumpeted and piped; and played a psalterion and a viol.]

He is, as Genius might say, following Orpheus, attempting to use the power of song to move objects and control nature as Orpheus did. He is also following Orpheus through his refusal to use his figurative hammers — testicles — to sculpt literal human beings in the 'natural', straight way commanded by Genius. He has, rather, used a literal hammer to make a figure of a human being. The metaphors are flying out of control here, as they do in the *De planctu* and the only way they can be resolved is through silence or by paradox. Where Alain opted for *aporia* at the end of his work, Jean de Meun grasps the paradox with both hands. Through the intervention of Venus — or, metonymically, sexual desire — Pygmalion's misuse of his hammer, in sculpting an artificial object for his lust *contra naturam*, leads to a parodically queer kind of reproduction. The sculpture comes to life. At this stage, the *Rose* surpasses the *De planctu naturae*. Where the Latin text has suggested that figurative, poetic writing is hopelessly shot through with queerness, the French poem takes the idea further and shows how queerness, how art/sodomy, how the pursuit of pleasure following a passion that is undoubtedly *contra naturam* — 'ceste amour ne vient mie de Nature' — can lead to reproduction outside of 'natural' heterosex; it can lead to the production of art. Rather than the shadowy images drawn with Genius's left hand as depicted by Alain, Jean shows the power of individuated desire, of the ego, to combine with Genius to produce art that, speaking metaphorically of course, has a life of its own.

The association between sexual intercourse and art does not stop there, however. Pygmalion marries his now living but nameless sculpture and they have children. The artist has sexual intercourse, possibly incestuously,[37] with his unnatural offspring, a living work of art, in order to continue his lineage. If, as has often been suggested,[38] the Pygmalion story emblematizes the process of poetic creation, the artist having sex with his creation can be read metaphorically as a writer spawning textual offspring, reproducing new versions of his own text through translating, adapting or continuing it. It is far less incestuous, however, to have sex with someone else's work of art. Jean de Meun has taken the first part of the *Roman de la Rose*, written by Guillaume de Lorris, and like Pygmalion having sex with his sculpture has caused the text to reproduce, to produce a new *Rose*, just as the *Rose* would be continued, adapted, abridged, or aped in the centuries that were to follow. Sexual intercourse can be just as much a metaphor for writing as the other way around. Medieval authorship and creation, and indeed translation, involve taking earlier materials and reworking them through the mediation of an author into something new. If, for the *De planctu*, poetry, and by extension art, is queer, then the *Rose* shows how queer art can be productive and life-giving as well as pleasurable and unsettling. Artistic or literary creation, with the attendant pleasure that it causes, preserves an idea and transverses it, transmits it in a new way through new texts just as sexual reproduction, with the attendant pleasure that it causes, continues the human species by resulting in new individuals. The author, inescapably gendered as masculine, metaphorically couples with the female body of the text and queerly creates his literary offspring.

Both the *De planctu naturae* and the *Roman de la rose* wrestle, or play, with the question of excluding queerness from a vision of 'natural', perfectly heterosexual, sexual activity, and, possibly despite themselves, both demonstrate the productive paradoxes of the restless deviation of figurative language. They indicate that the only way to remain totally straight is to abolish the ego, and to avoid writing, speaking or thinking, to be no more than an unindividuated sex-machine. This kind of untroubled total heterosexuality is shown to be impossible for humans, certainly for fallen sinful humans. Queerness and artistic creation go hand in hand, and the more original the piece of art the queerer it is.

Notes to Chapter 13

1. While I am principally interested in metaphor in this essay, the deviation entailed by metaphor is equally a phenomenon related to all the other devices that Quintilian categorizes under the heading of 'trope' in Book IX of his *Institutio oratoria*, including metonymy, antonomasia, metalepsis, synecdoche, catachresis and allegory. All tropic or figurative language is understood by Quintilian as a departure from natural, straight meaning, and it is the larger genus of a trope that is used as a metaphor for deviant sexual pleasure by Alain de Lille, rather than metaphor itself (see n. 20 below).
2. Gary Cestaro, 'Is Ulysses Queer? The Subject of Greek Love in *Inferno* XV and XXVI', in *Dante's Plurilingualism: Authority, Knowledge, Subjectivity*, ed. by Sara Fortuna, Manuele Gragnolati and Jürgen Trabant (Oxford: Legenda, 2010), pp. 179–202 (p. 180), and Eve Kosofsky Sedgwick, *Tendencies* (London: Routledge, 1994), p. XII.

3. *Oxford English Dictionary*, transverse, v. 1 (second edition, 1989; online version, March 2011). <http://www.oed.com:80/Entry/205123> [accessed 31 May 2011].

4. *Oxford English Dictionary*. transverse, v. 2 (second edition, 1989; online version, March 2011). <http://www.oed.com:80/Entry/205124> [accessed 31 May 2011].

5. Lee Edelman, *No Future: Queer Theory and the Death Drive* (Durham, NC, and London: Duke University Press, 2004), p. 60.

6. William E. Burgwinkle, *Sodomy, Masculinity and the Law in Medieval Literature* (Cambridge: Cambridge University Press, 2004), p. 2.

7. In Sedgwick's phrase; see Sedgwick, *Tendencies*, p. 8.

8. Edelman, p. 60.

9. Cited from Alain de Lille, *De planctu naturae* (hereafter *DPN*), ed. by N. Häring, *Studi Medievali*, 19 (1978), 797–879 (p. 878). All translations taken from Alain de Lille, *The Plaint of Nature*, ed. and trans. by James Sheridan (Toronto: Pontifical Institute of Mediaeval Studies, 1980). Page numbers in the body of the text refer to Sheridan's translation, which uses a different structure to Häring's edition.

10. Jacques Chiffoleau, '*Contra naturam*: Pour une approche casuistique et procédurale de la nature médiévale', *Micrologus*, 4 (1996), 265–312 (p. 268).

11. See John Boswell, *Christianity, Social Tolerance and Homosexuality: Gay People in Western Europe from the Beginning of the Christian Era to the Fourteenth Century* (Chicago, IL: University of Chicago Press, 1981), pp. 277–78.

12. Here I am drawing particularly on Paul Ricœur's definition of catachresis in *La Métaphore vive* (Paris: Seuil, 1975), pp. 84–85. See also Eva Feder Kittay, *Metaphor: Its Cognitive Force and Linguistic Structure* (Oxford: Clarendon Press, 1987), p. 296: 'Catachresis is, literally, a misuse of language. It is sometimes taken to refer to those cases of metaphor which arise out of a need to name some unnamed entity — standard examples include "the leg of a chair" or the "foot of a mountain" — or it is sometimes said to be an *abuse* of language' (original emphasis).

13. See Mark D. Jordan, *The Invention of Sodomy in Christian Theology* (Chicago, IL: University of Chicago Press, 1996), pp. 41–44.

14. Jordan, p, 42 . See also p. 52 for the example of Burchard of Worms' *Decretum*, which includes some description of sodomitical acts yet still avoids explicit clarity. Cf. Michel Foucault's famous description of sodomy as 'cette catégorie si confuse' [that utterly confused category]: Michel Foucault, *Histoire de la sexualité, I: La Volonté de savoir* (Paris: Gallimard, 1976), p. 134; translation from Michel Foucault, *The History of Sexuality, Vol. 1: An Introduction*, trans. by Robert Hurley (Harmondsworth: Penguin, 1984), p. 101.

15. Alain de Lille, *Liber Poenitentialis*, ed. by Jean Longère, 2 vols (Louvain: Nauwelaerts; Lille: Giard, 1965), II, 27 (my translation).

16. See Jordan, p. 5.

17. For a detailed investigation both of the implications of using writing as a metaphor for sex in the *De planctu naturae* and of the threatening and pleasurable blurring of gender boundaries in Alain de Lille and Jean de Meun, see David Rollo's *Kiss My Relics: Hermaphroditic Fictions of the Middle Ages* (Chicago and London: University of Chicago Press, 2011).

18. See *DPN* VIII, 78–80; p. 136.

19. Alain is using the terms 'predicate' and 'subject' in their formally logical sense. The role of the predicate is to modify the passive subject and is thus employed as a metaphor for the active, male principle.

20. Translation emended. See Quintilian, *Institutio oratoria*, ed. and trans. by Donald A. Russell, 5 vols (Cambridge, MA, and London: Harvard University Press, 2001), IV: 'Est igitur tropos sermo a naturali et principali significatione tralatus ad aliam ornandae orationis gratia, vel, ut plerique grammatici finiunt, dictio ab eo loco in quo propria est tralata in eum in quo propria non est' [A Trope, then, is language transferred from its natural and principal meaning to another for the sake of embellishment, or (as most *grammatici* define it), 'an expression transferred from a context in which it is proper to one in which it is not'] (IX.1.4). Alain leaves implicit Quintilian's discussion of natural and unnatural language and its parallels with the sin *contra naturam*: man is turned from his proper place — that is, engaged in vaginal sex with a woman for the continuation of the species — and has become attracted to unnatural sexual practices.

21. Alain places the male part of the syllogism, the *predicatum*, in the grammatical role of the female passive, acted upon by Venus who might transfer (*alienet*) him, just as the queer transferral or translation effected by sodomy turns active men into passive women (cf. *DPN* I, 5: 'Venus in Venerem pugnans illos facit illas').

22. See Burgwinkle, *Sodomy*, p. 191.

23. The issue of explicitly describing that which is thought to be obscene is approached in the *Roman de la rose* when Raison and Amant discuss the appropriateness or otherwise of articulating the word 'testicles'; see Guillaume de Lorris and Jean de Meun, *Le Roman de la rose* (hereafter *RR*), ed. by Félix Lecoy, 3 vols (Paris: Champion, 1965–70), 6898ff. Amant's complaint about the impropriety of testicles appearing in a maiden's mouth seems to recall Natura's words on improper speech cited here. For discussion of this issue, see Alastair Minnis, 'From *Coilles* to *Bel Chose*: Discourses of Obscenity in Jean de Meun and Chaucer', in *Medieval Obscenities*, ed. by Nicola McDonald (York: York Medieval Press, 2006), pp. 156–78 (esp. pp. 157–59). See also Jan Ziolkowski, 'The Obscenities of Old Women: Vetularity and Vernacularity', in *Obscenity: Social Control and Artistic Creation in the European Middle Ages*, ed. by Jan M. Ziolkowski (Leiden: Brill, 1998), pp. 73–89 (p. 76), and John V. Fleming, *Reason and the Lover* (Princeton, NJ: Princeton University Press, 1984), p. 106, n. 9.

24. Jacques Derrida, *Qu'est-ce qu'une traduction 'relevante'?* (Paris: L'Herne, 2005), pp. 19–20. Translation from Jacques Derrida and Lawrence Venuti, 'What is a "relevant" translation?', *Critical Inquiry*, 27.2 (2001), 174–200 (pp. 178–79).

25. See Roger Dragonetti's remark that '[l]e discours doctrinal sur le "Singe de Nature" est structuré selon une antithèse qui ouvre un intervalle infranchissable entre la fécondité de l'imitation par *Nature* et l'impouvoir qui caractérise le mode mimétique du praticien de l'art' [The doctrinal discourse concerning the 'Monkey of Nature' is structured according to a dichotomy which opens up an uncrossable gap between the abundance of the imitation carried out by *Nature* and the impotence which is the defining factor of the mimetic mode practised by the artist]. Roger Dragonetti, 'Le "Singe de Nature" dans le *Roman de la Rose*', in *La Musique et les Lettres: Études de littérature médiévale* (Geneva: Droz, 1986), pp. 369–80 (p. 369). The translation is my own.

26. Both metaphor and translation have their etymological roots in metaphors of carrying something away from its original context. Metaphor, from the Greek 'μεταφέρειν' ('to carry away' or 'to transfer'), sees the name of one thing taken from its original, natural subject onto something new. Translation, from the Latin 'transferre' ('to carry away'), sees a text carried from its original language and setting into a new one.

27. While I largely agree with Susan Schibanoff's analysis of Alain's use of metaphor, I disagree with her argument that Jean de Meun 'attempted — but failed — to rewrite the *Plaint* in order to forestall sodomy's return.' Susan Schibanoff, 'Sodomy's Mark: Alan of Lille, Jean de Meun and the Medieval Theory of Authorship', in *Queering the Middle Ages*, ed. by Glenn Burger and Steven F. Kruger (Minneapolis and London: University of Minnesota Press, 2001), pp. 28–56 (p. 29).

28. Ernest Langlois, *Origines et sources du 'Roman de la rose'* (Paris: Ernest Thorin, 1891), p. 102.

29. See Rita Copeland, *Rhetoric, Hermeneutics and Translation in the Middle Ages: Academic Traditions and Vernacular Texts* (Cambridge: Cambridge University Press, 1991), p. 2.

30. Copeland, p. 7.

31. Copeland, p. 30.

32. All translations from the *Rose* are my own.

33. Scanlon, p. 244.

34. Giorgio Agamben, *Profanazioni* (Rome: Nottetempo, 2005), pp. 10–11. Translation from Giorgio Agamben, *Profanations*, trans. by Jeff Fort (New York: Zone, 2008), p. 11.

35. Agamben, p. 13.

36. Sylvia Huot, *Dreams of Lovers and Lies of Poets* (Oxford: Legenda, 2010), p. 56.

37. Incest recurs later in the family tree in *Metamorphoses*, when Pygmalion's great-granddaughter, Myrrha, ends up tricking her father into sleeping with her. Huot notes that 'Jean's Pygmalion absorbs the tainted aura of "unnaturalness" that Ovid identified with Myrrha' (p. 78).

38. See, for example, Thomas D. Hill, 'Narcissus, Pygmalion, and the Castration of Saturn: Two Mythographical Themes in the *Roman de la Rose*', *Studies in Philology*, 71.4 (1974), 404–26; Kevin

Brownlee, 'Orpheus' Song Re-sung: Jean de Meun's Reworking of *Metamorphoses*, x', *Romance Philology*, 36.2 (1982), 201–09; and, more recently, Reinier Leushuis, 'Pygmalion's Folly and the Author's Craft in Jean de Meun's *Roman de la Rose*', *Neophilologus*, 90.4 (2006), 521–33.

CHAPTER 14

Desiring Tales:
Two Vernacular Poetics of Desire

Monika Otter

It is almost certain that the German Gottfried von Strassburg and the English Laȝamon could not have known of each other and could not have seen each other's work. They inhabited different countries, different social spheres, different political contexts, different languages, although their engagement with French courtly literature tenuously connects them. For us today, they inhabit different academic departments and critical discourses. Yet there are striking points of contact. The two poets are near or fairly near contemporaries (Laȝamon being notoriously hard to date).[1] They both are, self-consciously and explicitly, translators from French, concerned with a still relatively new and untested literary vernacular but also confident of its possibilities. They both explicitly formulate a programmatic poetics based on desire: famously so in Gottfried, who coins the term *senemaere*, 'desire-tale'; a bit less obviously perhaps in Laȝamon, who is known more for a deliberately archaizing, epic streak that can be quite violent and brutal. And yet 'love' or 'lufelich' are key words whenever he begins to talk about his craft. The objection that they are working in different genres, that Gottfried's is, declaredly, a *senemaere*, a love story or romance, whereas Laȝamon aspires to historiography, need not stop us. The overlap between romance and historiography, here and elsewhere, is conspicuous and programmatic. In fact, both poets use the notion of desire to negotiate a complicated view of historicity and fictionality, of 'truth', as they both say. Both propose a poetics based on affective bonds, on multiple homologies, congruences, coincidences of desire. Both go so far as to invoke Eucharistic language to state that ideal concord; and both distance it indefinitely — for if it were ever reached, the narrative would collapse. Desire, asymptotic and deferred, is the basic metaphor for describing the continuous tension that keeps both texts open and going.

I am, of course, echoing a classic description of romance: it is that narrative which consists of the deferral of its own ending.[2] It is worth noting that here, it is deferred indefinitely: neither of these very long poems has a romance ending. Gottfried's *Tristan*, for reasons endlessly and inconclusively debated, breaks off well short of the story's projected ending. Laȝamon's *Brut* ends by reminding us of the prophecy that one day the Britons will again regain power in their own land; but this day has not yet arrived, and, we have come to understand, probably never will:

> þa ȝat ne com þæs ilke dæi . be heonne-uorð alse hit mæi
> Iwurðe þet iwurðe . iwurðe Godes wille.
> Amen[3]

[That day has not come yet . be it henceforth as it may
What shall come to pass, shall come to pass . God's will be done. Amen.]

It is in the nature of a history that it is not over at the point the author chooses to end it. The apparent finality of the 'Amen' only patches over an ending that could not be more open or more inconclusive.

But Gottfried and Laȝamon are interested in the appetitive and distancing function of desire not only linearly, as it describes the narrative progress. For them, desire operates in all other spatial directions and informs all the relations in the text: between characters; characters and narrator; readers and characters; readers and narrator — as well as the narrator-translator with his source, and/or the historical truth. Together these form a web of desires, affective bonds and obstacles that subtend the text and ultimately make it possible.

Gottfried and Laȝamon both employ what I think of as figures of these networked desires, disparate though they are: Laȝamon's Merlin, much altered from his source; and Gottfried's little lap-dog, Petitcreiu. All they have in common is that, on one hand, they are somewhat incidental and peripheral to the narrative and in fact strangers to it. On the other hand, they are urgently sought for and invested with a sudden, surprising, and seemingly out-of-place burst of affectivity. That would seem to be a clue to their real function, which is to refuse closure or overly neat correspondences, and hence to enable the narrative.

Gottfried's celebrated, difficult, and much-commented prologue postulates a series of ideal correspondences, and, in his characteristic style, cements them with multiple word-plays, often at the cost of violent neologisms.[4] There is correspondence between his text and its one correct source, Thomas ('daz ich in sîner rihte | rihte dise tihte' [that I may 'right' this poem according to his right version | his direction]).[5] There is an ideal concord between lovers and love-stories ('der edele senedaere | der minnet senediu maere' [the noble desirer loves desiring tales]) (lines 121–22). There is correspondence, chiastically and multiply, between the two lovers and their readers:

> Von diu swer seneder maere ger
> der envar niht verrer danne her.
> ich wil in wol bemaeren
> von edelen senedaeren
> die reiner sene wol tâten schîn:
> ein senedaere und ein senedaerin,
> ein man ein wîp, ein wîp ein man
> Tristan Isolt, Isolt Tristan. (lines 123–30)

[Therefore, he who craves a desiring tale,
Let him look no further than here.
I will be-tale him well
Of noble desirers
who well exemplified pure desire:
a desirer and a desireress,

> a man and woman, a woman a man,
> Tristan Isolde, Isolde Tristan.]

Further, the poet vows to throw in his lot with the lovers and the readers — the right kind of readers, those who can live with sorrow, tension, and contradiction:

> Dem lebene sî mîn leben ergeben,
> der werlt wil ich gewerldet wesen,
> mit ir verderben oder genesen. (lines 64–66)

> [To that life let my life be dedicated;
> to that world let me be worlded,
> to perish with it or prosper with it.]

This is the famous 'edele herzen' conceit, the 'noble hearts' who enjoy a special, quasi-sacred communion, culminating in the almost explicitly eucharistic vision that ends the prologue:

> Deist aller edelen herzen brôt.
> hie mite sô lebet ir beider tôt.
> wir lesen ir leben, wir lesen ir tôt
> und ist uns daz süeze alse brôt.
> Ir leben, ir tôt sint unser brôt.
> sus lebet ir leben, sus lebt ir tôt.
> sus lebent si noch und sint doch tôt
> und ist ir tôt der lebenden brôt. (lines 233–40)

> [Here is bread for all noble hearts.
> Hereby lives the death of these two.
> We read their life, we read their death
> and that is sweet to us as bread.
> Their life, their death is our bread.
> Thus lives their life, thus lives their death,
> Thus live they still and are yet dead,
> and their death is bread to the living.]

Gottfried's romance also desires an ideal correspondence between words and meanings, language that is transparent onto its referent.[6] In his celebrated 'literary excursus', a sweeping critical overview of the literary scene of his day, Gottfried satirizes an unnamed poet (traditionally identified as Wolfram von Eschenbach), deliberately obscure, who has us scurrying to the Black Magic books in search of glosses (lines 4689–90).[7] By contrast, he praises Hartmann, the great master of the previous generation, for his 'crystal-clear' words ('cristallînen wortelîn') (line 4629). The image of crystal, as well as clearly coordinated meanings, recurs in the equally famous allegory of the love grotto, the utopian vision of the paradisiacal love, where Tristan and Isolde find, briefly, their ideal existence ('wunschleben') (line 16846): the bed in the grotto is made of crystal, for 'diu minne sol ouch cristallîn | durhsihtic und durchlûter sîn' ('Love, too, ought to be crystal-clear | transparent and translucent') (lines 16983–84). And in describing the love grotto, Gottfried resorts to pure allegory: every feature of the cave, every detail corresponds exactly to a clear, nameable meaning.

Much of this ideal clarity is beyond our reach. 'Crystal' transparency and purity certainly is not realized on the level of narrative events, where both love and language are endlessly complicated, slippery and devious. The love grotto is clearly framed as utopian and aspirational, not part of the chronotope of the romance, known to us all no matter where we are, yet never completely available (lines 17100–38). Likewise, the correspondences and rapports of the prologue are in no way easy or harmonizing; on the contrary, Gottfried stresses their difficulty and tension. Those who 'cannot bear any sorrow and only want to hover in happiness' are explicitly excluded from the compact, although the poet wishes them all the best. Only those who can withstand 'sweet sour, pleasurable sorrow, death and life together in one heart' need apply. And although the 'desiring tale' is supposed to both nourish and soothe the desiring reader's desire, it will leave things suspended: it will bring their 'near-going sorrow' only 'zu halber senfte' (lines 74–75), it will half-way assuage it.

Gottfried's discourse of desire is very conspicuous and very famous indeed: nothing I have said so far will surprise anyone familiar with the text. Not so Laʒamon. His book is very largely an Early Middle English translation of Wace's *Roman de Brut*, in its turn a translation of Geoffrey of Monmouth's *Historia Regum Britanniae*. He casts himself as a chronicler, not a romancier, often described by critics as an archaic bardic figure, who re-Germanicizes and re-epicizes what the French court poet Wace had made courtly, polite and non-threatening to the Norman elites.[8] And yet, in his prologue, Laʒamon begins with a surprisingly affective, indeed sensuous, narrative of his book's genesis.[9] Having obtained his sources,

> Laʒamon leide þeos boc . 7 þa leaf wende.
> he heom leofliche bi-heold . liðe him beo Drihten.
> Feðeren he nom mid fingren . 7 fiede on boc-felle
> 7 þa soþere word . sette to-gadere .
> 7 þa þre boc . þrumde to are. (lines 24–28)

> [Laʒamon laid out these books . and turned the leaves.
> He lovingly beheld them . may God be kind to him.
> Feathers he took with fingers . and wrote on book-skins
> And the truer words . he set together
> And those three books . pressed into one.]

The first burst of affect, then, is directed by the writer at his books, the sources as well as his own still empty parchment. Laʒamon travels after his sources, 'wide ʒond þas leode', widely throughout the land — as, indeed, does Gottfried (lines 157–63). The phrase 'lufliche beheold', here describing his fond gaze on the books, is formulaic; it recurs several times in the poem, usually in an erotic context.[10] The onset of his own writing is described in tactile, concrete, and bodily terms: feathers, not quills; 'book-skins', not pages or parchments. Even his fingers are mentioned, explicitly and unnecessarily: what else would he grip a quill with? Michael Camille has noted that even now, many of us can get a rush of emotion from touching manuscript parchment, as we cannot from printed paper: just nostalgia, the joy of handling an ancient object, or a recognition of its organic, animal origin?[11]

In Laʒamon's other major poetological statement, his account of Arthur's Round Table, love is also the central term. To be sure, that love is far from warm and consoling. In his version, uniquely, the Round Table is a kind of civilization myth: it is imposed almost forcibly after a brawl among the knights, but not before Arthur has meted out punishments of startling brutality (lines 11390–11407).[12] Yet the table is also Eucharistic:

> swa him sæide Merlin . þe witeʒe wes mære
> þat a king sculde cume . of Vðere Pendragune.
> þat gleomen sculden wurchen burd . of þas kinges breosten.
> and þerto sitten . scopes swiðe sele
> and eten heore wullen . ær heo þenne fusden
> and winscenches ut teon . of þeos kinges tungen
> and drinken and dreomen . daies 7 nihtes. (lines 11492–98)

> [Thus said about him Merlin . who was a great soothsayer
> That a king should come . of Uther Pendragon
> That minstrels should fashion a board . of that king's breast
> And at it sit . very happy scops
> And eat their fill . before they hurried away
> And draw draughts of wine . from this king's tongue
> and drink and rejoice . day and night.]

This quasi-Eucharistic scene completes a defence of fiction, and particularly of the Celtic legends of Arthur's messianic return. As Elizabeth Bryan shows, by turning the meal into poetry, and Arthur into host and table, eater and eaten simultaneously, Laʒamon takes the doubtful legends out of the realm of historical fact altogether.[13] What holds these stories together, and justifies them, is a bond not of mimetic correspondence, but of affect:

> swa deð auer-ale mon . þe oðere luuien con
> ʒif he is him to leof, þenne wule he liʒen [...]
> Aeft ʒif on uolke . feond-scipe arereð [...]
> me con bi þan læðe . lasinge suggen. (lines 11456–62)

> [Thus does ever any man . who loves another
> If he is too dear to him, then he will lie [...]
> Also, if among people . enmity arises [...]
> one will through loathing . tell lies.]

Unlike Wace, his source, who suspects the popular fabulists of either venality or fear,[14] Laʒamon sees their motivation as emotional: excess love or excess hate. He distances himself from the most explicitly Messianic fictions, those of Arthur's non-death and eventual return:

> Ne al soh ne al les . þat leod-scope singeð
> ah þis is þat soððe . bi Arðure þan kinge
> nes næuer ar swulc king . swa duhti þurh alle þing...
> Ah Bruttes hine luueden swiðe . 7 ofte him on liʒeð
> and suggeð feole þinges . bi Arðure þan kinge
> þat næuere nes i-wurðen . a þissere weorlde-richen.
> inoh he mai suggen . þe soð wule uremmen
> seolcuðe þinges . bi Arðure kinge. (lines 11465–75)

> [Neither all truth nor all lies . what the people's scops sing
> But this is the truth . about Arthur the king

> Never before was any such king . so brave in all things...
> But the Britons loved him so much . and often lied about him
> And said many things . about Arthur the king
> That never happened . in this world-realm
> Enough may he say . who would tell the truth
> Wonderful things . about Arthur the king.]

But he lets it stand; the Britons may keep their loving belief, even in Arthur's messianic return: 'þis ilefde Bruttes . þet he uule comen þus' (line 11515).

It is that excess of affection and of story-telling that I believe Merlin stands for. In the figure of Merlin, as has been noted before, Laȝamon is quite independent of his immediate sources. He derives his Merlin, it seems, directly from Geoffrey's lesser-known *Vita Merlini*, an odd and hard-to-pinpoint text that overflows with apparently aimless and literally insane desire and movement, to unload the energy thus generated in a burst of obscure prophecies in the Celtic tradition.[15] Laȝamon does not choose that outlet; he has more in the way of prophecy than Wace does in his *Brut* (where he famously refuses to translate Merlin's prophecies), but certainly not on the same scale as the *Vita Merlini*. But he does carefully replicate the *Vita*'s gesture of building up excess energy. It is important to remind oneself that in the early Arthurian histories (unlike in some popular Arthurian material nowadays), Arthur and Merlin never meet; by Arthur's time, Merlin is nothing but a remembered prophetic voice whose presence is sorely missed. As Schirmer noted, Merlin and Arthur function as twin high points of the Brut chronicles, related but not coinciding, connected by a system of desires, anticipatory and prophetic as well as nostalgic and elegiac.[16] Merlin makes his first appearance as a child-prophet, in the scene that leads to Vortigern's fiery demise; he reappears a few times thereafter, to help Uther rape Ygerne and beget Arthur, to transport Stonehenge from Ireland. Each time, he is portrayed as lost and needing to be re-found, persuaded to appear before the king, coaxed to act on the king's behalf. Laȝamon, at least in the so-called Caligula version, makes the most of this narrative motif, in anaphoric, heavily rhymed and rhythmic style, as often when the emotional temperature rises in the *Brut*:

> θa sonden gunnen riden . widen 7 siden
> summe heo uerden riht norð . 7 summe heo uerden suð forð
> summe heo uerden riht æst . 7 summe heo uerden riht west
> summe heo uerden a-nan . þat heo comen to Alæban. (lines 8493–96)

> [Then messengers rode out . far and wide
> Some traveled due north . and some traveled southward
> Some traveled due east . and some traveled due west
> Some traveled straight ahead . until they came to Alæban.]

When he gets to Aurelius's court,

> næuer ær an his liue . nes þe king swa bliðe
> for næuere nanes monnes cume . þe him to come [...]
> He hine iclupte . he hine custe
> he hine cuð-læhte
> Muchel wes þe murhȝe . i þan mon-uerede
> al for Marlines cume . þe nes nanes monnes sune. (lines 8530–38)

[Never in his life . was the king so glad
for no man's coming . that came to him [...]
He hugged him . he kissed him
He called him dearest friend
Great was the gladness . among his retinue
All for Merlin's coming . who was no man's son.]

These frantic scenes of urgent searching, finding, coaxing, welcoming fit perfectly in the *Vita Merlini*, where Merlin 'Silvester' is a wild man, at times a madman, who continually schemes and negotiates to be allowed to return to the woods. Here, the motif is (almost) blind, unmotivated; there is, at the plot level, no real reason for the King's desire or for the urgency of the search.

But there may be a poetological reason. Merlin, for his part, is both over- and under-involved in Aurelius's affairs. He knows the messengers' errand without being told — he foresaw that they would come, and when — but he is hesitant to leave his beloved spring and bathing-hole, unmoved by promises and love, unemotional amid the urgent affection of king and court. His estrangement is emphasized by the here unnecessary reminder that 'he was no man's son'. From the *Vita Merlini*, Laȝamon inherits a figure who is literally and explicitly a madman. If we were diagnosing him in modern terms we would say that at least part of what's wrong with him is some sort of relational or affective disorder: he responds oddly when spoken to, he laughs in the wrong places, is inappropriately affectless in other situations, and most of the time cannot bear human companionship, even that of his select few loved ones.

Laȝamon, too, keeps his distance, and that distance is in part cultural or even ethnic: the promised end is a Welsh hope, and he is not Welsh (although, like so many great writers of that era, he is from the border region). Like his Merlin, he is both over- and under-involved in the affairs of his narrative. He will not participate in the Welsh messianic narrative, but he will tolerate it in a neutral, friendly, neighbourly spirit. In this respect, the narrative closure is deferred. As Laȝamon says, even-handedly, if we take the Celtic narrative even somewhat seriously, we simply cannot say if Arthur did or did not die, or whether the messianic hope of his return is at all reasonable. At the same time, the Celtic version stands for an emotional closeness of love and hope that contrasts with Laȝamon's gentle standoffishness. Merlin, the Welsh prophet, seems to me to enable both these things. He embodies the narrative of love and messianic hope. But in his restiveness and his reluctance to join those who desire him so much, Merlin also stands for Laȝamon's inability — or unwillingness — to play that game.

Any transition from Laȝamon's prophet to our second figure of desire, Gottfried's little lapdog Petitcreiu, is bound to be wrenching; I ask readers to bear with me. The story — extant in this form only in Gottfried[17] — is this: on his wanderings in exile, Tristan stays for a while with Count Gilan, who has a magic dog from fairyland. Petitcreiu is of delightful but near-miraculous appearance: his coat is all colours and no colour, literally indescribable, although the narrator spares no words in trying. Above all, he wears a magic bell that will instantly make everyone forget their sorrow and be happy. Tristan decides he must get Petitcreiu for Isolde, to console her. He has to trick the Count into parting with the dog, by trapping him in the familiar 'Rash Promise'; and Gilan is devastated. Tristan sends Petitcreiu to Cornwall by ingenious means. Isolde cherishes him but cannot accept the instant consolation of the magic bell. She destroys the bell, and 'no one is ever consoled by it again'. She prefers, as she reasons to herself, to suffer when Tristan suffers; all else would be disloyal (lines 15791–16402).

This episode sits rather oddly within the narrative as a whole. As many critics have objected, it comes at a point where Petitcreiu cannot do much good and where there is no special need for magical mood-lifters, or for heroic emotional sacrifice on anyone's part. The preceding crisis that has led to Tristan's temporary exile has already been resolved; in fact, Tristan learns by return messenger that it is safe for him to return to Cornwall, and he does so.[18] The frantic activity and the high emotion surrounding the dog seem superfluous and isolated — as Petitcreiu is, in fact, always visually isolated, radiating his own strangeness into the space surrounding him. Before Gilan has him brought in, a special, luxurious cloth is spread for the dog to be set on, and it is this cloth, not the dog, that is first described with the two key terms that come to characterize Petitcreiu: 'vremde' and 'wunderlich', strange or alien, and wonderful (line 15802). Isolde, too, spends much of her time with the wondrous pet, fashioning a similar presentation cloth for him.

But despite his extraneousness, the little dog cries out to be 'read': he is, quite overtly, a rhetorical creature, for the 'colours' cannot but evoke those of rhetoric or poetics (lines 15811–44).[19] For all his cuteness, he verges on the uncanny — or the comical. This is in part because he is so precious as to appear almost artificial, a mechanical animal. Yet Petitcreiu is invested with enormous significance; Gilan, pleading with Tristan not to take the dog away from him, calls him 'my eyes' best delight and the joy of my heart' ('daz beste mîner ougen spil | und mînes herzen wunne vil'; lines 16261–62) and ranks him above his realm and his sister, just below his 'honour' and his life. On the other hand, the dog is nothing — not sayable, not visible. His name is a non-name, meaning simply 'little creature'; and the giant from whom Petitcreiu is won taunts Tristan with once again fighting 'umbe niht', for no reason or for nothing (line 16001).

Petitcreiu is rather transparently a miniature, a mise-en-abîme, of Gottfried's poem.[20] Gottfried goes out of his way to pack the episode with cross-references to other events of the poem, before and after. But Petitcreiu is a disturbing representation of the poem: artful but artificial, affecting yet alien, all colours and no colour, everything and nothing. If the bell magic were allowed to work as advertised, the story would grind to a halt: Tristan would no longer be *triste*, his eponymous and determining quality; everyone's desire, their 'senede swaere' would evaporate. Petitcreiu seems an almost rudely concrete, cynically funny embodiment of our desires, and the text's desires, for harmony, homology, closure: there, you asked for it — here it is. It is as when one suddenly realizes that what one always wanted is in fact attainable — and therefore all of a sudden not nearly as desirable as previously imagined. That prospect of a sudden, but final, fulfilment of all desires is what makes Petitcreiu faintly monstrous, and we are partly relieved as Isolde destroys the magic bell. Almost comically, the dog refers back to the Prologue. A *senemaere* works, Gottfried promises, by *half* assuaging longing, 'ze halber senfte bringen'. Petitcreiu is that unspeakable thing that would bring it to *full* 'saenfte' and thus destroy the tension that keeps the story going. Isolde wisely chooses to use the dog/poem differently: having 'dedicated her life to desire and Tristan' ('diu haete ir vröude unde ir leben | sene unde Tristande ergeben') she keeps the dog, sans bell, 'ze niuwenne ir senede leit', to renew her desiring sorrow.

We may conclude by noting briefly that even the framing trope of translation — the overt announcement by both authors that they are translating a preceding text — establishes and grounds the tensions of desire. In both medieval and modern understandings, translation lives by its unresolvable paradoxes of sameness and difference: its asymptotic desire to completely match, even become identical with the source, and its simultaneous recognition that attaining that identity would be both impossible and counterproductive. By casting themselves as translators rather than originator of their text, as its readers as well as its writers, Gottfried and Laȝamon distance and objectify the story. At the same time, they make it the object of their own yearning desire. Both Gottfried and Laȝamon assert their source with great urgency and affectivity. We have seen Laȝamon's loving, tactile attention to his source texts. The equivalent in Gottfried would be his explicit choice of Thomas over other sources, his declared and even combative allegiance and loyalty to that source, his desire to 'right' his poem according to Thomas's *rihte*.

To be sure, what both poets practice here is not strictly 'translation' as understood by either modern or medieval readers.[21] The modern idea of translation relies on an unresolved and usually unnoticed paradox of subservience, substitution, and identity. The translator is to substitute the original with closely equivalent linguistic material in the target language, *sensus pro senso*, one unit of meaning at a time. She is to do so without asserting her own voice, deixis, or presence; where Gottfried, for instance, says 'I', the translator is to reproduce that 'I' without comment.[22] The result is felt to be, and marketed as, a complete substitute of the original, while at the same time professing to be entirely at its service, indeed practically identical with it. If you have read *Tristan*, for instance, in A. T. Hatto's English translation for Penguin Classics, you will say and feel, with no sense of irony, that you have read Gottfried, not Hatto.

To medieval publics, *c.* 1200, this conception of translation is available, if at all, only for the 'vertical' translation from authoritative Latin to popular vernacular. 'Horizontal' translation, from one vernacular to the other, does not practice sense-for-sense substitution, or even the reproduction of the original's deixis. When Laȝamon renders an authorial intervention by Wace, he will either work around it, or he will mark it as Wace's, and comment on it in his own voice; he will not adopt Wace's 'I'.[23] It may not even have occurred to Laȝamon and Gottfried to consider their work analogous to what Jerome did with the Bible. They do not proceed sense for sense, much less word for word; they work in much larger units, scenes perhaps, or narrative ideas. To them it is probably closer to the kind of imitative writing one learned in school, based on the techniques of *amplificatio* and, less often, *abbreviatio*. The term 'translation', or the verb *vertere*, sometimes used for 'turning' Latin to vernacular, does not seem to have been used for horizontal translation of this sort.[24] Recent scholarship has proposed not calling vernacular-to-vernacular transfer 'translation' at all, but to see it together with imitation, retelling, adapting, as one of many techniques of 'retextualization'.[25] Both Laȝamon and Gottfried stress that they produce a text of their own, and both do so with words that suggest condensing, compressing, making something tighter or tauter: Laȝamon's *þrumde to are* ('pressed into one') and Gottfried's *tihte*.[26] The process is effortful; the translator feels the constraint of staying closely alongside the source, and he needs to constrain his text (especially since he is writing in verse).[27] Yet that procedure also, potentially, yields something autonomous. Gottfried emphatically offers '*mín* lesen' (*my* reading), which is his gift to the noble hearts. Laȝamon produces 'truer words' (*soþere word*) and a bardic *loft-song*.

Nonetheless, there is a close, even loving relationship between the translators and their sources, and fidelity matters. Both authors stress that they follow their source precisely. Laȝamon does so as a kind of scribe, using an exemplar ('þe he to bisne inom'; line 37). Or else he is taking oral dictation: the priest who picks up a pen and 'says' 'al swa the book speketh' [exactly as the books speak] (line 37) suggests nothing so much as an evangelist portrait. He is physically channelling his source, a ceremonial and priestly action. Gottfried is perhaps more of an academic, a commentator, who reads and critiques how others 'read' the matter of Tristan ('die von Tristande hant gelesen'; line 132). Yet his claim to superior reading comes from Thomas's *rihte*, a word that points in a number of semantic directions: 'rightness' as well as 'direction' (*Richtigkeit* and *Richtung*, in modern German).

Gottfried, in his customarily dense wordplay, sums it up perfectly: 'daz ich in sîner rihte | rihte dise tihte'. *Rihte/tihte* is a standard rhyme; other Middle High German translators use it too.[28] But Gottfried has carefully prepared and contextualized it, and exploits it fully. It takes up the strand of 'rehte/rihte' that has been going on for some lines, condenses it into a couplet where it rhymes with 'tihte' [poem] and repeats exactly across the line break but with a significant variation of meaning. The first 'rihte', at the end of the first line, is the noun, 'right-ness' or 'direction' or perhaps as in 'Richtschnur', a 'guideline'; the second 'rihte' that starts the next line, is a verb, by this time so polysemous that I have capitulated and simply rendered it 'to right'. (The pun that results in English, with 'write', is not possible in German — it is just about the only pun that will *not* work.) The word *rihte*, then, can be read in many senses, some of them standard dictionary meanings, others ad-hoc ones Gottfried has engineered: 'to prepare, to put together'; 'to judge'; it can mean 'to right' as righting a listing ship; it can mean 'to orient, point in the right direction' or 'to make right', 'to do correctly'. This polysemy encapsulates both his dependence and his independence, his agency and his subservience, his closeness to Thomas and his own creation. He sees his activity less as a transfer and more as a writing-alongside, even writing inside the source: the preposition, significantly, is 'in' not 'after' or 'according to' (*in* rather than *nach siner rihte*). His conformity to Thomas's *rihte* produces his own rightness; and conversely his own rightness guarantees his closeness to the *rihte*. It is not so much a wholesale 'turning', a carrying-across a divide; it is both something more distant and at the same time something closer, more intimate, where the translator never quite detaches from the model, let alone fully substitutes or supplants it. There is a productive and emotional tension between source and text that arises, in Susan Stewart's formulation, from their mutual inherence and their 'mutual exteriority':[29] a strangeness and a closeness, a striving for nearness and a striving for emancipation. Maybe even more than our kind of translation, this medieval translation keeps things open and maintains a space for desire.

Notes to Chapter 14

1. Gottfried's *Tristan* is usually dated *c.* 1210. Datings for Laȝamon's *Brut* have ranged from the late twelfth century to *c.* 1275 (the approximate date of both manuscripts in which the poem survives). Many scholars now appear to have settled on the early thirteenth century.

2. Patricia Parker, *Inescapable Romance: Studies in the Poetics of a Mode* (Princeton, NJ: Princeton University Press, 1979).

3. Laȝamon, *Brut*, ed. by G. L. Brook and R. F. Leslie, 2 vols, EETS 250, 277 (London: Early English Text Society, 1963–78), lines 16094–96. References in the text, by line number, will be to this edition, Caligula text (left-hand side). Translations are my own, although I have consulted Rosamund Allen's translation: Lawman, *Brut* (New York: St. Martin's Press, 1992).

4. See, among others, Nicola Kaminski, 'Zeichenmacht: Gottfrieds *Tristan*', *Oxford German Studies*, 37 (2008), 3–26.

5. Gottfried von Strassburg, *Tristan*, ed. and trans. by Rüdiger Krohn, 3rd edn, 3 vols (Stuttgart: Reclam, 1984), lines 161–62. This edition will henceforth be cited in the text, by line number. Translations are my own, although I have consulted Krohn's facing-page modern German translation. The most convenient English translation is Gottfried von Strassburg, *Tristan*, trans. by A. T. Hatto (Harmondsworth: Penguin, 1978).

6. On Gottfried's theory of signification, see Christoph Huber, 'Wort-Ding-Entsprechungen: Zur Spruch- und Stiltheorie Gottfrieds von Straßburg', in *Befund und Deutung: Zum Verhältnis von Empirie und Interpretation in Sprach- und Literaturwissenschaft*, ed. by Hans Fromm (Tübingen: Niemeyer, 1979), pp. 268–302; Mark Chinca, *History, Fiction, Verisimilitude: Studies in the Poetics of Gottfried's 'Tristan'* (London: Modern Humanities Research Association, 1993), particularly pp. 71–81.

7. For a very different reading of this much-discussed passage, see Ursula Liebertz-Grün, 'Selbstreflexivität und Mythologie: Gottfrieds *Tristan* als Metaroman', *Germanisch-romanische Monatsschrift*, n.f. 51 (2001), 1–20.

8. An influential formulation of this view is E. G. Stanley, 'Laȝamon's Antiquarian Sentiments', *Medium Aevum*, 38 (1969), 23–37.

9. See also Alice Sheppard, 'Love Rewritten: Authorizing History in the Prologue to Laȝamon's *Brut*', *Mediaevalia*, 23 (2002), 99–121. For another important discussion of affectivity in the *Brut* — in an episode not directly related to the argument here — see Lucy Perry, 'The Life of Brian: A Loyal Retainer and a Loving Subject', in *Laȝamon: Contexts, Language, and Interpretation*, ed. by Rosamund Allen, Lucy Perry, and Jane Roberts (London: King's College Centre for Late Antique and Medieval Studies, 2002), pp. 385–411.

10. Kenneth J. Tiller, *Laȝamon's Brut and the Anglo-Norman Vision of History* (Cardiff: University of Wales Press, 2007), pp. 103–05.

11. Michael Camille, 'The Book as Flesh and Fetish in Richard de Bury's *Philobiblon*', in *The Book and the Body*, ed. by Dolores Warwick Frese and Katherine O'Brien O'Keeffe (Notre Dame, IN: University of Notre Dame Press, 1997), pp. 34–77 (pp. 40–42).

12. Tiller, pp. 194–98.

13. Elizabeth J. Bryan, 'Truth and the Round Table in Lawman's *Brut*', *Quondam et Futurus*, 2 (1992), 27–35.

14. *Le Roman de Brut de Wace*, ed. by Ivor Arnold, 2 vols (Paris: SATF, 1938–40), lines 9785–98.

15. Geoffrey of Monmouth, *Life of Merlin—Vita Merlini*, ed. and trans. by Basil Clarke (Cardiff: University of Wales Press, 1973).

16. Walter F. Schirmer, *Die frühen Darstellungen des Arthurstoffes*, Arbeitsgemeinschaft für Forschung des Landes Nordrhein-Westfalen, Geisteswissenschaften, Heft 73 (Köln: Westdeutscher Verlag,

1958), p. 13; see also Jeff Rider, 'The Fictional Margin: The Merlin of the "Brut"', *Modern Philology*, 87 (1989), 1–12.

17. Petitcreiu clearly figured in Thomas's *Tristran* — he is represented in its Old Norse adaptation, the *Tristramssaga*. But Werner Schröder doubts — persuasively I think — that Thomas's Petitcreiu played the same role, or nearly as elaborate a role: 'Das Hündchen Petitcreiu im *Tristan* Gotfrids von Strassburg', in *Dialog: Literatur und Literaturwissenschaft im Zeichen deutsch-französischer Begegnung. Festgabe für Josef Kunz*, ed. by Rainer Schönhaar (Berlin: Schmidt, 1973), pp. 32–42 (pp. 40–41). On Petitcreiu, see also Silke Philipowski, 'Mittelbare und unmittelbare Gegenwärtigkeit, oder: Erinnern und Vergessen in der Petitcriu-Episode des "Tristan" Gottfrieds von Straßburg', *Beiträge zur Geschichte der deutschen Sprache und Literatur*, 120 (1998), 29–35; Marion E. Gibbs, 'The Medieval Reception of Gottfried's *Tristan*', in *A Companion to Gottfried von Strassburg's 'Tristan'*, ed. by Will Hasty (Rochester, NY: Camden House, 2003), pp. 261–84 (p. 280).

18. Schröder, p. 38.

19. See Andrew Cowell, 'The Dye of Desire: The Colors of Rhetoric in the Middle Ages', *Exemplaria*, 11 (1999), 115–39.

20. Cowell, p. 124. See the suggestive comments on miniatures in Susan Stewart, *On Longing: Narratives of the Miniature, the Gigantic, the Souvenir, the Collection* (Durham, NC: Duke University Press, 1993), pp. 37–69.

21. Tiller, *Laȝamon's Brut and the Anglo-Norman Vision of History*, offers an important reading of the *Brut* as a translation, political and historical, in terms of post-colonial translation theory.

22. Lawrence Venuti, *The Translator's Invisibility: A History of Translation* (London: Routledge, 1995).

23. See Franz Josef Worstbrock, 'Wiedererzählen und Übersetzen', in *Mittelalter und frühe Neuzeit: Übergänge, Umbrüche und Neuansätze*, ed. by Walter Haug, Fortuna Vitrea, 16 (Tübingen: Niemeyer, 1999), pp. 128–42 (p. 129).

24. Martina Backes, '"Ich buwe doch die strazzen | die sie hant gelazzen": Überlegungen zu Selbstverständnis und Textkonzept deutscher Bearbeiter französischer Werke im Mittelalter', in *Retextualisierung in der mittelalterlichen Literatur*, ed. by Joachim Bumke and Ursla Peters, Zeitschrift für deutsche Philologie, Sonderheft zu Bd., 124 (Berlin: Schmidt, 2005), pp. 345–55; Monika Unzeitig-Herzog, 'Zu Fragen der Wirkungsäquivalenz zwischen der altfranzösischen "Queste del Saint Graal" und den deutschen Fassungen der "Gral-Queste" des "Prosa-Lanzelot"', in *Übersetzen im Mittelalter: Cambridger Kolloquium 1994*, ed. by Joachim Heinzle, L. Peter Johnson and Gisela Vollmann-Profe, Wolfram-Studien, 14 (Berlin: Schmidt, 1996), pp. 149–70 (pp. 154–55); Monika Unzeitig, 'tihten–diuten–tiutschen: Autor und Translator: Textinterne Aussagen zu Autorschaft und Translation in der mittelhochdeutschen Epik', in *Edition und Übersetzung: Zur wissenschaftlichen Dokumentation des interkulturellen Transfers*, ed. by Bodo Plachta and Winfried Woesler, Beihefte zu Editio, 18 (Tübingen: Niemeyer, 2002), pp. 55–69.

25. Joachim Bumke, 'Retextualisierungen in der mittelalterlichen Literatur, besonders in der höfischen Epik', in Bumke and Peters, eds, *Retextualisierung in der mittelalterlichen Literatur*, pp. 6–46.

26. The etymology of German *dichten*, despite its homophony with *dicht* [dense], points to Latin *dictare*, cf. the obsolete English word *endite*. But the pun is irresistible. On *þrumde*, see Tiller, p. 105.

27. The usage is not unparalleled; another Middle High German translator, Conrad the Priest, says he has 'forced' his French source into *Latin* before then translating that into German verse — 'in die Latînsche betwungen'. See Unzeitig-Herzog, p. 154.

28. Unzeitig, 'Tihten', pp. 58–61.

29. Stewart, p. 45.

SELECTED BIBLIOGRAPHY

*The bibliography lists the main primary texts analysed by the essays in the volume,
as well as a selection of critical studies which relate to the various aspects of desire*

Texts

ALAIN DE LILLE, *Liber Poenitentialis*, ed. by Jean Longère, 2 vols (Louvain: Nauwelaerts; Lille: Giard, 1965)

—— *De planctu naturae*, ed. by N. Häring, *Studi Medievali*, 19 (1978), 797–879

—— *The Plaint of Nature*, ed. and trans. by James Sheridan (Toronto: Pontifical Institute of Mediaeval Studies, 1980)

ALBERTUS MAGNUS, *Super Dionysium De Divinis Nominibus*, ed. by Paulus Simon (Aschendorff: Monasterii Westfalorum, 1972)

ALIGHIERI, DANTE, *Dante's Lyric Poetry*, ed., trans., and with a commentary by Kenelm Foster and Patrick Boyde, 2 vols (Oxford: Oxford University Press, 1967)

—— *The Divine Comedy*, trans. and with a commentary by Charles S. Singleton (Princeton, NJ: Princeton University Press, 1970–75)

—— *Convivio*, ed. by Cesare Vasoli and Domenico De Robertis (Milan and Naples: Ricciardi, 1988)

—— *Il Convivio/The Banquet*, trans. by Richard Lansing (New York: Garland, 1990)

—— '*La Commedia*' *secondo l'antica vulgata*, ed. by Giorgio Petrocchi, Società Dantesca Italiana, Edizione Nazionale, 2nd rev. edn, 4 vols (Florence: Le Lettere, 1994)

—— *De vulgari Eloquentia*, ed. and trans. by Steven Botterill (Cambridge: Cambridge University Press, 1996)

—— *Vita Nova*, ed. by Guglielmo Gorni (Turin: Einaudi, 1996)

—— *Commedia*, ed. by Anna Maria Chiavacci Leonardi, 3 vols (Milan: Mondadori, 1991–97)

—— *Vita Nuova*, trans. by Mark Musa (Oxford: Oxford University Press, 1999)

—— *Vita Nova*, ed. by Luca Carlo Rossi (Milan: Mondadori, 1999)

—— *The Divine Comedy*, trans. by Robert Hollander and Jean Hollander, 3 vols (New York: Doubleday, 2000–07)

—— *The Divine Comedy*, trans. by Robin Kirkpatrick, 3 vols (London: Penguin Books, 2006–07)

—— *Rime giovanili e della Vita Nuova*, ed. by Teodolinda Barolini, with notes by Manuele Gragnolati (Milan: Rizzoli, 2009)

—— *The Divine Comedy of Dante Alighieri*, ed. and trans. by Robert Durling and Ronald Martinez, 3 vols (Oxford and New York: Oxford University Press, 1996–2011)

AMBROSE, SAINT, *Hexameron, Paradise, and Cain and Abel*, trans. by John J. Savage (Washington, DC: Catholic University of America Press, 1961)

AQUINAS, THOMAS, *In librum beati Dionysii de Divinis Nominibus expositio*, ed. by Ceslai Pera (Turin and Rome: Marietti, 1950)

—— *Summa theologica*, trans. by Fathers of the English Dominican Province, 5 vols (New York: Benziger Brothers, 1948)

—— *Summa theologiae* (1888–1906; rev. edn, Rome: Editiones Paulinae, 1962)

ARNAUT DANIEL, *Le canzoni di Arnaut Daniel*, ed. by Maurizio Perugi (Milan and Naples: Ricciardi, 1978)

—— *The Poetry of Arnaut Daniel*, ed. by James J. Wilhelm (London and New York: Garland, 1983)

—— *Sirventese e canzoni*, ed. by Giosuè Lachin (Turin: Einaudi, 2000)

'Attār, *The Conference of the Birds*, trans. by Dick Davis (Harmondsworth and New York: Penguin Books, 1984)

AUGUSTINE, *De trinitate libri xv*, ed. by W. J. Mountain, 2 vols, Corpus Christianorum 50–50A (Turnhout: Brepols, 1968)

—— *The Trinity (De Trinitate)*, ed. by John E. Rotelle, trans. by Edmund Hill (New York: New City Press, 1991)

—— *Confessions*, ed. and trans. by Henry Chadwick (Oxford: Oxford University Press, 1992)

—— *Confessions*, ed. with commentary by James J. O'Donnell, 3 vols (Oxford: Clarendon Press, 1992), available at: <http://www.stoa.org/hippo>

—— *Vingt-six sermons au people d'Afrique: Retrouvés à Mayence*, ed. by François Dolbeau (Paris: Institut d'Études Augustiniennes, 1996)

BOCCACCIO, GIOVANNI, *Vite di Dante*, ed. by Pier Giorgio Ricci (Milan: Mondadori, 2002)

BONCOMPAGNO DA SIGNA, *Rhetorica Novissima*, in *Scripta Anecdota Glossatorum*, ed. by A. Gaudenzi (Bologna: 1896)

CAVALCANTI, GUIDO, *Complete Poems*, ed. and trans. by Marc Cirigliano (New York: Italica Press, 1992)

CONTINI, GIANFRANCO, ed., *Poeti del Duecento*, 2 vols (Milan and Naples: Ricciardi, 1960)

FOLCHETTO DI MARSIGLIA, *Le poesie di Folchetto di Marsiglia*, ed. by Paolo Squillacioti (Pisa: Pacini, 1999)

GERTRUDE VON HELFTA, *Œuvres spirituelles*, ed. and trans. into French by Pierre Doyere and others, Sources chrétiennes: Série des textes monastiques d'Occident, 5 vols (Paris: Editions du Cerf, 1967–86)

GOTTFRIED VON STRASSBURG, *Tristan*, trans. by A. T. Hatto (Harmondsworth: Penguin, 1978)

—— *Tristan*, ed. and trans. by Rüdiger Krohn, 3rd edn, 3 vols (Stuttgart: Reclam, 1984)

GUILLAUME DE LORRIS and JEAN DE MEUN, *Le Roman de la rose*, ed. by Félix Lecoy, 3 vols (Paris: Champion, 1965–70)

HADEWIJCH, *De Visionen van Hadewijch*, ed. by Jozef van Mierlo (Löwen: De Vlaamsche Boekenhalle, 1924–25)

—— *Die Erlösung: Eine geistliche Dichtung des 14. Jahrhunderts*, ed. by Friedrich Maurer, Deutsche Literatur. Sammlung literarischer Kunst- und Kunstdenkmäler in Entwicklungsreihen. Reihe: Geistliche Dichtung des Mittelalters, 6 (Leipzig: Reclam, 1934)

—— *Strophische gedichten*, ed. by Josef van Mierlo, Leuvense studiën en tekstuitgaven, 13, 2 vols (Antwerp: Standaard-Boekhandel, 1942)

—— *Mengeldichten*, ed. by Jozef van Mierlo (Antwerpen: N. V. Standaard Boekhandel, 1952)

—— *Strofische gedichten: Middelnederlandse tekst en moderne bewerking met een inleiding*, ed. by Edward Rombauts and Norbert de Paepe (Zwolle: Tjeenk Willink, 1961)

—— *The Complete Works*, trans. by Mother Columba Hart (London: SPCK, 1981)

—— *Liederen*, ed. and trans. by Veerle Fraeters and Frank Willaert, with a reconstruction of the melodies by Louis Peter Grijp (Groningen: Historische Uitgeverij, 2009)

IBN 'Arabî, *The Bezels of Wisdom*, trans. by R. W. J. Austin and with a preface by Titus Burkhardt (Mahwah, NJ: Paulist Press, 1980)

ISIDOR OF SEVILLE, *Isidori Hispalensis Episcopi Etymologiarvm sive originvm libri XX*, ed. by Wallace Martin Lindsay, 2 vols (Oxford and New York: Oxford University Press, 1985)

LAȜAMON, *Brut*, ed. by G. L. Brook and R. F. Leslie, 2 vols, EETS 250, 277 (London: Early English Text Society, 1963–1978)

LAWMAN, *Brut*, trans. by Rosamund Allen (New York: St. Martin's Press, 1992)

MECHTHILD VON MAGDEBURG, *Das fließende Licht der Gottheit*, ed. by Hans Neumann with Gisela Vollmann-Profe, Münchener Texte und Untersuchungen, 100 (Munich: Artemis, 1990)

PETRARCA, FRANCESCO, *Le Familiari: libri I–IV*, ed. and Italian trans. by Ugo Dotti (Urbino: Argalìa, 1970)

—— *Rerum familiarium libri I–VIII*, trans. by Aldo S. Bernardo (Albany, NY: SUNY Press, 1975)

—— *Petrarch's Lyric Poems: The 'Rime sparse' and Other Lyrics*, trans. by Robert M. Durling (Cambridge, MA: Harvard University Press, 1976)

——FRANCESCO PETRARCA, *Canzoniere*, ed. by Marco Santagata, rev. edn (Milan: Mondadori, 1989)

—— *Canzoniere*, ed. by Gianfranco Contini (Turin: Einaudi, 1992)

—— *Trionfi, rime estravaganti, codice degli abbozzi*, ed. by Vinicio Pacca and Laura Paolino; introduction by Marco Santagata (Milan: Mondadori, 1996)

—— *The Essential Petrarch*, ed. and trans. by Peter Hainsworth (Indianapolis, IN, and Cambridge, MA: Hackett, 2010)

PSEUDO-DIONYSIUS AREOPAGITA, *The Complete Works*, trans. by Colm Luibheid and ed. by Paul Rorem (New York and Mahwah, NJ: Paulist Press, 1987)

—— *De Divinis Nominibus*, ed. by Beate Regina Suchla (Berlin and New York: Walter de Gruyter, 1990)

QUINTILIAN, *Institutio oratoria*, ed. and trans. by Donald A. Russell, 5 vols (Cambridge, MA, and London: Harvard University Press, 2001)

SEUSE, HEINRICH, *Seuses Leben*, in *Heinrich Seuse: Deutsche Schriften*, ed. by Karl Bihlmeyer (Stuttgart: Kohlhammer, 1907; repr. Frankfurt: Minerva, 1961)

SHAKESPEARE, WILLIAM, *Hamlet*, ed. by Harold Jenkins (London: Arden Shakespeare, 1982)

VIRGIL, *Eclogues, Georgics, Aeneid 1–6*, trans. by H. R. Fairclough (Cambridge, MA: Harvard University Press, 1960)

Critical literature

ABARDO, RUBY, ed., *Omaggio a Beatrice (1290–1990)* (Florence: Le Lettere, 1998)

AGAMBEN, GIORGIO, *Stanzas: Word and Phantasm in Western Culture*, trans. by Ronald L. Martinez (Minneapolis and London: University of Minnesota Press, 1993)

—— *The End of the Poem*, trans. by Daniel Heller-Roazen (Stanford, CA: Stanford University Press, 1999)

—— *Ninfe* (Turin: Bollati Boringhieri, 2007)

—— *Profanazioni* (Rome: Nottetempo, 2005); in English as *Profanations*, trans. by Jeff Fort (New York: Zone, 2008)

AKBARI, SUZANNE CONKLIN, *Seeing through the Veil: Optical Theory and Medieval Allegory* (Toronto and London: University of Toronto Press, 2004)

ALLEN, ROSAMUND, LUCY PERRY, and JANE ROBERTS, eds, *Laȝamon: Contexts, Language, and Interpretation* (London: King's College Centre for Late Antique and Medieval Studies, 2002)

ANTONELLO, PIERPAOLO, and SIMON A. GILSON, eds, *Science and Literature in Italian Culture from Dante to Calvino* (Oxford: Legenda, 2004)

ARDIZZONE, MARIA LUISA, *Dante, Il paradigma intellettuale: Un'inventio degli anni fiorentini* (Florence: Olschki, 2011)

ASCOLI, ALBERT RUSSELL, *Dante and the Making of a Modern Author* (Cambridge: Cambridge University Press, 2008)

ASPERTI, STEFANO, 'Dante, i trovatori, la poesia', in *Le culture di Dante: Studi in onore di R. Hollander: Atti del quarto Seminario dantesco internazionale*, ed. by Michelangelo Picone, Theodore J. Cachey, Jr, and Margherita Mesirca (Florence: Cesati, 2003), pp. 61–92

ASTELL, ANN W., *The Song of Songs in the Middle Ages* (Ithaca, NY, and London: Cornell University Press, 1990)

AVALLE, D'ARCO SILVIO, *Ai luoghi di delizia pieni: Saggio sulla lirica italiana del XIII secolo* (Milan and Naples: Ricciardi, 1977)

AYRES, LEWIS, *Augustine and the Trinity* (Cambridge: Cambridge University Press, 2010)

BADIOU, ALAIN, *Saint Paul et la fondation de l'universalisme* (Paris: Presses Universitaires de France, 1997); in English as *Saint Paul: The Foundation of Universalism*, trans. by Ray Brassier (Minneapolis: University of Minnesota Press, 2000)

——and NICOLAS TRUONG, *Éloge de l'amour* (Paris: Flammarion, 2009)

BAILEY, ELIZABETH, 'Raising the Mind to God: The Sensual Journey of Giovanni Morelli (1371–1444)', *Speculum*, 84 (2009), 984–1008

BARAŃSKI, ZYGMUNT G., 'Dante's Biblical Linguistics', *Lectura Dantis*, 5 (1989), 105–43

——'The "New Life" of "Comedy": The *Commedia* and the *Vita Nuova*', *Dante Studies*, 113 (1995), 1–29

——*Dante e i segni: Saggi per una storia intellettuale di Dante Alighieri* (Naples: Liguori, 2000)

——'"Per *similitudine* di abito scientifico": Dante, Cavalcanti and the Sources of Medieval "Philosophical" Poetry', in *Science and Literature in Italian Culture from Dante to Calvino*, ed. by Pierpaolo Antonello and Simon A. Gilson (Oxford: Legenda, 2004), pp. 14–52

——and THEODORE J. CACHEY, JR, eds, *Petrarch & Dante: Anti-Dantism, Metaphysics, Tradition* (Notre Dame, IN: University of Notre Dame Press, 2009)

BARNES, JOHN C., and JENNIFER PETRIE, eds, *Word and Drama in Dante: Essays on the Divina Commedia* (Dublin: Irish Academy, 1993)

——and JENNIFER PETRIE, eds, *Dante and the Human Body: Eight Essays* (Dublin: Four Courts Press, 2007)

——ed., *Dante and the Seven Deadly Sins* (Dublin: Four Courts Press, forthcoming)

BAROLINI, TEODOLINDA, *Dante's Poets: Textuality and Truth in the 'Comedy'* (Princeton, NJ: Princeton University Press, 1984)

——'The Making of a Lyric Sequence: Time and Narrative in Petrarch's *Rerum vulgarium fragmenta*', *MLN*, 104.1, Italian issue (Jan. 1989), 1–38

——*The Undivine 'Comedy': Detheologizing Dante* (Princeton, NJ: Princeton University Press, 1992)

——'Dante and Cavalcanti (On Making Distinctions in Matters of Love): *Inferno* V in its Lyric Context', *Dante Studies*, 116 (1998), 31–63

——'Dante and Francesca da Rimini: Realpolitik, Romance, Gender', *Speculum*, 75 (2000), 1–28

——and H. WAYNE STOREY, eds, *Dante for the New Millennium* (New York: Fordham University Press, 2003)

——*Dante and the Origins of Literary Culture* (New York: Fordham University Press, 2007)

BARRY, MICHAEL, *Figurative Art in Medieval Islam and the Riddle of Bihzâd of Herât* (Paris: Flammarion, 2004)

BARTOLI, VITTORIO, and PAOLA URENI, 'Controversie medico-biologiche in tema di generazione umana nel XXV del Purgatorio', *Studi danteschi*, 68 (2003), 83–111

——'La dottrina di Galeno in "sangue perfetto" (Purg. XXV 37)', *Studi danteschi*, 70 (2005), 335–44

BELTRAMI, PIETRO, 'Arnaut e la "bella scola" dei trovatori di Dante', in *Le culture di Dante*, ed. by Michelangelo Picone, Theodore J. Cachey, Jr, and Margherita Mesirca (Florence: Cesati, 2003), pp. 29–59

BERRA, CLAUDIA, and PAOLO BORSA, eds, *Le Rime di Dante*, *Quaderni di Acme*, 117 (2010)

BERSANI, LEO, *Is the Rectum a Grave? and Other Essays* (Chicago, IL, and London: University of Chicago Press, 2010)

BERTONE, GIORGIO, *Lo sguardo escluso: L'idea del paesaggio nella letteratura occidentale* (Novara: Interlinea, 2000)

BOCCASSINI, DANIELA, *Il volo della mente: Falconeria e Sofia nel mondo mediterraneo: Islam, Federico II, Dante* (Ravenna: Longo, 2003)

—— ed., *Sogni e visioni nel mondo indo-mediterraneo*, *Quaderni di Studi Indo-Mediterranei*, 2 (2009), 1–20

BOLZONI, LINA, 'Dante o della memoria appassionata', *Lettere Italiane*, 60 (2008), 169–93

—— *Il cuore di cristallo: Ragionamenti d'amore, poesia e ritratto nel Rinascimento* (Turin: Einaudi, 2010)

BOSWELL, JOHN, *Christianity, Social Tolerance and Homosexuality: Gay People in Western Europe from the Beginning of the Christian Era to the Fourteenth Century* (Chicago, IL: University of Chicago Press, 1981)

BOYDE, PATRICK, *Perception and Passion in Dante's 'Comedy'* (Cambridge: Cambridge University Press, 1993)

BRENKMAN, JOHN, 'Writing, Desire, Dialectic in Petrarch's "Rime 23"', *Pacific Coast Philology*, 9 (April 1974), 12–19

BRONFEN, ELISABETH, *Over her Dead Body: Death, Femininity and the Aesthetic* (Manchester: Manchester University Press, 1992)

BROWNLEE, KEVIN, 'Orpheus' Song Re-sung: Jean de Meun's Reworking of *Metamorphoses*, x', *Romance Philology*, 36.2 (1982), 201–09

——, MARINA BROWNLEE, and STEPHEN NICHOLS, eds, *The New Medievalism* (Baltimore, MD: Johns Hopkins University Press, 1991)

BRYAN, JENNIFER, *Looking Inward: Devotional Reading and the Private Self in Late Medieval England* (Philadelphia: University of Pennsylvania Press, 2008)

BURGER, GLENN, and STEVEN F. KRUGER, eds, *Queering the Middle Ages* (Minneapolis, MN, and London: University of Minnesota Press, 2001)

BURGIN, VICTOR, JAMES DONALD and KARA CAPLAN, eds, *Formations of Fantasy* (London and New York: Methuen, 1986)

BURGWINKLE, WILLIAM E., *Sodomy, Masculinity and the Law in Medieval Literature* (Cambridge: Cambridge University Press, 2004)

—— 'Ethical Acts and Annihilation: Feminine Heroics in "Girart de Roussillon"', in *Women and Medieval Epic: Gender, Genre and the Limits of Epic Masculinity*, ed. by Sara S. Poor and Jana K. Schulman (New York and Basingstoke: Palgrave Macmillan, 2007), pp. 159–82

BUTLER, JUDITH, *Gender Trouble: Feminism and the Subversion of Identity* (New York and London: Routledge, 1990)

—— *Bodies That Matter: On the Discursive Limits of 'Sex'* (New York and London: Routledge, 1993

BYNUM, CAROLINE WALKER, *Holy Feast and Holy Fast: The Religious Significance of Food to Medieval Women* (Berkeley, Los Angeles, and London: University of California Press, 1987)

—— *Fragmentation and Redemption: Essays on Gender and the Human Body in Medieval Religion* (New York: Zone Books, 1992)

—— *The Resurrection of the Body in Western Christianity, 200–1336* (New York: Columbia University Press, 1995)

CAMILLE, MICHAEL, 'Before the Gaze: The Internal Senses and Late Medieval Practices of Seeing', in *Visuality before and beyond the Renaissance: Seeing as Others Saw*, ed. by Robert S. Nelson (Cambridge: Cambridge University Press, 2000), pp. 197–223

——'The Book as Flesh and Fetish in Richard de Bury's *Philobiblon*', in *The Book and the Body*, ed. by Dolores Warwick Frese and Katherine O'Brien O'Keeffe (Notre Dame, IN: University of Notre Dame Press, 1997), pp. 34–77

CAMILLETTI, FABIO, 'The Golden Veil: Purezza e malinconia in un racconto di Dante Gabriel Rossetti', *Rivista di Studi Vittoriani*, 8.15 (2003), 77–93

——'Dante's *Vita Nova* and the Victorians: The Hidden Image behind Rossetti's *Giotto Painting the Portrait of Dante*', in *The Victorians and Italy: Literature, Travel, Politics and Art*, ed. by Alessandro Vescovi, Luisa Villa and Paul Vita (Monza: Polimetrica, 2009), pp. 181–92

——*Dante's Book of Youth: The 'Vita Nova' and the Nineteenth Century 1840–1907* (London: igrs books, forthcoming)

CAMPBELL, JOSEPH, ed., *The Mysteries: Papers from the Eranos Yearbooks* (Princeton, NJ: Princeton University Press, 1955)

CESTARO, GARY, *Dante and the Grammar of the Nursing Body* (Notre Dame, IN: University of Notre Dame Press, 2003)

——'Is Ulysses Queer? The Subject of Greek Love in *Inferno* XV and XXVI', in *Dante's Plurilingualism: Authority, Knowledge, Subjectivity*, ed. by Sara Fortuna, Manuele Gragnolati and Jürgen Trabant (Oxford: Legenda, 2010), pp. 179–202

CHIAMENTI, MASSIMILIANO, 'The Representation of the Psyche in Cavalcanti, Dante and Petrarch: the *Spiriti*', *Neophilologus*, 82 (1998), 71–81

CHIFFOLEAU, JACQUES, '*Contra naturam*: Pour une approche casuistique et procédurale de la nature médiévale', *Micrologus*, 4 (1996), 265–312

COPELAND, RITA, *Rhetoric, Hermeneutics and Translation in the Middle Ages: Academic Traditions and Vernacular Texts* (Cambridge: Cambridge University Press, 1991)

CIOFFI, CARON ANN, 'St. Augustine Revisited: On "Conversion" in the *Commedia*', *Lectura Dantis Virginiana*, 5 (1989), 68–80

COGLIEVINA, LEONELLA, and DOMENICO DE ROBERTIS, eds, *Sotto il segno di Dante: Scritti in onore di Francesco Mazzoni* (Florence: Le Lettere, 1998)

CORBIN, HENRY, *L'Imagination créatrice dans le soufisme d'Ibn 'Arabi* (Paris: Entrelacs, 2006)

CORNISH, ALISON, *Reading Dante's Stars* (New Haven, CT, and London: Yale University Press, 2000)

CORTI, MARIA, *La felicità mentale: Nuove prospettive per Cavalcanti e Dante* (Turin: Einaudi, 1983)

——*Dante a un nuovo crocevia* (Florence: Sansoni, 1981)

COWELL, ANDREW, 'The Dye of Desire: The Colors of Rhetoric in the Middle Ages', *Exemplaria*, 11 (1999), 115–39

CURTI, ELISA, 'Un esempio di bestiario dantesco: La cicogna o dell'amor materno', *Studi Danteschi*, 67 (2002), 129–60

DAGENAIS, JOHN, *The Ethics of Reading in Manuscript Culture: Glossing the 'Libro de buen amor'* (Princeton, NJ: Princeton University Press, 1994)

DAVID, BENJAMIN, 'The Paradisal Body in Giovanni di Paolo's Illuminations of the *Commedia*', *Dante Studies*, 122 (2004), 45–69

DE BRUIJN, T. P., *Persian Sufi Poetry: An Introduction to the Mystical Use of Classical Poems* (Richmond, UK: Curzon Press, 1997)

DELEUZE, GILLES, and FÉLIX GUATTARI, *A Thousand Plateaus: Capitalism and Schizophrenia*, trans. by Brian Massumi (Minneapolis, MN: University of Minnesota Press, 1987)

DENERY II, DALLAS G., *Seeing and Being Seen in the Later Medieval World: Optics, Theology, and Religious Life* (Cambridge: Cambridge University Press, 2005)

DE PAEPE, NORBERT, *Hadewijchs Strofische Gedichten: Een studie von de minne in het kader der 12e en 13e eeuwse mystiek en profane minnelyriek* (Gent and Leuven: Wetenschappelijke uitgeverij en boekhandel, 1967)

DERRIDA, JACQUES, *Qu'est-ce qu'une traduction 'relevante'?* (Paris: L'Herne, 2005)

——and LAWRENCE VENUTI, 'What is a "relevant" translation?', *Critical Inquiry*, 27.2 (2001), 174–200

DIDI-HUBERMAN, GEORGES, *Fra Angelico: Dissemblance and Figuration*, trans. by Jane Marie Todd (London: University of Chicago Press, 1995)

DIETRICH, PAUL, 'The Wilderness of God in Hadewijch II and Meister Eckahrt and His Circle', in *Meister Eckhart and the Beguine Mystics: Hadewijch of Brabant, Mechtild of Magdebrug and Marguerite Porete* (New York: Continuum, 1997), pp. 31–43

DRAGE HALE, ROSEMARY, 'Rocking the Cradle: Margaretha Ebner (Be)Holds the Divine', in *Performance and Transformation: New Approaches to Late Medieval Spirituality*, ed. by Mary A. Suydam and Joanna E. Ziegler (Basingstoke: Macmillan, 1999), pp. 211–39

DRAGONETTI, ROGER, 'Le "Singe de Nature" dans le *Roman de la Rose*', in Roger Dragonetti, *La Musique et les Lettres: Études de littérature médiévale* (Geneva: Droz, 1986), pp. 369–80

DRONKE, PETER, 'The Song of Songs and Medieval Love-Lyric', in *The Bible and Medieval Culture*, ed. by W. Lourdaux and D. Verhelst (Leuven: Leuven University Press, 1976), pp. 256–62

——*Dante's Second Love: The Originality and Contexts of the 'Convivio'* (Exeter: Society for Italian Studies, 1997)

DURLING, ROBERT M., and RONALD L. MARTINEZ, *Time and the Crystal: Studies in Dante's 'Rime petrose'* (Berkeley and Oxford: University of California Press, 1990)

EDELMAN, LEE, *No Future: Queer Theory and the Death Drive* (Durham, NC, and London: Duke University Press, 2004)

EISENBICHLER, KONRAD, ed., *Petrarch's Triumphs: Allegory and Spectacle* (Ottawa: Dovehouse Editions, 1990)

ELIOT, T. S., *The Waste Land*, in *The Annotated Waste Land with Eliot's Contemporary Prose* (New Haven, CT: Yale University Press, 2005)

EMERSON, JAN SWANGO, and HUGH FEISS, OSB, eds, *Imagining Heaven in the Middle Ages: A Book of Essays* (New York and London: Garland, 2000)

FAESEN, ROB, *Begeerte in het werk van Hadewijch* (Antwerp: Peeters, 2000)

FERGUSON, MARGARET W., *Dido's Daughters: Literacy, Gender, and Empire in Early Modern England and France* (Chicago, IL, and London: University of Chicago Press, 2003)

FERRUCCI, FRANCO, *Il poema del desiderio* (Milan: Leonardo, 1990)

FLEMING, JOHN V., *Reason and the Lover* (Princeton, NJ: Princeton University Press, 1984)

FOUCAULT, MICHEL, *The History of Sexuality*, trans. by Robert Hurley, 3 vols (New York and Toronto: Random House, 1970–85)

FORTUNA, SARA, MANUELE GRAGNOLATI, and JÜRGEN TRABANT, eds, *Dante's Plurilingualism: Authority, Knowledge, Subjectivity* (Oxford: Legenda, 2010)

——and MANUELE GRAGNOLATI, 'Dante after Wittgenstein: "Aspetto", Language, and Subjectivity from *Convivio* to *Paradiso*', in *Dante's Plurilingualism*, ed. by Sara Fortuna, Manuele Gragnolati, and Jürgen Trabant (Oxford: Legenda, 2010), pp. 223–48

FRECCERO, JOHN, ed., *Dante: A Collection of Critical Essays* (Englewood, NJ: Prentice-Hall, 1965)

——*Dante: The Poetics of Conversion*, ed. by Rachel Jacoff (Cambridge, MA: Harvard University Press, 1986)

——'The Fig Tree and the Laurel: Petrarch's Poetics', *Diacritics*, 5.1 (Spring 1995), 34–40

FRESE, DOLORES WARWICK, and KATHERINE O'BRIEN O'KEEFFE, eds, *The Book and the Body* (Notre Dame, IN: University of Notre Dame Press, 1997)

FULTON, RACHEL, *From Judgment to Passion: Devotion to Christ and the Virgin Mary, 800–1200* (New York: Columbia University Press, 2002)

——and BRUCE W. HOLSINGER, eds, *History in The Comic Mode: Medieval Communities and the Matter of Person* (New York: Columbia University Press, 2007)

GILLESPIE, VINCENT, 'The Study of Classical Authors: From the Twelfth Century to *c.* 1450', in *The Cambridge History of Literary Criticism: Volume II: The Middle Ages*, ed. by Alastair J. Minnis and Ian Johnson (Cambridge: Cambridge University Press, 2005), pp. 145–235

GILSON, SIMON A., 'Dante and the Science of "Perspective": A Reappraisal', *Dante Studies*, 115 (1997), 185–219

—— *Medieval Optics and Theories of Light in the Works of Dante* (Lewiston, NY, Queenston and Lampeter: Edwin Mellen Press, 2000)

—— 'The Anatomy and Physiology of the Human Body in the *Commedia*', in *Dante and the Human Body: Eight Essays*, ed. by John C. Barnes and Jennifer Petrie (Dublin: Four Courts Press, 2007), pp. 11–42

GIUNTA, CLAUDIO, *La poesia italiana nell'età di Dante: La linea Bonagiunta-Guinizzelli* (Bologna: Il Mulino, 1998)

GLISSANT, ÉDOUARD, *Poetics of Relation*, trans. by Betsy Wing (Ann Arbor: University of Michigan Press, 1997)

GORNI, GUGLIELMO, 'Beatrice agli Inferi', in *Omaggio a Beatrice (1290–1990)*, ed. by Rudy Abardo (Florence: Le Lettere, 1998), pp. 143–58

—— 'La Beatrice di Dante, dal tempo all'eterno', in Dante Alighieri, *Vita Nova*, ed. by Luca Carlo Rossi (Milan: Mondadori, 1999), pp. v–xl

—— *Dante prima della* Commedia (Fiesole: Cadmo, 2001)

GRAGNOLATI, MANUELE, *Experiencing the Afterlife: Soul and Body in Dante and Medieval Culture* (Notre Dame, IN: Notre Dame University Press, 2005)

—— 'Gluttony and the Anthropology of Pain in Dante's *Inferno* and *Purgatorio*', in *History in the Comic Mode: Medieval Communities and the Matter of Person*, ed. by Rachel Fulton and Bruce W. Holsinger (New York: Columbia University Press, 2007), pp. 238–50

—— 'Nostalgia in Heaven: Embraces, Affection and Identity in the *Commedia*', in *Dante and the Human Body: Eight Essays*, ed. by John C. Barnes and Jennifer Petrie (Dublin: Four Courts Press, 2007), pp. 117–37

—— '(In-)Corporeality, Language, Performance in Dante's *Vita Nuova* and *Commedia*', in *Dante's Plurilingualism: Authority, Knowledge, Subjectivity,* ed. by Sara Fortuna, Manuele Gragnolati and Jürgen Trabant (Oxford: Legenda, 2010), pp. 211–22

GRAYSON, CECIL, '*Nobilior est vulgaris*: Latin and Vernacular in Dante's Thought', in *Centenary Essays on Dante by Members of the Oxford Dante Society* (Oxford: Oxford University Press, 1965), pp. 54–76

GUEST, TANIS M., *Some Aspects of Hadewijch's Poetic Form in the 'Strofische gedichten'* (The Hague: Martinus Nijhoff, 1975)

HAHN, CYNTHIA, '*Visio dei*: Changes in Medieval Visuality', in *Visuality Before and Beyond the Renaissance*, ed. by Robert S. Nelson (Cambridge: Cambridge University Press, 2000), pp. 169–96

HAINSWORTH, PETER, *Petrarch the Poet: An Introduction to the 'Rerum vulgarium fragmenta'* (London: Routledge, 1988)

HAMBURGER, JEFFREY, 'The Visual and the Visionary: The Image in Late Medieval Devotions', *Viator*, 20 (1989), 161–82

—— and ANNE-MARIE BOUCHÉ, eds, *The Mind's Eye: Art and Theological Argument in the Middle Ages* (Princeton, NJ: Princeton University Department of Art and Archaeology in Association with Princeton University Press, 2006)

—— and others, eds, *Frauen, Kloster, Kunst: Neue Forschungen zur Kulturgeschichte des Mittelalters: Beiträge zum internationalen Kolloquium vom 13. bis 16. Mai 2005 anlässlich der Ausstellung 'Krone und Schleier'* (Turnhout: Brepols, 2007)

HARRISON, ROBERT POGUE, *The Body of Beatrice* (Baltimore, MD: Johns Hopkins University Press, 1988)

HASEBRINK, BURKHARD, and others, eds, *Innenräume in der Literatur des deutschen Mittelalters. XIX: Anglo-German Colloquium Oxford 2005* (Tübingen: Niemeyer, 2008)

HAWKINS, PETER S., 'Dido, Beatrice, and the Signs of Ancient Love', in *The Poetry of Allusion: Virgil and Ovid in Dante's 'Commedia'*, ed. by Rachel Jacoff and Jeffrey T. Schnapp (Stanford, CA: Stanford University Press, 1991), pp. 113–30 and pp. 274–76

——*Dante's Testaments: Essays in Scriptural Imagination* (Stanford, CA: Stanford University Press, 1999)

HILL, THOMAS D., 'Narcissus, Pygmalion, and the Castration of Saturn: Two Mythographical Themes in the *Roman de la Rose*', *Studies in Philology*, 71.4 (1974), 404–26

HOLLANDER, ROBERT, '*Purgatorio* II: Cato's Rebuke and Dante's *scoglio*', *Italica*, 52 (1975), 348–63

——'Dante's Reluctant Allegiance to St. Augustine in the *Commedia*', *L'Alighieri*, 32 (2008), 5–16

HOLMES, OLIVIA, *Dante's Two Beloveds: Ethics and Erotics in the 'Divine Comedy'* (New Haven, CT: Yale University Press, 2008)

HUOT, SYLVIA, *Dreams of Lovers and Lies of Poets* (Oxford: Legenda, 2010)

IDEL, MOSHE, and BERNARD MCGINN, eds, *Mystical Union in Judaism, Christianity and Islam: An Ecumenical Dialogue* (New York: Continuum, 1999)

IRIGARAY, LUCE, *Speculum of the Other Women*, trans. by Gillian C. Gill (Ithaca, NY: Cornell University Press, 1985)

JACOFF, RACHEL, 'The Post-Palinodic Smile: *Paradiso* VIII and IX', *Dante Studies*, 98 (1980), 111–22

——'Transgression and Transcendence: Figures of Female Desire in Dante's *Commedia*', in *The New Medievalism*, ed. by Kevin Brownlee, Marina Brownlee, and Stephen Nichols (Baltimore, MD: Johns Hopkins University Press, 1991), pp. 183–90

——and JEFFREY T. SCHNAPP, eds, *The Poetry of Allusion: Virgil and Ovid in Dante's 'Commedia'* (Stanford, CA: Stanford University Press, 1991)

——'"Our Bodies, Our Selves": The Body in the *Commedia*', in *Sparks and Seeds: Medieval Literature and its Afterlife. Essays in Honor of John Freccero*, ed. by Dana E. Stewart and Alison Cornish (Turnhout: Brepols, 2000), pp. 119–37

JORDAN, MARK D., *The Invention of Sodomy in Christian Theology* (Chicago, IL: University of Chicago Press, 1996)

JUNG, JACQUELINE E., 'Crystalline Wombs and Pregnant Hearts: The Exuberant Bodies of the Katharinenthal Visitation Group', in *History in the Comic Mode: Medieval Communities and the Matter of Person*, ed. by Rachel Fulton and Bruce W. Holsinger (New York: Columbia University Press, 2007), pp. 223–37

KAY, TRISTAN, 'Redefining the "matera amorosa": Dante's *Vita Nova* and Guittone's (anti-) Courtly "canzoniere"', *The Italianist*, 29 (2009), 369–99

——'Dante's Ambivalence towards the Lustful', in *Dante and the Seven Deadly Sins*, ed. by John C. Barnes (Dublin: Four Courts Press, forthcoming)

——'Dido, Aeneas, and the Evolution of Dante's Poetics', *Dante Studies*, 129 (forthcoming 2011)

KITTAY, EVA FEDER, *Metaphor: Its Cognitive Force and Linguistic Structure* (Oxford: Clarendon Press, 1987; repr. 1989)

KOOPER, ERIK, ed., *Medieval Dutch Literature in its European Context* (Cambridge: Cambridge University Press, 1991)

KRISTEVA, JULIA, *La Révolution du langage poétique: L'Avant-garde à la fin du XIXe siècle: Lautréamont et Mallarmé* (Paris: Seuil, 1974)

——*Soleil noir: Dépression et mélancolie* (Paris: Gallimard, 1987); in English as, *Black Sun: Depression and Melancholia*, trans. by Leon S. Roudiez (New York: Columbia University Press, 1989)

KUON, PETER, *L'aura dantesca: Metamorfosi intertestuali nel 'Rerum vulgarium fragmenta' di Francesco Petrarca* (Florence: Cesati, 2004)

LACAN, JACQUES, 'The Mirror Stage as Formative of the Function of the I as Revealed in Psychoanalytic Experience' (1949); repr. in his *Écrits: A Selection*, trans. by Alan Sheridan (New York: Norton, 1977), pp. 1–7

—— *The Four Fundamental Concepts of Psycho-Analysis* (1973), ed. by Jacques-Alain Miller, trans. by Alan Sheridan (New York: Norton, 1978)

—— 'The Meaning of the Phallus', in *Feminine Sexuality: Jacques Lacan and the École Freudienne*, ed. by Juliet Mitchell and Jacqueline Rose, trans. by Jacqueline Rose (New York: Norton, 1985), pp. 74–85

—— *The Seminar of Jacques Lacan, Book I: Freud's Papers on Technique* (1975), trans. by John Forrester (New York: Norton, 1988)

—— *The Seminar of Jacques Lacan, Book 7: The Ethics of Psychoanalysis 1959–1960*, ed. by Jacques-Alain Miller and trans. by Dennis Porter (New York and London: Norton, 1992)

—— *Écrits*, trans. by Bruce Fink (New York and London: Norton, 2006)

LÄHNEMANN, HENRIKE, and SANDRA LINDEN, eds, *Dichtung und Didaxe: Lehrhaftes Sprechen in der deutschen Literatur des Mittelalters* (Tübingen: de Gruyter, 2009)

LANSING, RICHARD, ed., *The Dante Encyclopedia* (New York: Garland, 2000)

LAPLANCHE, JEAN, and J. B. PONTALIS, 'Fantasy and the Origins of Sexuality', in *Formations of Fantasy*, ed. by Victor Burgin, James Donald, and Kara Caplan (London and New York: Methuen, 1986)

—— *Seduction, Translation, Drives*, ed. by John Fletcher and Martin Stanton, trans. by Martin Stanton (London: Institute of Contemporary Arts, 1992)

LARGIER, NIKLAS, *Die Kunst des Begehrens: Dekadenz, Sinnlichkeit und Askese* (Munich: C. H. Beck, 2007)

LAUDE, PATRICK, *Divine Play, Sacred Laughter, and Spiritual Understanding* (New York: Palgrave Macmillan, 2005)

—— 'Creation, Originality and Innovation in Sufi Poetry', *The Eye of the Heart*, 2 (2008), 112–30

LAZZERINI, LUCIA, 'L'"allodetta" e il suo archetipo: La rielaborazione di temi mistici nella lirica trobadorica e nello stil novo', in *Sotto il segno di Dante: Scritti in onore di Francesco Mazzoni*, ed. by Leonella Coglievina and Domenico De Robertis (Florence: Le Lettere, 1998), pp. 165–88

—— 'La trasmutazione insensibile: Intertestualità e metamorfismi nella lirica trobadorica dalle origini alla codificazione cortese', *Medioevo Romanzo*, 18 (1993), 153–205 and 313–69

LECHNER, GREGOR MARTIN, *Maria Gravida: Zum Schwangerschaftsmotiv in der bildenden Kunst* (Munich: Schnell und Steiner, 1981)

LEDDA, GIUSEPPE, *La guerra della lingua: Ineffabilità, retorica e narrativa nella 'Commedia' di Dante* (Ravenna: Longo, 2002)

LEO, ULRICH, 'The Unfinished *Convivio* and Dante's Rereading of the *Aeneid*', *Medieval Studies*, 13 (1951), 41–64

LEUSHUIS, REINIER, 'Pygmalion's Folly and the Author's Craft in Jean de Meun's *Roman de la Rose*', *Neophilologus*, 90.4 (2006), 521–33

LEWISOHN, L., and C. SHACKLE, eds, *'Attār and the Persian Sufi Tradition: The Art of Spiritual Flight* (London and New York: The Institute of Ismaili Studies, 2006)

LINDBERG, DAVID C., *Theories of Vision from Al-Kindi to Kepler* (Chicago, IL: University of Chicago Press, 1976)

LOMBARDI, ELENA, *The Syntax of Desire: Language and Love in Augustine, the Modistae, Dante* (Toronto: University of Toronto Press, 2007)

—— 'Plurilingualism *sub specie aeternitatis* and the Strategies of a Minor Author', in *Dante's Plurilingualism: Authority, Knowledge, Subjectivity*, ed. by Sara Fortuna, Manuele Gragnolati, and Jürgen Trabant (Oxford: Legenda, 2010), pp. 133–48

——— The Wings of the Doves: Love and Desire in Dante and Medieval Culture (Montreal: McGill University Press, 2012)

LÓPEZ CORTEZO, CARLOS, 'Metapoetica della lussuria: Le gru di Purgatorio XXVI', Tenzone, 6 (2005), 121–41

LOURDAUX, W., and D. VERHELST, eds, The Bible and Medieval Culture (Leuven: Leuven University Press, 1976),

MANDELBAUM, ALLEN, ANTHONY OLDCORN, and CHARLES ROSS, eds, Lectura Dantis: Purgatorio (Berkeley, Los Angeles, and London: University of California Press, 2008)

MARCHESI, SIMONE, Dante and Augustine: Linguistics, Poetics, Hermeneutics (Toronto, Buffalo and London: University of Toronto Press, 2011)

MARCOS, SYLVIA, 'Embodied Religious Thought: Gender Categories in Mesoamerica', in Gender/Bodies/Religion: Adjunct Proceedings of the XVIIth Congress on the History of Religions, ed. by Sylvia Marcos (Cuernavaca, Mexico: ALER Publications, 2000), pp. 93–114

——— Taken from the Lips: Gender and Eros in Mesoamerican Religions (Leiden and Boston: Brill, 2006)

MATTER, E. ANN, 'The Voice of My Beloved': The Song of Songs in Medieval Christianity (Philadelphia: University of Pennsylvania Press, 1990)

MAZZEO, JOSEPH ANTHONY, 'The Augustinian Conception of Beauty and Dante's Convivio', The Journal of Aesthetics and Art Criticism, 15.4 (1957), 435–48

McDONALD, NICOLA, ed., Medieval Obscenities (York: York Medieval Press, 2006)

McGINN, BERNARD, The Flowering of Mysticism: Men and Women in the New Mysticism (1200–1350) (New York: Schuster, 1998)

——— 'Love, Knowledge and Unio mystica in the Western Christian Tradition', in Mystical Union in Judaism, Christianity and Islam: An Ecumenical Dialogue, ed. by Moshe Idel and Bernard McGinn (New York: Continuum, 1999), pp. 59–86

——— ed., The Presence of God: A History of Western Christian Mysticism, 4 vols (New York: Herder & Herder, 2005)

McGOWAN, TODD, The Real Gaze: Film Theory after Lacan (Albany: State University of New York Press: 2007)

MAZZOTTA, GIUSEPPE, The Worlds of Petrarch (Durham, NC: Duke University Press, 1993)

MEIER, FRITZ, 'The Mystery of the Ka'ba: Symbol and Reality in Islamic Mysticism', in The Mysteries: Papers from the Eranos Yearbooks, ed. by Joseph Campbell (Princeton, NJ: Princeton University Press, 1955)

MENGALDO, PIER VINCENZO, Linguistica e retorica di Dante (Pisa: Nistri-Lischi, 1978)

MESSINESE, LEONARDO, and CHRISTIAN GÖBEL, eds, Verità e responsibilità: Studi in onore di Aniceto Molinaro (Rome: Centro Studi S. Anselmo, 2006)

MILBANK, ALISON, Dante and the Victorians (Manchester: Manchester University Press, 1998)

MILES, MARGARET, Image as Insight: Visual Understanding in Western Christianity and Secular Culture (Eugene, OR: Wipf and Stock, 1985)

MINNIS, ALASTAIR J., Medieval Theory of Authorship: Scholastic Literary Attitudes in the Later Middle Ages (Aldershot: Wildwood house, 1984)

——— 'Amor and Auctoritas in the Self-Commentary of Dante and Francesco da Barberino', Poetica, 32 (1990), 25–42

——— and A. B. SCOTT, eds, Medieval Literary Theory and Criticism c. 1100–1375: The Commentary Tradition (Oxford: Oxford University Press, 1998)

——— and IAN JOHNSON, eds, The Cambridge History of Literary Criticism: Volume II: The Middle Ages (Cambridge: Cambridge University Press, 2005)

——— 'From Coilles to Bel Chose: Discourses of Obscenity in Jean de Meun and Chaucer', in Medieval Obscenities, ed. by Nicola McDonald (York: York Medieval Press, 2006), pp. 156–78

MISSIRINI, MELCHIOR, *Dell'amore di Dante Alighieri e del ritratto di Beatrice Portinari* (Florence: Ciardetti, 1832)

MÖLK, ULRICH, *Trobadorlyrik* (Munich and Zurich: Artemis, 1982)

MOEVS, CHRISTIAN, *The Metaphysics of Dante's* Comedy (Oxford and New York: Oxford University Press, 2005)

——'Subjectivity and Conversion in Dante and Petrarch', in *Petrarch & Dante: Anti-Dantism, Metaphysics, Tradition*, ed. by Zygmunt G. Barański and Theodore J. Cachey, Jr (Notre Dame, IN: University of Notre Dame Press, 2010), pp. 226–59

MOONEY, CATHERINE M., ed., *Gendered Voices: Medieval Saints and their Interpreters* (Philadelphia: University of Philadelphia Press, 1999)

MULDER-BAKKER, ANNEKE, *Lives of the Anchoresses: The Rise of the Urban Recluse in Medieval Europe* (Philadelphia: University of Pennsylvania Press, 2005)

MULVEY, LAURA, *Visual and Other Pleasures*, 2nd edn (Basingstoke and New York: Palgrave, 2009)

MURK JENSEN, SASKIA, *The Measure of Mystic Thought: A Study of Hadewijch's Mendeldichten* (Göppingen: Kümmerle Verlag, 1991)

NARDI, BRUNO, *Nel mondo di Dante* (Rome: Edizioni di Storia e Letteratura, 1944)

——*Dal 'Convivio' alla 'Commedia'* (Rome: Istituto Storico Italiano per il Medio Evo, 1960)

——*'Lecturae' e altri studi danteschi*, ed. by Rudy Abardo (Florence: Le Lettere, 1990)

NASR, SEYYED HOSSEIN, *Knowledge and the Sacred* (Albany, NY: SUNY Press, 1989)

NASTI, PAOLA, *Favole d'amore e 'saver profondo': La tradizione salomonica in Dante* (Ravenna: Longo, 2007)

NELSON, ROBERT S., ed., *Visuality before and beyond the Renaissance: Seeing as Others Saw* (Cambridge: Cambridge University Press, 2000)

NEWHAUSER, RICHARD G., 'Peter of Limoges, Optics, and the Science of the Senses', in *Pleasure and Danger in Perception: The Five Senses in the Middle Ages and the Renaissance*, ed. by Corine Schleif and Richard G. Newhauser, special issue of *The Senses and Society*, 5.1 (March 2010), 28–44

NICHOLS, STEPHEN G., ANDREAS KABLITZ, and ALISON CALHOUN, eds, *Rethinking the Medieval Senses: Heritage / Fascinations / Frames* (Baltimore, MD: Johns Hopkins University Press, 2008)

NOBLE, DAVID, *A World Without Women: The Christian Clerical Culture of Western Science* (New York and Oxford: Oxford University Press, 1992)

——*The Religion of Technology: The Divinity of Man and the Spirit of Invention* (Harmondsworth: Penguin, 1997)

O'DALY, GERARD, *Augustine's Philosophy of Mind* (Berkeley and Los Angeles: University of California Press, 1987)

OTTER, MONIKA, 'Closed Doors: An Epithalamium for Queen Edith, Widow and Virgin', in *Widows and Virgins in the Middle Ages*, ed. by Angela Jane Weisl and Cindy Carlson (New York: St. Martin's Press, 1999), pp. 63–92

——'Entrances and Exits: Performing the Psalms in Goscelin's *Liber confortatorius*', *Speculum*, 83 (2008), 283–302

OYEWUMI, OYERONKE, *The Invention of Women: Making an African Sense of Western Gender Discourses* (Minneapolis: University of Minnesota Press, 1997)

PALMER, NIGEL F., 'Herzeliebe, weltlich und geistlich: Zur Metaphorik vom "Einwohnen im Herzen" bei Wolfram von Eschenbach, Juliana von Cornillon, Hugo von Langenstein und Gertrud von Helfta', in *Innenräume in der Literatur des deutschen Mittelalters. XIX: Anglo-German Colloquium Oxford 2005*, ed. by Burkhard Hasebrink and others (Tübingen: Niemeyer, 2008), pp. 197–224

PAOLINI, SHIRLEY J., *Confessions of Sin and Love in the Middle Ages: Dante's 'Commedia' and St. Augustine's 'Confessions'* (Washington, DC: University Press of America, 1982)

PARK, KATHARINE, *Secrets of Women: Gender, Generation and the Origins of Human Dissection* (New York: Zone Books, 2006)

PARKER, PATRICIA, *Inescapable Romance: Studies in the Poetics of a Mode* (Princeton, NJ: Princeton University Press, 1979)

PARRONCHI, ALESSANDRO, *Studi su la dolce prospettiva* (Milan: Aldo Martello, 1964)

PASSERINI, LUISA, *L'Europa e l'amore: Immaginario e politica fra le due guerre* (Milan: Il Saggiatore, 1999)

PERRY, LUCY, 'The Life of Brian: A Loyal Retainer and a Loving Subject', in *Laȝamon: Contexts, Language, and Interpretation*, ed. by Rosamund Allen, Lucy Perry, and Jane Roberts (London: King's College Centre for Late Antique and Medieval Studies, 2002), pp. 385–411

PERTILE, LINO, 'Paradiso: A Drama of Desire', in *Word and Drama in Dante: Essays on the Divina Commedia*, ed. by John C. Barnes and Jennifer Petrie (Dublin: Irish Academy, 1993), pp. 143–80

—— *La puttana e il gigante: Dal 'Cantico dei cantici' al 'Paradiso terrestre' di Dante* (Ravenna: Longo, 1998)

—— 'Does the *Stilnovo* Go to Heaven?', in *Dante for the New Millennium*, ed. by Teodolinda Barolini and H. Wayne Storey (New York: Fordham University Press, 2003), pp. 104–14

—— *La punta del disio: Semantica del desiderio nella 'Commedia'* (Florence: Cadmo, 2005)

PICH, FEDERICA, 'L'immagine *donna della mente* dalle Rime alla *Vita Nova*', in *Le Rime di Dante*, ed. by Claudia Berra and Paolo Borsa, *Quaderni di Acme*, 117 (2010), pp. 345–76

PICONE, MICHELANGELO, THEODORE J. CACHEY, JR, and MARGHERITA MESIRCA, eds, *Le culture di Dante: Studi in onore di R. Hollander: Atti del quarto Seminario dantesco internazionale* (Florence: Cesati, 2003)

—— 'La *Vita nova* nella prospettiva della *Commedia*', *Letture classensi*, 38 (2008), 7–15

—— 'Guittone, Guinizzelli e Dante', *L'Alighieri: Rassegna dantesca*, 18 (2001), 5–19

—— 'Paradiso IX: Dante, Folchetto e la diaspora trobadorica', *Medioevo romanzo*, VIII (1981–83), 47–89

POOR, SARA S., and JANA K. SCHULMAN, eds, *Women and Medieval Epic: Gender, Genre and the Limits of Epic Masculinity* (New York and Basingstoke: Palgrave Macmillan, 2007)

PRIGOGINE, ILYA, *The End of Certainty: Time, Chaos, and the New Laws of Nature* (New York: Bantam Books, 1984)

PSAKI, REGINA, 'The Sexualized Body in Dante and the Medieval Context', *Annali di storia dell'esegesi*, 13 (1996), 539–50

—— 'Dante's Redeemed Eroticism', *Lectura Dantis*, 18/19 (1996), 12–19

—— 'The Sexual Body in Dante's Celestial Paradise', in *Imagining Heaven in the Middle Ages: A Book of Essays*, ed. by Jan Swango Emerson and Hugh Feiss, OSB (New York and London: Garland, 2000), pp. 47–61

—— 'Love for Beatrice: Transcending Contradiction in the *Paradiso*', in *Dante for the New Millennium*, ed. by Teodolinda Barolini and H. Wayne Storey (New York: Fordham University Press, 2003), pp. 115–30

PULEGA, ANDREA, *Amore cortese e modelli teologici: Guglielmo IX, Chrétien de Troyes, Dante* (Milan: Jaca Book, 1995)

PURCELL, WILLIAM M., '*Transsumptio*: A Rhetorical Doctrine of the Thirteenth Century', *Rhetorica*, 5.4 (1987), 369–411

RAFFA, GUY, *Divine Dialectic: Dante's Incarnational Poetry* (Toronto: University of Toronto Press, 2000)

RAFFI, ALESSANDRO, *La gloria del volgare: Ontologia e semiotica in Dante dal 'Convivio' al 'De Vulgari Eloquentia'* (Soveria Mannelli, Calabria: Rubbettino, 2004)

REYNOLDS, SUSAN, *Medieval Reading: Grammar, Rhetoric and the Classical Text* (Cambridge: Cambridge University Press, 1996)

REYNAERT, JORIS, 'Hadewijch: Mystic Poetry and Courtly Love', in *Medieval Dutch Literature in its European Context*, ed. by Erik Kooper (Cambridge: Cambridge University Press, 1991), pp. 208–25

RICŒUR, PAUL, *La Métaphore vive* (Paris: Seuil, 1975)

ROLLO, DAVID, *Kiss My Relics: Hermaphroditic Fictions of the Middle Ages* (Chicago and London: University of Chicago Press, 2011)

ROSSETTI, DANTE GABRIEL, *The Collected Works*, ed. by William Michael Rossetti, 2 vols (London: Ellis and Elvey, 1890)

—— *The Paintings and Drawings 1828–1882: A Catalogue Raisonné*, ed. by Virginia Surtees, 2 vols (Oxford: Clarendon Press, 1971)

ROSSI, ALBERT L., ' "E pos d'amor plus no·m cal": Ovidian Exemplarity and Folco's Rhetoric of Love in *Paradiso* IX', *Tenso: Bulletin of the Société Guilhem* IX, 5 (1989), 49–102

ROSSINI, ANTONIO, *Il Dante sapienziale: Dionigi e la bellezza di Beatrice* (Pisa and Rome: Fabrizio Serra, 2009)

RUBIN, MIRI, *Mother of God: A History of the Virgin Mary* (London: Allen Lane/Penguin, 2009)

RUBLACK, ULINKA, 'Female Spirituality and the Infant Jesus in Late Medieval Dominican Convents', *Gender and History*, 6 (1994), 37–57

RUTLEDGE, MONICA, 'Dante, the Body and Light', *Dante Studies*, 113 (1995), 151–65

SANTAGATA, MARCO, *Amate e amanti: Figure della lirica amorosa fra Dante e Petrarca* (Bologna: Il Mulino, 1999)

SAYCE, OLIVE, *The Medieval German Love Lyric 1150–1300: The Development of its Themes and Forms in their European Context* (Oxford: Clarendon Press, 1982)

SBACCHI, DIEGO, *La presenza di Dionigi Areopagita nel Paradiso di Dante* (Florence: Olschki, 2006)

—— 'Il linguaggio superlativo e gerarchico del *Paradiso*', *L'Alighieri*, 31 (2008), 5–22

SCANLON, LARRY, 'Unspeakable Pleasures: Alain de Lille, Sexual Regulation and the Priesthood of Genius', *Romanic Review*, 86.2 (1995), 213–42

SCHIBANOFF, SUSAN, 'Sodomy's Mark: Alan of Lille, Jean de Meun and the Medieval Theory of Authorship', in *Queering the Middle Ages*, ed. by Glenn Burger and Steven F. Kruger (Minneapolis, MN, and London: University of Minnesota Press, 2001), pp. 28–56

SCHLEIF, CORINE, and RICHARD G. NEWHAUSER, eds, *Pleasure and Danger in Perception: The Five Senses in the Middle Ages and the Renaissance*, special issue of *The Senses and Society*, 5.1 (March 2010)

SCHNAPP, JEFFREY, 'Dante's Sexual Solecisms: Gender and Genre in the *Commedia*', in *The New Medievalism*, ed. by Kevin Brownlee, Marina Brownlee and Stephen Nichols (Baltimore, MD, and London: Johns Hopkins University Press, 1991), pp. 201–25

SCHUON, FRITHJOF, *The Transcendent Unity of Religions*, rev. edn with an intro. by Huston Smith (Wheaton, IL: Quest Books, 1997)

SCIUTO, ITALO, 'Agostino fra Dante e Petrarca', in *Verità e responsibilità: Studi in onore di Aniceto Molinaro*, ed. by Leonardo Messinese and Christian Göbel (Rome: Centro Studi S. Anselmo, 2006), pp. 381–89

SEDGWICK, EVE KOSOFSKY, *Between Men: English Literature and Male Homosocial Desire* (New York: Columbia University Press, 1985)

—— *Epistemology of the Closet* (Berkeley and Los Angeles: University of California Press, 1990)

—— *Tendencies* (London: Routledge, 1994)

SELLS, MICHAEL, *Mystical Languages of Unsaying* (Chicago, IL: University of Chicago Press, 1994)

SHAPIRO, MARIANNE, IN *Hieroglyph of Time: The Petrarchan Sestina* (Minneapolis: University of Minnesota Press, 1980)

SHAW, PRUE, 'Canto XXVI: The Fires of Lust and Poetry', in *Lectura Dantis: Purgatorio*, ed.

by Allen Mandelbaum, Anthony Oldcorn, and Charles Ross (Berkeley, Los Angeles, and London: University of California Press, 2008), pp. 288–302

SHEPPARD, ALICE, 'Love Rewritten: Authorizing History in the Prologue to Laȝamon's *Brut*', *Mediaevalia*, 23 (2002), 99–121

SINGLETON, CHARLES S., '"In exitu Israel de Aegypto"', in *Dante: A Collection of Critical Essays*, ed. by John Freccero (Englewood, NJ: Prentice-Hall, 1965), pp. 102–21

SPELMAN, ELIZABETH V., *Inessential Woman: Problems of Exclusion in Feminist Thought* (Boston, MA: Beacon Press, 1988)

SPITZER, LEO, 'Speech and Language in *Inferno* XIII', *Italica*, 19.3 (Sept. 1942), 81–104

SQUILLACIOTI, PAOLO, 'Folchetto di Marsiglia "Trovatore di Dante": *Tant m'abellis l'amoros pessamens*', in *Rivista di letteratura italiana*, 11 (1993), 583–607

STABILE, GIORGIO, 'Teoria della visione come teoria della conoscenza', *Micrologus*, 5 (1997), 225–46

STATEN, HENRY, *Eros in Mourning: Homer to Lacan* (Baltimore, MD: Johns Hopkins University Press: 1995)

STEINBERG, JUSTIN, 'Dante *Estravagante*, Petrarca *Disperso*, and the Spectre of the Other Woman', in *Petrarch & Dante: Anti-Dantism, Metaphysics, Tradition*, ed. by Zygmunt G. Barański and Theodore J. Cachey, Jr (Notre Dame, IN: University of Notre Dame Press, 2009), pp. 263–89

STEWART, DANA E., and ALISON CORNISH, eds, *Sparks and Seeds: Medieval Literature and its Afterlife: Essays in Honor of John Freccero* (Turnhout: Brepols, 2000)

—— *The Arrow of Love: Optics, Gender, and Subjectivity in Medieval Love-Poetry* (Lewisburg, PA: Bucknell University Press, 2003)

STEWART, SUSAN, *On Longing: Narratives of the Miniature, the Gigantic, the Souvenir, the Collection* (Durham, NC: Duke University Press, 1993)

STOCK, BRIAN, *Augustine's Inner Dialogue: The Philosophical Soliloquy in Late Antiquity* (Cambridge: Cambridge University Press, 2010)

STONE, LUCIAN, 'Blessed Perplexity: The Topos of *Hayrat* in 'Attār's *Mantiq al-Tayr*', in *'Attār and the Persian Sufi Tradition: The Art of Spiritual Flight*, ed. by L. Lewisohn and C. Shackle (London and New York: The Institute of Ismaili Studies, 2006), pp. 95–111

STRAUB, JULIA, *A Victorian Muse: The Afterlife of Dante's Beatrice in Nineteenth-Century Culture* (London: Continuum, 2009)

STURGES, ROBERT S., 'Visual Pleasure and *La Vita nuova*: Lacan, Mulvey, and Dante', in *Pleasure and Danger in Perception: The Five Senses in the Middle Ages and the Renaissance*, ed. by Corine Schleif and Richard G. Newhauser, special issue of *The Senses and Society*, 5.1 (March 2010), pp. 93–105

SUERBAUM, ALMUT, 'Die Paradoxie mystischer Lehre im *St. Trudperter Hohenlied* und im *Fließenden Licht der Gottheit*', in *Dichtung und Didaxe: Lehrhaftes Sprechen in der deutschen Literatur des Mittelalters*, ed. by Henrike Lähnemann and Sandra Linden (Berlin: de Gruyter, 2009), pp. 27–40

—— '"O wie gar wundirbar ist dis wibes sterke": Discourses of Sex, Gender and Desire in Johannes Marienwerder's Life of Dorothea von Montau', in *Dorothea von Montau and Johannes Marienwerder: Constructions of Sanctity*, ed. by Almut Suerbaum and Annette Volfing, *Oxford German Studies*, 39.2 (2010), 181–97

SUITNER, FRANCO, 'Due trovatori nella *Commedia*: Bertran de Born e Folchetto di Marsiglia', *Atti della Accademia nazionale dei lincei: Memorie: Classe di scienze morali, storiche e filologiche*, 24 (1980), 579–643

SUYDAM, MARY A., and JOANNA E. ZIEGLER, eds, *Performance and Transformation: New Approaches to Late Medieval Spirituality* (Basingstoke: Macmillan, 1999)

TACHAU, KATHERINE H., 'Seeing as Action and Passion in the Thirteenth and Fourteenth Centuries', in *The Mind's Eye: Art and Theological Argument in the Middle Ages*, ed. by

Jeffrey F. Hamburger and Anne-Marie Bouché (Princeton, NJ: Princeton University Department of Art and Archaeology in Association with Princeton University Press, 2006), pp. 336–59

TESTAFERRI, ADA, ed., *Donna: Woman in Italian Culture* (Toronto: Dovehouse, 1989)

TOOK, JOHN, 'Dante and the *Confessions* of St. Augustine', *Annali d'Italianistica*, 8 (1990), 360–83

TORRE, ANDREA, *Petrarcheschi segni di memoria: Spie, postille, metafore* (Pisa: Edizioni della Normale, 2007)

TURNER, DENYS, *Eros and Allegory: Medieval Exegesis of the Song of Songs* (Kalamazoo, MI: Cistercian Publications, 1995)

VANCE, EUGENE, 'Seeing God: Augustine, Sensation, and the Mind's Eye', in *Rethinking the Medieval Senses: Heritage / Fascinations / Frames*, ed. by Stephen G. Nichols, Andreas Kablitz, and Alison Calhoun (Baltimore, MD: Johns Hopkins University Press, 2008), pp. 13–29

VESCOVI, ALESSANDRO, LUISA VILLA and PAUL VITA, eds, *The Victorians and Italy: Literature, Travel, Politics and Art* (Monza: Polimetrica, 2009)

VILLA, CLAUDIA, 'Tra affetto e pietà (per *Inferno* v)', *Lettere Italiane*, 51 (1999), 513–41

WALLER, MARGUERITE, *Petrarch's Poetics and Literary History* (Amherst, MA: University of Massachusetts Press, 1980)

——— 'Seduction and Salvation: Sexual Difference in Dante's *Commedia* and the Difference It Makes', in *Donna: Woman in Italian Culture*, ed. by Ada Testaferri (Toronto: Dovehouse, 1989), pp. 225–43

——— 'The Spectacle of Society: The Semiotics of Renaissance Pageantry and the Triumphs of Petrarch', in *Petrarch's Triumphs: Allegory and Spectacle*, ed. by Konrad Eisenbichler (Ottawa: Dovehouse, 1990)

WARNAR, GEERT, *Ruusbroc: Literature and Mysticism in the Fourteenth Century* (Leiden: Brill, 2007)

WEBB, HEATHER, *The Medieval Heart* (New Haven, CT: Yale University Press, 2010)

WEINRICH, HARALD, *La memoria di Dante* (Florence: Accademia della Crusca, 1994)

WEISS, BARDO, *Ekstase und Liebe: Die unio mystica bei den deutschen Mystikerinnen des 12. und 13. Jahrhunderts* (Paderborn: Schöningh, 2000)

WEISL, ANGELA, and CINDY CARLSON, eds, *Widows and Virgins in the Middle Ages* (New York: St. Martin's Press, 1999)

WELLS, MARION A., *The Secret Wound: Love-Melancholy and Early Modern Romance* (Stanford, CA: Stanford University Press, 2007)

WHARTON, EDITH, *The House of Mirth* (1905; repr. New York: Collier, 1987)

WILLAERT, FRANK, 'Hadewijch und ihr Kreis in den *Visionen*, *Abendländische Mystik im Mittelalter: Symposion Kloster Engelberg 1984*, ed. by Kurt Ruh (Stuttgart: Metzler, 1986), pp. 368–85

WILLIAMS, PAMELA, *Through Human Love to God: Essays on Dante and Petrarch* (Troubador: Leicester, 2007)

WITTGENSTEIN, LUDWIG, *Remarks on the Philosophy of Psychology* (Oxford: Blackwell, 1980)

WOOLGAR, CHRISTOPHER M., *The Senses in Late Medieval England* (New Haven, CT: Yale University Press, 2006)

WRIGHT, ELIZABETH, and EDMOND WRIGHT, eds, *The Žižek Reader* (London: Blackwell, 1989)

ZEEMAN, NICOLETTE, *Piers Plowman and the Medieval Discourse of Desire* (Cambridge: Cambridge University Press, 2006)

ZIOLKOWSKI, JAN, 'The Obscenities of Old Women: Vetularity and Vernacularity', in *Obscenity: Social Control and Artistic Creation in the European Middle Ages*, ed. by Jan M. Ziolkowski (Leiden: Brill, 1998), pp. 73–89

ŽIŽEK, SLAVOJ, 'Courtly Love, or Woman as Thing', in *The Žižek Reader*, ed. by Elizabeth Wright and Edmond Wright (London: Blackwell, 1989), pp. 148–73

INDEX